The Image in Print

The Image in Print

BOOK ILLUSTRATION IN LATE MEDIEVAL ENGLAND AND ITS SOURCES

Martha W. Driver

The British Library

2004

First published 2004 by
The British Library
96 Euston Road
London NW1 2DB

© Martha W. Driver 2004

British Library
Cataloguing in Publication Data
A CIP record for this volume is
available from The British Library

ISBN 0-7123-4833-6

Designed by John Trevitt
Typeset in Sabon by
Norman Tilley Graphics,
Northampton
Printed in England by
St Edmundsbury Press,
Bury St Edmunds

For Ian and Alex, alpha and omega

CONTENTS

ACKNOWLEDGEMENTS

THANKS are due to many, many people who have assisted me with a project that has been in the making over the last decade. Most of all, I thank Derek Pearsall, who read and commented on early drafts of this book. William Chester Jordan also kindly read the initial draft and directed my revision in a most helpful way. Lotte Hellinga provided erudite comments throughout the draft, as well as bibliographical references, and gave me the full benefit of her great expertise in the field. Alexandra Gillespie aided greatly by checking all the STC numbers and plates in the collections of the British Library, while Ian Doyle has commented on various of my essays over the years, offering excellent advice as an intellectual mentor and guide. Gill Kent helped to make the spelling more British and, finally, Gavin Lewis has not only encouraged me but has helped bring the project to birth.

Among the many librarians and curators who have been helpful far beyond the call of duty over many years, I especially thank the reading room librarians at the Pierpont Morgan Library, Inge Dupont and Sylvie Merian, who have become good friends, along with the curatorial staff, especially Roger Wieck, and Marilyn Palmieri in photographic services. At the British Library, I must thank David Way, editor and midwife, along with Kathleen Houghton and John Trevitt who meticulously oversaw the reproduction and careful placement in the text of the many images that are represented here. At Pace University, so many friends have been supportive, but special thanks are due to Elisabeth Birnbaum and the interlibrary loan staff of the Birnbaum Library at Pace University in New York who have been instrumental in locating important reference works. The book could not have been completed without the generous support of my former dean Gail Dinter-Gottlieb (now president of Acadia University) and President David Caputo, both of whom understand the value and time-consuming nature of archival research. Finally, I wish to thank friends and family who have put up with my various projects over the years, especially my father who reads them all.

The research for this book was supported by grants from the National Endowment for the Humanities, the American Council of Learned Societies, the American Philosophical Society, the Bibliographical Society of America, and Pace University. I thank all these institutions for their most generous help. Parts of earlier chapters draw on the following previously published essays: 'Illustration in Early English Books: Methods and Problems', *Books at Brown* 33 (1986), pp. 1-57; 'Pictures in Print: Late Fifteenth- and Early Sixteenth-Century English

Acknowledgements

Religious Books for Lay Readers: Illustration and Layout', in *De Cella in Seculum*, ed. Michael G. Sargent (Cambridge, 1989), pp. 229-244; 'The Image *Redux*: Pictures in Block-books and What Becomes of Them', in *Blockbücher des Mittelalters: Bilderfolgen als Lektüre*, ed. Cornelia Schneider (Mainz, 1991), pp. 341-352; 'Nuns as Patrons, Artists, Readers: Bridgettine Woodcuts in Printed Books Produced for the English Market', in *Art into Life: Collected Papers from the Kresge Art Museum Medieval Symposia*, ed. Carol Garrett Fisher and Kathleen L. Scott (East Lansing, Mich., 1995), pp. 237-267; 'The Illustrated de Worde: An Overview', *Studies in Iconography*, Medieval Institute Publications, 17 (1996), pp. 349-403; 'Christine de Pisan and Robert Wyer: *The .C. Hystoryes of Troye*, or *L'Epistre d'Othea* Englished', *Gutenberg-Jahrbuch* 72 (1997), pp. 125-139; 'Ideas of Order: Wynkyn de Worde and the Title Page', in *Texts and Their Contexts: Papers from the Early Book Society*, ed. Julia Boffey and V. J. Scattergood (Dublin, 1997), pp. 87-149; 'Mirrors of a Collective Past: Re-Considering Images of Medieval Women', in *Women and the Book: Assessing the Visual Evidence*, ed. Lesley Smith and Jane Taylor (London, 1997), pp. 75-93; and 'Medievalizing the Classical Past in Morgan M 876', in *Middle English Poetry: Texts and Traditions, Essays in Honour of Derek Pearsall*, ed. A. J. Minnis (York, 2001), pp. 211-239.

ABBREVIATIONS

BL	The British Library, London.
BNF	Bibliothèque Nationale de France, Paris.
Dodgson, *Ashm.*	Campbell Dodgson, ed., *Woodcuts of the Fifteenth Century in the Ashmolean Museum, Oxford* (Oxford: Clarendon Press, 1929).
Dodgson, 'Bodl.'	Campbell Dodgson, 'English Devotional Woodcuts of the Late Fifteenth Century, with Special Reference to Those in the Bodleian Library', *The Walpole Society* 17 (1928-1929), pp. 95-108.
Goff	F. R. Goff, *Incunabula in American Libraries; a Third Census* (Millwood, New York: Kraus, 1973).
GW	*Gesamtkatalog der Wiegendrucke. Bd. I* (Leipzig, 1925-1938; repr. Stuttgart, 1968). Vols 1-7 reproduced with additions and corrections from the original edition.
Hind	A. M. Hind, *Introduction to a History of Woodcut*, 2 vols (1935; repr. New York: Dover, 1963).
Hodnett	Edward Hodnett, *English Woodcuts, 1480-1535* (1935; repr. Oxford: Oxford University Press, 1973).
PML	Pierpoint Morgan Library, New York.
Schreiber	Wilhelm L. Schreiber, *Handbuch der Holz- und Metallschnitte des XV. Jahrhunderts*, completed by Heinrich Theodor Musper, 3rd edn, 11 vols (Stuttgart: Anton Hiersemann, 1969-1976).
STC	*A Short-Title Catalogue of Books Printed in England, Scotland, & Ireland and of English Books Printed Abroad 1475-1640*, first compiled by A. W. Pollard and G. R. Redgrave, 2nd edn, rev. and enlarged, begun by W. A. Jackson and F. S. Ferguson, completed by Katharine F. Pantzer, 3 vols (London: The Bibliographical Society, 1976-1991).

INTRODUCTION

[Prints] are like old books of letters and recollections: if the information they give us is curious and worth having, it is all the same their pungent, plain-speaking style that brings us to them.

James Schuyler, ARTnews, Summer 1956

WOODCUTS have long been the poor relations of manuscript miniatures in the study of book illustration. Every manuscript miniature is, as an individually made picture, unique, and every one is in colour. Woodcuts are mechanically reproduced and are generally not in colour unless they have been coloured in by hand. Yet they too are a valuable resource in the study of late medieval and early modern books: they have much to tell us about how books were produced and for what purposes, about reading habits and developments in literacy, and about the part that books played in social, political and religious change. In this book, the study of woodcuts, and of the texts in which they appear, especially as they are seen to relate to and contrast with manuscript miniatures and drawings, will be used to argue for a radically new understanding of book illustration. The central focus here is on the physical evidence – pictures and texts – provided by books produced during the pre- and early Reformation periods, ranging from the products of the earliest English printers such as William Caxton, Richard Pynson and Wynkyn de Worde, through woodcut images of holy women and black people, to books that were censored, defaced and glossed by Protestant reformers. Reconsideration of this rich raw material can lead us to broader views of manuscript and book production, of reading and the development of literacy, and of the impact of the book on social change as well as on religious and political trends.

Illustration in printed books produced for the English market in the late fifteenth and early sixteenth centuries had a variety of functions. It has often been said that the early printers were haphazard in their use of woodcuts, but careful observation of illustration in English printed books indicates that this is not the case.[1] Even as they lost the distinctiveness of miniatures, woodcuts gained increased functional value; they were used more methodically to divide and organise text, to make text and meaning more accessible. Above all, through the study of images, one may begin to reconstruct the reading process and reading habits of a partially literate English lay audience prior to, and during, the early Reformation period. As William M. Ivins has remarked, 'the history of the cheap illustrated book and its role in the self-education of the multitude has yet to be written'.[2]

This book is a contribution to this as yet unwritten history. It considers the continued existence of earlier book production and illustration technologies in the fifteenth and early sixteenth centuries – manuscript media, woodcut illustrations and block-books – and how these technologies helped shape the development of books printed with movable type. It discusses several aspects of the reading of images, for example: how was reading represented for the first audiences of the early printed book? What is the function of the book or text in the representation of reading? Can we learn something of the medieval experience of reading from visual representation? It looks at book illustration as a way of reconstructing social history: what do pictures help us to recover about common social rituals, marriage, for example? What do woodcut images teach us about the work-place? And how do images help to promote ideas about contemporary culture? Finally, the book examines images in books as a force for social and political change, concluding with questions of control and ownership of information.

Printing increased the availability of books, and readership, or at least ownership, of books was made possible for a large number of people for the first time. Consideration of the introduction of printing and its effects on potential audiences for early printed books raises a number of questions concerning printing's impact on the growth of literacy in England, lay readership of books formerly read by the religious, and the role of book illustration and layout in promoting literacy among lay people. Who was the intended audience for the inexpensive, illustrated printed paper quartos and folios, written mainly in the vernacular, that were produced by the hundreds in the late fifteenth and early sixteenth centuries? Some evidence may be found in ownership marks or in mention of readers or patrons in book prefaces, dedications, or colophons. It is possible, in some cases, to deduce audience from subject-matter and presentation of text. For example, William Lyndewode's *Constitutiones provinciales*, a Latin legal text printed in many editions which have minimal or no illustration, was clearly directed at the educated lawyer and perhaps his assistants. *Historia Maioris Britanniae*, a history of England and Scotland (with a title-page woodcut and woodcut initials throughout), written by John Major and published in Paris in 1521, was again produced for an educated, predominantly male English audience, well versed in Latin. On the other hand, heavily illustrated vernacular miscellanies, such as *The Kalender of Shepherds*, and Books of Hours produced in less than de luxe formats, seem destined for an audience without university education and without Latin, that is, for women and lay readers.[3]

Constructing reader profiles for specific texts without specific provenance can be a chancy business, but some generalisations may occasionally be made. Two parallels might be drawn from contemporary publishing practice. *The New York Times* and *Publishers Weekly* bestseller lists indicate, to some extent, popular tastes in reading and what sells, if not specifically who is reading what. Similarly, some judgements about a book's popularity and its saleability in the early days of printing can be deduced from the number of reprints and competitive copies that were issued. At least nineteen editions of *The Kalender of Shepherds*, for example, were printed by competing publishers in English from 1503 through 1631; the numerous issues attest to this book's popularity.[4]

As for individual reading tastes, another look at present-day readers reveals how difficult this is to predict or determine. Presumably there is a small overlap of readers of Jackie Collins novels or paperback romances – the kind with the lurid covers generally read on the New York subways – with readers of bestsellers with more intellectual content. But, in general, the readers in the first category are separated from readers in the second by class, education, and to some extent gender. The same basic factors determined the tastes of readers of early printed books, but there were also some important differences.

Books for educated readers in the late fifteenth and early sixteenth centuries were written mainly in Latin, and readers with training in Latin tended also to be literate in English. Whether readers without knowledge of Latin had a basic grasp of written English is, however, debatable. Literacy, then as now, varied from individual to individual. Judging again from titles of printed books that seem mainly directed at a lay readership and from their presentation of vernacular text as well as from types of illustration, the audience would seem to have been partially or newly literate. People without Latin who were fully literate in the written vernacular did, of course, exist, as exemplified by Margaret Beaufort and her London circle, or by the Bridgettine nuns of Syon Abbey who were strongly encouraged to own and to read books in English. The development of vernacular literacy among women and the laity, which was gradually achieved in the years just prior to and during the early Reformation, was directly tied to the increased production of books, their often simplified text layout and their numerous illustrations. Printing is seen as a cheaper and faster form of publication than producing books by hand. Woodcut images, often drawn from manuscript exemplars, were readily reused in the early printed book, allowing for 'rapid communication of visual information and ideas', with familiar pictures from familiar stories contributing to the development of literacy.[5] The repetition of woodcuts created, perhaps not entirely intentionally, networks of meaning across a variety of contexts, testing the ingenuity of early printers to transmit visually the message of the word. When we look at book illustration in particular, the movement from manuscript to print can be traced as a political act, with the print medium empowering newly literate readers, both women and men, to read and think for themselves.

Chapter 1

EARLY ILLUSTRATION IN PRINT

SINGLE LEAVES, BLOCK-BOOKS
AND THEIR PRINTED PROGENY

JUST HOW UNUSUAL WAS IT to own a printed book in the late fifteenth century? For the modern reader, the latest bestseller is as close as the Internet or the corner bookshop. The process of acquiring a book in the early days of printing in England was far more complex, even if one happened to live in Westminster where books were produced or in one of the university towns where imported books were offered for sale. Still, the introduction of printing into England by William Caxton in 1476 dramatically increased the number and availability of books. Ownership of books was suddenly possible in a way it had not been before. The printed book, in fact, gradually changed the world of the private individual in the fifteenth century just as computers have changed ours today.

Like any technology, however, printing began conservatively, becoming gradually more innovative and experimental as new applications were found. In the fifteenth century, as today, we find old and new media co-existing. Manuscript and print were produced together, with more or less equal value attached to them. Print met with less resistance than modern electronic media, at least initially, perhaps because it was first used to produce conservative publications such as the Gutenberg Bible (Fig. 1). The Church required uniformity in its bibles, missals and prayer-books, and printing supplied that need. But the Church could not foresee print's capacity to reach a mass audience outside its direct control, an aspect later exploited by Martin Luther and later Protestant reformers, and by every entrepreneur who turned to printing in the early years, producing a readily affordable product for increasingly literate audiences.

Not surprisingly, most of what was first printed in England had previously circulated in manuscript; works popular in manuscript were popularised further by print. Among the earliest works printed in England were Chaucer's *Canterbury Tales* and *The Parliament of Fowls*; Ranulf Higden's *Polychronicon* (translated by John Trevisa); the encyclopedia of Bartholomeus Anglicus; the compilation of saints' lives called the *Golden Legend*; and numerous works translated, written by or attributed to John Lydgate, the prolific court poet to Henry V and Humphrey, Duke of Gloucester, including the *Fall of Princes*, the *Pilgrimage of the Life of Man*, *The Siege of Thebes*, *The Churl and the Birde*, *The Horse, the Sheep and the Goose*, *The Temple of Glas*, *The Court of Sapyence*, *The Lyf of our lady*, and *The medicyne of the stomache*, all published between 1476 and 1515. In western Europe, during the first fifty years of printing, then,

Fig. 1. Biblia Latina [Gutenberg Bible] (Mainz: Johann Gutenberg, *c.* 1454-5),
fol. A1[r]. BL C.9.d.3, 4.

very little appeared in print that had not previously appeared in manuscript. The Bible, the *Canterbury Tales*, Aesop's *Fables*, the *Golden Legend* and prayer-books, or Books of Hours, were among the earliest works in England with a continuous publishing history from manuscript to print, making the jump from being copied by hand into printed books called 'incunabula' (literally, 'from the cradle').[1] Caxton's early output mirrored a similar conservatism in continental practice.

At the outset, printing was a costly enterprise, requiring a large financial outlay. Printers who survived the early years took few risks, printing what had proved successful and reliable in manuscript exemplars. Printed books were made to look like manuscripts, incorporating details of manuscript format and presentation, such as page-ruling as a guide for written script, which printing with set type had made obsolete. Illumination and coloured initials were supplied by hand in printed books to make them seem similar to manuscripts. This 'hand-finishing' might have occurred in the printing house or have been supplied by stationers; it could have been collectively bespoke or ordered by individual owners. We find, for example, hand-supplied paraph marks and initials on a page from William Caxton's 1483 printed edition of Chaucer's *Canterbury Tales* (Fig. 2). Printed books were at first directed at an elite, wealthy, educated

Fig. 2. Geoffrey Chaucer, *Canterbury Tales* (Westminster: William Caxton, 1483), sig. a3ᵛ. *STC* 5083. BL G. 11586 (or IB 55095).

audience, well versed in Latin, and judging from the many incunables printed in English, in the vernacular as well. This was essentially the same group of readers as for manuscripts, which, of course, did not die out with the invention of printing, but existed alongside printed books in England for another 150 years or so. Later, in the sixteenth and seventeenth centuries, printing became devalued precisely because of its mass appeal and affordability; sonnets were circulated in manuscript among aristocratic intimates, presumably never intended to be printed, though most sonnet sequences were subsequently printed and read by those not known personally to the poet.[2] Earlier on, an elite audience for the printed book is indicated, in part, by the fact that, like many Latin incunabula produced on the continent, the first books printed by Caxton after he returned to England with the new technology have no pictures. The first big book Caxton published at Westminster was his *Canterbury Tales* edition of 1476/7. This appeared without woodcut illustrations or initials, and director letters for initials occur throughout, indicating that, at some point after printing, initials were to have been added by hand. In the well-known preface to his second *Canterbury Tales* edition of 1483, Caxton explains that the manuscript 'by whiche I haue corrected my book' was brought to him by a dissatisfied purchaser of the first edition. This manuscript is described in the preface as 'a book whyche hys fader had and moche louyd / that was very trewe', but Caxton does not mention whether it was illustrated.[3] Caxton's 'corrected' second edition of *Canterbury Tales*, however, appeared with 22 woodcuts of the pilgrims on horseback, along with the famous illustration of the dinner at the Tabard Inn. The second edition of the *Canterbury Tales* thus established a pictorial tradition of pilgrim illustration in print that was followed, somewhat sporadically, by the printed editions of Chaucer's *Works* through the eighteenth century.[4]

Caxton's illustrated *Canterbury Tales* is representative of an increasing trend toward illustration that occurred some years after printing came to England. When Caxton established his press at Westminster, it is highly probable that he lacked the artists, wood-blocks and expertise to produce illustrated books; Caxton's first book with illustrations, *The Mirror of the World* (1481), appeared with eleven diagrammatic woodcuts after he had been in the business of editing, translating and printing books in England for five years. In his introduction to the first edition, Caxton stipulates that this particular text, which he has also translated, requires 'figures / without whiche it may not lightly be vnderstande'.[5]

But most experimentation with the possibilities of illustration and layout occurred later, being mainly the province of the printers who came after Caxton: Wynkyn de Worde, the foreman who took over Caxton's shop after his death early in 1492; and his chief rival, Richard Pynson, a Norman who probably learned printing at Rouen. This experimentation seems at least partly motivated by these printers' attempts to broaden the audience for books; producing attractive, inexpensive illustrated books was one way to develop readership. Perhaps the earliest forerunners of these illustrated printed books that began to circulate in the late fifteenth century appeared even before the actual invention of printing with movable type in the form of single-leaf prints, which started to be produced around 1400.

Single-leaf prints were multiple reproductions of the same image, often accompanied by xylographic text, that is, with text produced in relief print from a wood-block, painstakingly hand-cut letter by letter. They were created originally as *ephemerae*, or 'matter of current and passing interest', that is, like holy cards today or even a leaflet one might be handed on the street. Single-leaf prints had a variety of uses: they might be hung on the walls of rooms in the home or sewn into clothes, purchased as indulgences or bought and sold as souvenirs of pilgrimages. We find them pasted on travelling or dispatch boxes, adorning 'countless little tracts, boxes, drawers, clothes and personal articles of the fifteenth century', or, in the city of Florence, lining the interiors of coffins. They quickly became either bound in with or pasted into manuscripts – or at least, that is where we usually find them today, their survival aided, if not guaranteed, by having been bound into a book. A little later in the fifteenth century, we also find them interleaved with or pasted into books printed with movable type. However, 'By 1500 only modest, private devotional tracts were ornamented by pasted-in woodcuts and engravings; most such objects were being produced by commercial printers.'[6]

As pious objects, single-leaf woodcuts were early associated with women owners or patrons. In *Portrait of a Female Donor* (Fig. 3), painted *c.* 1450 by Petrus Christus, for example, we see a woodcut of St Elizabeth tacked to the wall above a prie-dieu at which an unidentified noblewoman kneels.[7] There are many other examples of prints associated with or sometimes made by women.

On the continent, the Bridgettine order, founded by St Bridget of Sweden in the fourteenth century, was well known for designing and producing single-leaf woodcuts for devotional purposes, some before the invention of printing with movable type. Several important examples are now in the Ashmolean Museum, Oxford, including a single-leaf print of Bridget with her daughter, also a saint, made in Augsburg *c.* 1490 to 1500. Both women are shown holding books, and their haloes are inscribed with the xylographic captions 'S. Birgitta' and 'S. Katerina B. tochter' (Fig. 4). Dodgson comments that 'The production of very numerous woodcuts relating to [Bridget] in Germany at the end of the fifteenth century may be connected with a general chapter of the Brigittine order which was held in 1487 at Gnadenberg in the Upper Palatinate.'[8] Single-leaf prints such as this example were typically made to commemorate and publicise such an occasion.

A triptych woodcut of Bridget (Fig. 5), which shows her giving the rule to her order, was also produced in Augsburg. At the bottom of the woodcut is the xylographic inscription: 'Da gibt sant birgita us3 die regel saluatoris den schwestern vvnd brudern' ('Here St Bridget issues the Rule of the Saviour to the sisters and brothers'). This woodcut also promoted the sanctity and cult of the saint, showing her blessed from above by Christ and the Virgin Mary as the dove of the Holy Spirit emerges from the clouds. The kneeling nun in the left foreground, shown with a halo, was probably intended to represent Bridget's daughter, St Catherine. Two other impressions of this woodcut occur in the Munich University Library and in a manuscript derived from the Bridgettine convent of Altomunster, where the woodcuts were probably produced.[9] In the fifteenth century, it became common practice to insert ready-made single-leaf prints into plain paper manuscripts as an inexpensive method of illustration.[10]

A *Pietà* with the instruments of the Passion in 26 compartments (Fig. 6), also produced by the Bridgettines, was originally intended as an indulgence. Bridget herself was 'an eminent propagandist for indulgences', and a number of surviving indulgences can be traced to Bridgettine workshops both in England and on the continent.[11] Three lines of xylographic text beneath the image ('Who sum euer deuoutly beholdith these armys off cristis passyon hat ... yeris off pardon') have been dutifully scratched out, perhaps by some sixteenth-century Reformer. This woodcut, along with two others, has been inserted as an illustration into MS Rawlinson D. 403, a fifteenth-century paper manuscript with Bridgettine prayers written in Latin, now in the Bodleian Library, Oxford.[12] Like the manuscript, the woodcuts were made in England, most likely at the Bridgettine house of Syon in Isleworth, just outside London.[13] A. I. Doyle has described two other Syon-related indulgences, one of the fallen Christ, the Virgin and St Bridget, and

Fig. 3. Petrus Christus, Portrait of a Female Donor, *c.* 1450 (detail).
Washington, D.C., National Gallery of Art.

Fig. 4 (*above left*). St Bridget and
St Catherine of Sweden (Augsburg,
c. 1490-1500). Douce coll. Oxford,
Ashmolean Museum. Dodgson 38,
Schreiber 1311-1313.

Fig. 5 (*above right*). St Bridget Giving the
Rule to her Order (Augsburg, fifteenth
century). Douce coll. Oxford, Ashmolean
Museum. Dodgson 37, Schreiber 1293a.

Fig. 6 (*below left*). Pietà. English, fifteenth
century. Inserted into MS Rawl. D. 403.
Oxford, Bodleian Library. Schreiber 976,
Dodgson, Bodl. 21.

another showing Christ seated on a Cross surrounded by the instruments of the Passion, that have been bound into a copy of Walter Hilton's *Scale of Perfection*, published by Wynkyn de Worde in 1525. Doyle comments that the presence of these woodcuts 'suggests that this was a Syon-owned book; not only its subject, but the very presence of these cuts, for the Brigittines and Carthusians seem to have been very prominent in the use and importation of such things into England'.[14]

Block-books, printed from wood-blocks, were once thought to represent an interim stage between single-leaf prints and books printed with movable type. Paper analysis has shown, however, that block-books cannot be dated any earlier than 1460 to 1470, post-dating the invention of printing with movable type by at least a decade.[15] Xylography, producing text in relief print from a wood-block, has generally been considered a more primitive technology than printing with movable type, but it may not have been so regarded when the two technologies were new and existed side by side. Johannes Regiomontanus, for example, a mathematician and printer from Nuremberg (fl. 1474), first produced a calendar printed with movable type, and then, some months later, a completely xylographic calendar. And then there are curious hybrid productions dating from this early period of printing, such as the *Speculum humanae salvationis* in the Pierpont Morgan Library in New York, the second Latin edition of this work to appear in print. This particular edition, printed by an anonymous printer about 1474 to 1475, has twenty xylographic leaves, that is, leaves in which illustration and text are both produced from wood-blocks. The rest of the text is set in movable type with woodcut illustrations.[16]

As these examples suggest, neither xylographic reproduction nor printing with movable type seems to have been valued over the other in the incunable era. Block-books, however, are primarily pictorial with minimal text, while illustration is not, at least initially, the primary emphasis in books printed with movable type. As one technology gradually overtakes the other, illustrations from block-books are appropriated to new uses, finding their way into vernacular printed books directed at a predominantly lay audience.

Block-books are important because they preserve and act as conduits for popular religious themes and imagery. These include Apocalypse sequences, the Fifteen Signs of Doomsday (preserved in the last leaves of the German Antichrist block-book), the *Oracula Sibyllina*, the typological *Biblia pauperum*, the *Speculum humanae salvationis* and the *Ars moriendi*. Pictures in block-books became models for later illustration in books printed from movable type; though block-books as such were not produced in England and only minimally in France, images from them proliferated in popular vernacular handbooks and in the margins of printed Books of Hours in the late fifteenth and early sixteenth centuries.[17] Block-book formats and presentation were also adapted to new uses. As this and subsequent chapters will demonstrate, illustration found initially in block-books would retain its vitality well after printing with movable type became the technology of choice.

One very well documented example of the fluid movement between books printed xylographically and those produced typographically is the Art of Dying, or *Ars moriendi*. Block-books on this theme, which became popular in the 1470s, were derived from the *Tractatus*, or *Speculum*, *artis bene moriendi*, which was probably written in the first quarter of the fifteenth century, most likely 'between 1414 and 1415 by order of the Council of Constance, which included among its reforming concerns an "emphasis on more devout Christian living"'.[18] The *Ars moriendi* text opens by saying it was intended not only for 'religious and devout men but also for carnal and secular men'. The anonymous author wished to provide Christians, both religious and lay, with a handbook of practical as well as spiritual aid, guiding them through the stages of dying.[19]

The *Tractatus* was, in turn, based on the writings of Jean Gerson, chancellor of the University of Paris in the early fifteenth century. In a section on the art of dying in his *Opusculum tripartitium*, Gerson addressed himself first to priests, then to laymen caring for the poor and sick; this portion of the treatise was based directly on the liturgy for visiting the sick (*De visitate infirmorum*). According to Mary Catharine O'Connor, in what is still the most authoritative study, the *Tractatus* is the earlier of the two popular versions; the block-book is not a source for the longer work, as once was thought, but an abridgement derived from it.[20] Based on just one chapter of the *Tractatus*, the block-book *Ars moriendi* consists of eleven woodcuts depicting, in expanded and animated form, the temptations and the spiritual recovery of the dying man. Each woodcut is accompanied by a single page of text. The illustrations dramatise each temptation, stage by stage, and then provide spiritual comfort as revealed in Scripture and interpreted by the Church.

Two pages from a German block-book *Ars moriendi*, issued *c.* 1475, illustrate scenes which will be used elsewhere. In the Temptation to Impatience (Fig. 7), Moriens, or the dying man, 'having overturned the bedside table and with it a bowl, a glass and a spoon, is now kicking the doctor, who is retreating in alarm'.[21] In this picture one woman, presumably the dying man's wife, sympathetically (or perhaps ironically) says, 'Behold how he bears his suffering' ('Ecce quantam penam patitur'), while the demon exclaims, 'How well I have deceived him!' ('Quam bene decepi eum'). In the foreground, another woman holds a glass in one hand, and in the other a plate on which is the leg of a fowl, domestic details which may also refer to the importance placed on diet by medieval medical practitioners when treating illness.

The other page (Fig. 8) illustrates the Death of Moriens in the eleventh and final scene of the volume: 'In this scene, the only one in which Moriens is at the left, the soul, in the form of a small child, is passing from his body to one of the group of four angels behind the bed. ... On the right side stands a crucifix between two groups of saints, Our Lady, St Mary Magdalene and St Peter (here distinguished by a sword) foremost in one group, St John in the other. At the right of the bed six demons are departing in fury.' By ending the *Ars moriendi* text with this powerful image of the Final Moment, the anonymous author extends hope for salvation to all Christians in their last earthly battle, the soul shown here as having successfully passed all the temptations of the previous scenes.[22]

The *Ars moriendi* is known in 21 printings reproduced from 13 distinct sets of blocks.[23] Perhaps the most beautiful illustrations are the copper engravings made by Master E. S. around 1450, one very likely pictorial source for the woodcuts that later appear in block-books.[24] With the increasing use of movable type, these pictures are taken from their block-book contexts and put to new uses; many find their way into English vernacular religious texts via French intermediaries. The entire *Ars moriendi* block-book series was copied and reproduced in 1492 in *L'Art de bien vivre et de bien mourir*, published in Paris for the prolific French editor and bookseller Antoine Vérard; in this and in later Vérard editions, the Latin text has been translated into French.

In the French text accompanying the scene of Impatience, for example (Fig. 9), Satan says to the dying man: 'You suffer too much; God is not just. Look at these people around you. They pretend to sympathize with your ills, but they really are thinking only of your money.'[25] This reference to the barely concealed venality of the mourners clustered about the dying man's bed is a late medieval common-place, illustrated visually in Books of Hours such as the *Hours of Catherine of Cleves*, though perhaps most fully realised in later seventeenth-century plays from John Webster's *Duchess of Malfi* to Ben Jonson's *Volpone*. In the final scene, the death of Moriens, the soul of the dying man is shown reborn as a child into eternal life. The dying man has used his free will responsibly, 'made a good death', and found eternal salvation.

Ars moriendi images in England are derived from Vérard's *L'Art de bien vivre et de bien mourir* and from another book published in Paris by Vérard in 1503, a peculiar English translation called *The book intytulyd the art of good lywyng and good deying*.[26] Illustrations based on Vérard and indirectly on continental block-books then appear in English books, for example, in the *Boke named the Royall*, a religious vernacular prose manual printed collaboratively by Wynkyn de Worde and Richard Pynson in 1507. The English text was translated by William Caxton from the *Somme le Roi*, composed in 1279 by Frère Laurent for King Philippe III of France, and printed by Caxton *c*. 1485-1486.[27]

The manuscripts of the *Somme le Roi* quickly developed a picture cycle of fifteen miniatures which was firmly established by the end of the 1200s. The manuscripts uniformly illustrated the how-to-die-well chapter of text with a Last Judgement scene.[28] In the *Boke named the Royall*, however, de Worde and Pynson depart from the manuscript tradition, looking to more recent printed models which derive from the block-book *Ars moriendi* (Fig. 10).

An evocative image (Fig. 11) appears on the verso of the final folio of *ThOrdynary of Crysten Men*, a vernacular prose handbook printed in 1506 by de Worde.[29] This was Andrew Chertsey's translation of Vérard's *L'Art de bien vivre et de bien mourir*. De Worde printed two editions of the Chertsey translation, in 1502 and again in 1506. The title-page of *ThOrdynary of Crysten Men* consists of two blocks, one with the xylographic title of the book

Fig. 7 (*above right*). Temptation to Impatience. *Ars moriendi* block-book, 1st edition (Rhine district: *c.* 1465), fol. 21ʳ (fol. 11ᵛ, modern foliation in right corner). BL IB 18. Schreiber iv.257.
Fig. 8 (*above left*). Death of Moriens. *Ars moriendi* block-book, 1st edition (Rhine district: *c.* 1465), fol. 41ʳ (fol. 23ᵛ, modern foliation, right corner). BL IB 18. Schreiber iv. 257.
Fig. 9 (*below left*). Temptation to Impatience. *L'Art de bien vivre et de bien mourir* (Paris: for Antoine Vérard, 1492), sig. ciiʳ. IB 40027.

and another of the Sacrament of Confession. On the verso of the last leaf, the xylographic title of the book is repeated, along with the woodcut derived from the *Ars moriendi* of the death of Moriens. Repetition of the title on the verso of the last leaf may be connected to the way early books were sold, usually in paper covers to be bound elsewhere. This repetition gives a sense of closure to the volume, encapsulating the information the book contains.[30]

We find the *Ars moriendi* images again copied in *The crafte to lyue well and to dye well* (Fig. 12), another translation from Vérard, which was printed by de Worde in 1505. In the Temptation to Impatience woodcut, the scrolls have been filled in with movable type rather than xylographic lettering. This is a good example of what is called factotum printing, where pieces of type were inserted into spaces within the wood-block.[31] Still other copies from the block-book *Ars moriendi* turn up on the title-pages of *The deyenge creature*, printed by de Worde in 1507 and again in 1514, and of the *Rote or myrour of consolacyon & conforte*, which appeared in 1511 and in 1530. Other copies of *Ars moriendi* images occur in numerous other English books, including the *Complaynt of the Soule*, printed c. 1519 and 1532; the *Doctrynall of dethe*, printed in 1532; and in later issues of the English *Ars moriendi*.[32]

Ars moriendi images were both common and popular in early printed books for the laity, and their continued reuse by French and English printers should not be attributed to printerly expediency or unimaginative copying of what had come before. Instead, these are images with a history, with associations. Behind them lies a consciousness of *Ars moriendi* block-books and manuscript miniatures – for example, those which occur in the Litany and Office of the Dead in Books of Hours. These pictorial guide-books were practical as well as popular, leading the dying person visually through series of steps, showing the human response to sickness and approaching death (kicking the doctor, for example) and offering various consolatory motifs. If one can judge a culture from its how-to books, what one sees in French and English handbooks for the laity in the later fifteenth and early sixteenth centuries is an honest acceptance of the inevitability of death in books that tell one how to live well and die well, and how to find consolation and comfort in the process of dying. *Ars moriendi* images retained their potency because they were immediately recognisable to contemporary readers, identifying and introducing the contents of the text.

Though block-books and books printed with movable type emerged simultaneously, they seem (at least on first glance) to have been directed at two very different types of audience. Picture books represented a transitional phase between hearing a story and reading it; illustrated books were generally designed for lay use, for readers more adept at interpreting visual than verbal signs. While some block-books are very simple, however, others, like the *Biblia pauperum* (Fig. 13), are directed at a more sophisticated reader and were very probably employed for the private devotion of the educated lay person, that is, a reader adept at interpreting complex visual signs. Avril Henry has pointed out in her recent facsimile edition of the *Biblia pauperum* that 'The medieval user of the

Fig. 10 (*above left*). How to Die Well. *Boke named the Royall*, trans. William Caxton
(London: Wynkyn de Worde and Richard Pynson, 1507), sig. J5ʳ. *STC* 21430. C.11.a.23.
Fig. 11 (*above right*). End-leaf, *ThOrdynary of Crysten Men*, trans. Andrew Chertsey
(London: Wynkyn de Worde, 1506), sig. PP6ᵛ (endleaf). *STC* 5199. BL C.25.f.7.
Fig. 12 (*below left*). Temptation to Impatience. *The crafte to lyue well and to dye well*
(London: Wynkyn de Worde, 1505), sig. Bb6ᵛ. *STC* 792. BL C.132.h.40.

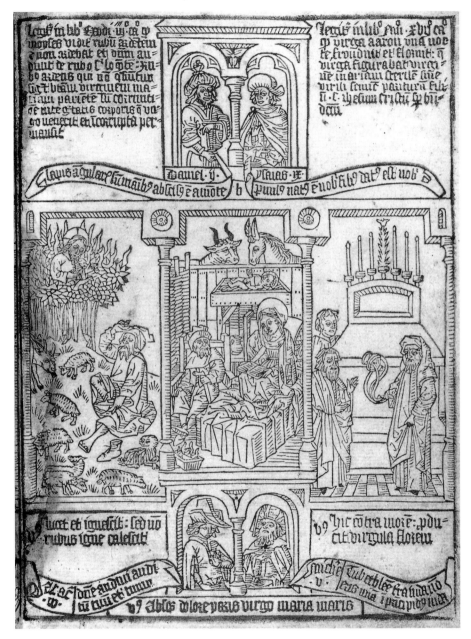

Fig. 13. Moses, the Nativity and Aaron. *Biblia pauperum* (Netherlands: *c.* 1470),
fol. 3ʳ. BL G 12090. Schreiber edition IX.

forty-page block-book *Biblia pauperum* must have possessed remarkable skills in reading its pictures, let alone its heavily abbreviated Latin text. Such a combination of skills is rare today.'[33] In light of these observations, Henry has suggested that the *Biblia pauperum* images, with their truncated texts, were primarily meditative, meant to be savoured and contemplated rather than quickly perused.

The reading of visual and/or verbal signs becomes a question of perception as well as of literacy. Certainly, in the premodern world where there were fewer images (and they were therefore much more significant), the reading of pictures was a complex and subtle process. In early printed books, pictures can trigger the memory of heard text; visual signs aid in deciphering the meaning of verbal signs. (Ironically, with increased literacy, pictures become secondary, reliance on memory less crucial, and memory weaker.) Reading the image not only aids in reading the text, but fixes the contents of the text in the memory.

Memory is a key element in understanding the role of pictures in the reading process. According to medieval and Renaissance commentaries, memory is centred on the image.[34] Modern studies have also demonstrated that memory is closely tied to the use of synesthesia, turning sounds into vivid visual imagery.[35] It is no coincidence that texts of the *Ars memorativa* proliferated in block-book form in the fifteenth century, and that images from them were copied in memory books printed with movable type in the sixteenth century. One example (Fig. 14), from the *Ars memorandi* printed by Thomas Anshelm at Pforzheim in 1502, combines illustrations reproduced from block-books with typographic text.[36] The picture may initially puzzle a literate person who is accustomed to reading without pictures; in this case, the visual image is used to spark memory of heard text, immediately communicating the idea of the text, chapter and verse, to an image-oriented, non-linear thinker.

Here is the way this particular picture might be decoded. The eagle, symbol of John, represents St John's Gospel. To the right of the eagle's head is the head of an old man with flowing beard; to the left is the head of a man, and standing on the eagle's head, a dove, with the number '1' beside it. These represent the secret of the Trinity, visual shorthand for the contents of the first chapter of the Gospel of John. A lute on the eagle's chest, inscribed with the number '2', and accompanied by little money bags, represents the second chapter, and recalls the marriage at Cana (the lute is traditionally a marriage instrument) and the driving of the money-changers from the Temple. Other images accompanied by numbers designate the main events of each chapter. For example, the loaves and fishes over the eagle's right wing represent the miraculous feeding of the five thousand in the sixth chapter. The wafer, with the image of the Crucifixion, refers to John 6:35, where Jesus tells the apostles, 'I am the bread of life.' Chapter and verse of the other Gospels are similarly displayed; the other main figures are the lion, bull and angel, representing Mark, Luke and Matthew respectively, with smaller figures representing chapters arranged on and around them.[37] Such pictures operate

Prima viden Aquilę facies : ſed imago Iofiannis
Hec docet immēſi que genitura dei   a iij

Fig. 14. The Gospel of John. *Ars memorandi* (Pforzheim:
Thomas Anshelm, 1502), sig. a3^r. BL 689.C.7.

quite differently from pictures in our modern culture, which generally communicate new information; the function of woodcuts in the *Ars memorandi* is to remind the reader of what he or she already knows.

The presentation of typological scenes in the *Biblia pauperum* and *Speculum humanae salvationis* also implies a degree of pictorial literacy on the part of the observer or reader.[38] The meaning of 'typology' is relatively simple; it is defined as the study of types, most frequently as the use of Old Testament images or texts to prefigure or prophesy those of the New, thus linking past, present and future as part of God's plan. Typological imagery, however, in its many combinations can become quite complex to decipher. As Avril Henry comments, 'pictures in this mode only "instruct" if you already know what they mean. They then act as reminders of the known truth. It is not a bit of good staring at a picture of a man carrying two large doors on the outskirts of a city and expecting it to suggest the risen Christ. You are likely to take him for a builder's merchant or a removal man unless you already know that this is always Samson with the gates of Gaza and that like Christ he has, as it were, broken gaol.'[39]

Though their meaning and intention are difficult for the modern scholar fully to grasp and identify, typological block-books like the *Speculum humanae salvationis* and the *Biblia pauperum* draw on a world of images that seems to have been readily recognisable to their fifteenth-century readers. It is now thought that such books were texts for meditation with mnemonic elements used in the private devotions of educated lay people. Their page presentation is non-linear; the interplay of text and image on each page can be read and interpreted in a variety of ways. Henry compares this to 'a series of chords – comprehensible only because based on recognized relationships, exciting in unexpected modulations by Prophecies and tituli'.[40] Non-linear thinking is often associated with an intuitive grasp of the whole, in which, as Rudolf Arnheim notes, 'the components of intuitive thought processes interact within a continuous field'.[41] The printing of texts with movable type, on the other hand, tends to fix linearity of thought, which 'transforms all linear relations into one-dimensional successions – the sort of event we represent by an arrow'.[42]

Appropriating typological block-book images to illustrate vernacular books later in the sixteenth century was not, however, a retrogressive exercise. Such images were still vital, fulfilling important cultural functions. As Keith Moxey has remarked more generally about woodcuts, 'we need to understand their cultural significance for those who produced and acquired them and thus demonstrate the ways these images actively articulated the structure of social relations'.[43] The continued reproduction of typological images implies a thought process in transition; though readers of sixteenth-century illustrated vernacular books are a generation away from the block-book audience, the emphasis on the image continues to suggest a readership more pictorially than verbally literate.

About 1504, Antoine Vérard published *Les figures du Vieil Testament et du Nouuel*, with illustrations copied from those in the block-book *Biblia pauperum* (Fig. 15). The British Library has a paper fragment as well as a presentation or

Fig. 15. Moses, the Nativity and Aaron. *Les figures du Vieil Testament et du Nouuel*
(Paris: for Antoine Vérard, *c.* 1504), sig. a.iiii^r. BL C.22.b.7.

Fig. 16. Moses and the Nativity.
*The crafte to lyue well and to dye
well* (London: Wynkyn de Worde,
1505), sig. D3ʳ. *STC* 792.
BL C.132.h.40.

de luxe copy printed on vellum with hand-coloured full-page images. Lengthy
vernacular verses and text accompany the illustrations (though Latin captions
appear in the pictures themselves). The verses here, however, differ from the
vernacular verse captions of similar typological scenes in *L'Art de bien vivre et de
bien mourir*, published for Vérard in 1492, though the relationship between
illustrations in these two books, as well as their links with *Biblia pauperum*
block-books, is worth further inquiry.[44] Vérard clearly knew the images from the
Biblia pauperum and reproduced them in his books, and the picture copies
in his *L'Art de bien vivre et de bien mourir* were the immediate model for
typological scenes in *The crafte to lyue well and to dye well*, printed by Wynkyn
de Worde in 1505 (Fig. 16).

In de Worde's version, typological two-block illustrations accompany a
lengthy exposition of the Creed. The text is English and includes Latin Bible

verses and commentaries on each article. To create many of these typological scenes, de Worde combines woodcuts and metalcuts, the latter from a Book of Hours series, clearly French in style, the provenance of which has yet to be identified.[45] In an illustration of Moses and the Nativity (Fig. 16), the text in the scrolls of the prophet ('Ego autem in domino gaudeo') and of the apostle, identified in the text as St James ('Qui conceptus est de spiritu'), has been inserted into the factotum block. The typological significance of the story of Moses before the Burning Bush and its relation to the conception of Christ is clarified by the verses beneath the illustration:

> Moyses sawe the busshe/enflammed all with fyre.
> A voyce also he herde but nothynge he perceyued.
> Mary þe mayden as was her desyre.
> Without mannes sede the sone of god conceyued.[46]

This simple poetry, along with the image, acts as a mnemonic trigger. In the miracle of the Burning Bush, Moses is shown the prefiguration of Christ's conception, which is represented by the metalcut of the Nativity beneath the Moses woodcut.

In the French version (Fig. 17) published for Vérard, the prophet and apostle are given more detailed scripts; the central scene is a conflation of the Annunciation, with the angel before Mary at the left and the Nativity at the right; and the entire illustration is cut from one block. Beneath the picture are French verses which are closely related to the English ones. Both the English and French versions have a common source in block-books, in the typological illustrations presented in the *Speculum humanae salvationis* (which pairs Moses before the Burning Bush with the Annunciation) and even more directly with those in the *Biblia pauperum*.

In the complex pictorial narrative of the *Biblia pauperum* (Fig. 13), the Nativity is presented as the central scene flanked by illustrations of Moses before the Burning Bush and of the flowering rod of Aaron, which miraculously blossomed one night, another Old Testament prefiguring of the Conception. Four figures, identified as Daniel, Isaiah, Habakkuk and Micah (the latter text quoted, however, from Matthew 2:6), appear in architectural frames with scrolls containing quotations pertinent to the pictures. The choice of the Nativity as the central illustration in both the Vérard and the de Worde texts, with their inclusion of two figures with scrolls – a prophet from the Old Testament and an apostle from the New – seems modelled on the presentation of typological scenes in the *Biblia pauperum*. All these texts pictorially refer to the Old Testament prefiguring of New Testament events, the ideas then made simplified and more explicit in these later vernacular copies.

Another typological illustration from *The crafte to lyue well and to dye well* (Fig. 18) again consists of two blocks. The woodcut above shows Samson carrying off the Gates of Gaza. At the left is a prophet, and at the right, the

Fig. 17. Moses, Annunciation, Nativity. *L'Art de bien vivre* (Paris: for Antoine Vérard, 1492), sig. dd3ʳ. BL IB 40027.

Apostle Thomas with his piece of the Creed. The association of each Apostle with a specific line of the Creed was commonplace by the fifteenth century, used as a mnemonic device and teaching tool. The Apostles regularly appear with their lines of the Creed in painted glass, manuscripts and printed books. Thomas is here appropriately given the line referring to Christ's Descent into Hell.[47] The woodcut beneath depicts the Harrowing of Hell. Although the pairing of Samson with the Harrowing is not precisely incorrect, when examined in the larger context of earlier models – the *Biblia pauperum*, for example, shows us Samson, the release of Jonah, and as the central scene, the Resurrection – the English example is perhaps overly anticipatory. The Vérard woodcut in *L'Art de bien viure et de bien mourir* (Fig. 19) shows Samson with the prophet and apostle above the central scene of the Resurrection. The Harrowing is conflated with this central image, taking place in the left background. Both the *Speculum humanae salvationis* and the *Biblia pauperum* consistently use the Old Testament types of Samson carrying off the gates and Jonah emerging from the whale as pre-figurations of the Resurrection. The Harrowing, in the block-book exemplars, is

Fig. 18. Samson and the Harrowing of Hell. *The crafte to lyue well and to dye well* (London: Wynkyn de Worde, 1505), sig. D4^r. *STC* 792. BL C.132.h.40.

always accompanied by scenes of David cutting off the head of Goliath and Samson killing the lion.

The linking of Samson with the Harrowing in the de Worde illustration is not an error but one example of his resourcefulness in illustrating texts. De Worde inherited the Harrowing woodcut from the former master of his shop, Caxton. It is one of several woodcuts, all designed by the same artist, used to illustrate Caxton's two editions of Nicholas Love's translation of *Speculum vitae Christi*.[48] This group of woodcuts once included a Resurrection woodcut as well, which may have been broken, worn down or lost by 1505, the date of *The crafte to lyue well and to dye well*. It does not appear after 1498. But the substitution of the

26

Fig. 19. Samson, Resurrection and Harrowing of Hell. *L'Art de bien… mourir* (Paris: for Antoine Vérard, 1493), sig. d2ʳ. BL C.22.b.3 (imperf.).

Harrowing illustration makes good sense when read in the context of the descriptive verse beneath:

> Thre dayes ionas was closed in þe se
>
> Samson brake ye yates & bare them away
>
> Jhesu heryed hell that dyed on a tre.
>
> And the thyrde day arose in þe sprynge of the daye.

The verse connects the two Old Testament types, Jonah and Samson, who are familiar from block-book models, with the twin themes of the Harrowing and the Resurrection. In this example, as in other typological illustrations, we see de Worde's reliance on and reinterpretation of his sources, and his inventiveness in economically using the blocks he had on hand, characteristics which are more fully explored elsewhere in this volume. Whether he knew the *Biblia pauperum* and *Speculum* at first hand is another matter; it is more likely that the English printers came to their imagery through other intermediaries produced on the

Fig. 20. Joseph, the Entombment and Jonah. *Biblia pauperum* (Netherlands, 1470?),
p. 27. BL G 12090.

continent, either in books like Vérard's or through the typological marginalia commonly found in Books of Hours printed in France.

Block-books also serve as sources for Hours marginalia, just as they do for illustrations found in vernacular handbooks for the laity. Pictures of sibyls and narrative illustrations from the Apocalypse derived from block-book models occur frequently in the margins of Books of Hours printed in Paris for the English and French markets, as do the Fifteen Signs of Doomsday and Last Judgement, the Dance of Death, and various typological scenes.[49]

Since block-books were not printed in England, I suspect that block-book images were conveyed en masse to the English reading public by way of the narrative and typological borders in printed Books of Hours. One comparison may be apt. On one page from the *Biblia pauperum* (Fig. 20), the scene on the left shows Joseph put down the well; the central panel illustrates Christ's Entombment; and the right panel shows Jonah cast into the sea. Beneath are two prophets with xylographic text in banderoles. In another example from a printed Book of Hours (Fig. 21), we see the same scenes running down the right margin: Joseph in the well, the Entombment and Jonah. This repetition of scenes is simply conventional typology, but what is significant (and points to the block-book *Biblia pauperum* as the immediate source) is the text spoken by the two prophets in the lower margin, which, though abbreviated differently, matches that in the *Biblia pauperum*; texts differ slightly from block-book to block-book and from Book of Hours to Book of Hours, but this seems more than a coincidence.[50]

Typological scenes like these appeal to a particular type of reader. The images in de Worde's *Crafte to lyue well*, for example, are drawn from block-book models, by way of Vérard and Hours marginalia, and have several functions. De Worde's homely two-block illustrations stand in complex relation to the text: there are connections between Old Testament and New Testament scenes; between illustration and verse; and between illustration, verse and the prose commentary on each article of the Creed. In these examples, visual images lend another level of meaning to the main text, acting as marginal commentaries as well as mnemonic devices which help the reader hold the main ideas in mind. And, in these pages, two modes of thought and perception stand side by side: the ideas are communicated through the linearly presented prose text, the non-linear typological scenes, and finally, through the mnemonic verses that tie the two together.

We find another kind of non-linearity in the early history of publishing, when manuscripts, single-leaf prints, block-books and books printed from movable type co-existed. As printing with movable type became dominant, some of these earlier forms were incorporated into it. Just as manuscript details were included in print formats, manuscripts also began to be copied from printed books, and the two media were at first given equal weight in a non-linear progression in the fifteenth and early sixteenth centuries. Though originally directed at an educated class of readers adept in Latin, printed books began to be illustrated, an excellent

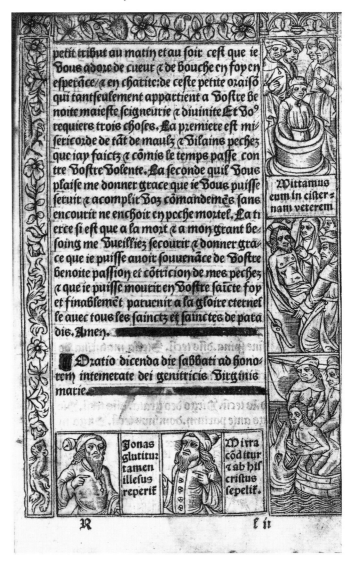

Fig. 21. Joseph, the Entombment and Jonah. *Horae ad usum Sarum* (Paris: Philippe Pigouchet, Pro iohanne ricardo: Rothomagi, 1494), sig. E8ᵛ. BL IA.40311.

marketing device in the selling of a new product, as we shall see. The abundant illustration in printed vernacular books produced for the laity in the late fifteenth and early sixteenth centuries became an intellectual tool, making the meaning of text more readily accessible. The image served as stimulus for meditation, memory, reading and thinking. Block-book images represent an important stage in the movement from visual to verbal literacy because they preserved and promoted popular religious themes. With the increasing use of movable type, these images were removed from their block-book contexts and put to new uses. Block-book illustration was copied in later books because it was familiar, a known quantity, an available model for printers to use. The reprinting of these pictures, particularly those with mnemonic or typological elements, points to gradual changes in thought and perception in the late fifteenth and early sixteenth centuries. The pervasive reproduction of block-book images in later printed books indicates that these pictures still fulfilled a vital function, appealing to a large audience in the years following the invention of printing.

Chapter 2

WOODCUTS IN EARLY ENGLISH BOOKS
SOURCES AND CIRCULATION

F ROM THE START, printing in England was derivative. William Caxton, the first English printer, brought his texts, his type, many of his wood-blocks and his foreman, Wynkyn de Worde, from the continent. Caxton is better known for his translations, prologues and prose style than for the beautiful appearance of his books. While his type is cleanly designed and distinctive, his attention to illustration seems rather cursory at best (though there are exceptions, for example, *The Golden Legend*).[1] And, from the point of view of illustration, execution and layout, English printed books are generally regarded as inferior to their continental counterparts until well into the seventeenth century. Whether this reputation is entirely merited is debatable – there were some extremely ugly books produced on the continent in the early days of printing – and the English sense of inferiority may have been perpetuated, to some extent, by the printers themselves. Many commissions for Books of Hours, for example, were given to continental printers with English printers and stationers acting as middlemen, though the resulting products were hardly more handsome than Books of Hours printed in England.[2]

Then there is the later case of the Great Bible commissioned by Henry VIII in the 1530s, on the face of it the most nationalistic of projects – an English translation of the Bible to be distributed to all English churches, the English people being freely permitted to read or hear the text. But even this was sent initially to Paris to be printed at the shop of François Regnault. When the Paris press was threatened by the Inquisition, the printed sheets had to be smuggled across the Channel for the completion of the Great Bible in England.[3] Still, the fact is that at the start of the project, the Great Bible was given to the French, on the assumption that English presses were less capable of fine printing.

If even the English were sceptical about their own presses, why study illustration and layout in the early English printed book? There are several reasons. First, printers working in England were survivors in a tough trade. The man who misjudged his readership or who staked his funds on an unlikely project quickly went bankrupt. There are countless examples of early continental printers who produced two or three books and were never heard from again. But, for some reason, English printers were particularly tenacious: Wynkyn de Worde, who inherited Caxton's shop, survived an early legal wrangle with Caxton's daughter, and stayed in business until his death 44 years later, publishing nearly one thousand separate titles.[4] Plentiful, if not always beautiful, illustration, provided in ingeniously economical ways, seems to have been one key to de Worde's success. With the introduction of printing, books were suddenly available to people who could not previously afford them, people who were often partially literate or literate only in the vernacular. In many cases, the woodcuts, initials and page layout in books produced by the English printers act as guides through difficult or partially comprehended texts, indirectly promoting literacy by acting as signals or symbols of the texts and inviting the reader to read them. In this way, pictures functioned as a vital part of the reading process in the early printed book, and the plentiful reproduction of images seems to have built readership for books produced in England from the late fifteenth century onward.[5] Finally, in the study of English book history, Caxton has long been in the limelight. The importance of second- and third-generation British printers – men like de Worde, Richard Pynson, Julian Notary, Robert Copland, Robert Wyer and Thomas Godfray – is just now beginning to be fully evaluated.

In this chapter we will examine illustration and some of its sources in books produced by the second generation of printers in England, with emphasis on those produced by de Worde. Continental picture models, particularly those illustrating books published by the enterprising French bookseller and Parisian publisher Antoine Vérard, will also be more fully explored. Here we will trace as an example the peregrinations of two generic woodcut figures of continental origin, a man and a woman who sometimes appear together, sometimes separately and sometimes reversed, through a multitude of contexts in books printed for English readers over a sixty-year span from 1503 right through to 1566. The wanderings of the two figures exemplify both the ways in which context – the relationship between an image and a given text – influences the reading of that image, as well as the wide range of functions an image can perform. Likewise, the illustrations in English editions of works originally composed on the continent, notably by the fifteenth-century author Christine de Pizan, will shed light on attitudes toward translation, book illustration and authorship, as well as further demonstrate the ingenuity (and economical practices) of the English printers in visually transmitting the message of the printed word.

Among the earliest printers in England, Wynkyn de Worde seems to have been far more experimental than William Caxton or his contemporary and rival printer, Richard Pynson.[6] Whereas Caxton was more concerned with text, particularly with his translations, de Worde experimented with visual aspects of the book, the page layout, the effect of borders and initials and new methods of creating economical woodcut illustration. But de Worde's aesthetic sense has not received much praise. H. S. Bennett comments on the 'inferior quality' of de Worde's books, and Henry R. Plomer more scathingly remarks that de Worde had 'no artistic taste … nor did he trouble himself as to whether the blocks or ornaments he used were suitable to the text or type of book he was printing. … Anything that happened to be on the shelves at the time was inserted.'[7]

These appraisals seem unfair as well as incorrect. We find in many of de Worde's books not only a crude, vigorous skill in copying popular continental picture models but also thoughtful, purposeful presentation of illustration. Most woodcuts are either employed appropriately or are innocuous enough to illustrate nearly any scene imaginable. De Worde's illustrated books reflect his ingenuity and economy in the use of woodcuts and ornaments. Further, de Worde had a tremendous variety of blocks on hand, drawing on 'a stock of woodblocks which could not have numbered less than 1,000. It is (also) known that he took cuts here and there from foreign books printed in France and Flanders.'[8]

De Worde's ingenious use of pictures signals a new way of thinking about the book, the possibilities of the printed page, the function of illustration and the book's intended audience. His business acumen and his willingness to experiment with page design are shown in his use of an innovation which gradually becomes a standard feature after the introduction of printing – the title-page, a subject that will be discussed at more length in the next chapter. Here I shall analyse de Worde's adaptation of woodcuts, suggest probable sources for some of his illustrations, and describe what is surely not a random, careless placement of illustrations but the beginning of a thoughtful pictorial methodology that de Worde developed in the early years of his career.

De Worde seems to have had access to a large variety of picture sources. Prior to 1501, he made imaginative and economical use of the wood-blocks he inherited from Caxton: blocks were reused both within the same text and in separate texts, and slightly different copies of old or worn-out blocks were used to illustrate a variety of texts. After 1500, de Worde's methods were further revolutionised by his connection with Vérard.

When de Worde took over Caxton's shop in 1491, he inherited Caxton's blocks, many of which then made reappearances in de Worde's books. Perhaps the most famous woodcut to be reused by de Worde was originally employed by Caxton in his *Canterbury Tales* of *c.* 1483 to illustrate the Pilgrims at Table (Fig. 1). The woodcut shows people from all walks of life, with tonsured monks, yeomen, a fool, a figure wearing a liripipe, and a woman in hat and veil representing the pilgrims, seated at a round table on which are a variety of foods, including a boar's head complete with a tusk on a platter. De Worde then appropriated this woodcut to represent the Feast of the Immortals in his edition of Lydgate's *Assembly of Gods*, printed *c.* 1500.[9] Other Caxton cuts used by de Worde include the prefatory woodcut that appeared in Caxton's *Golden Legend* of 1483, the Trinity Adored by the Assembly of Saints. This makes several reappearances in de Worde's *Golden Legend* editions of 1493, 1498 and 1527. The same woodcut also appears as the frontispiece to the first edition of John of Tynemouth's *Nova legenda Angliae*, printed by de Worde in 1516 (Fig. 2).[10] By reusing this image, de Worde links John's work, which describes the lives of English saints, with his (and Caxton's) earlier editions of Voragine's very popular *Golden Legend*, an effective marketing technique.

One particularly durable woodcut, depicting the Crucifixion, was used first by Caxton (*c.* 1491) as a frontispiece to the *Fifteen Oes*, a collection of fifteen

Fig. 1. Pilgrims at Table. Geoffrey Chaucer, *Canterbury Tales* (Westminster: William Caxton, 1483), sig. c4ʳ. STC 5083. BL G. 11586.

meditations widely ascribed to St Bridget of Sweden in books and manuscripts produced in the fourteenth through sixteenth centuries. The Crucifixion then turns up on the verso of the title-page of de Worde's 1496 edition of the *Abbaye of the Holy Ghost*, as well as in de Worde's *Golden Legend* edition of 1493 (Fig. 3).[11] Edward Hodnett first noticed that the Crucifixion cut was stylistically related to four other woodcuts that would also be used later by de Worde. These are a woodcut of Dives and Lazarus with a scene of devils in the margin beneath; a two-panelled woodcut of David and Goliath, and David and Bathsheba; a Jesse Tree; and an illustration of the Three Living and Three Dead.[12] The style of all five woodcuts is clearly continental, although they do not, to the best of my knowledge, appear in any surviving continental book. Although Arthur Hind speculates that these woodcuts come from a French source, both Hodnett and George Painter call them Flemish, which seems more likely given their style and general composition.[13] I have made a case elsewhere for placing the *Fifteen Oes* series in or around the workshop of the Master of the *Virgo inter Virgines*, an artist who originated in Delft, was active in the 1480s as a painter, and also supplied drawings and woodcut designs over a twenty-year span to Delft printers, although his blocks enjoyed a much wider circulation. Designs by or copied from the Virgo Master appear in books printed by Gerard Leeu in Antwerp, and his blocks were circulated to Jacob Bellaert of Haarlem; his designs turn up also in books printed in Delft by Christiaen Snellaert and in Zwolle by Pieter van Os. M. J. Schretlen comments that the Virgo Master, or a related designer, once worked for Gerard Leeu in Antwerp, 'and consequently it is probable that the Antwerp craftsmen took his woodcuts as patterns'.[14]

Related stylistically to the *Fifteen Oes* Crucifixion are the sinuous and ornate initials of de luxe books printed by de Worde. The exquisite initial *T* on the final page of de Worde's *Golden Legend* (Fig. 3) has a history even longer than that of

Fig. 2. Assembly of Saints. John of Tynemouth, *Nova legenda Angliae* (London: Wynkyn de Worde, 1516), frontispiece. STC 4601. BL G.11925, C.48.h.2.

Fig. 4 (*above*). Woodcut of initial 'G' ('Generacio'). Werner Rolewinck, *Fasciculus Temporum* (Utrecht: Johann Veldener, 1480), fol. 2^r. BL IB 47086.

Fig. 3 (*left*). Crucifixion, initial 'T'. Jacobus de Voragine, *Legenda Aurea* (Westminster: Wynkyn de Worde, 1493), endleaf. *STC* 24875. Providence, R.I., John Carter Brown Library, Brown University.

the Crucifixion woodcut. It has been copied from initials which occur in several volumes produced by the printer Johann Veldener. A similarly designed initial *N* occurs in a folio copy of the *Legenda aurea* produced in Utrecht by Veldener on 12 September 1480, recently acquired by the Pierpont Morgan Library.[15] A very similar *G* (Fig. 4) opens the text in Veldener's second edition of Werner Rolewinck's chronicle of world history, the *Fasciculus temporum* (Utrecht, 1480), in Dutch translation. In copying the style of this initial, de Worde is drawing from Caxton's original source, for Veldener cut Caxton's first supply of type and designed 'Caxton Type 2', which was Caxton's most important type in his early Westminster years.[16]

Among other blocks that de Worde reused was a rather undistinguished landscape copied from a Dutch source, which he first employed to illustrate 'Of partyes of the erthe' at the beginning of Book 15 of his 1495 edition of *De proprietatibus rerum* by the great encyclopedist Bartholomaeus Anglicus. Three years later it reappeared (Fig. 5), this time as a representation of the English countryside in *The descrypcyon of Englonde*.[17] The caption now reads: 'Here foloweth a lytell treatyse the whiche treateth of the descrypcyon of this

Fig. 5. Landscape. *The descrypcyon of Englonde.* (Westminster:
Wynkyn de Worde, 1498), sig. A1ʳ. *STC* 13440b. New York,
Pierpont Morgan Library PML 735.2, ChL f1814.

londe which of olde tyme was named Al-byon And after Brytayne And now is
called Englonde.'

Woodcuts were also adapted and recut to suit specific purposes. The wood-
cut of a bishop on the title-page of the *Constitutiones provinciales ecclesiae
Anglicanae*, printed by de Worde in 1496, was intended to represent William
Lyndewode (d. 1446), Bishop of St David's and author of this commentary
on English church law (Fig. 6).[18] De Worde first used the Lyndewode cut to
represent St Nicholas in his 1493 and later in his 1498 and 1512 editions of the
Golden Legend. A very similar woodcut of a pope, probably by the same artist
(Fig. 7), portrayed St Urban in de Worde's 1493 and 1498 editions of the *Golden
Legend*; it later appeared as Lyndewode in de Worde's 1499 edition of the
Constitutiones. The free interplay between images of saints and those of lesser
men not only demonstrates the versatility of these woodcuts; there is also a
suggestion of a more casual approach toward early portraiture.[19]

In a Sarum Hours published by de Worde in 1494, we find a small, decorative
illustration of St Andrew, which is painted over in the Bodleian Library copy. The

Fig. 6. A Bishop.
William Lyndewode,
*Constitutiones
provinciales ecclesie
Anglicanae*
(Westminster: Wynkyn
de Worde, 1496), sig.
A1ʳ. *STC* 17103. BL
IA.55185.

Fig. 7. A Pope. Jacobus de
Voragine, *Legenda aurea*
(Westminster: Wynkyn de
Worde, 1493). *STC* 24875.
Providence, R.I., John Carter
Brown Library, Brown
University.

Fig. 8. St Andrew. John Mirk,
Liber festivalis (Westminster:
Wynkyn de Worde, 1496), sig.
i4ᵛ. *STC* 17962. BL C.11.a.20.

unpainted woodcut (Fig. 8) occurs as the sole illustration in de Worde's 1494 edition of John Mirk's *Liber festivalis*, probably included as an afterthought.[20] The woodcut was also used to illustrate another Book of Hours printed by de Worde in the same year. After 1496 the block seems to have been acquired by Julian Notary. It does not appear again in de Worde's books, but does occur in a Book of Hours produced by Notary *c.* 1503 and in Notary's edition of the *Legenda aurea*, printed *c.* 1504. The image of St Andrew is, in fact, a reversed copy of an illustration first used in the 1486 edition of Mirk's *Liber festivalis*, printed in Oxford by Rood and Hunte. Copied by one of the cutters working for Caxton, the wood-block came into de Worde's possession when he took over Caxton's shop.[21]

The adaptation and recutting of wood-blocks is evident also in de Worde's 1495 edition of *De proprietatibus rerum*. This medieval encyclopedia covers a range of subjects, including the nature of God, angels and time; the composition of the elements and the human body; and the varieties of plants, animals, gems and eggs. The book had first been printed by Caxton at Cologne in 1471 – a magnificent edition, but without illustrations.[22] Subsequent editions by other printers were illustrated, however, and de Worde drew upon two of them in particular for his woodcuts.

One of these, the first illustrated edition, was produced by a German printer,

Fig. 9. Frontispiece to Book I of Bartholomaeus Anglicus, *De proprietatibus rerum* (Westminster: Wynkyn de Worde, 1495), sig. A3ʳ. STC 1536. BL IB. 55242.

Fig. 10. Frontispiece to Book I of Bartholomaeus Anglicus, *De proprietatibus rerum* (Haarlem: Bellaert, 1485), sig. A1ᵛ (following paratext). BL IB. 48508.

Mathias Huss, who was working in Lyon. This was a French translation, published in 1482 with full-page woodcuts at the start of each book. Huss reprinted this edition in 1485, and many of the same cuts, with new decorative work and borders, also appeared again in his edition of 15 March 1491 or 1492. To complicate matters, the same woodcuts, copied by what Hind terms 'a more powerful cutter', appeared in Jean Syber's Bartholomaeus edition of 1485 or 1486, also printed in Lyon.[23] Meanwhile, in Haarlem, on Christmas Eve of 1485, Jacobus Bellaert published a Dutch edition of Bartholomaeus, the *Boeck van de proprieteyten des dinghen*. This, too, had woodcuts at the start of various books, though Bellaert did not illustrate all the books like Huss, Syber and de Worde. This was the second version that de Worde seems to have used as a source of woodcuts when he put out his edition.[24]

The first woodcut in de Worde's edition (Fig. 9) illustrates the first book of text, which opens with an exposition of the Trinity: 'The fader – the sonn – the holy ghost.' This woodcut seems modelled on Bellaert (Fig. 10). But the de Worde cutter is not so sure-handed as his Dutch counterpart and perhaps spoils the stark drama of the composition by adding medallions of the four Evangelists in the corners of his illustration. However, he does retain the three-circle aureole and the general shapes of God and his throne.

The Bellaert edition omits some of the most striking scenes in the French and later editions – for example the illustration of the dissection of a corpse. In the

Huss edition (Fig. 11), this picture introduces Book 5, dealing with the human body. Here we see five physicians examining a corpse on a table. Notice also the diamond pattern on the floor. In the de Worde copy (Fig. 12), we again see five physicians examining a corpse on a table placed on a diamond-patterned floor. But, in this case, windows and an architectural frame have been added to the scene. Note also that the corpse has been reversed, and the physician standing at its feet on the right side of the Huss woodcut now appears on the left. Though de Worde's image has several modifications, this reversal of the corpse is suspicious, suggesting that its basic composition is a direct copy of the Huss original. When copying woodcuts, cutters commonly traced the picture, then cut the block from the tracing, thereby reversing the image. To complicate matters further, there is another version of the dissection scene (Fig. 13), which appears in the first Spanish edition of Bartholomaeus, produced at Toulouse in 1494 by the German printer Heinrich Mayer. The woodcut was probably designed and cut by a Spanish craftsman and is also the first representation of a dissection to be printed in a Spanish book.[25] Here, too, the corpse is pointed in the same direction as that in the Huss cut, and there is a black-and-white patterned floor. However, in this copy, more emphasis is placed on architectural detail, and a sixth physician stands in the doorway.

It would seem logical for the de Worde artist, or the artist of the prototype used by de Worde, to have turned to the Huss copy for inspiration, since the Bellaert edition has only eleven pictures while the Huss edition has twenty. The de Worde artist, however, does not consult Huss only when a scene has been omitted in Bellaert. Quite often, the Huss edition or editions are used as a model even when Bellaert also illustrates the scene.

For example, prefacing Book 9 in the Bellaert edition is an orderly rendering of the Divisions of Time (Fig. 14), which does not seem to be the direct model for pictures in either the de Worde (Fig. 15) or the Spanish edition (Fig. 16). James Snyder describes the corresponding woodcut in the Lyon edition of Huss as 'a large circle of the zodiac with inner compartments marked off by the spokes of the wheel of time and containing illustrations of the 12 labors of the months'.[26] This certainly appears to be the programme followed by the de Worde artist (Fig. 15). In this woodcut, we see the labours of the months circling around a central medallion, not mentioned by Snyder, of a maiden holding a wreath, or perhaps a martyr's crown, as a man appears to drown in a river. This scene is perhaps reminiscent of the dreamer's experience in the Middle English poem *Pearl*, but it has no clear connection to the text at hand, which deals mainly with the nature of time. The Spanish cutter, meanwhile (Fig. 16), seems to have also followed the Huss model but has overestimated the space on his page. Notice that the woman is there, but the figure of the man in the central medallion has been botched, and is covered over with abstract lines. Examination of the prototype of both images in Huss's edition (Fig. 17) suggests the likely identity of the two figures. Here we see in the upper half of the medallion a woman who appears to be making a garland. In the lower half, a man sits in a barren field,

Fig. 11. Frontispiece to Book V
(on surgery) of Bartholomaeus
Anglicus, *De proprietatibus
rerum* (Lyons: Mathias Huss,
12 October 1485), sig. d8ᵉ BL IB.
41702.

Fig. 12. Frontispiece to Book V
(on surgery) of Bartholomaeus Anglicus,
De proprietatibus rerum (Westminster:
Wynkyn de Worde, 1495), sig. f6ᵛ.
STC 1536. BL IB. 55242.

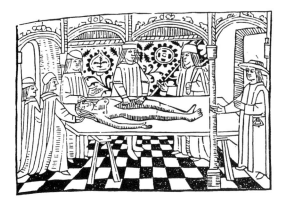

Fig. 13. Frontispiece to Book V
(on surgery) of Bartholomaeus
Anglicus, *De proprietatibus rerum*
(Toulouse: Heinrich Mayer,
1494), sig. e8ʳ. BL IB 42456.

Fig. 14. Frontispiece to Book IX (on the labours of the months) of Bartholomaeus
Anglicus, *De proprietatibus rerum* (Haarlem: Bellaert, 1485), sig. u2ᵛ. BL IB. 48508.

warming his hands by a fire and looking upward. Around the edges of the
medallion are the words 'Le Jour, La nuit, Le Jour, La nuit', an inscription which
suggests that the image represents day and night, and perhaps also alludes to
summer and winter. In any case, this ties the image to the theme of Book 9,
namely time. The copies found in the editions of de Worde and Heinrich Mayer
have lost the original sense of picture and text, being copies of copies in which
the man warming himself before a fire in winter has become a man holding his
hands up in supplication out of a rocky landscape or perhaps ocean waves.

Fig. 15. Frontispiece to Book IX (on the labours of the months) of Bartholomaeus Anglicus, *De proprietatibus rerum* (Westminster: Wynkyn de Worde, 1495), sig. y1ᵛ. *STC* 1536. BL IB. 55242.

Fig. 16. Frontispiece to Book IX (on the labours of the months) of Bartholomaeus Anglicus, *De proprietatibus rerum* (Toulouse: Heinrich Mayer, 1494), sig. C2ʳ. BL IB 42456.

Fig. 17. Frontispiece to Book IX (on the labours of the months) of Bartholomaeus Anglicus, *De proprietatibus rerum* (Lyon: Mathias Huss, 12 October 1485), sig. p3ᵛ. BL IB. 41702.

Fig. 18. Frontispiece to Book XVIII (on the kingdom of the animals) of Bartholomaeus Anglicus, *De proprietatibus rerum* (Lyon: Mathias Huss, 12 October 1485), sig. G2ʳ. BL IB. 41702.

Fig. 19. Frontispiece to Book XVIII (on the kingdom of the animals) of Bartholomaeus Anglicus, *De proprietatibus rerum* (Westminster: Wynkyn de Worde, 1495), sig. x5ᵛ. *STC* 1536. BL IB. 55242.

In a final example from the Bartholomaeus, an illustration of the Kingdom of Animals appears in the Huss edition (Fig. 18) at the beginning of Book 18. The artist has creatively rendered the major animals, including the elephant, giraffe, camel and lion; notice the lion's long beard. In the de Worde copy, note that these animals are again reversed (Fig. 19), and they are in slightly different positions from those they occupy in the original. In this case, the de Worde artist has had the good sense to limit the number of animals for his smaller space and to focus mainly on copying the most exotic ones: he has also elaborated a little, giving the elephant a cornucopia-shaped trunk and distinct toes, and elongating the lion's claws.

Using earlier copies of Bartholomaeus as models for illustration makes sense – though consulting several sources for artistic inspiration indicates, perhaps, an impractical, even obsessive thoroughness, and de Worde did not always follow this practice. Let us turn now to his two editions of Andrew Chertsey's translation of the immensely popular *L'Art de bien vivre et de bien mourir*, published in Paris by Antoine Vérard from around 1492.[27] The Vérard edition went through five printings in five years. De Worde printed two editions of the Chertsey translation, one titled *Ordynarye of Crystyanyte or of Crysten Men* in 1502 and another titled *ThOrdynary of Crysten Men* in 1506. Except for their titles and some variant spelling, both de Worde editions include precisely the same text but illustrate it with different woodcuts.

For example, two woodcuts function as borders on either side of the Ten Commandments (Fig. 20) in the 1502 edition of the *Ordynarye*. On the left is Moses, his hands against the edge of the border, seeming to display or hold up the Commandments. On the right is a bishop, holding a wand or rod, with a multitude behind him. Notice the bold lines of the figures here. In the 1506 edition, de Worde substitutes a weak rendering of the original (Fig. 21); Moses seems to simper, and the detail is sloppy. Also compare the thin lines in both these woodcuts to the stronger, surer ones in the prototypes. Why include new illustrations, in most cases inferior ones, in an edition of the same text printed four years after the first? Perhaps some light might be shed on this problem by examining the pattern of repetition of these woodcuts in other de Worde books. The 1502 Moses was not reused. But copies of the weak copy turn up in de Worde's *Floure of the commaundements* and the *Kalender of shepeherdes*.[28] Thus, the 1502 blocks show minimal reuse, while the 1506 blocks show maximum reuse.

According to Edward Hodnett, in his *English Woodcuts 1480-1535*, the majority of woodcuts in the 1502 *Ordynarye* were made for that edition, though many of their borders are broken.[29] A broken border in a woodcut usually indicates wearing of the wood-block and is a fairly reliable sign of previous use (though how much previous use is uncertain). If the majority of wood-blocks were indeed made for the 1502 edition of the *Ordynarye*, why do some of these reappear only once and the majority not at all? The breaks suggest that the 1502 blocks were originally cut for an earlier book, probably produced on the continent – from the style I would guess in Paris, copied from originals in books published by Vérard. Their minimal reuse implies that they were returned to the original owner – printer or publisher – or perhaps shelved shortly after the printing of the 1502 *Ordynarye*. The blocks may have been borrowed by de Worde expressly to illustrate the first of these two books, copied and returned, and then the poorer copies used to illustrate the 1506 edition. But, without the appearance of the original blocks elsewhere, this remains conjecture.

Many early printers reused the blocks they had on hand and copied images from other books, but de Worde was among the first to explore the limits of the image and to exploit its possibilities. Like his experiments with title images, at which he becomes increasingly proficient, de Worde's use of composite and factotum pictures was directly related to the new technology of printing, which made such methods practicable for the first time. A composite picture was made from two or more wood-blocks which were 'movable' like text type itself – that is, they could be reused and recombined to form different pictures. Because the combinations of figure and scene were nearly endless, pictures could appropriately illustrate a variety of scenes while simultaneously being economically reproduced. Factotum printing goes one step beyond the Moses example we have just discussed, in which the text of the Ten Commandments is bracketed by

Fig. 20. Woodcuts for the Ten Commandments. *Ordynarye of Crystyanyte or of Crysten Men*, trans. A. Chertsey (London: Wynkyn de Worde, 1502), sig. h6ʳ. *STC* 5198. BL G.11739.

Fig. 21. Woodcuts for the Ten Commandments. *ThOrdynary of Crysten Men*, trans. A. Chertsey (London: Wynkyn de Worde, 1506), sig. g8ʳ. *STC* 5199. BL C.25.f.7.

images. This type of printing is done by inserting metal type into a space left in a wood-block. Study of the ink patterns suggests that the type rested on a groove cut into this opening and was held in place by pieces of metal, probably malleable lead. De Worde employs the factotum method of inserting movable type into wood-blocks chiefly to identify figures in his composite illustrations or to render what they are saying, as in *The crafte to lyue well and to dye well* discussed in Chapter 1, although examples may also be found on his title-pages and else-where. The importance of the process to de Worde is indicated by Plomer's discovery of an inventory believed to be that of de Worde's shop, cited by James Moran. Written in Latin, French and English, the inventory cites 'quatuor les pryntyng presses duo par de cases wythe letters to prynte *cum* pyctures'; that is, two of the four presses may have had cases with letters to print with pictures.[30]

De Worde first began to experiment with factotum printing in the 1490s. In genealogical charts illustrating his 1497 edition of the *Cronycle of Englonde* (Fig. 22), words are printed in and around rather crudely carved woodcut boxes.[31] In this example, the name 'Noe' is printed within the box and sur-rounded by a circle and little ornaments. These diagrams were very probably modelled on those in Werner Rolewinck's world history, the *Fasciculus Temporum*. An edition of the Latin *Fasciculus* (Fig. 23), with similar, though more gracefully executed charts, was printed in 1480 by Johann Veldener, who, as we have seen, was also the source for the woodcut initial on the final leaf of de Worde's *Golden Legend*. They also occur in Veldener's 1478 edition, printed in Louvain.[32] De Worde's charts continued to be reprinted in his four subsequent editions of the *Cronycle of Englonde*, which were issued through 1528.[33]

After 1500 de Worde quickly moved to a more sophisticated style of factotum printing. In *The crafte to lyue well and to dye well*, besides the Temptation to Impatience image discussed in Chapter 1, there is a woodcut of Christ preaching to the Apostles (Fig. 24) accompanying a vernacular exposition of the Lord's Prayer. The text of the prayer has been set in type within the scroll. It is highly abbreviated and has been printed on a slight curve. A paraph mark appears at the beginning of the text. The inking of the letter *e* in the word 'name' at the end of the first line is faint; and the word 'Thy', used twice in line 2, begins both times with a capital *T*. The same woodcut occurs in de Worde's edition of the *Floure of the commaundements* (Fig. 25), which was printed in 1510, although presentation of the inset text is slightly different. The Lord's Prayer has again been inserted into the scroll, but with some modifications; the paraph at the start of text is missing; the *e* in the word 'name' has been well inked; and the words 'thy', again repeated in the second line, have been left in lower case. Just how this type was set into the curving text space of the block is a matter for conjecture.[34] De Worde's sources for the woodcut and method of text presentation may be found in French illustrations, for example Guy Marchant's *Kalendrier des bergeres*, Antoine Vérard's *L' Art de bien vivre* and perhaps most directly in *The book intytulyd the art of good lywyng and good deyng* (Fig. 26), a peculiar English translation published by Vérard in Paris in 1503.[35] Although de Worde's

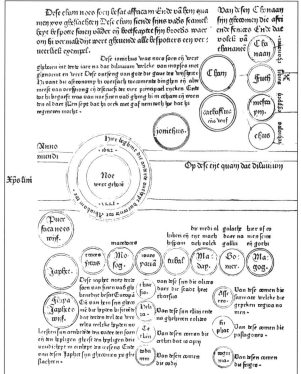

Fig. 22 (*above*). The Line of Noe. *Cronycle of Englonde* (Westminster: Wynkyn de Worde, 1497), sig. aiii[v]. STC 9996. BL C.11.b.1. (1).

Fig. 23 (*right*). The Line of Noe. Werner Rolewinck, *Fasciculus Temporum* (Utrecht: Jan Veldener, 1480), fol. 4[v]. BL C.15.b.8.

illustrations are, as usual, somewhat less gracefully executed than the continental ones, he demonstrates the same virtuosity at setting type within the block and the same economical reuse of the image. Printing with a factotum block seems to have ensured the block's longevity. De Worde continued to use the Lord's Prayer woodcut, resetting the text as appropriate, in a number of vernacular religious handbooks through 1528.

Vérard was also de Worde's most immediate continental source for composite images. The practice of using separate blocks to form a composite picture began in Holland, spread first to Germany and then moved across the continent, coming to England by way of Paris. One of the earliest examples of composite illustration appears in the *Boeck des gulden throens*, a folio printed in Utrecht on 30 March 1480 by a printer known only as 'tC', the initials on his devices. Each illustration is very simple, consisting of a male figure, the Elder, and a female figure, the Soul, framed by an architectural border. There are six varieties of Elder, five types of Soul and four border-pieces; these are arranged in numerous ways 'with up to 120 non-repeating combinations', making variations in the scenes (see Figs 27 and 28).[36] In this way, the printer, or an artist associated with his shop, was able to create a variety of illustrations to fit variations in the text while maintaining a consistent and pleasing page design throughout the

50

Fig. 24. The Lord's Prayer. *The crafte to lyue well and to dye well* (London: Wynkyn de Worde, 1505), fol. xvʳ. *STC* 792. BL C.132.h.40, C.53.e.4.

Fig. 25. The Lord's Prayer. *The Floure of the Commaundements of God* (London: Wynkyn de Worde, 1510), fol. xxxviʳ (sig. F6ʳ). *STC* 23876. BL Huth 30.

Fig. 26. The Lord's Prayer. *The book intytulyd the art of good lywyng and good deyng* (Paris: for Antoine Vérard, 1503), sig. d1^r. STC 791. BL C.70.g.14.

book. The woodcuts are painted in some copies, adding further variation and the illusion of dimension; hand-painting makes the picture more pleasing, and there is some attempt at creating shadow in the folds of the gowns and in the architectural borders.[37]

Schretlen says the artist responsible for the blocks illustrating the *Boeck des gulden throens* also designed the blocks for Veldener's Utrecht edition of the *Fasciculus Temporum*.[38] Although neither of these books necessarily served as direct models for de Worde's illustrations, there does seem to be a well-established link, which occurs quite early on, between factotums and composites. The Veldener artist moves from designing factotum-block genealogical charts, which are printed along with movable type, to creating interchangeable composite images, a connection de Worde will also make.

A more sophisticated method of creating a picture out of separate wood-blocks was used by the German printer Johann Grüninger, who employed this practice in a variety of books from surgical treatises to classical works. In 1497, Grüninger printed the first treatise on surgery (*De chirurgia*) by the Strasbourg surgeon Hieronymus Brunschwig, which is abundantly illustrated with composite wood-blocks. Grüninger used the same method to illustrate Brunschwig's plague tractate (*Pestbuch*) and the *Medicinarius* (*Kleines Destillierbuch*), both printed in 1500.[39] Perhaps the most amusing demonstration of the versatility of composites might be found in Grüninger's edition of the works of Horace,

Fig. 27. Elder and Soul (one variant). Otto von Passau, *Dat boeck des gulden throens* (Utrecht: tC, 1480), fol. 28ᵛ. Goff O-124, AmBM 467. Providence, R.I., Annmary Brown Memorial, Brown University.

Fig. 28. Elder and Soul (another variant). Otto von Passau, *Dat boeck des gulden throens* (Utrecht: tC, 1480), fol. 40ᵛ. Goff O-124, AmBM 467. Providence, R.I., Annmary Brown Memorial, Brown University.

published in 1498. In one illustration (Fig. 29), which is made up of three separate blocks, we see at the left a rocky landscape, a building and a piece of the ship's prow. The centre cut shows seven travellers, men and women, amidships. The block on the right depicts the ship's stern and more rocky landscape with trees. In other examples the ship recurs (Fig. 30), with the central block replaced by one showing three travellers and a man rowing. Here the image is slightly amended to suit the immediate text.

The Horace was one of three classical volumes Grüninger brought out in quick succession, the others being his Terence of 1496 and his 1502 Virgil. The most influential of these, at least from the point of view of illustration, was the Terence, which is heavily illustrated with composites.[40] For his pictures, Grüninger drew on a Terence published in Lyon in 1493, illustrated, however, with conventional one-block images. Hind comments that Grüninger's Terence is 'the first important work with cuts in the new style. ... [V]arious characters, properties and backgrounds reappear in a variety of combinations.'[41] A typical picture (Fig. 31) from Grüninger's Terence is comprised of five blocks, with scrolls above the heads of the various characters; these are generally blank,

Fig. 29. Seven Travellers Aboard Ship. Horace, *Opera*
(Strassburg: Johann Grüninger, 1498), fol. 14ʳ. BL IB 1471.

Fig. 30. Three Travellers with a Man Rowing. Horace, *Opera*
(Strassburg: Johann Grüninger, 1498), fol. 43ʳ. BL IB 1471.

though some are occasionally filled in by hand. Antoine Vérard may have come across a copy of this Terence, for he quickly picked up Grüninger's method of illustration, using it in his French translation of Terence, *Therence en françois*, printed in 1500, and again in *Le Jardin de Plaisance et Fleur de Rhetorique* of 1501.[42] In these books Vérard tends to employ Grüninger's five-block format, following 'Grüninger in his composite subjects, making up his subjects by fitting together a limited number of block-pieces with figure, architecture, or landscape', a variation of the same method of composing an illustration used twenty years before by the Utrecht printer tC.[43]

Vérard's *Therence en françois* also marks the first appearance of two 'movable' figures that had a long history ahead of them in both French and English book illustration. One of them appears, for example, as Pamphile in a picture of Davus, Pamphile and Symon (Fig. 32) that illustrates Terence's *Andria* in Vérard's *Therence en françois*. Notice that the three figures and two buildings are printed from separate blocks. Note also that a scroll accompanies each figure, identifying it. The scrolls are factotums that can be filled in with the appropriate name, so that the images can depict almost anyone, as we see in the next example. Here (Fig. 33) Pamphile is again the central figure, but he has now taken on the identity of Cherea in the *Eunuchus*. The buildings are the same position as in the previous example, but Davus and Symon have been replaced by two women – including the other recurring figure, the courtesan Thais.

Some of Vérard's 'movable' figures also make their way separately into other volumes published by Vérard in the early 1500s, among them Pamphile-Cherea. For example, in an allegorical work entitled *L'amoureux Transy sans Espoir*, by Jean Bouchet, printed on vellum and published for Vérard in 1502, we find the familiar woodcut now representing L'amant, or L'amoureux, the lover (Fig. 34). In this anthology, the author Bouchet is 'identified as the "Amoureux transy", the name in fact given to the first of the poem's unhappy lovers. Whereas Bouchet states that he has merely recorded this character's lament as he heard it, Vérard has equated author with character. Moreover, by using this name as the title of the book, Vérard creates an ambiguity which masks the nature both of the individual work and of the printed volume.'[44] The same woodcut again represents the lover, who is also apparently the author, at the end of the poem, when he looks beyond the transient loves of this world to that of the Queen of Heaven, represented in the volume by a scene of the Annunciation.

The Pamphile–Cherea–Lamant figure began its move to England a year later when Vérard used it in *The Kalendayr of the shyppars* (Fig. 35), printed in 1503. This was a peculiar English translation produced for the English market in which the L'amant figure regularly appears, assuming a variety of identities. Like the Terence editions, the *Kalender* is not original with Vérard, but is another of the many works published by him that had the status of bestsellers in their day. As a publisher, Vérard was a successful entrepreneur, republishing books that had previously circulated in manuscript (often in de luxe illuminated manuscripts), as well as in block-book formats, drawing, in this case, from previous printed

Fig. 31. Composite illustration. Terence, *Comoediae* (Strassburg: Johann Grüninger, 1496), sig. s4ᵛ. BL C.3.c.16. Note the blank scroll filled in by hand.

Fig. 32. Dauus, Pamphile and Symon. *Therence en françois* (Paris: for Antoine Vérard, *c.* 1500), sig. d2ᵛ. BL IB 41244.

Fig. 33. Pithias, Cherea and Thais. *Therence en françois* (Paris: for Antoine Vérard, *c.* 1500), sig. s1^v. BL IB 41244.

Fig. 34. L'amant (or L'amoureux). Jean Bouchet, *L'amoureux Transy sans Espoir* (Paris: for Antoine Vérard, *c.* 1502/3), sig. a3^r. BL C.34.g.6 (1). Painted copy courtesy of San Marino, Calif., Huntington Library.

Fig. 35. Two Men. *The Kalendayr of the shyppars* (Paris: for Antoine Vérard, 1503), sig. 1 4v. *STC* 22407. BL C.132.i.2.

editions published by Guy Marchant and others. Judging from its reprint history, the *Kalender* was extremely popular, with eight editions in Paris and Geneva between 1493 and 1500. Guy Marchant's editions appeared in 1493 and 1500. Richard Pynson, who became the official printer to Henry VII in 1506/7, brought out his edition in 1506. De Worde then published *The Kalender of shepeherdes*, first in 1508, then in 1511 and 1528, after which it continued to be published by a variety of printers until 1631.[45]

A miscellany of shepherd's lore, tables for finding the dates of movable feasts, descriptions of the torments of Purgatory, and explications of the Ten Commandments, Lord's Prayer and Creed, the *Kalender* was heavily illustrated, the pictures in the English editions deriving from those in the Marchant and Vérard versions. Both the text and the iconography of these in turn derived from an illuminated manuscript now in the Fitzwilliam Museum, Cambridge (MS 167). Written in French with later notations in Italian, this manuscript is dated *c.* 1486, and it has not previously been connected with the print editions.[46] Compare, for example, the miniature of the shepherd with his plumb-line (Fig. 36) with the woodcut on de Worde's title-page (Fig. 37). Many images in the manuscript clearly served as models for the woodcuts, which were, in turn, copied and recopied from edition to edition.

Fig. 36. A Shepherd.
Le Calendrier des Bergers
(French, *c.* 1486?), fol. 86^r.
Fitzwilliam Museum MS 167.
Courtesy of Cambridge,
Fitzwilliam Museum.

The Pamphile–Cherea–Lamant woodcut (Fig. 35), however, originated with Vérard, and was also used by Richard Pynson. It was subsequently employed repeatedly by de Worde in a variety of contexts and continued to be reused by a number of later English printers well into the sixteenth century. For example, the figure turns up in *Boke named the Royall* (Fig. 38), on which Pynson and de Worde collaborated in 1507, confronting Death as he rides out from Hell-mouth.[47] He reappears in a similar context in de Worde's edition of *The Kalender of shepeherdes* (Fig. 39). Illustrating the text, 'Man loke þu be ware. I do smyte all unware', he represents, in this case, the reader to whom the caption is addressed (along with the verses beneath, which are also spoken to the reader by Death), functioning here as a kind of Everyman. The printer John Skot, in fact, used a copy of this figure to represent Everyman on both title-pages of his two editions of the play of that name, which were printed *c.* 1528 and *c.* 1535.[48] The

Fig. 37. A Shepherd. *The Kalender of shepeherdes* (London: Wynkyn de Worde, *c.* 1508). *STC* 22409. C.I.1.18. Oxford, Magdalen College.

figures and title-page in Skot's *Everyman* editions were, in turn, very probably based on those used by Pynson in his two editions of the play, published *c.* 1515 and 1526-28?, though their title-pages no longer exist.[49]

The tougher lines of Everyman's face than in Vérard's version, and the careless rendering of the plants at his feet, seem to indicate that the cut was copied by de Worde's 'chief hand', who has been described as 'A fairly successful cutter but not a trained draughtsman – his effects, however, are often strong and neat'.[50] His neatness of execution is evident in this illustration, though the two blocks here are not as artfully arranged as those in the Vérard or Grüninger editions. Their alignment, for example, is slightly uneven.

After his English debut in Vérard's version of the *Kalender*, the Pamphile–Cherea–Lamoureux–Everyman figure then makes a multitude of appearances in de Worde's books. He represents both the young lover and, later, the beleaguered

Remembre frendes grete and small.
For to be redy whan dethe doth call.

Fig. 38. Everyman Confronting Death. *Boke named the Royall*, trans. William
Caxton (London: Wynkyn de Worde and Richard Pynson, 1507),
sig. J5ʳ. STC 21430/21430a. BL C.21.c.1, C.11.a.23.

Man loke ȝ beware. I do smyte all vnware.

Aboue this hors blacke and hedyous
Dethe I am that spersly doth sytte
There is no fayrnes but fyght tydyous
All gaye colours I do it
My horse rennes by dales and hylles
And many he smyteth deed and kylles
In my trappe I take some by euery way
By townes and castelles I take my rente
I wyll not respecte one an houre of a day
Before me they must nedes be present
Ka. of She.
K.I.

Fig. 39. Everyman Confronting Death. *The Kalender of shepeherdes* (London: Wynkyn
de Worde, *c*. 1508), sig. K1ʳ. STC 22409. RRW 139. Oxford, Magdalen College.

Fig. 40. Guenellet and Sydoyne.
*The noble hystory of ... kynge
Ponthus* (London: Wynkyn de
Worde, 1511), sig. E3ʳ. *STC*
20108. Bodleian Library Douce
PP 214. Oxford, Bodleian Library.

Fig. 41. Titus and Emperor Vaspazyan. *The
Destruction of Jerusalem* (London: Wynkyn de
Worde, 1528), fol. f3ʳ. *STC* 14519. PML 21134.
New York, Pierpont Morgan Library.

husband in *The fyftene Joyes of maryage*, printed by de Worde in 1509. This text,
a satirical look at marriage from the perspective of a put-upon husband,
was taken from a popular French work attributed to Antoine de La Sale and
translated by an anonymous English translator.[51] The figure also represents the
young lover Troilus in de Worde's *Troilus and Criseyde*, published in 1517, but,
like Bottom in *Midsummer Night's Dream* in his desire to play every part, he can
also portray knights or tyrants. He appears reversed, for example, as Guenellet
in de Worde's 1511 edition of *Kynge Ponthus* (Fig. 40).[52] In yet another incarnation, the Everyman figure returns in the guise of Titus, son of the evil 'Emperor
Vaspazyan', in de Worde's 1528 edition of the *Destruction of Jerusalem* (Fig. 41).
In this illustration, we see the emperor seated on the throne, a knight and the
emperor's son, Titus. The disregard for careful composition on the part of de
Worde's 'chief hand' is evident in this example. The Everyman figure in his new
identity as Titus has undergone some subtle changes: the figure is reversed and
wears slightly modified shoes, and the braid on his tunic is not as prominent.
This reversed copy occurs as well in the *Gesta Romanorum* of *c.* 1510.[53] It further
appears on the title-pages of *The contrauersye bytwene a louer and a iaye*, of
c. 1532, and of *The complaynt of a louers lyfe* (Fig. 42), printed *c.* 1531.[54] A very
rough copy of the figure represents the eponymous hero of the late medieval
drama *Hycke scorner*, printed *c.* 1515, and we find other rough copies of this
woodcut illustrating English books through the middle of the sixteenth century.[55]

Fig. 42. Title-page, *The complaynt of a louers lyfe* (London:
Wynkyn de Worde, *c.* 1531), sig. A1ʳ. *STC* 17014.7. BL C.132.i.43.

The Everyman figure and copies of it often represent personifications of Love
and/or Folly on the title-pages or opening leaves of English books, with the image
serving as a marketing device for the volume. For example, the figure represents
Desire in the frontispiece to William Nevill's undated romance *The Castell of
Pleasure*, and also turns up as Grand Amour, the young hero of the allegorical
Pastime of Pleasure, written by Stephen Hawes, presented by him to Henry VII
and printed in 1517 by de Worde.[56] The woodcut appears again in *Thenterlude
of Youth*, printed by de Worde in 1528.[57]

Fig. 43. Desyre with Beaute. William Nevill, *The Castell of Pleasure* (London: Wynkyn de Worde, n.d.), title-page. *STC* 18475. San Marino, Calif., Huntington Library.

In many cases, in accordance with de Worde's (and Vérard's) practice of using the factotum and composite methods together, the woodcut of Everyman has a banderole, or scroll, above his head with inserted type which variously identifies him to fit the text. The banderoles themselves are woodcuts, and the caption texts are produced with inset metal type. They range from a simple scroll to an ornate winding banner with interior shading. Like composites (to which they are sometimes attached), the banderoles are used and reused for a number of purposes. On the frontispiece of William Nevill's romance *The Castell of Pleasure* (Fig. 43), for example, titles within banderoles, printed from three separate wood-blocks, identify the name of the work and those of the allegorical figures; banderoles above the figures' heads introduce the main players, Desire and Beauty, whom we recognise from their previous incarnations as Everyman and the courtesan Thais from the Vérard Terence.[58] The titles have been printed with movable type, which has been neatly fitted within the woodcut scroll.

The fortunes of this female figure (Fig. 33), which we will call 'Everywoman' here, may likewise be traced through a variety of popular fifteenth- and sixteenth-century printed texts well into the 1560s. For example, we find the familiar figures of Everyman and Everywoman representing Bohemians, in *The Fyrste Boke of the Introduction of Knowledge* (Fig. 44), by Andrew Boorde, a volume printed *c.* 1562 in London.[59] The career of Everywoman is slightly longer than that of Everyman, ending in 1566 with an appearance as 'the ill-starred

Fig. 44. Bohemians. Andrew
Boorde, *The Fyrste Boke of
the Introduction of Knowledge*
(London: William Copland,
c. 1562), sig. M5^r. *STC* 3383.
Providence, R.I., John Hay
Library, Brown University.

Mother Waterhouse', the heroine of *The Ende & Confession of Mother Waterhouse.*[60] By that time, she had also represented Beauty, as we have seen, as well
as the beautiful widow Criseyde in Chaucer's *Troilus and Criseyde* in the
woodcut prefacing Book 3 of de Worde's 1517 edition, and the tormenting and
haughty wife from *The fyftene Joyes of maryage*. In a double image from the
Destruction of Jerusalem (Fig. 45), she represents both 'the quene' and, reversed,
with some modifications, Claryce. In this portion of text, Mary, the queen and
widow of the king of 'Affrycke', has travelled with her friend and confidant
Claryce to Jerusalem where they are starving during the city's siege. The incident
described in the caption for this illustration – 'How as two ladyes were in
counsayll [and] the queen in swoune an aungell badde the quene roste and ete her
chylde' – is fortunately not shown (though it does appear in some manuscript
illustrations of the scene).[61] Instead, we see Claryce and the queen 'in counsayll',
attended by an anonymous group of small people, perhaps intended to represent
children.

We find the same figure, again named Clarysse, in de Worde's 1512 edition of
The Knight of the Swanne, addressing the same representation of a king that
formerly portrayed the wicked Emperor 'Vaspazyan' in the *Destruction of
Jerusalem*. In the copy printed by William Copland *c.* 1560 (Fig. 46), she appears
again on sig. G4^v as 'Beatryce' under the caption 'How king Oriant sent for the

Fig. 45. Claryce with the Quene. *The Destruction of Jerusalem*
(London: Wynkyn de Worde, 1528), fol. d8ᵛ. STC 14519. BL C.25.k.5.

good quene Beatrice his wife for to expose to her þe wherof she was accused &
to condemyne her to death. And how Helias his son*n*e ariued at þe Palais of his
father for to defende & succour his mother fro death'. In this story, the 'good
spouse Queene Beatrice' is accused by 'the false Makaire' in this scene of sleeping
with a dog and conceiving by it: 'Syr I haue tolde you & yet wyll vpholde before
all here present, that I haue seen her haue compani & habitacion with a dogge,
wherof she hath conceyued .vii. whelpes, the whiche sith ben yssued of her owne
bodye.' He further accuses Beatrice of attempting to poison himself and the
king's 'Mother my lady Matabrune'. Later in the volume (sig. O2ʳ), this woodcut
represents the wife of Helyas, illustrating the caption, 'How the duchesse of
Boullon complayned to the emperor for the departiug [*sic*] of Helyas.'[62] She
appears as well in the *Gesta Romanorum* of *c.* 1510 and in the *Chronicles of
England*, printed in 1520, where she represents Octavian's daughter (Fig. 47).[63]
The Everywoman figure further personifies the female speaker in the text of *An
interlocucyon with an argument betwyxt man and woman & whiche of them
could proue to be most excellent*, printed by de Worde about 1528.[64]

   Although it is difficult to pinpoint precisely when de Worde began to use
composite images, all examples I have found occurred after Pynson's publication
in 1506 of the *Kalender of shepherdes*, which is illustrated with copies of the
original Vérard woodcuts.[65] But in some cases, de Worde uses composites
that appear only in Vérard's books, and for which there are no prior English

Fig. 46. Beatryce. *The knyght of the swanne* (London: William Copland, *c.* 1560), fol. G4ᵛ. STC 7572. BL C.21.c.67.

examples, which implies that he was familiar not only with Pynson's copies but also with the French editions. Once in England, copies of Vérard's blocks continue to be used, and for good reason. First, the figures could be made 'to represent almost anybody by inserting the necessary inscription into the scroll'.[66] Second, as is evident from these few examples, the figures had tremendous mobility and could be widely adapted. They were also convenient and economical to use.

De Worde's use of interchangeable blocks indicates his willingness to experiment with picture layout, sequence and the latest techniques from the continent. Even more important, the appearance of composites in de Worde's books reveals his awareness of a rapidly expanding, fiercely competitive book market – one that William Caxton had had almost to himself only a few years earlier. Immediately after Caxton's death, the publisher Gerard Leeu of Antwerp quickly reprinted three Caxton editions and cut in on de Worde's trade.[67] De Worde, however, ultimately succeeded by offering his customers an affordable product. And the woodcuts illustrating this product were plentiful (if occasionally repetitive), drawn from a wide variety of sources, and produced in the most economical way.

These lessons in producing an attractive illustrated volume were also learned

Fig. 47. Octavian's Daughter.
The Chronicles of England
(London: de Worde, 1520).
STC 1000. Providence, R.I.,
Annmary Brown Memorial,
Brown University.

by the third generation of English printers, which included Robert Copland, Julian Notary, John Rastell, John Skot and Henry Pepwell. We have seen that Julian Notary reused the wood-block of St Andrew that first belonged to Caxton, then to de Worde. Factotums were particularly popular with third-generation printers. As previously noted, John Skot used the Everyman figure on the title-pages of his published editions of the play. The Everywoman figure was used perhaps most provocatively in English editions of works originally composed by Christine de Pizan and published in the sixteenth century for middle-class readers. The figure illustrates *The .C. Hystoryes of Troye*, the English version of Christine de Pizan's *Letter of Othea to Hector*, which was printed between 1540 and 1550 in London by Robert Wyer, and again appears in Christine's *Boke of the Cyte of Ladyes*, printed in 1521 for the first time in English by Henry Pepwell.[68]

Wyer was a very successful printer, producing, according to Gordon Duff, 'a very large number of small popular books' over his long career.[69] With the majority of third- and second-generation English printers, Wyer shares the tendency to appropriate French text and picture models, and to copy earlier illustrations.[70] Like many other early English printers, Wyer also tends to use the wood-blocks he has on hand to illustrate the text, rather than acquiring new blocks which might be more appropriate. Careful consideration of the text–picture relationships in his inexpensive and rather scruffy English edition of the *Epistre* (*Letter of Othea to Hector*) shows that Wyer is also very familiar with his text, not blindly illustrating it. He is, in fact, the translator, as one can deduce from the translator's lengthy *Apologia* at the beginning of the poem. In this prefatory verse, Wyer opens with a conventional trope, asking his book to make 'excusacion / To all to whom thou shalt they selfe present'. He then explains that 'thy translatour hath þe wryte / Not to obtayne thankes or remuneracions / But to the entent, to do the to be wryten / As well in Englande, as in other nacyons', thereby claiming Christine's work for English readers.[71]

The *Apologia* replaces Christine's dedication to her patron, effectively, if not intentionally, erasing Christine as author of the book. Examination of Wyer's translation activity, and of text and image, shows that his version of the *Epistre* is very much a product of its time. The suppression of Christine in Wyer's edition is not to be read as a purposeful erasure of a female author, but rather derives from typical sixteenth-century publishing practice. To explain this in techno-logical terms, the overwriting of Christine as author, in Wyer's as well as in other early printed editions of her works, becomes the typical default position. In the first hundred years of printing, the printer, the new maker, superseded the author in the transmission of texts, just as Hollywood overwrites literary authors today.[72]

The French models for Wyer's *.C. Hystoryes* were supplied by one or more printed editions. The *editio princeps* was published in Paris *c.* 1500 by Philippe Pigouchet, after which there were at least four subsequent editions.[73] The second (or possibly the third) Paris edition appeared on 30 November 1522, printed by Philippe Le Noir. The page layouts of the two title-pages are quite similar: each has a title, and then the printer's mark, with a subtitle that is similar in both books. Pigouchet simply tells us his book has been newly printed in Paris: 'Lepistre de Othea deesse de prudence enuoyee / a lesperit cheualereux Hector de troye / auec cent hystoires. Nouuellement imprimee a Paris.' Le Noir supplies his full address for the interested purchaser, the title-page functioning as advertisement as well as announcing the title of the text: 'Lepistre de Othea deesse prudence enuoyeea lesperit cheualereux Hector de troye / auec cent hy-stoires. Nouuellement imprimee a Paris par Philippe le noir libriare [*sic*] demourant a la rue sainct Jacques a lenseigne dela Rose blanche coutonnee.'

On his version of the title-page, Wyer follows the basic French formula, giving first the title in English ('here foloweth / the .C. Hystoryes / of Troye') above a woodcut of two knights jousting before a fountain, and then, curiously, using Pigouchet's wording, in somewhat mangled French, beneath, though he leaves off the reference to Paris, simply saying the text has been newly printed: 'Lepistre de Othea deesse de Prudence / Enuoyee a tesperit cheualereux Hector / De Troye / auec cent Histoires. / Nouuellement imprimer.'

Characteristically, however, Wyer throws something of a curveball: instead of supplying his printer's mark, he substitutes a woodcut of knights jousting, a narrative image referring no doubt to the first *Epistre* text which, according to Wyer's translation, is addressed 'To the noble Hector, prynce of moste excellence / Which flouryssheth in Armes / Hast so great puyssaunce / That whom thou encountrest / Thou puttest to vtterance / Sone to the mighty Mars god of battayle'.

For the printed *Epistre*, Pigouchet sets the pattern for the layout of text and image in subsequent French editions, with the verse text beneath a woodcut in the centre of the page, and the surrounding gloss in the margins. Le Noir slavishly follows Pigouchet's format, but Wyer very definitely does not. He adapts the text to fit his octavo format by presenting first the image, then the verse text, then the gloss – a layout more like that found in the English manuscripts of the poem which had been made for the aristocracy.[74] Wyer's rather humble printed translation was directed at a very different kind of audience, middle-class readers with social aspirations who might learn refinement from the moral stories presented by Christine or might simply enjoy them as they read them through the intermediary of an English translator of the same social class as themselves. The French texts, while closer to Christine's original, show some confusion about the relation of text and image, which Wyer overcomes by substituting another method of illustration.

The story of Narcissus (Texte 16), for example, is conventionally illustrated by Pigouchet with a woodcut showing a young man gazing at his reflection in a fountain. The Le Noir edition instead supplies a woodcut of a man seducing a queen in a forest that bears at best a loose relation to the theme of the text, the downfall of the presumptuous knight through pride and vanity. Le Noir uses the same image elsewhere, for example, to illustrate Texte 63, a verse on the goddess Diana that warns against the pleasures of hunting, where the image perhaps alludes to the familiar metaphor of the hunt of love.

A better choice to illustrate the Narcissus story would have been a woodcut Le Noir unaccountably uses later to illustrate Texte 69, the story of Actaeon, showing a young man gazing into a fountain as a woman speaks to him with a pleading gesture. A more conventional representation of the Actaeon story, showing the young hunter riding into a part of the forest where Diana is bathing, illustrates Texte 69 in Pigouchet's edition. Le Noir will, however, reuse his image of the woman and the young man to illustrate the story of Echo (Texte 86), where image and text make sense together. Three points are pertinent here: Le Noir clearly had the block representing Echo and Narcissus to hand; the image has nothing to do with the story of Actaeon; and Le Noir was unaware of the connection between the story of Echo and the story of Narcissus. Judging from this and other mistakes Le Noir makes in the placement of pictures, one has the impression of an illiterate printer, unconcerned with text/image relations, copying the layout of his exemplar but careless about which images he uses to introduce texts.[75] Following the model set by Pigouchet, Le Noir's edition is slicker and cleaner than Wyer's, but the relationship between text and images in it is often tenuous.

To illustrate his Narcissus text, Wyer bypassed all the confusion of his French models by avoiding a narrative scene altogether and using a composite image made up of two blocks (Fig. 48). In Wyer's text, we see two courtly, if crudely

Fig. 48. Narcissus. Christine de Pizan, *Here foloweth the .C. Hystoryes of Troye*, trans Robert Wyer (London: Robert Wyer, *c.* 1540-50), sig. E2ʳ. *STC* 7272. PML 40646. New York, Pierpont Morgan Library.

Fig. 49. Semele and Juno. Christine de Pizan, *Here foloweth the .C. Hystoryes of Troye*, trans Robert Wyer (London: Robert Wyer, *c.* 1540-50), sig. N5ʳ. *STC* 7272. BL C.21.a.34.

drawn, male figures based on those used earlier by Wynkyn de Worde in a number of books. The figure at the left holds his hands in a gesture like that of our Everyman figure and the figure on the right, holding an axe, wears a short tunic similar to Everyman's. The text itself describes Narcissus as a 'prideful knight', a bachelor destroyed by vanity. Presumably the figures here are intended to represent Narcissus himself and his pride, allegorised in the figure of another young man.

To illustrate the story of Semele, Texte 62 (Fig. 49), Wyer again employs factotums, so as to portray the two female characters in the text, Semele and Juno. Christine tells us that Juno visited Semele in the guise of an old woman and heard Semele's confession of her affair with Juno's husband, Jupiter, thus enabling Juno to take revenge. Like the other composites we have seen, these derive from originals first used by Vérard around 1500 and are debased copies of his Everywoman figure.

71

A composite illustration of two women, copies of the Everywoman figure, beside a walled town appears on the title-page of Pepwell's 1521 edition of the *Boke of the Cyte of Ladyes*. The volume closes with an illustration of two female figures, mirror images of each other, on the final leaf, which also contains the place and date of the book's publication, and on the verso, Pepwell's printer's mark (Fig. 50). Because of their position in the book, on the colophon page, these images of women may be read as visual signifiers of Christine herself, who is consistently identified as the author in the *Cyte of Ladyes* narrative, including in the list of chapter headings at the beginning of the book; the name, however, is shortened to 'Xpine'.

In a parallel position to Pepwell's printer's mark at the end of the volume is the woodcut portrait of Christine (Fig. 51), which appears on the verso of the title-page of the *Cyte of Ladyes*, before the main text begins. She is shown at a reading desk beside a cupboard filled with books, greeting the Three Virtues in procession at left, carrying their attributes. The woodcut of Christine at her desk seems to draw on two woodcuts used earlier by de Worde. The strongly rendered features of Christine's face bear a striking resemblance to the portrait of St Catherine of Siena on the frontispiece of *The Orcharde of Syon*, printed by de Worde in 1519, while the depiction of Christine's study calls to mind a similar woodcut of Bridget used by de Worde to illustrate a number of volumes. More generally, the busyness of detail, the tiled floor, the awkward perspective and the compactness of the scene echo the style of both these predecessors.[76] Both of these images, in fact, were to be copied by Pepwell, and it has been noticed elsewhere that 'both are extremely close copies of De Worde's designs'.[77] Judging from the style of the Christine woodcut, it is, in fact, very likely that the artist who copied the de Worde woodcuts for Pepwell also executed the illustration of Christine and the Three Virtues.

Unlike many of the other images we have seen, the woodcut of Christine meeting the Three Virtues was made specifically for this volume and recurs at the start of each of the three books. Repeating an image, or linking related images, at the beginning and end of a volume, at the start and close, is typical sixteenth-century printing practice, originating in the fact that books were not usually printed and bound in the same shop. In the Pepwell examples, the images function as visual pointers at beginning and end to the two makers of the book, creating links between author and printer (with emphasis on the printer).

The study of types of illustration can pinpoint influential prototypes such as Grüninger's Terence, Vérard's *Kalendayr of the shyppars* or the Huss edition of the Bartholomaeus. Observation of picture types can also give insight into production and cost of early printed books and, more obscurely, into relationships between printers such as the Pynson–de Worde collaboration on the *Boke named the Royall*. Finally, illustration is often intimately connected with the way a printer perceives a text, as is true in particular of de Worde, and with the way he chooses to present this text to his audience. In English printed books of the late fifteenth and early sixteenth centuries, particularly in religious and

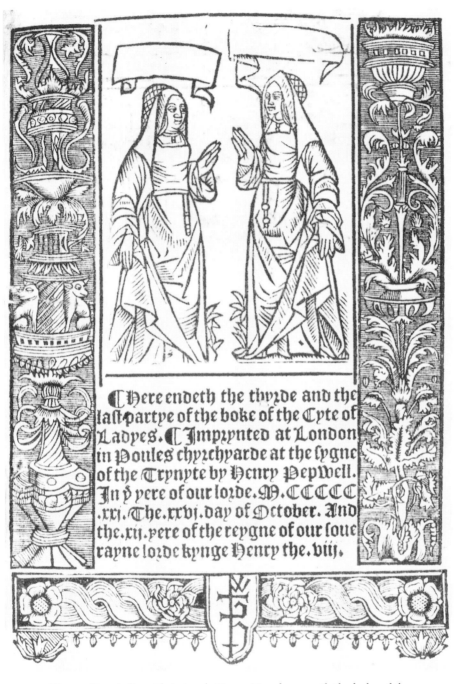

Fig. 50. Two ladies. Christine de Pizan, *Here begynneth the boke of the Cyte of Ladyes*, trans. B. Anslay (London: Henry Pepwell, 26 October 1521), sig. z4ʳ. *STC* 7271. BL C.13.a.18.

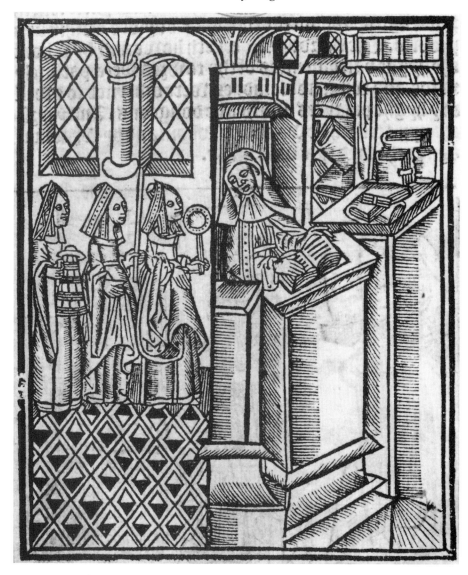

Fig. 51. Christine de Pizan at her Desk. Christine de Pizan, *Here begynneth the boke of the Cyte of Ladyes*, trans. B. Anslay (London: Henry Pepwell, 26 October 1521), sig. Aa1ᵛ. *STC* 7271. BL C.13.a.18.

devotional handbooks produced for lay readers, there is a conscious construction of a grammar of images, which is directly connected to the rise of literacy.

Like well-loved actors, the figures of Everyman and Everywoman traverse the printed page over a sixty-year span – the leading man and leading lady, if you will, of early English print illustration. Their persistent repetition implies a visual language with which sixteenth-century readers were familiar. They are not just actors but pictographs, representing the generic man or woman appropriate to a variety of scenes, often appearing in the first pages of a volume or on the title-page to entice a prospective buyer. For a short time in the sixteenth century, movable pictures illustrate books printed with movable type, and word and image have equal power to convey meaning. Though factotums were less frequently employed on the continent after 1510, they continued to be used in English books through the 1560s, perhaps indicating an innate conservatism of the print medium in England. Or perhaps we are seeing in these examples a healthy willingness by English printers to experiment with what they could make woodcuts say and do.

Chapter 3

WYNKYN DE WORDE
AND THE TITLE-PAGE

Among early English printers who experimented with visual aspects of the book, the most active was Wynkyn de Worde. His use of pictures signals a new way of thinking about the book, the possibilities of the printed page, and the function of illustration – both as a way of increasing the impact of text upon the reader, and as a means of selling books and developing a recognisable 'image' for the printer himself. This can be plainly seen in de Worde's development of what might be called the 'labelling' features of the book: his printer's mark, the repetition of images at openings and endings of texts, and above all the title-page, of which he was the main pioneer in England. Examination of de Worde's title-pages gives us some idea of the way in which de Worde's books were conceptualised, marketed and organised, as well as insight into the beginnings of a thoughtful pictorial methodology which de Worde developed in the early years of his career. The packaging of the book, in this case, is an important aspect of its formal and external structure rather than embedded in the text. The same applies to de Worde's concern with another field of book packaging, that is, the binding. The attention he gave to this area can be seen both from his activities as an employer of binders and member of the Leatherseller's Company Guild, and from what can be traced of his use of visual images in bookbinding panels.

Using a woodcut mark or device to identify the producer of a book was a new idea that came along shortly after the invention of movable type. Printers' marks seem to have been related to the monograms that began to occur in single-leaf prints in the 1450s, which were, in turn, related to merchants' and to goldsmiths' and silversmiths' marks. Such marks were not found in manuscripts, and scribes rarely revealed their names. Printed books, however, needed to be actively sold, and printers therefore needed to be known and recognised by the public. By identifying the maker of a book for prospective customers, the printer's mark functioned as both a label and an advertisement.

When de Worde took over Caxton's shop in 1491, among the assets that he inherited was Caxton's printer's device, which he persistently reused and later incorporated into his own devices (Fig. 1). De Worde presumably retained Caxton's mark initially to ensure continued sales and to reassure old customers that his books would be of the same high quality as Caxton's had been. De Worde would continue to use Caxton's device in some form to the end of his own career, however, even incorporating it into border-pieces, where it appears on shields in

Fig. 1. Device. Bartholomaeus Anglicus, *De proprietatibus rerum* (Westminster: Wynkyn de Worde, 1495), sig. oo6ᵛ. *STC* 1536. BL IB. 55242.

the margins (Fig. 2). These borders were used to adorn title-pages, end-leaves – as in this example – or the margins of Books of Hours. They occur, for example, with de Worde's printer's mark on the verso of the final leaf of *The mirroure of golde for the Synfull soule*, a work translated by Margaret Beaufort, and in margins throughout a Book of Hours printed by de Worde in 1526. They appear as well on the title-page of John Fisher's *Sermon agayn M. Luther* (see Fig. 11). The device was usually printed in black, but occasionally appears in a striking red ink, as on both recto and verso of the last leaf of de Worde's 1496 edition of the *Book of Hawking, Hunting, and Heraldry*.[1]

De Worde employed several variations on Caxton's device: early examples may be seen in Robert Whittinton's popular grammar books, *Synonyma*, printed by de Worde in 1510, and *De nominum generibus* of *c.*1510-1511. In *Synonyma*, de Worde's device appears on the title-page as well as on the final folio, both opening and closing the text.[2] A somewhat later use of the printer's mark on the title-page occurs in the *Colloquies* of Erasmus, printed by de Worde in 1519 (Fig. 3), and there are many other examples. This placement of the printer's mark is typical as well of continental productions. The printer's mark of Berthold Rembolt appears, for example, on the title-page of a Sarum Missal printed for de Worde on 2 January 1497/8 by Ulrich Gering and Rembolt, printers to the University of Paris (Fig. 4), through the agency of the Paris printer Pierre Levet. This folio, printed in two colours with woodcuts and musical notation, was published for de Worde and Michael Morin, a London stationer who, along with

Fig. 2. Device (end-leaf). Desiderius Erasmus, *Familiarium colloquiorum formulae* (London: Wynkyn de Worde, 1519). *STC* 10450.6. By permission of the Houghton Library, Harvard University, Cambridge, Mass.

Fig. 3. Device (title-page). Erasmus, *Familiarium colloquiorum formulae*
(Westminster: Wynkyn de Worde, 1520). *STC* 10450.7.
By permission of the John Rylands Library, Manchester.

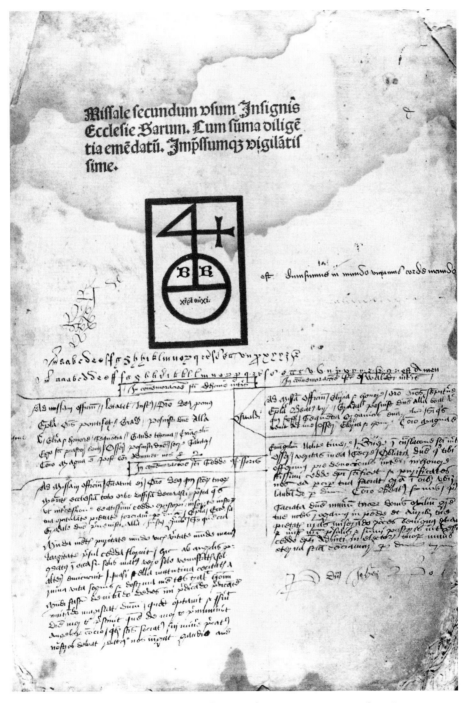

Fig. 4. Device (title-page). *Missale Secundum vsum Insignis Ecclesie Sarum*
(Paris: for Wynkyn de Worde, 1497/8), sig. A1ʳ. STC 16169. BL IB. 40686.

de Worde, commissioned several other books in Paris and imported them into London.[3] Originally, then, there seems to have been no fixed placement for the printer's mark, which could occur at the start, the close or even in the margins of a volume.

A similar impulse to label and advertise his products is at work in de Worde's development of the title-page. His work in this area was not entirely without precedent. He was perhaps following the lead of William Machlinia who, in about 1480, printed in London a treatise on the plague with a separate title-page. Caxton, it is true, has been seen as more conservative and more influenced by manuscript practice. As A. W. Pollard says in a much-quoted passage: 'Machlinia's example was never followed by Caxton, who, though one of the most chatty and communicative of printers, preferred to tell his readers the name of his book and the date of its printing, at the beginning or end of prologue, table of contents, text or epilogue, anywhere in fact rather than on an otherwise blank first page.'[4] But some of Caxton's books, like the *Golden Legend* or the *Fifteen Oes*, include a frontispiece, or a prefatory woodcut illustration, which are clearly attempts to introduce the matter of the text visually. The famous engraving of Caxton presenting his book to Margaret of York opens the *Recuyell of the Historyes of Troye*, its preface printed in red on a separate page at the beginning of the volume.[5] These seem to me to be early and effective experiments with the presentation and promotion of the printed book.

Still, it is de Worde who is credited with producing the first book with a title-page, *The Chastising of God's Children*, printed at Westminster in 1493, and it was he who more than any other printer developed the possibilities afforded by this new feature.[6] At first de Worde's title-pages are crude and perfunctory. That of St Jerome's *Lives of the Fathers*, published by de Worde in 1495, consists of two words ('Vitas [*sic*] Patrum') printed from a metal stencil plate. The same method is used for the title-page of Bartholomaeus Anglicus' encyclopedia *De proprietatibus rerum* (Fig. 5). The 'label-title', as this type of title is called, is customarily brief, generally consisting 'of a short version of the title of the book, and [sometimes] the author's name'. It is characteristic of printed books produced at the end of the fifteenth century.[7] The stark simplicity of these title-pages may be further explained by the fact that de Worde took both projects over from Caxton. The *Vitas Patrum* was Caxton's last translation, as indicated by its colophon: 'Thus endyth the moost vertuouse hystorye of the devoute and right renommed lyves of holy faders lyvynge in deserte, ... out of whiche hath be translated out of Frensshe into Englysshe by Wyllyam Caxton of Westmynstre late deed and fynysshed it at the laste daye of his lyff.' Caxton had earlier been involved in the publication of the Latin version of the Bartholomaeus encyclo-paedia in Cologne. Again, according to de Worde's colophon, Caxton was 'first printer of this book, in Latin tongue at Cologne'. By the time de Worde took over Caxton's press, the market for Caxton's books was well established, and buyers would be drawn to purchase a book previously printed by Caxton or one trans-lated while he was on his deathbed. In order to generate readership for his own

Fig. 5. Title-page. Bartholomaeus Anglicus, *De proprietatibus rerum*
(Westminster: Wynkyn de Worde, 1495), sig. A1ʳ. *STC* 1536. BL IB. 55242.

publications, however, de Worde rethinks the visual possibilities of the title-page.

One important way de Worde uses visual images is to identify the author or the contents of a book. Among the authors portrayed on de Worde's title-pages are St Bridget of Sweden, St Catherine of Siena, St Bernard, St Francis and St Jerome, as well as the bishop and jurist William Lyndewode, Thomas Trumpyngton, prior of the Coventry charterhouse, John Alcock, bishop of Ely, and the grammarians John Stanbridge and Robert Whittinton.[8] One illustration probably intended as an authorial (if not authoritative) portrait is the depiction of Richard Rolle, which may appear on the title-page, or just after, as a kind of frontispiece (Fig. 6). In four of the five times this woodcut is used, it is clearly depicting Rolle. The woodcut appears first in de Worde's 1506 edition of *Rycharde Rolle hermyte of Hampull in his contemplacyons of the drede and loue of God*. It also illustrates the 1519 edition of the *Contemplations*, again ascribed to Rolle, as well as de Worde's 1508 and 1519 editions of *The Remedy Against the Troubles of Temptations*, another work commonly attributed to Rolle in the fifteenth and sixteenth centuries – though now, ironically, neither the *Contemplations* nor the *Remedy* is thought to have been written by Rolle.[9]

On the title-page of the 1508 edition of the *Remedy* is a woodcut of the badge of Margaret Beaufort, countess of Richmond and Derby, and de Worde's royal patron (Fig. 7). A. I. Doyle has pointed out that two copies of de Worde's edition belonged to laymen, 'but there can be little doubt that a number went to religious purchasers, who may have instigated the editions and provided the text for the

Fig. 6. Representation of Richard Rolle. *Contemplacyons of the drede and loue of God* (London: Wynkyn de Worde, 1506), sig. a1ʳ. *STC* 21259. BL G. 12058, C.21.c.22.

purpose'.[10] It is, in fact, quite probable that Margaret herself directed the publication of this particular volume in the year before her death. De Worde uses her badge elsewhere in his books to indicate a connection between Margaret and the text. It occurs, for example, on both recto and verso of the title-page of *The mirroure of golde for the Synfull soule* (Fig. 8), a work which opens as follows: 'This presente boke is called the Myrroure of golde to the synfull soule / the whiche hath ben translated at paryse oute of latyn in to frensshe / and after the translacion seen and corrected at length of many clarkes Doctours and maisters *in* deuinite / & now of late tra*n*slated out of frensshe in to englisshe by þᵉ right excellent pryncesse Margarete moder to our souerayn lorde Kynge Henry þᵉ .vii. & cou*n*tesse of Rychmond & derby.'

This translation was made by Margaret from the French of a rather conventional Carthusian *contemptu mundi* work, with chapters beginning, for example, 'How we ought to dyspyse and hate the worlde', 'How men ought alwaye to attende and dreade dethe', 'Of the Joyes of paradyse and paynes of hell'. *The mirroure of golde* was printed by de Worde in 1522.[11] That it is Margaret's own translation is the most compelling aspect of the book, and the prominent placement of the king's mother's badge on the title-page, or near the beginning of a volume, is also good advertising, underscoring de Worde's royal connections.

Fig. 7. Badge of Margaret Beaufort (title-page). *The Remedy Against the Troubles of Temptations* (London: Wynkyn de Worde, 1508), sig. A1^r. *STC* 20875.5. BL G. 12058, C.21.c.22.

Margaret's badge appears as well on the opening leaf (Fig. 9) of John Fisher's sermons on the Penitential Psalms, which were made, as the introductory text states, 'at the exhortacyon and sterynge of the moost excellent pryncesse Margaret countesse of Rychmount and Derby'. John Fisher and Margaret are also found together, in a manner of speaking, on the title-page of *A mornynge remembrau[n]ce*, printed by de Worde in 1509 (Fig. 10). A realistic title-page portrait of John Fisher preaching in St Paul's introduces Fisher's eulogy for

Fig. 8. Badge of Margaret Beaufort (title-page). Margaret Beaufort, trans., *The mirroure of golde for the Synfull soule* (London: Wynkyn de Worde, 29 March 1522), sig. A1^r. *STC* 6895. BL G. 12042

DIEV ET MON DROIT

℮ This treatyse concernynge the fruytfull
saynges of Dauyd the kynge & prophete in
the seuen penytencyall psalmes. Deuyded
in seuen sermons was made and compyled
bz the ryght reuerente fader in god Johan
fyssher doctoure of dyuynite and bysshop of
Rochester at the exortacion and sterynge of
the moost excellēt pryncesse Margarete cōū
tesse of Rychemoūt and Derby/& moder to
our souerayne lorde kinge Henry the. vij.

Fig. 9. Badge of Margaret Beaufort. John Fisher, *the fruytfull saynges of Dauyd …
in the seuen penytencyall psalms* (London: Wynkyn de Worde, 1508), sig. aa1ʳ.
STC 10902, 10903. BL G.12026.

87

¶Here after foloweth a mornynge remembraũce had at the moneth mynde of the noble pzynces Margarete counteſſe of Rychemonde ⁊ Darbye moder vnto kynge Henry the. vii. ⁊ grandame to oure fouerayne lozde that nowe is/vppon whoſe ſoule almyghty god haue mercy.

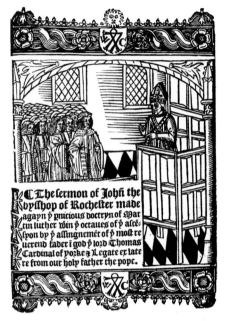

¶The ſermon of Johñ the byſſhop of Rocheſter made agayn þ pnicious doctryn of Mar tin luther wiin þ octaues of þ aſcẽ ſpon bp þ aſſingnemẽt of þ moſt re uerend fader i god þ lozd Thomas Cardinal of Yozke ⁊ Legate ez late re from our holy father the pope.

Fig. 10. Title-page. John Fisher,
A mornynge remembrau[n]ce (London:
Wynkyn de Worde, 1509). *STC* 10891.
BL G. 1202.

Fig. 11. Title-page, John Fisher, *Sermon
agayn M. Luther* (London: Wynkyn de
Worde, 1522). *STC* 10894.5.
BL C.25.e.20.

Margaret.[12] The woodcut appeared first in de Worde's 1509 printings of Fisher's *Sermon for kynge Henry vii* on the occasion of the king's funeral. The wood-block was then reused, representing Fisher each time, over a period of about twenty years.[13]

The Fisher woodcut had, in fact, been designed for reuse. In the lower left foreground, we see a cloth-covered coffin with four candles. This replaced the effigy of a king with crown, sceptre and orb lying on a pall in the original woodcut, a picture illustrating, quite literally, Fisher's sermon, which was delivered, as the text tells us, 'the body beynge present'. Henry's effigy and royal hearse were then cut out, and Margaret's coffin was 'neatly inserted'.[14] This section of the block was removed entirely when the block was used as the title-page illustration in three consecutive printings of Fisher's *Sermon agayn M. Luther* (Fig. 11), which were published *c.* 1521, in 1522 and *c.* 1527.[15] In these editions, the portion of the block illustrating Margaret's coffin was replaced by type for the title.

The consistent use of this block to illustrate Fisher's works suggests that it was intended as a specific portrait, a suggestion confirmed by examination of the image. In the woodcut, Fisher's facial features are carefully delineated. He is given a lined, serious face with heavy-lidded eyes, high cheekbones and a strong square jaw. The same features are shown in another contemporary portrait of Fisher, a chalk drawing at Windsor Castle made by Hans Holbein when the bishop was about 57 years old.[16] The woodcut is also interesting because, as Pollard and others have pointed out, there is a very close fit between the main part of the block and the movable sections, which implies that these were made in England.[17] This surmise, along with the realistic delineation of Fisher's features, argues that the artist may have seen Fisher preaching in his pulpit and rendered him from life.

In presenting these works to the public, de Worde takes care to identify the author with his book, labelling the product for its potential customers by illustrating its title-page with an idealised author portrait, as in the case of Rolle, or with what could be seen as an active narrative sequence – Fisher preaching the funeral sermon for the king and his mother, for instance. And, as in the case of *The Remedy Against Temptations*, a book's patron might also be advertised on the title-page, an astute marketing device using the built-in cachet of the patron's prominence to promote and sell the printed word.

Narrative representations of the contents of the book are also commonly found on de Worde title-pages. For example, the title-page of *The fyftene Joyes of maryage*, translated from a popular French work by an anonymous English translator and printed by de Worde in 1509 (Fig. 12), is illustrated with a generic wedding scene based on French picture models, appropriately introducing this satiric look at marriage described from the perspective of the long-suffering husband. The marriage woodcut, first used by de Worde here, appeared subsequently in *The payne and sorowe of euyll maryage*, a translation by John Lydgate from *De coniuge non ducenda*, printed c. 1509; in the *Gesta Romanorum*, printed about 1510; in the *Knyght of the swanne*, translated by Robert Copland and printed 6 February 1512; and in the romance *Olyuer of Castylle*, printed 1518.[18] Thereafter, the block is not seen again. In *The fyftene Joyes* the same woodcut is repeated on the final leaf, after the colophon, with de Worde's printer's mark on the verso. As we have seen elsewhere, the repetition of the image encapsulates the text, and we are beginning to find a pattern of enclosure in these images that open, then close text.

A very poor copy of the marriage woodcut (Fig. 13) appears in *Syr Degore*, an illustrated romance printed by de Worde about 1528.[19] This image illustrates 'How syr Degore wedded his moder the kynges doughter of Englonde'. Incest themes recur throughout this unlikely romance in which a king's daughter, raped in the woods, becomes pregnant and laments that everyone will think she has been sleeping with her father:

> For I haue ben euer meke and mylde
> And truly nowe I am with chylde
> And yf ony man it vnder yede
> Euery man wolde tell in euery stede
> That my fader on me it wan
> For I loued neuer other man

Fig. 12. Wedding scene (title-page). Antoine de La Sale, *The fyftene Joyes of maryage* (London: Wynkyn de Worde, 1509). *STC* 15258. PML 21589. By permission of the Pierpont Morgan Library, New York.

After the birth of the baby, who will become Syr Degore, his mother leaves him at a hermitage, and the child is subsequently adopted. At the age of twenty, Syr Degore leaves home to seek his fortune and slays a dragon in a forest, fighting Percival-like with only a club in his hand, 'A full good sapelyng of an oke'. He jousts with the King of England, wins his daughter, and marries her, only to find that she is his mother, after which revelation Degore rides off to various adventures with a dwarf and a giant, then finds his father and marries a 'lady bryght'. The title-page of this neglected classic (Fig. 14) advertises only a knightly romance, showing a well-dressed Syr Degore on a richly caparisoned steed with a companion in armour. This woodcut appears also on the end-leaf of the British Library copy of *The Dystruccyon of Jherusalem*, another sort of knightly romance, with de Worde's printer's mark on the verso – a further example of using images to enclose text.[20]

The marriage woodcuts employed by de Worde are derived from print models of the sacraments which appeared in a number of books published by Antoine Vérard. Vérard's beautifully produced books provided a range of illustrations which were then copied by de Worde, Richard Pynson and other English printers.

Fig. 13. Wedding scene. *Syr Degore* (London: Wynkyn de Worde, *c.* 1528), fol. 62ᵛ. *STC* 6470. PML 21135. By permission of the Pierpont Morgan Library, New York.

The marriage scene from *L'Art de bien vivre et de bien mourir* (Fig. 15), published for Vérard in Paris in 1492, and the illuminated woodcut of the sacrament of confession from the vellum copy printed on 15 December 1492 by Gillet Couteau and Jean Menard for Antoine Vérard (Fig. 16) are two examples from the sacrament series popularised by this book. Illustrations from Vérard's sacrament series were subsequently copied by the Parisian printers Le Petit Laurens and Philippe Pigouchet, and then by de Worde in his editions of *The crafte to lyue well and to dye well* (Fig. 17), and his 1502 and 1506 editions of *ThOrdynary of Crysten Men* (Fig. 18), Andrew Chertsey's translation of Vérard's *L'Art de bien vivre et de bien mourir*. The title-page of *ThOrdynary of Crysten Men* consists of two woodcuts, one with the xylographic title – lettering which has been cut from a wood-block, not set in movable type – and another of the Sacrament of Confession. The source for Vérard's sacrament series remains unidentified, though some comparison may be made with the much simpler and more roughly rendered illustrations by the Gouda artist of *Van den Seven Sacramenten*, printed by Gerard Leeu in 1484.[21] As we have seen in prior chapters, Vérard was a successful Parisian entrepreneur who habitually published books that had been popular previously, whether in manuscript or in print. In several cases he looked to block-book models for inspiration, and it is not impossible that his sacrament series derives from a lost block-book source.[22]

In his edition of *L'Art de bien vivre et de bien mourir*, Vérard also includes an entire set of *Ars moriendi* illustrations which have certainly been drawn from block-book exemplars. These also appear in another edition published in Paris by Vérard in 1503, a peculiar English translation called *The book intytulyd the*

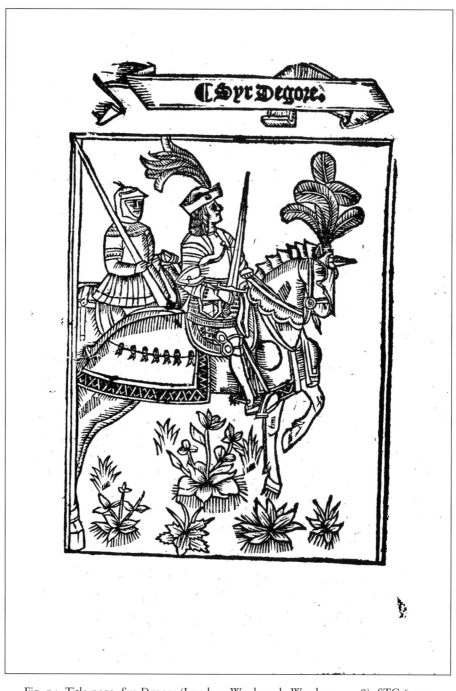

Fig. 14. Title-page. *Syr Degore* (London: Wynkyn de Worde, *c.* 1528). STC 6470.
PML 21135. By permission of the Pierpont Morgan Library, New York.

Fig. 15. Wedding scene. *L'Art de bien vivre et de bien mourir* (Paris: for Antoine Vérard, 1492). BL IB. 40027.

Fig. 16. Confession scene. *L'Art de bien viure et de bien mourir* (Paris: Gillet Couteau and Jean Menard for Antoine Vérard, 15 December 1492), sig. h2ʳ. By permission of the Huntington Library, San Marino.

art of good lywyng and good deyng.[23] We further find the scene of the Death of Moriens, the final scene of the *Ars moriendi* series, on the verso of the final folio of *ThOrdynary of Crysten Men* (see Chapter 1, Fig. 11). Like *ThOrdynary* title-page, the verso of the end-leaf consists of two blocks: the xylographic title of the book, which is repeated, and the *Ars moriendi* woodcut.

De Worde uses other images from Vérard's *Ars moriendi* series on the title-pages of *The deyenge creature* (Fig. 19), printed in 1507 and again in 1514, and of *The Rote or myrour of consolacyon & conforte* (Fig. 20), which appeared in 1511 and again in 1530.[24] In each case, the image introduces main themes in the text. *ThOrdynary of Crysten Men* editions are literally enveloped in two powerful images, opening with a scene of confession and closing with the moment of death as the soul leaves the body.

Illustrated title-pages are typically found in other religious books printed by de Worde. A title-cut of the Trinity (Fig. 21) illustrates *The ymage of loue*, first printed by de Worde for John Gough, who translated the work in 1525.[25] Gough, a bookseller known also as a reformer, seems to have sponsored books rather

Fig. 17 (*above*). Wedding scene.
The crafte to lyue well and to dye well
(London: Wynkyn de Worde, 1505), fol.
xlvii^r. *STC* 792. BL C.132.h.40, sig. H5^r.
Fig. 18 (*right*). Title-page. Andrew
Chertsey, trans., *ThOrdynary of Crysten
Men* (London: Wynkyn de Worde, 1506).
STC 5199. BL C.25.f.7.

than printing them himself.[26] This particular edition landed de Worde in trouble
with the authorities, presumably because of its criticism of the use of religious
images.[27] The woodcut on the title-page of *The ymage of loue* may have been
made specifically for this volume; here, the image of the Trinity is used to
promote religious belief (and to sell the book) even as the text condemns the
unthinking worship of pictures.[28]

One year after the 1525 publication of the controversial *Ymage of loue*,
de Worde brought out his final edition of *The thre kynges of Coleyne*, attributed
to Joannes of Hildesheim. This work was clearly popular, for it was printed by
de Worde four times over a period of thirty years.[29] The title-page of the 1526
edition (Fig. 22) is illustrated by a woodcut of the Adoration of the Magi and is
further adorned with three border-pieces and metal ornaments. The image in this
case refers to the heroes of this apocryphal religious text, the Three Kings who,
as the preface relates, 'came to Bedleem and worshypped hym and offred to hym
/ vnto the tyme of theyr deth'. Unlike the unbelieving Jews (who are punished for
their doubt), the kings follow the prophecy of Balaam ('a sterre shall sprynge of
Jacob and a man shall ryse vp of Israell and shall be lorde of all folke') to find the
Christ child in Jerusalem.

The kings then meet St Thomas the Apostle, sending their archbishops 'aboute

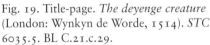

Fig. 19. Title-page. *The deyenge creature* (London: Wynkyn de Worde, 1514). *STC* 6035.5. BL C.21.c.29.

Fig. 20. Title-page. *The Rote or myrour of consolacyon & conforte* (London: Wynkyn de Worde, 1511). *STC* 21336. BL C.37.e.6.(2.).

cytees & townes & other dyuers places' who 'ordeyned many chyrches'. They also encounter 'Preter Johan', the mythic Nestorian Christian emperor of India who was associated early on with the Apostle Thomas. We then are told the story of St Helena, about the finding of the True Cross, and the collecting of relics, including the bodies of the three kings, to be housed in 'the chyrche of saynt Sophye'. Later, their bodies are transported to the 'Cyte of Coleyne', in accordance with a well-known prophecy. The title image of the 1526 edition also appears in three Books of Hours printed by de Worde in 1519, 1523 and 1526, illustrating Sext in the Hours of the Virgin; and in two editions of Nicholas Love's translation of the *Speculum vitae Christi* (7 September 1525 and 8 February 1530), a text de Worde had inherited from Caxton.[30] An earlier de Worde issue of *The thre kynges*, that of 1511, again fittingly employs a woodcut of the Adoration of the Magi on its title-page, an image which had been used earlier in de Worde's *c.* 1507 edition of Love's version of the *Speculum* and would be used again by him in another edition of that work in 1517.[31]

The woodcut of the Adoration of the Magi is appropriate to all of these works. In Books of Hours, whether in manuscript or print, the scene of the Adoration of the Magi traditionally introduces Sext, readings for the fifth canonical hour of the day, providing the reader or viewer with visual stimulus for meditation on the Epiphany. The opening images of each chapter in Books of Hours were typically used for meditations on the life of Christ and the Virgin, one form of popular affective piety. In Love's *Speculum*, the image seems also to have had meditative purposes as a literal picturing of the verbal directives to meditation set forth in the text: '... and so ymagyne we and sette we oure minde and oure thou3t as we

Fig. 21. Title-page. John Gough, trans., *The ymage of loue* (London: Wynkyn de Worde for John Gough, 1532). *STC* 21472. By permission of the Bodleian Library, Oxford.

Fig. 22. Title-page. Joannes of Hildesheim, *The thre kynges of Coleyne*
(London: Wynkyn de Worde, 1526). *STC* 5575. PML 20897.
By permission of the Pierpont Morgan Library, New York.

were present in the place there this was done at Bethleem / byholdynge how these
thre kinges comen with grete multitude and a worschipful companye of lordes
and othere seruauntes …'.[32]

Likewise, in *The thre kynges*, the picture introduces the story's protagonists,
'those thre gloryous kynges', as de Worde describes them in his colophon. They
are a powerful, evocative image used to focus the reader's attention on the central
religious moment of what is essentially a compilation of religious story, prophecy,
folklore and picaresque tale. On the verso of the end-leaf is de Worde's printer's
mark. This is yet another example of a printed text enclosed by images, the first
image related to the book's thematic content, and the last announcing its maker.

Fig. 23. Two debaters (end-leaf). Henry Parker [attrib.], *Diues & Pauper* (Westminster: Wynkyn de Worde, 3 Dec., 1496), fol. 195ᵛ. *STC* 19213. BL C.11.b.4.

Narrative representations of the contents of the book are typically found on de Worde's title-pages. These include a simple presentation of the two debaters in de Worde's 1496 edition of *Diues & Pauper* (Fig. 23), a commentary on the Ten Commandments in the form of a dialogue between a rich man and a poor man. The woodcut on the title-page has been described as 'open and simple', and 'large enough to fill the folio page without letterpress or miscellaneous orna-

98

Fig. 24. Title-page. *The crafte to lyue well and to dye well*
(London: Wynkyn de Worde, 1505), fol. xlvii^r. STC 792. BL C.132.h.40.

ments'.[33] The title itself is xylographic, cut from the same block of wood as the image. On the verso of the last leaf, the title-page occurs again.

Another very interesting example of a narrative sequence occurs in *The crafte to lyue well and to dye well*, printed by de Worde in 1505 (Fig. 24). Here we see a wormy corpse being carted off to burial by a gaily caparisoned, prancing horse. The picture is repeated on the verso of the title-page, accompanying a verse prologue that neatly summarises the book's theme:

O mortall man / lyfte up thyn eye
And put all vanytes out of thy mynde.
For as thou seest / this corse here lye
Euen shalt thou / by nature and kynde.
A mannes lyf / is but a blast of wynde ...

Take þu example / of this carkes here.
Whereon these wormes: do gnawe & fede
No man is sure / hourse daye / ne yere
In this worlde to lye: it is mater in dede
Hyder thou camest / without ony wede.

The lines 'For as thou seest / this corse here lye' and 'Take þu example / of this carkes here. Whereon these wormes: do gnawe & fede' seem to refer directly to the woodcut, strongly implying that the illustration was made with these verses in mind: the picture is a visual rendering of the message of the poem, and more broadly, of the text it introduces.[34]

The *Boke of Husbandry* (Fig. 25), a quarto printed *c.* 1508, had wide circulation in manuscript. Composed by Walter of Henley, this is the 'earliest work on agriculture written by an Englishman'.[35] As the preface states, the work 'techeth all maner of men to gouerne theyr londes tene // mentes / and demenes ordynatly as the chapytres euydently is shewed. The.i.chapytre telleth how ye shall spende your good and extende youre londes. The.ii.chapytre telleth how youre londe shall be mesured.' Further chapters discuss ploughing, sowing and 'how ye shall nourysshe youre dounge', along with care of cattle, pigs, sheep, geese and hens, while the final chapter addresses 'how ye shall take a compte of your balyf [bailiff] ones a yere'. The image on the title-page, the only picture in the book, fittingly shows two men at work, one chopping at a tree with his axe, as two deer graze among other trees. Like that of *ThOrdynary of Crysten Men* (see Fig. 18), the title lettering is xylographic, though this time with white letters on a black background. A later example of a xylographic white-on-black title occurs on the title-page of de Worde's *Nychodemus gospel* of 1509, which also is adorned with four borderpieces, de Worde's printer's mark and a woodcut of the Deposition that first appeared in Caxton's 1486 edition of the *Speculum vitae Christi*. The white-on-black format occurs as well in several variants of de Worde's printer's device.[36]

The chirche of the euyll men and women, a 1511 tract against gambling, is illustrated with metal-cuts and woodcuts drawn from French sources. The illustration on the title-page (Fig. 26) appears in several Books of Hours produced by the Paris printer Thielman Kerver. Its style is derived from cuts used by Philippe Pigouchet, and is distinctively French with its criblée background.[37] The image of the Man of Pity in the de Worde volume is quite similar to one that occurs, for example, in an Hours for Rome use, now in the Pierpont Morgan Library, printed in Paris by Kerver in around 1500. The woodcut of the *Pietà* on the verso of the last leaf of the volume (Fig. 27) is also French in style. Attributed

Fig. 25. Title-page. Walter of Henley, *Boke of Husbandry* (London: Wynkyn de Worde, *c.* 1508). *STC* 25007. By permission of Cambridge University Library, Cambridge.

in the preface to 'saynt Bernardyn', or Saint Bernardinus of Siena, *The chirche of the euyll men and women*, we are told, 'hathe ben translated out of laten in to Frensshe / and vysyted at Parys by foure venerable doctours in the faculte of Theologye /' after which 'Henry Watson symple of vnderstondynge' was commissioned 'to translate this lytell treatyse in to our maternal tongue of Englysshe'. Watson was a translator and journeyman printer, who worked for de Worde around 1509. After 1513, he went into partnership with Hugh Goes at Charing Cross.[38] It is thought that the work was possibly printed in Paris for de Worde, the *STC* making this ambiguous comment, 'While the types have considerable

Fig. 26. Title-page. Henry Watson, trans., *The chirche of the euyll men and women* (London: Wynkyn de Worde, 1511). *STC* 1966. By permission of Cambridge University Library, Cambridge.

resemblance to those of de Worde, the woodcuts, orn[ament]s, and init[ial]s are not part of his usual stock and are prob[ably] French; the colophon date may merely repeat that in a French ed[ition].'[39] Like the missal made in France for de Worde and Morin, this work may also have been produced in France for de Worde. And, like the other examples we have seen, the text is encased in images, which introduce and close the book.

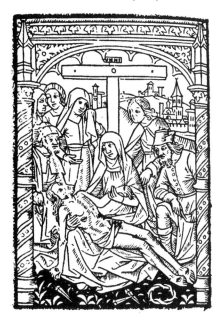

Fig. 27. End-leaf. Henry Watson, trans.,
The chirche of the euyll men and women
(London: Wynkyn de Worde, 1511).
STC 1966. By permission of Cambridge
University Library, Cambridge.

Notice that the image on the title-page of a slightly later work, *The Way to the holy lande* (Fig. 28), printed by de Worde in 1515, actually consists of three blocks. These are the central narrative scene as the pilgrim departs, staff in hand, and a small figure in the castle door seems to bid him adieu; the woodcut border beneath; and a banderole for the title, a decorative device de Worde used increasingly after 1500.[40] The title, in this case, has been printed from movable type that has been neatly fitted within the woodcut scroll. We have seen other examples of factotum printing like this, specifically on the title-page of William Nevill's romance *The Castell of Pleasure*, in which titles within banderoles identify the name of the work and those of the allegorical figures in the story (Chapter 2, Fig. 43).

On his title-pages, de Worde employs a number of different banderoles, ranging from a simple scroll to an ornate winding banner. Compare those found on the title-pages of *The Remedy Against the Troubles of Temptations* (Fig. 7), *The fyftene Joyes of maryage* (Fig. 12) and *Syr Degore* (Fig. 14), for example. De Worde uses banderoles as labels – another example of a visual translation of a rather literal concept, used also in manuscript illumination (and even today in the buttons used in computer displays). Their simplicity or complexity of design is not a reliable clue to date. However, breaks in the blocks, which are indicative of wearing, are often discernible. For example, the same banderole occurs on the title-pages of *The .vii. shedynges of the blode of Jhesu cryste* and *The lamentacyon of our lady*, where the title is accompanied by metal ornaments. *The .vii. shedynges* is dated 1509, while *The lamentacyon of our lady* is undated.

Fig. 28. Title-page. *The way to the holy lande* (London: Wynkyn de Worde, 1515).
STC 14082. PML 20898. By permission of the Pierpont Morgan Library, New York.

Careful comparison of the banderoles, in this case, is one important piece of
evidence that has led to a dating of the latter work by the *STC* as *c.* 1510.[41]

For his last edition of Aesop's *Fables*, an octavo printed in 1535, de Worde
combines new methods of title-page presentation with the tried and true. Aesop
was a perennial favourite with English printers. De Worde had earlier printed
quarto editions of the *Fabule Esopi cum commento*, in 1503, *c.* 1514 and 1516.
Pynson printed his first English edition of Aesop *c.* 1497, then several more, and
there are also editions by Henry Pepwell and Peter Treveris, produced through

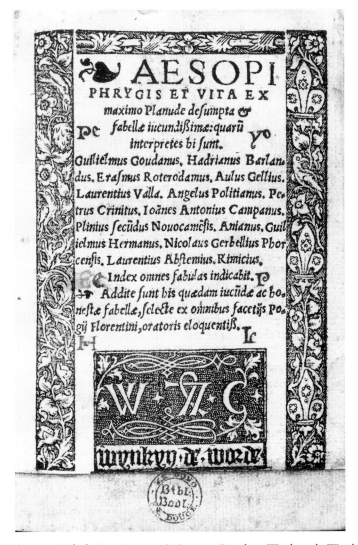

Fig. 29. Title-page. *Fabule Esopi cum co[m]mento* (London: Wynkyn de Worde, 1535). *STC* 171. By permission of the Bodleian Library, Oxford.

the 1530s. All of these draw from the first English edition, which was translated by Caxton and published by him on 26 March 1484.[42] De Worde's is a late example, a collection of Aesop's fables in Latin printed in the last year of his life.[43] The title-page (Fig. 29) shows humanist influence: it is set in roman and italic type, and is adorned with an ivy-leaf ornament derived from Italian models and with three borderpieces. The italic type has been copied from that used by the Aldus Manutius and his sons, and appears also in de Worde's editions of

William Lily's grammars and other school-books. Woodcut initials throughout the text are based on Italian models.[44] The French picture sources that served de Worde so well earlier in his career have here been discarded, perhaps in deference to the classical author and certainly in keeping with the fashionable trend of the times. However, we still find de Worde's mark at the foot of the title-page, the maker's sign being used repeatedly and prominently in books de Worde produced throughout his career.

The increasing use of the title-page after the introduction of printing was at least partially motivated by a new conception of the book. As Walter J. Ong remarks, 'Once print has been fairly well interiorized, a book was sensed as a kind of object which "contained" information, scientific, fictional, or other, rather than, as earlier, a recorded utterance.'[45] With printing, not only did perceptions of the book change, but there was a decided shift in the relationship between the producer of the book and his audience. The printer was a step away from the presumably close connection between scribe and patron. Labelling the book, advising a prospective buyer of its contents, made good business sense; it was an integral aspect of selling the product.[46] And, as we have seen, woodcuts, titles and/or printer's marks are frequently found at both the front and the back of a book, encapsulating and identifying the work.

In addition, there was another good reason for what might otherwise be seen as obsessive labelling of text: the technical requirements of the binding process. Bookbinding was a stage of finishing usually completed elsewhere than in the print shop. Howard Nixon comments that a printer would keep 'some bound copies in stock, if only as patterns for the customer to choose from', but the customer would purchase an unbound copy, taking the sheets 'to a bookbinder of his choice, or more frequently would probably ask the bookseller to arrange for the binding'. Paul Needham has pointed out that 'we know from surviving notes from inventories, [that printers] usually kept their stock in unbound sheets rather than ready-bound'.[47] This explains why so many of de Worde's books are labelled front and back, thereby setting off each volume as a distinct entity for the binder. Work by the 'Caxton binder' appears on a number of books printed by Caxton, on four books printed by de Worde, and on books printed by others, as well as on eight manuscripts: four of these manuscripts originated in Westminster, and several were copied by the English scribe William Ebesham.[48] The bindings date from 1477 to no later than 1511, after which most of the tools apparently went out of use. Thirty-nine bindings have so far been identified as having been produced by this shop, which is thought to have been located in Westminster: 'Of the bindings on books printed in Caxton's lifetime, fourteen are on Caxton's imprints, and five on books from other presses. Eight bindings of the group contain (or once contained) binder's waste from Caxton's press, and one other, waste from Wynkyn's press.'[49] The de Worde waste occurs in a 1503 edition of Joannes de Janua's *Catholicon*, printed by Nicholas Wolff in Lyon.[50] Other bindings contain printer's waste from Caxton's shop, and Nixon and

Mirjam Foot conjecture that Caxton and de Worde may, in fact, have owned this bindery: 'If they did not ... own this binder's shop it was certainly near their premises; all the printed waste found in its bindings comes from Caxton's press, and the shop also bound manuscripts for Westminster Abbey. But although one or two of the shop's kit of tools turn up alone considerably later, 1511 appears to be the latest date of printing of any book in the group. If the shop was de Worde's, it must have acquired a new set of tools about that time.'[51] Elsewhere, Foot has described the close connections between the printer's shop and the bindery in the early days of printing: 'In the late fifteenth century and during the beginning of the sixteenth, it seems as if the big stationers were instrumental in getting the books they sold bound, either by their own bindery on the premises or by a craftsman nearby. ... The same pattern can be seen earlier with books published by Caxton at Westminster and those associated with Theodoric Rood and Thomas Hunt at Oxford. In both cases one binder seems to have been most frequently employed and, in Caxton's case, had access to printer's waste.'[52]

The possibilities raised by specialists in the history of bookbinding are varied and often tantalising, based at least in part, as Needham has pointed out, on speculation: 'The association of the bindery with Caxton is based on circumstantial evidence.'[53] But it seems clear that the relationship between Caxton's shop, which de Worde took over in 1491, and the Westminster bindery was close, at least until 1511, when the tools ceased to be used. What was de Worde's relationship with the mysterious 'Caxton binder' after Caxton's death? Did de Worde himself own a bindery? Did Caxton? And what happened later, after 1511? While we cannot answer these questions for certain, we do know that de Worde maintained connections with binders, several of whom are mentioned in his will.

De Worde has been described as a man of diverse talents, as 'not only a stationer, printer and bookbinder, but also a member of the Leatherseller's Company'.[54] In his will, dated 5 June 1534 (proved 19 January 1535), de Worde mentions 'Alard bokebinder / now my seruante' who presumably worked on the premises, and 'Nowell [Havy] the bokebinder in / shoo lane', a binder with a separate shop in the leather district, to whom de Worde bequeathed 'xx s st in book*es*'.[55] From the mention of the two binders in de Worde's will, Nixon surmises, 'De Worde would be having books bound in his capacity as a retail bookseller' both in his shop and elsewhere.[56]

Apparently there were also binder's tools in de Worde's shop, or so it appears from an inventory of Wynkyn de Worde's house, made, however, in 1553, almost twenty years after his death. The inventory, written in a peculiar mixture of Latin, English and law French, cites, among other things, four printing presses, two pairs of cases with letters to print with, three shelves with pictures and fourteen 'historiis' (narrative images?) made of wood, along with 'the "toles" to bind with'.[57] Finally, returning to de Worde's will, we find that one of the executors came originally from a Ghent family of binders and had earlier been employed by de Worde, presumably in that capacity. James van Gaver, or 'Iames gauer', as he is called in the will itself, 'late my seruaunte', is bequeathed 'for his / labour in executing of this my present testament and last will as manny printed bookes as shall / amounte to the somme of twenty markes sterling /'. Duff describes Gaver as 'a member of the large family of Van Gavere, binders in the Low Countries'. After de Worde's death, 'He appears to have continued to live with Byddell in De Worde's house, the Sun in Fleet Street', and Gaver requested in his will that he 'be buried in St Bride's Church near Wynkyn de Worde'.[58] So it seems that binding tools may have been on the premises of de Worde's shop and that he employed at least two binders in house and another, Nowell Havy, in Shoe Lane. With all of the detail furnished by the will, and 'in spite of his enormous business, it is somewhat remarkable that de Worde does not seem to have ever used a panel with his name or device, at least so far not one has been found', as Duff pointed out in 1899.[59]

De Worde's connections with bookbinders date back to his early association with Caxton, and he is known to have produced between nine hundred and one thousand separate editions during his long, productive career.[60] Yet no de Worde binding has been identified. I have, however, come across a binding panel and some printer's waste that may be connected with de Worde's shop. In Archbishop Marsh's Library, Dublin, there are three books with a four-compartment binding panel containing the following images: John the Evangelist; Barbara holding an open book and a martyr's palm, with her tower at left; Catherine crowned, holding a sword and open book, standing on a broken wheel with the emperor beneath her feet; and Nicholas restoring the boys, who emerge from a pickling tub, to life.[61] G. D. Hobson reproduces this panel in his *Bindings in Cambridge Libraries*, from a binding of an edition of Paulus Orosius, *Opus prestatissimum*, printed by Jehan Petit in Paris in 1510, now in Corpus Christi College: 'The volume had formerly as flyleaves fragments from *Nova Statuta*, printed by W. Machlinia, London?, 1488.'[62] This binding, like Marsh's bindings, is apparently decorated with an English version of the panel that originated in France.

Hobson has found the French panel on seven books printed in Rouen, Paris and Lyon.[63] This French panel is also reproduced by Ruth Mortimer in her catalogue of French books, occurring on a volume of Beroaldo's commentary on Apuleius, printed in 1512 by J. Philippi for L. Hornken and G. Hittorp at Paris and Cologne.[64] The panel is described as well by E. Ph. Goldschmidt as: 'Brown polished calf on pasteboard, stamped on the upper cover with a large single panel of four compartments, a saint standing in each: St John the Evangelist, St Barbara, St Catherine and St Nicholas, each with appropriate symbols. The initials P G in the lower compartments. Lower cover: a plaque of five vertical strips of vine or flower ornament framed by a border of grape vines embracing birds, dragons, a snail and banderoles lettered with a motto and the name PIERRE GUIOT.'[65] The 'lower cover' here refers to the back cover of the book, and it is useful to note that in the French examples the four-compartment panel and the border always appear separately, that is, not on the same side of the book.

I have also found the French panel and/or its border on the bindings of three books in the Pierpont Morgan Library. The four-compartment panel occurs on the front cover of the *Epistolae* of the younger Pliny, printed in Paris by Francis Regnault and Gilles de Gourmont in 1510; the border with grapes, etc., is on the back cover. The French border panels again occur, without the four-compartment panel and along with other borders, on the front and back of the binding of an Hours for Rome use printed by Philippe Pigouchet for Simon Vostre in 1496. Finally, the binding panel and border appear on a copy of *Horae intemerate virginis Marie secundum vsum Romanum* printed by Thielman Kerver in 1500.[66] This book also includes the illustration of the Image of Pity, with criblée background, from which de Worde drew his image used on the title-page of the 1511 edition of *The chirche of the euyll men and women* cited earlier, which is thought perhaps to have been produced in Paris for de Worde.

As Hobson has noted, the French panel 'very closely resembles a panel which has in its lower border the initials S G' found on four books printed by de Worde.[67] But the two binding panels are not exactly the same. In the French version, the figure of St Nicholas, sometimes identified as Claude, is shown holding a staff cross with an open book. In the English version, Nicholas raises the boys from the tub. And, as noted earlier, in the French examples, the border and the panel occur separately, on the front and back of the book. In the English version, the four-compartment panel and its border always appear together (Fig. 30). The ornamental border is 'adorned with sprays of foliage and fruit, wiverns, and birds; at each angle is an artichoke', or possibly a pineapple.[68] In this border, the 'binder's cipher S G, formed by two dragons united by a knot', described by James Weale, has been cancelled or crossed out in the copies I have examined, but this is, according to Basil Oldham, the second and more common state, where the border is damaged in the middle 'at top and bottom, and the initials are almost, but not quite obliterated'.[69] Oldham places this binding panel in early sixteenth-century London, while Hobson identifies the panel as 'used in England, *c.* 1520'.[70]

The Marsh volumes on which the binding panel is found are an octavo Cassiodorus, printed by George Wolff in Paris *c.* 1490; two editions printed by de Worde in 1514, which have been bound together; and another edition, printed 1511 in Paris by Jehan Petit, with flyleaves from an early de Worde edition of the *Thre kynges of Coleyne*. There are also at least two volumes with this panel in the British Library: the *Synonyma* printed in London by de Worde in 1518, described by Weale, and a copy of the *Mirror of Our Lady*, printed by Richard Fawkes in 1530, wrongly ascribed to de Worde by Hobson. Hobson also cites editions printed by de Worde with this binding panel in the Society of Antiquaries, the Public Record Office and elsewhere.[71]

The English version of the binding panel appears, for example, on *De regimine ecclesie primitiue hystoria tripartita*, the Cassiodorus volume. The printer, Georg Wolff, was originally from Baden, and worked in Paris for several printers, including Ulrich Gering, who collaborated with Rembolt on the 1497 *Missale*

Fig. 30. Binding panel. *Expositio hymno[rum] totius anni secundum usum Sarum; Expositio Sequentiarum* (London: Wynkyn de Worde, 12 June 1514; 8 July 1514). *STC* 16125. By permission of the Governors and Guardians of Marsh's Library, Dublin.

secundum usum Sarum printed for de Worde and Michael Morin (see Fig. 4). Around 1490, about the time the Cassiodorus was printed, Wolff went to work for Thielman Kerver, going into partnership with Kerver after 1498.[72] In 1506, Kerver printed a Sarum Breviary for Morin and de Worde. Images in the Books of Hours produced by Kerver during this period seem to have influenced de Worde, as we have seen.

The 1514 quarto volume with the English panel consists of two works printed by de Worde which are bound together. These are *Expositio hymnorum totius anni secundum usum Sarum diligentissime recognitorum*, printed on 12 June 1514, and *Expositio sequentiarum &c*, printed on 8 July 1514. In the *Expositio hymnorum*, we find the ownership marks of 'Thomas hyll' and 'hugo heton', early sixteenth-century readers. And, as we have seen elsewhere, the title-page supplies the title and publishing details: 'Impressa Londini per Wynandum de Worde in parrochia scte brigide in vico anglice nuncupato (the fletestrete) ad signum solis commorantem'. Below this information is a variation of de Worde's printer's mark that we have also seen previously (see Fig. 3) with sun and stars, Caxton's mark, a banderole beneath inscribed 'wynkyn de worde', a dog and a centaur shooting an arrow. This same printer's mark, more heavily inked, appears on the final leaf verso of the volume, yet another example of a book identified, front and back, by the insignia of its maker. The *Expositio hymnorum* ends with this colophon: 'habes lector explanationes hymnorum se*cund*um vsum (vt dicunt) Sarum diligenter castigatas et auctas. Impressas Londonii per wynandum de worde comm*em*oratem in vico vulgariter nuncupato (the Fletestrete) in signo solis. Anno d*om*ini Millesimoquingentisimo decimo-quarto duodecima die mensis Junii. Laus deo.'

The title-page of the companion work in the volume, the *Expositio sequentiarum*, tells us that this too has been 'Impressa Londini per wynandum de worde in parrochia sancte Brigide in vico anglice nuncupato (the fletestrete) ad signum solis commorantem'. Beneath the title is a woodcut of a schoolmaster with his birch switch and three pupils. The colophon repeats the title and facts of publishing ('finis Londoni. per wynandum de worde impressa in vico anglice nuncupato (the fletestrete) ad signum Solis commorantem. Anno domini Millesimoquingentesimo decimoquarto. Die vero octaua mensis Julii'). On the verso of the final leaf of text, following the tabula, occurs this information: 'Ad lectorem. Splendidum pulchri specimen libelli / Lector inspectans: animos fauentes / Sume winando merito reponans. Era de worde'. De Worde's printer's mark recurs on the verso of the final leaf (the recto is blank). This repeated labelling of text is interesting. The two works seem to have been intended to be bound together, as they are here in this original binding, so that this naming and renaming of the text could be seen as obsessive self-identification by the printer, perhaps because the book was to be sent off in sheets to Shoe Lane or elsewhere.

The 1511 imprint, a copy of *Sermones in parabolam filii glutonis profusi atque*, a text by Johannes Medera, is perhaps even more interesting. Published in Paris by Jehan Petit, the book not only has the binding panel (which is, however,

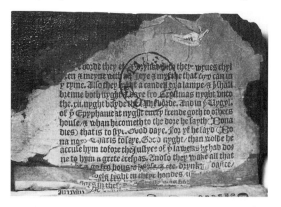

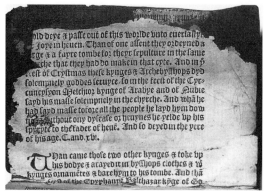

Figs 31-32. Waste. *Sermones in parabolum filii glutonis profusi* (Paris: Jehan Petit, 1511). By permission of the Governors and Guardians of Marsh's Library, Dublin.

much rubbed) but contains three flyleaves, originally included as printer's waste in a binding which has since split, from the de Worde edition of *The thre kynges of Coleyne* (Figs 31-34). The closest match is, in fact, the 1511 edition of de Worde's *Thre kynges*, and the leaves appear to be waste from that volume.[73]

There seems no doubt that the four-compartment panel of John the Evangelist, Barbara, Catherine and Nicholas originated in France and that a variant of this, with Nicholas raising the boys from the tub and an ornamental border, then circulated in England, appearing on the bindings of books printed by de Worde or on books produced by printers known to have associated with him. The appearance of the panel on the copy in the British Library of the *Mirror of Our Lady*, printed in 1530 by Richard Fawkes, further suggests that the panel continued to be used by English printers for over twenty years.

The evidence of de Worde's printer's waste found in a binding with the English panel seems particularly convincing of a direct link to de Worde's shop, particularly in light of the use of Caxton's waste as one source of proof that the 'Caxton

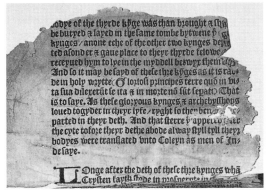

Figs 33-34. Waste. *Sermones in parabolum filii glutonis profusi* (Paris: Jehan Petit, 1511). By permission of the Governors and Guardians of Marsh's Library, Dublin.

binder' did exist. Mirjam Foot cites findings by William Ward and Christopher de Hamel of indulgence strips 'printed by Lettou and by Caxton used to strengthen the spines of bindings from the Rood and Hunt binder, who worked in Oxford'. From this evidence, however, Ward and de Hamel have cautioned against making quick conclusions: 'The discovery of indulgences printed by two different printers, one working in London, the other in Westminster, in a binding by an Oxford printer shows that such fragments cannot be used as proof either of the place of binding or of the identity of the binder', and I do not doubt that very little can be learned from the presence of binding strips alone.[74] But when a pattern begins to emerge, when one finds a binding panel or evidence of tools recurring, along with binder's waste, something more seems indicated. Printer's waste has clearly been one important clue in reconstructing the output of the Caxton's binder's shop. The question of de Worde's connection to this shop is less clear, and it may very well be that after 1511 he was looking to France, specifically Paris, rather than to Westminster. Certainly the year 1511 seems to recur in the evidence. In 1511, the tools associated with the 'Caxton Master' cease to be used. In 1511, *The chirche of euyll men and women* is published for de Worde, possibly in Paris, using illustrations typically found in Books of Hours printed by Thielmann Kerver, whose associate Georg Wolff published the copy of Cassiodorus on which the first known example of the English binding occurs. In 1511, de Worde printed *The thre kynges of Coleyne*, three leaves of which turn up in a *Sermones* also printed in 1511 by Jehan Petit in Paris, the binding of which is adorned with the English binding panel. These events do not seem coincidental but argue for a closer connection between de Worde and Parisian printers than has previously been assumed, perhaps consisting simply in the importation by de Worde of French-produced books into England and having them bound there.

De Worde's own tendency to label the text should also be borne in mind, with title-pages, images and printer's marks at beginning and end setting off each book as a discrete item. In addition to attracting customers with an appealing title-page, he is apparently labelling text for the bindery – the sheets to be bound as marked – which shows at the very least his awareness of the proper preparation of books for the binding stage. Just where these books were bound remains a mystery, and a complete picture of de Worde's activities remains to be drawn. As Howard Nixon has remarked, 'Future research must concentrate on the study of books printed by de Worde, which have survived in contemporary bindings, in the hope of identifying later work from his binding shop.'[75]

In a very brief span of time, de Worde found many ways to present the title-pages to his volumes, from author portraits to religious or lively narrative scenes. Subject, author and/or maker were graphically presented through the image, explaining at a glance what a book was about, who wrote it and in some cases, who made or commissioned it. Enclosing a printed text, front and back, with images was another method of ordering the text and preparing it for the binder, whether in-house or elsewhere.

All these methods are directly related to the technology of printing and to new ideas about the book. Movable pictures illustrate books printed with movable type; pictures may also be repeated in a variety of contexts. Books, illustrations, even binding panels seem to move readily between de Worde in England and several Paris printers. After assuming ownership of Caxton's shop, de Worde rapidly expanded the business, using the title-page to promote and sell his books. This was not only an effective marketing technique, but a new way of packaging, labelling and identifying the text for its potential readership. The title-page was an early innovation developed in England primarily by de Worde, so commonplace today that we take it completely for granted.

Chapter 4

REPRESENTATIONS OF SAINTLY WOMEN IN LATE MEDIEVAL WOODCUTS

Aᴍᴏɴɢ ᴛʜᴇ ɪᴍᴀɢᴇꜱ that found wide circulation in early print formats were those of women. In England, as on the continent, woodcuts of holy women provided visual models of exemplary behaviour and a focus for prayer and contemplation. Religious orders, above all the Bridgettines, were particularly active in circulating both single-leaf prints and illustrated books for their own use as well as for lay readers, both female and male. Through their repetition from book to book and context to context, these pictures created webs of meaning, acting on the viewer's imagination both associatively and mnemonically. Aspects of a saintly or holy life for women were defined and reinforced by images of the Virgin and other women saints, which were repeated in a variety of printed books produced for the reading public. Observation of these images enables us to explore the relationship between image and text in devotional reading as it appears in depictions of female saints, while also raising questions about the function of the book or text in each holy scene. Pictures of saintly women with their prayer books or Bibles show us how reading was represented for the first audiences of the early printed book.

It has recently been argued that late medieval mystical discourse was restricted to small groups surrounding the visionaries, who were focused not on the things or common people of this world but on transcendent experience: 'Far from being popular, late medieval mystical sanctity was, on the contrary, profoundly elitist. It claimed high ground and gloried in doing so. It flourished within restricted devout circles, groups of "friends of God" to which clergy and laity who longed for perfection came to seek the "spiritual consolations" which their parish or conventual communities could not provide.'[1] The great number of prints illustrating the holy or mystical experience of women that circulated, both separately and as part of the illustrative programs of printed books, throughout the fifteenth century, popularising and promoting the cults of contemporary saints such as Bridget of Sweden and Catherine of Siena as well as devotion to the Virgin (Fig. 1) and other holy women, would seem, however, to contradict this view of late medieval mysticism as inherently elitist and rarefied. The images themselves tend to represent the pathos of Christ's human suffering or the human relationships of women saints with one another and with the divine. In addition, print was most effectively employed when directed toward a wider audience, eager to receive the holy words attributed to the saints.

Fig. 1. Mary and Infant in mandorla. *The Remedy Against the Troubles of Temptations* (London: Wynkyn de Worde, 1508), sig. D2ᵛ. STC 20875.5. BL C.21.c.22.

Images of saintly women first began to circulate in the form of single-leaf prints, the original 'holy cards'. Single-leaf prints, each with a portrait of a saint or a holy scene, and sometimes with a short prayer attached, were used to commemorate a pilgrimage, or for private devotions or more public display on the wall of one's home, or sold as indulgences, a focal point for an owner's prayers for loved ones in Purgatory.[2] Single-leaf woodcuts 'spoke the complex language of saints' emblems and pictorial conventions ... which the medieval audience had learnt to "read"', though their grasp of written language may still have been limited.[3] Such woodcuts, in fact, seem to promote conventional hagiographic iconography, readily read by the fifteenth-century owner or viewer. Furthermore, as pious objects, single-leaf woodcuts were early associated with women owners or patrons, and their iconography often seems directed to a female audience.

Those that are still preserved were for the most part bound or pasted into books, serving as an inexpensive method of illustration, though there remain some rare extant examples of single-leaf woodcuts pasted into boxes, originally intended as travelling altars. One important example of such an altar may be seen in the Rosenwald Collection at the National Gallery of Art in Washington, D.C. Pasted into it is an image of the Lamentation copied from an engraving by Master E. S. The woodcut has the printer's mark of Lienhart Ysenhut, who was active in Basel *c.* 1489 to 1507, and is variously described in contemporary documents as a printer as well as a 'Heiligenmaler' ('painter of saints'), a 'Heiligendrucker' ('printer of saints'), a 'Briefmaler' ('letter painter') and a 'Kartenmacher' ('playing-card maker').[4] Another single-leaf woodcut in the Rosenwald Collection showing the Virgin and Child in a Rosary (Fig. 2a), made by an

Fig. 2a. Virgin and Child in a Rosary.
Anonymous French, fifteenth century
(Savoy school?, *c.* 1490). Schreiber 1130b.
By permission of the National Gallery of
Art, Washington, D.C.

Fig. 2b. Virgin and Child in a Rosary.
Anonymous French, fifteenth century
(Savoy school?, *c.* 1490). Schreiber
1130b. Arsène Bonafous-Murat,
Estampes 1490-1989 (Paris, 1989), no. 1.

anonymous French artist *c.* 1490, 'was discovered pasted into the lid of a strong box, which helped to preserve it'. A photograph of yet another extant example of this woodcut (Fig. 2b), still pasted into a box, recently appeared in a bookseller's catalogue.[5] Woodcuts like these 'were designed, cut, and printed in small monastic shops or by independent craftsmen, including playing-card makers'. Like Ysenhut, 'these craftsmen are often termed "Jesus makers" or "saint makers" in archival records'.[6] It is to the work of these 'Jesus makers' and small monastic shops that we shall now turn.

Most makers of wood-block images remain shrouded in obscurity, but examination of the function of the images, recovery of their meaning, and placing them into clear historical perspective can provide hard evidence about the range and scope of the activities of one group that was responsible for many such images, the Bridgettine order. Single-leaf prints made by or for the Bridgettines in England and on the continent are among the most important examples that survive. St Bridget of Sweden was born *c.* 1303, died in 1373 and was canonised in 1391. She herself was an active promoter of indulgences, and hers was a learned order. Syon Abbey, the Bridgettine house at Isleworth, just outside London, which was founded by Henry V, had a comprehensive library before the

Reformation, its volumes numbering close to 1400. A chapter in the *Mirror of Our Lady*, a Book of Hours and masses used at Syon, emphasises the private reading of books, which should be read and reread 'twyes or thryes', for comprehension. Edmund Colledge has remarked that 'Some of the most celebrated spiritual classics of the late Middle Ages can be shown to have been translated into English at Syon'.[7] Part of this activity can be reconstructed through examination of the woodcut evidence, which suggests that the Bridgettines were active not only in promoting vernacular translations but in selecting, commissioning and, to some extent, designing books thought appropriate to be read not only by themselves but by a larger lay audience outside Syon's walls.[8]

One single-leaf woodcut that at one time was probably incorporated into a manuscript shows St Bridget kneeling before Christ as the Man of Sorrows (Fig. 3), a woodcut attributed by Campbell Dodgson to Hans Burgkmair and dated about 1499 to 1501. Bridget is depicted in Bridgettine habit, her head veiled with a banded crown. The print in the Ashmolean Museum has been hand-coloured, and manuscript prayers in Latin are inscribed on the verso. Like the single-leaf prints ascribed to Ysenhut, this woodcut is exceptional in being attributed to a named artist. Burgkmair (1473-1531), who worked in Augsburg, was commissioned by Emperor Maximilian to produce drawings, woodcuts and paintings; he was also a leading figure in the development of the chiaroscuro woodcut.[9]

Another continental woodcut (Fig. 4) – made, in this case, by the Bridgettines themselves – a Virgin and Child in Glory with St Catherine and St Barbara, has also been hand-coloured. Anonymously produced at the Bridgettine convent of Marienwater in the Netherlands, the woodcut shows saints Barbara and Catherine, with their attributes of wheel, sword, tower and martyr's palm, and with books open in their laps, as the Virgin and Child appear in a mandorla before them. The text beneath, a prayer to the Virgin, is xylographic, cut from the block itself.[10]

One early example of the Bridgettine appropriation of images in England occurs in MS Rawlinson D. 403, a fifteenth-century paper manuscript with Bridgettine prayers written in Latin, now in the Bodleian Library. The first two leaves of this volume are woodcut Images of Pity: Christ as the Man of Sorrows with the emblems of the Passion and a *Pietà* (see Chapter 1, Fig. 6), originally intended as an indulgence. These single-leaf prints have been inserted as ready-made illustrations into the manuscript. Dodgson describes both of these as 'produced in the Brigittine convent of Syon'.[11] Both woodcuts in the Rawlinson volume are clearly indulgences.[12]

The third leaf of the Rawlinson manuscript has definite Syon connections. On fol. 3^r, on the back of a third inserted woodcut, seven prayers in Latin are written in the same hand as that which produced the rest of the manuscript. These are a series of meditative prayers on the Passion, reflecting on particular moments in the life of Christ (Crucifixion, Burial, Descent into Hell, Harrowing, Resurrection). The text moves from these moments to their applicability to the

Fig. 3. Bridget kneeling before the Man of Sorrows. Hans Burgkmair (?),
c. 1501. Dodgson 39. Douce Collection, Ashmolean Museum.

life of the individual. The final meditation reads, in part, 'have mercy on my soul
when it leaves my body'.

On the verso of folio 3 (Fig. 5) is a woodcut of the Last Judgement, with the
captions 'Surgite Mortui' and 'Venite ad Judicium' in the top margin, and at the
bottom 'Arma Beate Birgitte: De Syon', with a shield of the Swedish lion partially
cut off. These captions are not xylographic but set in type.[13] It is possible that

Fig. 4. Virgin and Child in Glory with St Catherine and St Barbara.
Marienwater, Netherlands, n.d. Schreiber 1154. BL.

the woodcut may have been made first, and the typographic captions, which specifically identify the woodcut as Bridgettine, added later. However, the xylographic 'S' on the right side of the image (which might stand for Syon) and, more tellingly, the iconography, make it more likely that the entire woodcut is of Bridgettine origin.

The iconography of this woodcut is, at first, somewhat puzzling. The central scene is the Last Judgement. Christ, revealing his five wounds, is seated on a rather abstractly rendered rainbow, His feet on the orb of the world. On either side are angels with trumpets, their banderoles depicting the Instruments of the Passion and the Five Wounds. In the scene below, Death assails a tonsured monk (in what looks to be Bridgettine habit) with an arrow. On the other side of Death, there is a demon holding up a book, representing either his legal claim to the soul or perhaps, as in the morality play *Everyman*, the account book recording the soul's earthly deeds. Two figures emerge from the earth, one praying (and presumably saved), the other falling at the feet of a demon. In the panel beneath, in an open grave, is a wormy corpse in its shroud with pickaxe and shovel, two skulls, bones, and in the upper right corner, a jawbone with teeth. These may allude to the pieces of the body which must be brought together again on the Day of Judgement.

Fig. 5. Last Judgement. Anonymous English, fifteenth century. MS Rawlinson D. 403, fol. 3ᵛ. Schreiber 608, Dodgson 15. *STC* 14077e. 18. By permission of the Bodleian Library, Oxford.

Though originally issued as a single-leaf print and intended as a single meditative image, the woodcut underscores the message of the meditative prayers inscribed on its verso, referring as well to an actual ceremony required by Bridgettine rule. Each day, after Terce, the lady abbess was to intone the 'De profundis' beside an open grave. This is still practised in modified form by Bridgettines today. The 'De profundis', memorialising members of the community, is recited as the lady abbess moves earth in an open casket with her fingers.[14] Thus the woodcut of the Last Judgement, with its emphasis on death, the open grave and the salvation of the individual, is linked, by its iconography as well as by its captions, to the fifteenth-century manuscript prayers ('have mercy on my soul when it leaves my body') and to actual daily practice at Syon. Like the two indulgences that precede it, there is no evidence that the Last Judgement woodcut was made to illustrate this manuscript. It seems to have been originally issued as a single-leaf print, and intended as a single meditative image produced for devotional purposes.

Another example of a single-leaf print used to illustrate a Syon manuscript is found in Oxford, St John's College MS 164, a Latin processional with English rubrics made for a sister of Syon. A crude but charming metal-cut of the Epiphany has been pasted into the margin of fol. 4ʳ beside the rubric: '¶Versicle and orison as uppon criste masse daye. ¶Vppon twelf daye res. at procession Responde'. The names of 'Syster Mare Neule', 'Sister Tomysyn Grove' and 'Brother James Stock' are written on the recto of the second flyleaf.[15] The metalcut itself is a type of 'dotted print', or *manière criblée*, a style most characteristic of German work of the later fifteenth century.[16]

A final example (Fig. 6) of single-leaf prints directed primarily to a female audience, sometimes attributed to the Master with the Mountain-Like Clouds, is a single-leaf metal-cut made in Germany between 1480 and 1490. The Virgin is the central figure, and at her left and right are women saints, including Catherine of Alexandria, identified by her wheel and sword; Barbara with her tower; Margaret with a tiny dragon sitting on her garment; Apollonia holding her tooth with tongs; and Lucia, her eyes embroidered onto her habit. As in many representations of saints, Catherine of Alexandria has been confused, or perhaps simply fused, with Catherine of Siena. She is shown holding up a ring to the Christ child, a visual reference to the mystic marriage of St Catherine of Siena, described in her *Miracoli*: 'in a transport of overwhelming love [she] called the mother of Christ, and with a childlike simplicity asked her to give to her in marriage her son Jesus; and praying thus she felt herself raised somewhat from the ground into the air, and presently there appeared to her the Virgin Mary with her son in her arms, and giving the young girl a ring he took her as his spouse and then suddenly disappeared'. Richard Field has further tentatively identified St Dorothy (holding a flower). The inscription beneath the image reads 'She is beautiful among the daughters of Jerusalem', a phrase that may derive from the apocryphal book of Judith 15:10 and from the Second Vespers for Holy Women.[17] Like the metalcut from the Syon manuscript, the print has a criblée ground. The abstract frame of clouds and stars surrounding the image is further adorned with signs of the Four Evangelists in the corners. The metal-cut, probably designed for devotional use, celebrates female virgin martyrs and saints of the Church, conventional iconography drawn from manuscripts and other media, and then further promoted by the circulation of single-leaf prints like this one.

Besides single-leaf prints, representations of holy women are also very often found as illustrations in books. The large group of early printed books dealing with religious subjects includes prayer-books, Books of Hours, and popular narratives of the lives of the Virgin and Christ, among them the *Speculum humanae salvationis*, the *Golden Legend*, and the pseudo-Bonaventuran

Fig. 6. The Virgin enthroned with eighteen holy women. Anonymous German, attrib.
Master with the Mountain-Like Clouds. Metal-cut, *c.* 1480-90. Schreiber 2519m.
By permission of the National Gallery of Art, Washington, D.C.

Meditationes vitae Christi, or Meditations on the Life of Christ, probably composed by Johannes de Caulibus, a Franciscan friar, and later translated into English in the fifteenth century by Nicholas Love, prior of Mount Grace Charterhouse in Yorkshire. These books are repositories of images of saintly women (and men). Just as the texts are of works that had circulated widely in manuscript, so most of them draw on manuscript exemplars for their iconography. Pictures of holy women, who 'are often themselves described typologically as patterned after figures such as earlier saints, biblical personages, or even God',[18] find their way into printed collections of saints' lives, mystical and meditative texts and the margins and central spaces of printed prayer-books.

Both emblematic and narrative scenes of the lives of women saints appear in printed editions of the *Legenda Aurea*, or *Golden Legend*, which circulated in Germany, Italy, France and England. These illustrations employ the standard iconography of saints with their attributes, so familiar to readers not only from single-leaf prints, but also from representations in churches and public spaces. In the pages of the *Golden Legend* printed by William Caxton, for example, we find static scenes of saints with their emblems: Catherine with the wheel that broke as she was being martyred upon it, Barbara with the tower in which she was imprisoned, and Margaret, patron saint of childbirth, calmly emerging unscathed from the curiously tame and dog-like dragon that had devoured her (Fig. 7).[19] Such images were visual shorthand for the lives of the saints who were instantly recognisable by their attributes to the medieval reader.

More active narrative scenes also occur in Caxton's *Golden Legend*: illustrations of the births of the Virgin and John the Baptist, the Nativity and Epiphany, the Assumption of the Virgin and occasionally the martyrdoms of specific saints. The latter sort of image is more commonly found in German printed editions of the *Legenda aurea*, though the murder of Thomas Becket is regularly shown in Caxton's and later English editions. These images are then repeated in other printed books. In a scene of Pentecost from an early continental imprint of the *Golden Legend* (Fig. 8), Mary is the central figure, a book open in her lap, surrounded by the Apostles as they receive the Holy Spirit in the form of a dove. This is in accord with the biblical text of Acts, where Mary is described as praying with other women 'and with his brothers', the Apostles, when the Holy Ghost descends, granting those present gifts of prophecy and vision: 'And your sons and daughters shall prophesy, and your young men shall see visions, and your old men shall dream dreams.' The illustration comprises three woodcuts, the central image framed by representations of two wall statues of a monk and a man on cornices, and occurs in an edition of the *Golden Legend* printed in 1490.[20]

The same central woodcut is repeated in printed editions of the *Vita Christi* of Ludolphus of Saxony (Fig. 9), though the two border pieces that frame the central scene are different. The *Vita Christi*, a fourteenth-century prose life of Christ, was among many narrative lives of the Virgin and Christ that circulated in the later Middle Ages, and draws partially on another such work, the

Fig. 7. St Margaret. Jacobus de Voragine, *Legenda Aurea*, trans. William Caxton
(Westminster: William Caxton, 20 November 1483), fol. 214^v (sig. B6^v).
STC 24873-24874. BL C.11.d.8, IB.55161.

Meditationes vitae Christi, a Franciscan text composed in the late thirteenth
century. There are some two hundred manuscripts of the *Meditationes* still
extant, twenty of them illustrated.[21] A French adaptation of the *Meditationes*,
now in the Bibliothèque Nationale, was compiled and illuminated in manuscript
for Jean, Duke of Berry, in 1380, and almost a hundred years later the Lyons
printers Guillaume Le Roy and Barthélémy Buyer published a version of it. This
was one of the earliest books printed in France.[22] A versified Life of Christ on the
same theme (though textually unrelated), titled *La Passion Jhesuscrist*, also in the
Bibliothèque Nationale, dates from between 1503 and 1508. This manuscript
was produced and presumably edited by Antoine Vérard to fit a set of engravings,
the Large Passion by Israhel van Meckenem, for presentation to 'a lady', that

Fig. 8. Pentecost. Jacobus de Voragine, *Legenda Aurea sanctorum* (Zwolle: Peter van Os, 1490), sig. v4ʳ. By permission of Chetham's Library, Manchester.

is, for Louise de Savoie. This is one of several known examples of manuscripts or printed books that were illustrated with engravings made separately.[23] Other manuscripts of the period were illustrated with prints by this artist rather than with miniatures.[24] Only a limited number of illustrated copies of the *Meditationes* circulated in France, but the text was given new life in England in its fifteenth-century adaptation by Nicholas Love, and it subsequently circulated widely in manuscript and print. Illustrated copies were published by the earliest English printers, including William Caxton, Wynkyn de Worde and Richard Pynson.

Caxton's first edition of Love's *Speculum vitae Christi* was printed in *c.* 1484, and the second in *c.* 1490.[25] The two *Speculum* editions printed by Caxton are virtually alike, differing only in placement of paraph marks and use of abbreviations, and both contain the same woodcut illustrations. The unique fragment of the first edition in Cambridge University Library lacks the first nine leaves but undoubtedly originally contained all the illustrations which appear in the second edition, a close reprint of the first. Though print historians generally say that Caxton illustrated his *Speculum* editions with 25 woodcuts, there

Fig. 9. Pentecost. Ludolphus de Saxonia, *Vita Christi. Tboeck vanden leven Jhesu Christi* (Antwerp: Gerard Leeu, 1487), fol. 145ʳ, sig. MM4. BL IB.49767.

are actually 29 pictures and two repeats. Caxton thus illustrates his book with almost twice the number of pictures found in the extant manuscripts. This picture cycle was repeatedly reused by both Caxton and de Worde,[26] and Caxton set the pattern of using it to organise and format a text that already had a fairly complicated apparatus built into the manuscript exemplars. The woodcuts were then used and reused or closely copied by Caxton's successors to illustrate a number of books, as Edward Hodnett points out, including *The Golden Legend* and *Boke named the Royall*, the two known collaborations of Richard Pynson and Wynkyn de Worde.

An immediate picture source perhaps used by Caxton's *Speculum* artist, or known to Caxton himself, seems to have been one or both of the two illustrated English manuscripts of Love's translation that have related picture cycles. These are Advocates 18.1.7, with seventeen pictures on inset leaves, made by a contemporary of William Abell, and Morgan M. 648 which has sixteen less inventive but similar illustrations.[27] Caxton, however, in addition to illustrating scenes also illustrated in the manuscripts (the Annunciation, for example), adds thirteen new pictures that focus on Christ's acts before the Passion and expand upon the Passion cycle as presented in the manuscripts. Caxton's intention was apparently to highlight Love's contributions, as translator, to the pseudo-Bonaventuran text while also making good use of the apparatus and *ordinatio* that Caxton had inherited from the manuscript exemplars.

The *Speculum* manuscripts are distinguished by a sophisticated layout and apparatus, designed apparently by Love himself to 'facilitate regular reading to a regular audience as well as periodic private meditation, both things characteristic of religious communities yet also found in devout lay households'.[28] Most copies of the 56 complete or orginally complete manuscripts include running titles which divide the text by days of the week and by chapter; chapter heads in the text; and descriptive rubrics as well as marginal notations throughout.[29] Caxton follows this layout, incorporating running titles, chapter heads, captions and marginal notes into his printed text, and using the rubrics, drawn apparently from the illustrated Love manuscripts, as picture captions for his woodcuts, setting these slightly apart from the main text. Caxton's use of rubric as picture caption is fairly consistent and occurs even when Caxton illustrates portions of text that are not illustrated in the manuscripts. This layout is then followed by both de Worde and Pynson, though somewhat haphazardly in the case of the Pynson edition.[30]

It is doubtful, however, whether Caxton acquired the woodblocks as 'a set', as N. F. Blake asserts, with the implication that this was a casually acquired generic set of images of the Life of Christ.[31] Some of the woodcut illustrations are both apt and fairly obscure, related to Love's own additions to and emendations of his pseudo-Bonaventuran source. In several specific instances, moreover, Caxton seems to have used the woodcuts intentionally to highlight Love's own contributions to this text.

For example, Love appends to his source text the Treatise on the Blessed Sacrament, which is illustrated in Advocates 18.1.7 by a remarkable picture of a priest carrying the sacrament under a canopy in a procession to a church. In Morgan M. 648 (Fig. 10), a similar scene, a procession in which a priest carries the sacrament under a canopy held by four angels, with a small figure carrying a censor just visible beside him, accompanies the rubric: 'A shorte tretise of þe hiest and most worthy sacrament of Crist is blessid body and þe miracles therof. ...' The Procession of the Holy Sacrament is illustrated in Caxton's edition of the *Speculum* (Fig. 11) accompanied by the same rubric, and the same woodcut will later illustrate the scene in the *Speculum* editions printed by de Worde and Pynson, as well as similar scenes in other books.[32]

Another addition made to the text by Love, in which Love is using St Augustine rather than the pseudo-Bonaventuran *Meditationes* as his source, is a description of the raising of the daughter of Jairus. Neither of the extant manuscripts illustrates this scene, but Caxton again includes a text-specific woodcut in his edition (Fig. 12), captioned by a rubric which does appear in the manuscript sources: 'Of the reysyng of lazar .& other two dede bodyes.'[33] The woodcut will be reused to illustrate the scene in later printed editions of the *Speculum*.

Among Love's most important expansions of his source is his discussion of the conversion of Mary Magdalene, a scene again illustrated by Caxton (Fig. 13) that is not illustrated in the manuscripts. Love makes a major addition to the text,

Fig. 10. Procession of the Holy Sacrament. Nicholas Love, *Mirrour of the blessed lyf of Jesu Christ* English, *c.* 1440, fol. 131ʳ. Morgan M.648. By permission of the Pierpont Morgan Library, New York.

adding a lengthy analogy between Mary Magdalene and the sinner in need of confession. The Magdalene, described elsewhere in the text as the 'twin sister' of Martha, becomes representative of the compassionate acceptance of all human-kind. Love describes Mary's humility in anointing Jesus' feet and wiping them with her hair as a mirror of Christ's humility:

as to a souereyn confort of alle sinful folke we haue here opunly shewede in our lorde Jesu þe abundance of his endles mercye, þat so sone & so gladly forȝafe so many grete sinnes & trespasses of þis sinful woman, ... [here] we haue ensaumple & techyng what tyme we bene temptede to iustifying of oure self & reproue of oþer, þen to þenk & haue in mynde þe gude dedes & vertues þat ben or mow be in þat oþere man, forȝetyng oure owne gude dedes or vertues, & bryngynge to mynde oure defautes, & trespasses, & so shole we vertuesely deme oure self & excuse oþere, & so profite in þe vertue of trewe mekenes, þat he graunt vs, mirrour of mekenes blessede Jesus.[34]

The moral lesson of this portion of Love's text is to put aside pride, to remember our weaknesses, to look for the good in others, and to practice humility as Mary Magdalene does, shown in the woodcut on her knees wiping Christ's feet with her hair. The woodcut vigorously and accurately illustrates the content of Love's text, the weeping Mary shown crouched beneath the table, bending over the feet of Christ, her jar of ointment on the floor beside her.

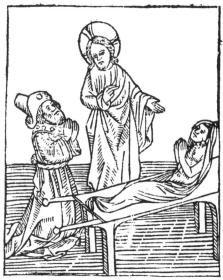

Fig. 11 (*above left*). Procession of the Holy Sacrament. Nicholas Love, *Speculum vitae Christi* (Westminster: William Caxton, 1490), sig. S1ᵛ. *STC* 3260. BL IB. 55119.

Fig. 12 (*above right*). Raising of the Daughter of Jairus. Nicholas Love, *Speculum vitae Christi* (Westminster: William Caxton, 1490), sig. K5ʳ. *STC* 3260. BL IB. 55119.

Fig. 13 (*below left*). Conversion of Mary Magdalene. Nicholas Love, *Speculum vitae Christi* (Westminster: William Caxton, 1490), sig. G8ʳ. *STC* 3260. BL IB. 55119.

Illustrations like these, then, are quite specific to the text and seem unlikely to have been part of a generic set of pictures bought wholesale by Caxton on the continent. The inclusion of woodcuts appropriate to the text seems to have been just as important to Caxton as the accurate representation of the original apparatus. If Caxton was indeed purposefully and intentionally using illustrations like these to highlight Love's contributions, then Caxton, or someone close to him, must have worked with an artist, a woodcutter or perhaps a purveyor of wood-blocks to specify just what scenes Caxton wanted to illustrate. Who might this person have been?

No one can quite agree on the source or even the style of the *Speculum* woodcuts.[35] Given the style of these illustrations, the artist/cutter (who may be the same person) of the *Speculum* woodcuts was very probably not Flemish or northern French, as has been previously supposed. It is tempting to locate this artist in Utrecht, a city in the central Netherlands which Caxton visited as governor of the English Nation in 1464 and 1465, and with which he retained important contacts. The picture evidence, in fact, logically points to the shop of Johann Veldener, who established his press in Utrecht in 1478 and initially supplied Caxton with his fonts. Originally from the diocese of Würzburg, Veldener began to print in Cologne, then set up a press in Louvain in 1473, and moved to Utrecht in 1478. In 1474, Veldener described himself 'as a master of his art, skilful in cutting, engraving, pressing and stamping, and also in designing and fashioning and whatever in the art is more closely hid'.[36] Veldener's words seem to suggest that he knew how to design and cut wood-blocks, though this suggestion needs further exploration.[37]

Caxton's *Speculum* editions were very influential in their text, layout and illustration. The woodcuts were reused by de Worde in his editions and loosely copied by Pynson. The woodcut of the Pentecost (Fig. 14), for example, appears in their editions of Love, the *Golden Legend* and the *Boke named the Royall*; Pynson also used a copy of this woodcut in his *Missale ad usum Sarum* of 1520 and in his 1526 edition of William Bonde's *Pylgrimage of Perfection*.

Nine printed editions of the *Speculum* were issued from 1484 to 1530. The later editions printed by de Worde and Pynson have 30 illustrations on average: Pynson's 1494 edition, for example, has 27 woodcuts, while de Worde's edition of 1517 has 35 woodcuts. By following the lead of Caxton and virtually doubling the number of illustrations from the number appearing in the extant manuscripts, de Worde and Pynson were responding to the broader requirements of a pious popular audience, supplying familiar visual signposts along with some simple verbal apparatus to help the reader through the terrain of the text.

The *Speculum vitae Christi* reached its peak of popularity about 1531, when St Thomas More 'recommended the reading of [this] work along with Hilton's *Scale*, as most profitable to the ordinary person'.[38] Several of the manuscripts travelled in aristocratic circles. Takamiya 8, for example, 'was owned by Joan, Countess of Kent, wife of the original founder of Mount Grace, and given by her to "Alice Belacyse", a member of an old Yorkshire family', while Advocates 18.1.7 may have been 'made for the marriage of Joan Percy to Edmund Grey'.[39] Print copies belonged to students, pious laypeople and nuns.[40] A copy of the 1490 edition of Caxton's *Speculum* printed on vellum, now in the British Library, was housed at Syon, indicating its appropriateness for reading by religious as well as by laywomen. At the suppression of the abbey in 1540, this book belonged to 'Susan Purefoy, a nun of Syon'.[41] This seems particularly appropriate as the

Fig. 14. Pentecost. Nicholas Love, *Speculum vitae Christi*
(Westminster: William Caxton, 1490), sig. R7ᵛ. *STC* 3260. BL IB. 55119.

Bridgettine nuns at Syon studied English, rather than Latin, texts and were eager
consumers of printed vernacular books, particularly those with helpful apparatus
and plentiful pictures.[42] While a direct print source for the woodcuts employed
by Caxton in his *Speculum* editions is yet to be conclusively found, there are
many clear connections between scenes of saints in English books and those
found in French printed books of the period, particularly in books produced for
Antoine Vérard.

We find, for example, a woodcut of Christ enthroned, flanked by Mary and
John the Baptist (Fig. 15), in an edition of *L'Art de bien vivre et de bien mourir*
printed for Antoine Vérard in 1492. The edition went through at least five
printings in five years; the copy in which this woodcut appears was printed for
Vérard by Pierre Le Rouge.[43] The female saints in the foreground are difficult to
identify because they lack their customary attributes, but Mary is clearly shown,

Fig. 15. Christ Enthroned. *L'Art de bien vivre et de bien mourir*
(Paris: for Antoine Vérard, 1492), sig. O6ᵛ. BL IB. 40027.

crowned in her role as Queen of Heaven. Vérard habitually reprinted books
that were already popular, whether in manuscript or in print, and in several cases
looked to block-books such as the *Ars moriendi*, the *Biblia pauperum* and the
Speculum humanae salvationis for inspiration. His beautifully produced books
provided a range of illustrations that were then copied by the English printers
de Worde and Pynson, among others. A close copy of this scene appears in the
edition of the *Golden Legend* produced collaboratively by Richard Pynson
and de Worde in 1507, while a modified copy illustrates the second edition of
ThOrdynary of Crysten Men (Fig. 16), a translation of *L'Art de bien vivre* by

Fig. 16. Christ Enthroned. *ThOrdynary of Crysten Men*, trans. A. Chertsey
London: de Worde, 1506), sig. MM7ᵛ. *STC* 5199. BL C.25.f.7.

Andrew Chertsey that was printed in London by de Worde in 1506. This woodcut of Christ enthroned with men and women saints introduces a text on the
'Joyes of paradyse' and is clearly modelled on that in the French edition.[44] The
1506 edition of *ThOrdynary* also includes English copies of Vérard's copies of
woodcuts from the German *Ars moriendi* block-book series.

Vérard is also the source for images of the Annunciation and Visitation
(Fig. 17) that are used later in English books, with the angel shown announcing
the news to Mary in a speech scroll at the left. In the right panel, the two pregnant
holy women, Mary and Elizabeth, greet one another. Conventionally in representations of the Visitation, the younger Mary is shown on the left, wearing a blue
cloak, as she is here. The older cousin, Elizabeth, pregnant with John the Baptist,
exclaims in a speech scroll: 'You are blessed among all women and blessed is the
fruit of your womb, Jesus.' A passage in Luke (1:39-44) describes John leaping
for joy in Elizabeth's womb when his mother hears Mary's voice.[45] The woodcuts
in the Huntington Library copy of *L'Art de bien viure et de bien mourir*, printed

Pres ce que larchãge gabriel eut ouytreceu le cōmādemēt de dieu dessusdit cestoit quil sen allast deuers la Vierge glorieuse iteneree marie en la cite de nazareth et quil lui annūcast la nouuelle de nostre reparation. Il partit et vola du ciel tresioyeusement acompaignie de chant ãgelicque melodieux ↄ delicieux et entra en forme humaine dedans la chambre et oratoire de la tresnoble ↄ glorieuse Vierge marie. Mais ledit archange gabriel ne sceut oncques si tost voler ne descendre deuers ladicte Vierge quil ne fust preuenu de dieu/car il trouua la saincte trinite laquelle preuit son messagier. Et indubitablement leuure excellēt de lincarnation fut seuure des trois psōnes ↄ la trinite: mais la seule psone du filz prit incarnation. O quelle maison et oratoire ou telz misterez sont faiz: Tantost ledit messagier tresfidele de dieu se huilia treshumblemēt deuant la sacree marie/et la salua treshumblemēt en lui disant. Aue gratia plena dominus tecum/benedicta tu mulieribus. Et pource que mon intention est en ce present liure

Fig. 17. Annunciation and Visitation. *L'Art de bien viure et de bien mourir* (Paris: for Antoine Vérard, 1492), sig. BB6ʳ. By permission of the Huntington Library, San Marino.

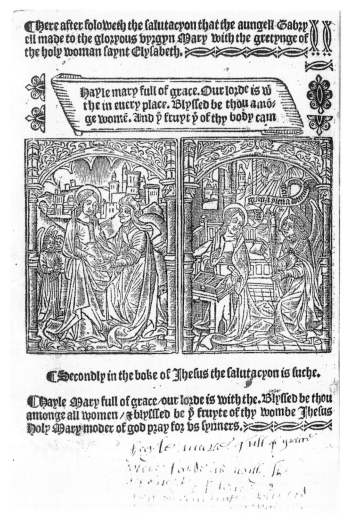

Fig. 18. Visitation and Annunciation. *The Kalender of shepeherdes*
(London: Wynkyn de Worde, 1508 [1516?]), sig. G3ᵛ. STC 22409.
CJ.1.18. By permission of Magdalen College, Oxford.

on vellum on 15 December 1492 by Gillet Couteau and Jean Menard for Antoine
Vérard, are illuminated.[46]

In the English copy illustrating the Hail Mary in de Worde's 1508 edition of
The Kalender of shepeherdes (Fig. 18), note that the order of the woodcuts has
been reversed so that the Visitation inexplicably precedes the Annunciation.
Among other variations, the speech scroll of Elizabeth has been modified, with a
verse prayer to the Virgin now serving as a label to both texts: 'Hayle mary full

Fig. 19 Annunciation. *Heures de nostre dame* (Paris: for Antoine Vérard, *c.* 1499), fol. 2ʳ. PML 1060. By permission of the Pierpont Morgan Library.

of grace. Our lorde is w*ith* the in euery place. Blyssed be thou amo*n*ge wome*n*. And þe fruyt þat of thy body cam.' De Worde will use the same pair of woodcuts, sometimes in the correct order, in a number of his books, including *The Arte to lyue well* editions of 1505 and 1506, his several editions of Love's *Speculum vitae Christi*, and Books of Hours printed in 1519 and *c.* 1526.

Aspects of a saintly or holy life for women were defined and reinforced by images of the Virgin and other women saints, which were repeated in a variety of printed books produced for the reading public. Readers were presented with pictures of holy women with their books, models of contemplation for the readers themselves. Fifteenth-century depictions of Mary, whether in manuscript or in print, typically show her reading, whether at Anne's knee, at the Annunciation, or as we have seen, at Pentecost. In the Annunciation (Fig. 19), as the angel announces the birth of Christ, Mary reads the text traditionally identified as that portion of Isaiah that predicts the birth of the Messiah.[47] The image becomes the prototype, the visual association, in the later Middle Ages that colours all other images of reading: the act of reading is presented as primarily meditative and prophetic, a holy activity that has urgent and undeniable connection with the event about to take place, the angel announcing Christ's conception. We know what follows, and it is interesting to note that very few books and fewer readers are shown in subsequent scenes of Christ's life and Passion. Action takes precedence over contemplation, although on the periphery patrons sometimes read or observe the holy scenes through the medium of the page. Like Mary, women saints are also shown reading in a variety of contexts, emulating the Virgin and showing their piety and learning: in a prayer-book printed in Ghent, for example, St Apollonia, patron of dentists, peruses the pages of a two-column prayer-book as she holds up her tongs and tooth (Fig. 20).

Most late medieval illuminations and prints show the reading process as silent rather than oral, without the speech scrolls and specific gestures that indicate that speech is occurring.[48] In the art of the later Middle Ages more generally, reading is for the most part shown as silent, with the readers portrayed as intensely concentrated and still, engaged in the moment. Does this represent the limitations of the visual medium? Or did the visual medium perhaps influence actual reading practice?

What is certain is that these images illustrate the reading process that came to be known as *lectio divina* – prayerful, serious study of Scripture and the Fathers. The inspiration for this manner of reading came from Augustine, who defined a *studiosus* as 'anyone who pursues God with intensity', and from Jerome, who is frequently portrayed in printed prayer-books, Bibles and works attributed to him in the later Middle Ages.[49] The book, sign of Jerome's *auctoritas*, is almost as much an attribute as his lion. Severus, a disciple of St Martin and a contemporary of Jerome, said: 'he was so learned, not only in Latin and Greek but also in Hebrew letters, that no one dares to compare himself with him in any branch of knowledge. ... He is totally absorbed in study, totally in books. ... he is always either reading or writing.' For St Jerome, 'to read without also writing' was 'to sleep'.[50]

In an early printed edition of the *Vitas Patrum*, or Lives of the Fathers, a work ascribed to Jerome in the Middle Ages, a woodcut of Jerome (Fig. 21) is repeated in the text at the beginning of each of the five parts of the volume and again on the end-leaf, along with the metalplate title. Jerome is depicted reading his own book; his gaze is upward, directed at the vision conjured by the book, of the saints whose lives it recounts. This edition, which was owned and read by women as well as by men, is illustrated with woodcuts of saintly fathers along with some holy mothers.[51] The saintly women described in the text include 'Saynt Maryne', 'Synt [*sic*] Eufrosyne' and 'Saynt Eufraxe'. The English translation from the French was made by William Caxton, who 'fynysshed it at the laste daye of his lyff', and it was printed in 1495 by Wynken de Worde.[52] In the picture of St Jerome, vision, reading, writing and seeing coincide. The woodcut conjures the

Fig. 20. St Apollonia. Fragment from a prayerbook (Ghent: Arend de Keysere, n.d.),
sig. B2ʳ. By permission of the Cambridge University Library, Cambridge.

conjunction of word and image that Richard de Fournival so succinctly described
in the 1250s: 'when one hears a story read aloud, listening to the events one sees
them in the present. ... And when you read, this writing with its *peinture*
(picture) and *parole* (word) will make me present to your memory, even when I
am not physically before you.' The book becomes the passage to vision.[53]

Beryl Smalley makes an apt analogy between the process of prayer, exegesis
and reading as shown in images like these, and the 'pierced technique' in
Carolingian art: 'It is as though we were invited to focus our eyes not on the
physical surface of the object, but on infinity as seen through the lattice. ... We
are invited to look not at the text, but through it.'[54] The book serves as a conduit
to transcendent vision, and there is also the suggestion that the prayer or Bible
text has been internalised. Reading, 'along with visualization of ... the central

139

Fig. 21. Jerome with Saints. Jerome (attrib.), *Vitas Patrum* (Westminster: Wynkyn de Worde, before 21 August 1495), sig. cccxxxvi^v. *STC* 14507. BL C.11.b.3.

episodes of the lives of Christ and Mary', can lead the pious to a direct and personal encounter with the divine.[55]

The indirection of a reader's gaze, the eyes partially closed or looking away from an open book, also manifests in visual form this concept of reading as a source of revelation. Several portraits of the author St Catherine of Siena appear in *The Orcharde of Syon* (Fig. 22), the Middle English translation of her *Dialogo* commissioned by Sir Richard Sutton, steward of the Bridgettine house of Syon, and printed in 1519 by de Worde.[56] De Worde's colophon says that Sutton, finding the text 'in a corner by it selfe, wyllynge of his greate charyte it sholde

Fig. 22. St Catherine of Siena receiving the stigmata. *The Orcharde of Syon*
(London: Wynkyn de Worde, 1519), title-page. *STC* 4815. BL C.11.b.6.

come to lyghte, that many relygyous and deuoute soules myght be releued and
haue comforte therby, he hathe caused at his greate coste, this booke to be
printed'. Just who these 'relygyous and deuoute soules' were, whether layfolk or
religious, is not specified, but the commissioning of this work by their steward
strongly implies that the Syon nuns were the primary audience.

The title-cut of the *Orcharde* (Fig. 22) shows St Catherine with her characteristic Crown of Thorns, displaying the stigmata and holding her attribute, the
heart. Dressed in the Mantellate habit of the Dominican tertiaries, she kneels
before an open book at a canopied prie-dieu as God the Father blesses her and
a dove descends from above. The title-page itself is printed in red and black – a
successful early experiment with two-colour printing – and the words 'Ecce
ancilla domini' appear, printed in red in a banderole above the woodcut. The
saint's gaze is directed upward, rapt in vision. The banderole echoes the words
of Mary at the Annunciation: 'Behold the handmaid of the Lord.' Then follows
a remarkable series of eight woodcuts illustrating Catherine's visions, where, in
virtually every scene, she is shown present before an open book, lifting her hands

Fig. 23. The Bridge. *The Orcharde of Syon* (London: Wynkyn de Worde, 1519),
sig. c6ᵛ. *STC* 4815. BL C.11.b.6.

in a gesture of prayer as the divinely inspired images unfold around her, a static
figure reading her book in a densely populated, supernaturally charged space.

The central portion of the text, called 'The Bridge', focuses on an extended
metaphor for Christ: 'how god made a brydge of his sone / whan the waye of
goynge to heuen was broke*n* by inobedyence of Adam by þe whiche brydge all
treue chryste*n* people maye ouerpasse'. The very complex visionary imagery of
the text is delineated in the prefatory illustration. Catherine in her habit (Fig. 23)
kneels before an open book, the gateway to vision, and holds up her hands in an
orans gesture, showing her stigmata. At the left Adam and Eve emerge from the
gates of Eden covering themselves with fig leaves. The bridge is made of stone,
'stones hewn on the body of the Word, my gentle Son', and a little house upon
the bridge represents 'the gate (which is, in fact, one with the bridge), which is
the only way you can enter'.[57] In the foreground, a demon plunges his pitchfork
into sinners in a bed of flames, torments described at some length in the text. God

explains the scene to Catherine: 'Daughter, words could never describe the suffering of these wretched little souls. ... Their suffering is even worse because they see the devil as he really is – more horrible than the human heart can imagine. ... This fire burns without consuming, for the soul cannot be consumed.'[58] There is also a river in the illustration, representing the transitory nature of the world, which Catherine says is the alternative route (that is, the road to hell), and a tree representing the tree of death, another metaphor that is greatly extended in the text, calling up the popular images of the trees of virtues and vices that circulated in manuscripts and printed books.[59]

Following Augustine, Jerome and others, the fourteenth-century mystic Walter Hilton, writing in *The Scale of Perfection*, described revelation as vouchsafed to those who studied scripture. Christ 'alone has the key of knowledge in his keeping, as Holy Scripture says, and he himself is the key, and he lets in whom he will through the inspiration of his grace, without breaking the seal. Jesus does this ... for those who are specially inspired to seek truth in holy scripture, with great devotion in prayer preceded by great diligence in study'. According to Hilton, the work of contemplation was 'to see Jesus in the scriptures after the opening of the spiritual eye'.[60] Reading, meditation and prayer were traditional means to the contemplation of the holy, as Catherine too suggests. In the *Orcharde*, Catherine describes some of the saints as lamps to open the mind's eye. Christ says to her:

By this great light set in the mind's eye Thomas [Aquinas] saw me and there gained the light of great learning. Augustine, Jerome, and my other holy doctors, enlightened by my Truth, understood and knew my Truth in the midst of darkness. I am referring to Holy Scripture, which seemed darksome because it was not understood. ... So I sent these lamps to enlighten the blind and dense understandings. ... All this light that is seen in the Old and New Testaments was seen and known by the eye of understanding through the light beyond natural light that I infused by grace.[61]

Catherine is told that learning 'in itself is good and perfect when the scholar is at the same time good and honorable and humble. But if learning is combined with pride, indecency, and sinful living, it is venomous and understands nothing but the letter of Scripture. It understands in darkness ... and its eye for understanding is clouded over.'[62] This theme is elaborated in the portion of text concerning good and bad priests (Fig. 24), which is introduced by this woodcut. Catherine is shown again praying before an open book as the priest celebrates Mass and wafers are given to kneeling men and women. Outside lovers (clerks?) embrace women lustfully as buildings crumble, and a man on his deathbed is threatened by a demon. In the text, Jesus says to Catherine: 'My ministers should be standing at the table of the cross in holy desire, nourishing themselves there on the food of souls for my honor. ... But instead these have made the taverns their table. ... They have become beasts in their sinning, lustful in word and deed.'[63] The woodcut again vividly communicates the message of Catherine's vision, which has been inspired by her prayer, meditation and reading.

Fig. 24. Holy Desire (Communion) and Lust. *The Orcharde of Syon*
(London: Wynkyn de Worde, 1519), sig. o5ᵛ. *STC* 4815. BL C.11.b.6.

A second author portrait of St Catherine with Twelve Nuns (Fig. 25)
occurs on the verso of the *Orcharde* title-page, functioning as a frontispiece. St
Catherine is again shown in Dominican habit, wearing the Crown of Thorns. She
is seated, her feet on a demon, with an open book in her lap, and she holds a heart
in her right hand. Surrounding her are twelve Dominican nuns, some of whom
carry books. They look away from the viewer, or at St Catherine, or modestly at
the ground, while St Catherine herself gazes directly from the page to the reader.
The book in her lap represents her *Revelations*, the book the reader is, in fact,
about to read. The same woodcut appears on the verso of the last leaf of the
volume (Fig. 26), illuminated in this example. The *Orcharde* text is thus enclosed
with repeated images of St Catherine, a practice probably related to the way early
books were bound, being printed in one shop to be bound elsewhere.[64] With the
exception of the title image, none of the other woodcuts was used again, a most
uncharacteristic move for de Worde, indicating that the woodcuts were made
expressly for this volume, perhaps at Syon itself. And, although we know that the

144

Fig. 25. St Catherine with Twelve Nuns. *The Orcharde of Syon* (London: Wynkyn de Worde, 1519), title verso. *STC* 4815. BL C.11.b.6.

Orcharde was commissioned by Sutton, the steward of Syon, presumably to be read primarily by the Syon nuns, marks in surviving volumes suggest that the work was also read by a lay audience. As in the woodcut of Jerome that we saw earlier (Fig. 21), the author, St Catherine, is shown with her book, the book that affords her visions authority and weight, the very book we are about to read.

The copy of *The Orcharde of Syon* in the Spencer Collection of the New York Public Library has a number of ownership marks, showing the book's rapid movement outward from the Syon community to lay readers.[65] First owned by 'Syster elyzabeth Stryckland professed in Syon', whose inscription appears on the flyleaf, the book was acquired after her death by her executor, Sir Richard Assheton, who gave it to his wife. The book then passed into the Sacheverall family, 'Katherin Sacheverall' having written her name on folio 3. It is interesting to note that, judging from the owner inscriptions, the book's predominant early readership was female. In her essay on *The Myroure of Oure Ladye*, Ellen Dunn says that the focus of Syon-sponsored translations was on 'the revelations of two great feminine mystics, St Bridget of Sweden and St Catherine of Siena. ... It is entirely appropriate that the spiritual reading given priority at Syon should be feminine in its origins, psychology, and manner of expression. The sisters of this community were simply having their turn at sharing in the long tradition of religious writing for English women.'[66]

The Syon community was particularly active in spreading images of St Bridget through numerous books, often depicting her as an inspired practitioner of *lectio*

Fig. 26. St Catherine with Twelve Nuns
(illuminated). *The Orcharde of Syon*
(London: Wynkyn de Worde, 1519),
endleaf (sig. B4ʳ). *STC* 4815. Formerly
in the collection of the Marquess of Bath,
Longleat House, Warminster, Wiltshire.

divina. According to her *Revelations*, the birth of St Bridget was foretold by the
local parish priest, who received a message sent by God: 'a man of proven life
and advanced age – while awake and praying, [he] saw in the night a shining
cloud, and, in the cloud, a virgin sitting with a book in her hand ... whose
wonderful voice will be heard throughout the world'.[67] Bridget founded an
important religious order, which was particularly significant, as we have seen,
for its emphasis on the learnedness of its monks and nuns as well as for its
production of single-leaf woodcuts. Bridget herself was well-read and more
literate than her contemporary Catherine of Siena, who dictated her works.
In her *Revelations*, Bridget includes references to the Pentateuch Paraphrase,
the Old Swedish Legendaries and Henry Suso's *Book Concerning the Eternal
Wisdom*, along with the writings of Ambrose, Augustine, Jerome and Gregory.[68]
Bridget herself tells us that 'when she was not occupied with manual labor, she
was continually re-reading the lives of the saints and the Bible, which she had
caused to be written out for herself in her own language'.[69]

Accordingly, Bridget is often shown in manuscript illuminations and woodcuts
writing or reading at her desk. One much-reprinted woodcut of Bridget (Fig. 27)
was, like the woodcuts in the *Orcharde of Syon*, probably produced by (and
certainly for) the nuns of Syon Abbey. Though Bridget is writing, she looks
upward, her inspiration divine as she contemplates the Trinity and Nativity. Yet
her vision also seems internally focused, as she records what she sees in the book

Fig. 27. St Bridget of Sweden. William Bonde, *Pylgrimage of perfection*
(London: Wynkyn de Worde, 23 February 1531), title-page. *STC* 3278. BL C.37.e.13.

before her and an angel whispers in her ear. This woodcut appeared in eighteen
printed books produced in England between 1519 and 1534, a period of fifteen
years, and was popular with a number of printers in the area of London,
including Wynkyn de Worde, Robert Redman, Lawrence Andrewe and Richard
Fawkes.

The Bridget woodcut follows conventional portrait models of Bridget in
manuscripts and printed books. Its immediate model is most likely the frontispiece of the 1481 edition of Bridget's writings, *Die Burde der Welt*, published in

Nuremberg by Conrad Zeninger, though there is also an extant fifteenth-century painting with very similar iconography in the Germanisches Nationalmuseum in Nuremberg. Images of Bridget writing at her desk also appeared in fifteenth-century English manuscripts.[70]

Just below the Virgin in the top right corner of this print are the pilgrim's staff and hat that represent Bridget's Roman pilgrimage undertaken in 1349, during which she worked for the return of the popes to Rome from Avignon. The woodcut image is a literal representation of the *Sermo Angelicus* portion of Bridget's revelations. Four years after she arrived in Rome, Bridget began to receive heavenly dictation from an angel as she gazed at the altar of the church of San Lorenzo in Damaso from her window in the building next door. According to the prologue to her *Revelations*, she would sit each day 'with pen, paper, and tablet ready'.[71] In the woodcut, at the bottom of the staff, we see 'the arms of Bavaria (Wittelsbach) and at the lower right those of the Counts Oettingen in whose territory the Bridgettine monastery of Maria-Maihingen was located', probably indicating the source image from which this English woodcut was copied.[72] The cross on the mantle of the kneeling monk is thought to allude to Bridget's voyage to Jerusalem and her death in Rome in 1373.

While in Rome, Bridget was further said to have prayed daily before a crucifix in St-Paul's-outside-the-Walls which was supposed to have spoken to her, and this story is one source for the prayer ascribed to Bridget, the *Fifteen Oes*, popular in English and continental prayer-books throughout and beyond the Reformation period.[73] Another of Bridget's visions was of St Francis in the church of San Francesco a Ripa, who said to her 'Come into my chamber to eat and drink with me', after which Bridget visited Assisi and then made a two-year tour of shrines in Italy.[74] Woodcuts of both of these miraculous scenes also figure prominently in Bridgettine iconography.

Fourteen of the books in which the Bridget woodcut appears have clear textual links to Syon. These include three works by William Bonde, who describes himself as a 'Brother of Syon', and seven separate editions of books produced by Richard Whitforde, the self-proclaimed 'wretch of Syon'.[75] For example, the Bridget woodcut is used to illustrate the title-page of *The Martiloge in englysshe after the vse of the chirche of salisbury / & as it is redde in Syon*, translated by Whitforde and published by Wynkyn de Worde in 1526. In his preface, Whitforde says that he has made his translation: 'for the edificacyon of certayne religyous persones vnlerned / that dayly dyd rede the same martiloge in latyn / not vnderstandynge what they redde' – a description that would fit the Bridgettine nuns who read English (rather than mainly Latin) texts.

The Bridget woodcut also illustrates the title-pages of the *Mirror of Our Lady*,[76] an English Book of Hours produced for Agnes Jordan, abbess of Syon, in 1530 by Richard Fawkes, and the *Myrrour or Glasse of Christes Passion*, published by Robert Redman in 1534, with a preface signed by the translator John Fewterer, the general confessor at Syon.[77]

By examining the patterns of use of this picture, I found that the repeated appearance of the St Bridget woodcut specifically in these fourteen works, which were published over a period of about fifteen years by a variety of printers, was not random. The Bridget woodcut links these texts and points to a common source: Syon Abbey. The woodcut functions as an imprimatur or seal of approval, a bookplate that assures the reader or purchaser of the authenticity of the text contents. This interpretation further implies that the Bridgettines had a wider influence on the English market for vernacular printed books and on what was being produced for English readers than has previously been supposed. The woodcut is not authorial – the books in which the bookplate appears were not written by Bridget – nor is it necessarily related thematically to the contents. Instead, the Bridget woodcut signifies Bridgettine approbation of certain texts.[78]

Reading was clearly important as a visual sign of female piety and authority. Throughout the writings of Bridget and Catherine, one finds images of writing and reading, and of Christ as a Book, as 'The Word ... incarnate in Scripture', which 'has a body and soul. The body is the words of the sacred text, the "letter" and literal meaning; the soul is the spiritual sense.' Those readers who are enlightened by God may transcend the text at hand to receive divine vision, as Christ tells Catherine: 'It was your mind's eye, with the pupil of holy faith that had vision in the end.'[79] Reading and meditation, the *lectio divina*, are emphasised as activities appropriate for holy persons, for nuns, saints and laywomen.

Perhaps the most famous woodcut of a woman writer and reader (or the best known today) is an engaging scene of a widow who was not a saint and was not canonised, though her literary canon has been rediscovered and much celebrated, particularly in the last decade. In manuscript miniatures and woodcuts, Christine de Pizan is often shown with books, though she is rarely reading them, which is conventional in author portraits. The famous miniature at the start of BL Harley MS 4431, for example, shows Christine offering her book to Queen Isabel of France, a book subsequently owned by Louis de Bruges, Seigneur de Gruuthuse, and by Elizabeth Woodville, wife of Edward IV. In this case, the book is a gift on the part of an artist presenting her work to a royal patron.[80] The manuscript depictions of Christine reading tend to occur in copies of the *Moral Proverbes*, where Christine is shown seated at a desk before an open book, instructing her son or a group of gentlemen from the text at hand.[81] On the verso of the title-page of the *Boke of the Cyte of Ladyes* (see Chapter 2, Fig. 51), printed in London by Henry Pepwell in 1521, is a woodcut portrait of Christine, shown distracted from the open copy of Mathéolus on the desk before her, her hand marking the place at which she has been interrupted.[82] The shelves and cupboards beside her desk are heaped with books in a rather disorganised way.[83] Her head turns toward the Three Virtues who process at left, carrying their attributes. As in the Annunciation, and the other woodcuts we have examined, here reading conjures up vision. The interior dialogues of Christine with the Three Virtues are inspired, in this case, rather than prophesied, by her reading the book, in a direct appropriation of the imagery of saintly reading.

Representations of Saintly Women in Late Medieval Woodcuts

Even a cursory examination of late medieval prints suggests that some religious cults, those of Bridget and Catherine for example, were popular rather than confined to the elite, and that some effort was made, through the production of single-leaf prints and illustrated printed books, to promote and publicise them. Popular devotion to female saints is more generally indicated by the surprisingly large number of single-leaf prints, essentially ephemera, that survive. Pictures of women saints helped to promote literacy among early readers of printed books, a woodcut of Margaret with her dragon or Apollonia with her tooth recalling at a glance the basic narrative to readers of texts like the *Golden Legend*. Repetition of images created contexts of meaning for fledgling readers. The images of women saints that illustrate the many popular printed narratives of the lives of the Virgin and Christ helped readers in their own process of holy reading and prayer: in the *lectio divina*, the 'prayerful reading' described by Augustine, Gregory and Jerome; and in affective prayer, visualising meditations on the holy stories, imagining themselves present at the sacred event. Using the model of the Annunciation, in which Mary's reading is shown as exemplary, meditative and prophetic, we have seen books linked with vision, sometimes prophetic vision, noting the indirection of the reader's gaze in relation to the open book, a sign of *meditatio*. Reading is shown as silent in these images; the reader's attention is distracted from the text at hand to the vision beyond, whether we consider Catherine's detailed vision of the Bridge or Christine's secular example. Finally, we have seen how the book itself might function as a bridge, or entrance to heaven, a gateway through which divine visions and prophecy might be revealed.

Chapter 5

RECONSTRUCTING
SOCIAL HISTORIES
READING IMAGES AS
HISTORICAL DOCUMENTS

In chapter 3, brief note was made of examples of the prestige given to books by some types of woodcut illustration – the incorporation, for instance, of the badge of Margaret Beaufort, Countess of Richmond and Derby, on a book's title-page or the inclusion of a realistic portrait of a famous preacher, such as that of John Fisher preaching his funeral sermon for Margaret at St Paul's. In order to fulfil their various roles in the illustration and marketing of books, pictures also had to reflect contemporary social attitudes and practice.

Pictures, of course, just like texts, are not necessarily to be interpreted as straight documentary evidence. The relationship of representation to historical reality is complex. A naive viewer tends to look at a picture as a direct rendering of reality, perhaps mistaking the immediacy of the image for accurate portrayal. An informed viewer, on the other hand, remains 'aware of his cultural pre-dispositions; that is, he is aware of the contemporary perspective he brings to the work of interpretation as a consequence of belonging to a culture different from the one under investigation, while the naive beholder is not'.[1] Though images may not directly record reality, they remain suggestive about practices and attitudes of the cultures producing them, appearing as projections of cultural consciousness. By looking at scenes of common social rituals such as marriage, of courtly pastimes such as jousting, or of everyday activities such as those of the writer, the schoolmaster and the printer, this chapter explores the boundaries of what pictures might suggest about the cultural ideas of late medieval Europe about its own society. By examining depictions of an exotic non-European group such as black Africans, we can also gain understanding of Europe's view of the outside world at the beginning of the age of exploration.

By the later fifteenth century the common social ritual of marriage is depicted fairly uniformly in the woodcuts illustrating books printed in France and England (see Chapter 3, Figs 12, 13, 15, 17). Though the ability of the woodcut designers and wood-block cutters varied, the scenes are iconographically the same. Holding the bride and groom by the wrist, a priest joins their right hands. The priest is dressed in an alb and stole, and is attended by a clerk. The bride wears a garland on her free-flowing hair, and the hatless groom a fur-lined coat. Male witnesses stand behind the groom; female witnesses attend the bride. The group stands just outside the church or in the church porch.[2] Marriages could still be contracted legally in a brief ceremony of agreement between partners before witnesses outside the church. This form of marriage was less common by the end of the fifteenth century when these woodcuts were produced, and 'no one doubts that it was the church's consistent aim through the centuries from the twelfth to the sixteenth and beyond to bring weddings into the church'.[3]

Because there were no customary wedding outfits, the fur-lined coat worn by the groom in all of these prints probably represents 'the best he had'.[4] His bare head signifies his respect for God and his bride, while her flowing hair represents her maiden status. The bride's garland also seems to have had significance; one case found by Richard Helmholz in the York records of 1372 describes a clandestine marriage in which William Burton, a tanner of York, married one Marjory by verbal agreement and then formally signified the new bond by kissing 'the said Marjory through a wreath of flowers, in English "Garland"'. The wearing of a garland for a wedding was a very ancient custom. It may have alluded to the garden and the vineyard, fertility images so prominent in the Song of Songs, which was often used in the Middle Ages as a marriage text.[5]

The joining of hands commonly seen in depictions of the marriage ceremony was called 'handfasting' in English, a 'venerable custom [that] was generally accepted in court as a sign of the mutual consent of the parties'.[6] In the French example (Chapter 3, Fig. 15) that appears in *L'Art de bien vivre et de bien mourir*, printed for Vérard in 1492, the marriage of Adam and Eve is shown in an arch above a contemporary ceremony below. God is the priest who joins the hands of Adam and Eve, prefiguring the earthly marriage in the lower scene. Adam and Eve are shown as unashamedly naked, and a fountain at the left symbolises the rivers of Eden. The image is copied in de Worde's edition of *The crafte to lyue well* (Chapter 3, Fig. 17), reduced to the basic figures of God joining the hands of the naked Adam and Eve, with the fountain roughly rendered at right.[7] The clasped hands of the bride and groom, 'the joining of right hands that is the central action of the marriage representations', were drawn from the story of the wedding of Sarah in the Book of Tobit, in which Raguel takes the right hand of his daughter and gives it to Tobit.[8]

Similarities in the iconography of English marriage woodcuts may in part result from the fact that they have been copied from a French model, and then from each other. However, the iconographic elements are also commonly found in wedding scenes in late medieval manuscript miniatures, and in sculpture and glass as well as in prints.[9] In any case, the English woodcuts circulated in a variety of contexts, promoting marriage practices that have come to be seen as traditional.[10] Scenes like these, which were readily reproduced in woodcut form, are generic and appropriate to illustrate virtually any wedding text. But there are also late medieval pictures that purport to be historical depictions.

A wedding scene (Fig. 1) is included, for example, in the well-known Beauchamp Pageants, a series of 53 pencil and brown ink drawings in a manuscript dated about 1483-1487 presenting 'pageants', or historic events in the life of Richard Beauchamp (1382-1439), Earl of Warwick. The iconography is similar

Fig. 1. The Wedding of Henry V and Katherine of Valois. Pageant 43, Beauchamp Pageants. English, *c.* 1480. BL Cottonian MS Julius E.IV, Article 6.

to that seen in the woodcuts, including the rich apparel of bride and groom, the clasped right hands, the priest standing just behind the couple, the male and female witnesses, even the architectural detail suggesting the porch of a church. In this case, however, the caption tells us: 'Here shewes howe kyng Henry the Vth was solempnely maried to Dame Kateryn, the kyng*es* doughter of Fraunce.'[11] Highlights from the Beauchamp Pageants include illustrations of Richard's first battle in 1403 ('the Warre of Wales by oone Owen of Glendour') with a comet (*stella comata*) above; Richard's service 'att the batell of Shrewesbury', fought on 21 July 1403, for which he received the Order of the Garter; his journey to Jerusalem in August 1408 and visit to the Holy Sepulchre; and drawings of the birth of Henry VI 'at Wyndsore on Seynt Nicholas day' in 1421, along with tournament and jousting scenes – another common theme of both manuscript and woodcut images.

Among tournament scenes from the Beauchamp Pageants is a drawing of jousters at the coronation of 'Quene Jane', or Joan of Navarre, Duchess of Brittany, who became Henry IV's queen. The king and queen watch from a gallery above the playing field, resting their arms on pillows. The queen wears butterfly veils, which will become more fashionable later in the century, and is accompanied by her ladies. Earl Richard is shown at the centre of the picture, engaged in the joust with the barrier, or tilt. He is identified by the crest on his helmet of the bear and the ragged staff, and is accompanied by his squire, who also wears his badge.

Sent on an embassy to the Council of Constance for a meeting with Pope John XXII and Emperor Sigismund in November 1414, Warwick again engaged in tournaments. One pageant shows the victorious Richard giving the Empress Barbara his badge ('And then the Emperesse toke the Erles lyvere a bere from a knyghtes shuldre / and for greet love and favor she sette hit on her shuldre') while still in the lists, where Richard has just slain his opponent, 'a myghty Duke'. Another pageant takes us to the Lollard uprising under Sir John Oldcastle, also in 1414: 'Henry the vth then beyng kyng of Englond was secretely enformed of a prevey and sodeyn insurreccione of traiterous heretikes', who were subdued by the armoured Earl Richard. There is also a scene of the siege of Calais in 1436: 'how Philip Duc of Burgoyne, beseged Caleys. And Humfrey Duc of Gloucestre, Richard Erle of Warrewik, and Humfrey Erle of Stafford, with a greet multitude, went over the see and folowed the Duc of Burgoyn, he ever fleyng before them. And there they sore noied the contrey with fire and swerde.' In the Beauchamp Pageants, history is recorded visually, if not always accurately. The editors of the 1914 facsimile say, for example, that 'The view of Calais is ... (though somewhat correct) a piece of artistic license.' The action is presented as a visual narrative in which the various exploits of the historical hero are readily seen through the immediacy of the image.[12]

We also find fine renderings of ships, tournaments, feats of arms and battle scenes in Morgan MS M. 775, a compendium containing Vegetius' *De re militari*, the *Ordinances of Chivalry*, treatises on navigation, Stephen Scrope's translation

Fig. 2. Seascape with Boats. *Ordonances of Chivalry &c.* (English, *c.* 1493?), fol. 130ᵛ. Morgan MS M. 775. By permission of the Pierpont Morgan Library, New York.

of Christine de Pizan's *Epistle of Othea*, and descriptions of ceremonial occasions, among other items, written and illuminated for Sir John Astley (d. 1486) in the fifteenth century.[13] Several miniatures from the Astley manuscript are intended as realistic portrayals, among them a picture of sailing ships with three rowing boats (Fig. 2) illustrating a text that gives sailing directions from Berwick-upon-Tweed to Holyhead and for the Bay of Biscay. Great attention has been given to detail: the furled and full sails on the five sailing ships, the carefully drawn rigging and crow's nests, the three boats, the pennants, and the windmill and flare in the foreground have been painstakingly delineated.

Fig. 3. Sir John Astley Battles Piers de Masse. *Ordonances of Chivalry &c.*
(English, *c.* 1493?), fol. 275ᵛ. Morgan MS M. 775.
By permission of the Pierpont Morgan Library, New York.

Like the Beauchamp Pageants, the Astley manuscript contains several illustrations that serve as visual records of an actual historical moment. For example,
a pen-and-ink drawing partially filled in with gouache (Fig. 3) details the
mounted combat between Piers de Masse and Sir John Astley in Paris in 1438
before the French king Charles VII, a combat for which Astley was later
knighted. The building from which the ladies watch the battle in their butterfly
veils is probably intended to represent the Bastille, erected by Charles V in 1369.

Just as Earl Richard is known by his badge or livery in the drawings comprising the Beauchamp Pageants, we can identify Astley by his arms; he is the figure on the near side of the tilt with his squire in the foreground. Beneath the windows at which the King and court are seen stand two heralds, one bearing the French arms on his tabard, and the other the arms of Astley. As in the examples from the Beauchamp Pageants, the heraldic insignia in the Astley illustration allow the viewer to identify real persons represented in the historical scene.

To some extent, then, whether an image might be said to be imaginary or historical is predicated on the text accompanying it and sometimes on signs within images indicating ties to a historical past, usually in the form of heraldic insignia.[14] The historical illustrations of the famous fights of Sir John Astley or the exploits of Earl Richard, which are intended to represent actual events, are accompanied by texts briefly explaining these events. Despite their seeming immediacy, however, the pictures of the Beauchamp Pageants were made some fifty years after the fact. The drawings of the birth of Earl Richard and later that of Henry VI, of the marriage of Henry V and Katherine of Valois and of the battles all look to be standard scenes taken from model books or other manuscript exemplars. In the case of the Astley manuscript, the fights are rendered elegantly and simply, the viewer being dependent to some extent on the heraldic signs to ascertain the action. But how long they were drawn after the historical event they purport to depict, or whether the drawings are factually accurate, no one can say. Though presented as eyewitness accounts, the illustrations in the Astley manuscript and the Beauchamp Pageants are also fictional reconstructions. Their purpose, I think, is in both cases memorial rather than strictly factual.

Extant woodcuts referring to actual events and people tend to be more scarce than drawings or miniatures, partly as a result of the visual constraints of the medium.[15] Woodcut images copied by English block-cutters are simplified even from their continental models. The pictures are emblematic, almost totemic, rather than naturalistic representations of reality, very much unlike the medieval drawings just discussed. Naturalism was also limited by the reuse of woodblocks, so essential for printers from a practical point of view. On the title-page of the *Pylgrymage of Sir Richarde Guylforde Knyght*, printed by Richard Pynson in 1511, for example, there is a conventional image (Fig. 4) of two courtiers shaking hands in the gateway of a castle. The same picture will be later used by Pynson to illustrate the *Hystorye of Troye* by Guido delle Colonne.[16]

Richard Guilford was a real person, and the story of his pilgrimage through France and Savoy to Venice and thence to Palestine is purportedly an eyewitness account by a priest who travelled with him. Guilford's arms appear on the verso of the title-page: two angels holding up a shield with three castles. But the title-image is generic. It is a scene of travellers either departing from or being met at the castle gates, its historical reference made clear only by the title above: 'This is the begynnynge, and contynuaunce of the Pylgrymage of Sir Richarde Guylforde Knyght / & controuler vnto our late soueraygne lorde kynge Henry

Fig. 4. Sir Richard Guilford on his Pilgrimage. *Pylgrymage of Sir R. Guylforde Knyght* (London: Richard Pynson, 1511), title-page. *STC* 12549. BL G.6719.

the .vii. And howe he went with his seruaun*tes* and company towardes Iherusalem.' As in the previous examples, language and heraldic reference fix the meaning of the image.

Despite the reduced detail in English woodcuts and their frequent reuse, however, we can learn much from them about one theme, at least: that of people at work.[17] It is precisely the totemic or reductive element in woodcuts that focuses attention particularly on the tools that people used in their daily work.[18] Like the fountain that represents Eden in the marriage woodcuts, tools come to signify trades or professions – for example, those of writers, teachers and printers.

Woodcuts of writers at work often feature, like their manuscript counterparts, the writer himself seated in a canopied chair, copying his text, with his books lying open or shut on a shelf or jumbled into a cabinet, and his inkpot and 'penner', or pen case, beside him. We see such details in an early German wood-cut (Fig. 5) illustrating Boccaccio's *De casibus virorum illustrium,* and in Caxton's *The book of the subtyl historyes and Fables of Esop.* In this example, the fabulist (sans pen case, however) writes at his desk, his copy-text before him (Fig. 6). In a second panel of the latter illustration, Aesop is shown offering his

Fig. 5. Writer at Work. Giovanni Boccaccio, *De Casibus Virorum Illustrium*
(Lyons: Mathias Huss and Iehan Schabeler, 1483), fol. 2ʳ. BL 86.h.18.

completed text on bended knee to his patron with a tip of the hat. Caxton's
woodcuts in this edition were drawn from German and French models.[19]

Ink containers like that shown in the German woodcut example were made
of horn, silver, tin or leather. Inkpots are also sometimes portrayed as portable,
since ink was kept in a powdered state and mixed with water only when needed
for use. Inkpots often appear in manuscript illuminations, paintings and prints
depicting the scribe or scholar in his study, and actual examples, as well as other
implements associated with these occupations, may still be seen in museums
today – metal pens, inkhorns and penners are extant, though no quill pens
survive.[20] The penner or pen case, most particularly, is regularly reproduced in
many manuscript miniatures and later in printed portraits of Geoffrey Chaucer,
which show the penner slung around his neck, an iconic reference that identifies
the author as directly and immediately as the attribute of a saint.[21]

Just as clearly identifiable is the schoolmaster with his switch or stick, the
emblem of his authority in the classroom (Fig. 7), who appears on the title-pages
of numerous schoolbooks produced by English printers in the late fifteenth
through the sixteenth centuries.[22] The master is generally shown seated on a large
and imposing chair, with the students seated around him on benches or even on
the floor. The students are comparatively smaller figures in most of these printed
images, perhaps intended to represent children, and are sometimes shown with
open books before them as they learn to read.

Fig. 6. Writer at Work and Presenting Book to Patron. Aesop, *Fables of Esop*, trans. William Caxton (Westminster: William Caxton, 26 March 1484), Liber Primus, fol. 31ʳ. *STC* 175. BL C.11.c.17.

The schoolmaster's switch, his chair and the open books of his students all suggest something of the actual experience of schooling in the later Middle Ages. The schoolmaster's switch, for example, simultaneously symbolises his authority and his capacity to punish, and accounts of students beaten in late medieval schools are numerous. Michael Clanchy cites the example of Robert Buck of Skipton in Yorkshire, who in 1304, recalled being beaten so badly at a school in Clitheroe that he ran away. In Albert W. Pollard's reconstruction of a popular late medieval Latin grammar, one of the dialogues includes the question: '"How often have you been punished to-day?"' and the answers '"semel-bis-ter-quarter"' and '"et iterum cras corrigeris"'. The dialogues also mention student 'custodes' or monitors, who were appointed in turns, among other things, to provide the schoolmaster with his instruments of punishment. When chosen for this job, one student says: '"it's not my turn". "Who ought to be appointed, then?" "This is the boy, Sir, both because it's his turn and because he knows how to get you long and nasty rods!"'[23] Writing in 1458, Agnes Paston told her son's schoolmaster not to spare the rod when sixteen-year-old Clement had not done well at his lessons. She asked that the master would 'truly belash him till he will amend. And so did the last master, and the best that ever he had, at Cambridge.' Sometimes, however, the tables were turned. Barbara Hanawalt, for example, mentions the delight that some schoolboys experienced 'when an Oxford master, out early one morning to collect willow twigs for a switch to beat them, fell into the river and drowned'.[24] The vengeance of schoolboys is beautifully expressed in the famous poem from the commonplace book of Richard Hill (Oxford, Balliol College, MS 354), citizen and grocer of London. After the boy has been punished by the schoolmaster, who has 'pepered my ars with well good speed' until it bleeds, he imagines that the master is a hare and his books are hounds, and the boy himself the hunter, who will blow his horn, hunting down the master and killing him.[25]

Examples of the corporal punishment of children in schools continued to appear in sixteenth-century accounts. We are told that 'In sixteenth-century Oxford, a man taking a degree in grammar was invested with a birch and a

Fig. 7. Schoolmaster with Students. John Stanbridge, *Vocabula magistri stanbrigi* (London: Wynkyn de Worde, 1510), title-page. *STC* 23178. BL G.7559.

"palmer", a stick with a round, flat head, specially designed for slapping hands.' In the Whitkirk grammar school, founded by Lord Thomas Darcy, a member of Thomas More's circle, 'The schoolmaster was specifically allowed to discipline with a stick.'[26] Nicholas Orme retells a story recounted by Henry Machyn, a London chronicler of the mid-sixteenth century, who reported that in 1563 a schoolmaster 'named Penred, who had a child to teach, beat him so severely with a buckled belt that the affair came to public notice. The master was set on the pillory, whipped till his blood ran down, and the boy's injuries were exhibited, "the pitiest [sight to] see at any time".'[27] The switch and rod were not, then, just hypothetical emblems of the schoolmaster but were apparently put to use in the classroom during the period in which the schoolmaster prints were circulating.

The schoolmaster's chair was a relatively recent innovation, for chairs were unusual items of furniture in or out of the classroom until the fifteenth century.[28]

The chair may be read as a signifier of the classroom itself, which might be located wherever the master chose to be. David Cressy has pointed out that 'Charters and charitable instruments alone did not determine where education took place. ... The crucial element was the presence of a competent teacher, whose school would operate for as long as he was available and which might fade from memory with his death or migration.'[29] In her study of pre-Reformation education in York, Jo Ann Hoeppner Moran concurs, further citing the prestige attached to grammar masters in the larger northern towns and the gratitude of some of their students for their instruction. She provides the example of Archbishop Thomas Rotherham, who, looking back to his boyhood (*c.* 1430), described the joy he and others felt at the arrival of a grammar master in their village:

We stood there in that time, without letters; we should have stood there untaught, illiterate, and rough for many years, had it not been that by God's grace a man learned in grammar arrived, from whom, as from a primal font we were, by God's will, instructed, and, under God's leadership came to the state in which we are now, and others arrived at great positions.[30]

Schoolmasters, then, were often mobile and could turn any spare room into a classroom, where they taught students of varying ages and sometimes of both genders. In the prints, the chair comes to symbolise the master's classroom, just as the switch signifies his authority. The chair literally represents a seat of authority, perhaps originally derived from a bishop's throne; the *Oxford English Dictionary* takes its earliest example of 'chair' meaning a 'place or situation of authority' from the 1382 Wycliffite New Testament. Another *OED* definition, 'The seat from which a professor or other authorized teacher delivers his lecture', is exemplified by the directive provided by Reginald Pecock (1395-1460) to his *c.* 1449 text *The Repressor of Over Much Blaming of the Clergy*: 'To be rad ... in the chaier of scolis'.[31] The chair here represents the seat of academic authority, a precursor perhaps to our contemporary 'chair' in the sense of 'professorship'.

In the prints, the students are usually shown with open books before them – perhaps a reference to schools that taught reading only, but more likely an allusion to the materials studied in grammar schools, where the main business was the teaching of Latin.[32] Though occasionally adorning the title-pages of books in English such as John Lydgate's *The chorle & the byrde* or Aesop, both presumably used as teaching texts in schools, the prints are most often found illustrating the numerous Latin editions of John Stanbridge's *Vocabula*, the *Synonyms* of John of Garland and the Latin grammar of Robert Whittinton printed in London by de Worde and Richard Pynson. The schoolmaster print occurs very often at the beginning or on the title-page of the volume and is usually the only illustration in the book. The image thus introduces the student of Latin to an imagined intellectual space, the classroom where Latin is learned and where the teacher is in authority. It functions, so speak, as a pictorial mirror presented at the beginning of the Latin text in which students see both themselves and their teacher portrayed.

Fig. 8. Death and the Printers. *La gra[n]t[e] danse macabre* (Lyon: Mathias Huss, February 18, 1499), sig. b1ʳ. BL IB 41735.

The makers of printed books themselves are also sometimes pictured in print. The wooden presses used by fifteenth- and early sixteenth-century printers have long since vanished. There is no printers' manual or description of a shop in English until the publication in 1677 of the first issue of Joseph Moxon's *Mechanick Exercises*.[33] Illustrations are therefore the only window we have into the early print shop, the equipment employed and the work at hand. How much can illustrations tell us about the earliest print shops? What are the limits of the woodcut image as an historical document? By analysing several prints of printers in their shops, we will find common elements that suggest historical fact, as well as serving as points of departure for speculation by book historians that is sometimes informed by their knowledge of later printing history.

The earliest depiction of the activities in a print shop is a woodcut showing Death and the Printers (Fig. 8), which appeared in *La grante danse macabre*, printed in Lyon by Mathias Huss in 1499. The scene at left shows the compositor seated at a trestle table before a case full of type. The case has compartments that separate the letters of type: 'the "upper case" contains the capitals, numerals and certain other characters, the "lower case" containing the "small" letters and the spaces', hence our common English names for upper-case and lower-case letters.[34] The compositor holds a composing stick and upon it is arranging types that he has taken one by one from the compartments in the case before him. He is shown using a printed page hanging from a stick in the case as his guide. He will put each stick-full of type, which is arranged in reverse order so that the lines read from right to left, along with wood-blocks for illustrations, into a metal frame or 'forme' that is lying next to him on the bench, and when he has accumulated a full two pages, he will lock them in securely.

Just behind the press, a man is shown waving an ink-ball, a leather-covered ball dipped in ink, with which he will ink the type in the forme. Ink-balls were in use from the late Middle Ages until the early nineteenth century. R. B. McKerrow points out that in the early printing process, 'Two workmen must always have been necessary, or at least one and a boy, as the same person could not ink the type and lay on the paper. In most of the pictures of early presses it seems that one man did the inking, the other laid on the paper and worked the machine.'[35] Using the 1499 Lyons woodcut as his evidence, Colin Bloy says that the use of ink-balls began with the invention of the printing press. In addition to this woodcut, he cites a deck of playing cards engraved by Jost Amman between 1560 and 1580 that has a suit of printers' ink-balls: 'These were a set of moralistic cards and the balls were intended to represent worthwhile industry.' He describes the inking process as follows: 'A ball was held in each hand and turned in a circular motion across the inking table, thereby picking up ink. This operation was repeated across the forme with both hands, and the balls moved in such a way that the type was not smeared with ink. This was called "beating the forme".'[36] The exact composition of these ink-balls and the precise process of inking cannot, of course, be determined from illustrations. The first detailed description of inking balls is that of Moxon, who advises that they be made of sheepskin treated so as not to resist the ink and then stuffed with wool or hair, with a long wooden handle made from alder or maple. The diameter of the ball at that time was seven inches. Later book historians have speculated that earlier ink-balls were composed of dog skin and stuffed with horsehair, or even sand.[37]

Next to the compositor's table, we see the two-pull wooden screw press, which was in use for about 50 years after Gutenberg first set up his shop.[38] The pressman (standing in front of the press) pulls the handle (or rounce), the rod protruding from the press above his head. By means of a screw mechanism, the rounce lowers a heavy horizontal plank, the platen, so that the dampened paper is pressed hard on to the inked forme. The printing process on this press is faster than on a single-pull press, since the forme holds two pages of type: once one page has been printed, instead of removing the forme and inserting another, the pressman will roll it further into the press so as to print off the second page.[39] We can also see in the print that the press is held to the ceiling by heavy beams so as to contain the pressure exerted by the platen.

The inspiration for the wooden printing press has been variously attributed (comparisons with contemporary woodcuts of other types of press might prove instructive). Most scholars say that the first printing presses were based on the wine presses then in use. Albert Kapr further conjectures that the early printing press may have developed from presses adapted for the printing of textiles from wooden patterns, while Seán Jennett suggests that 'The first presses were heavy, cumbersome affairs, perhaps converted cheese presses, or, what may be thought more likely, bookbinders' or papermakers' screw presses adapted or modified.'[40]

The last important element of the Lyons woodcut is the shop of the bookseller, seen at the right, his wares stacked on shelves behind him. These appear to be books that have already been bound. Headbands are visible on the spines of several bindings, and two volumes are shown with clasps. While it is generally thought that late medieval books were most commonly purchased in unbound sheets and then sent out to be bound elsewhere, this might not always have been the case. De Worde's will, for example, cites a servant of his who was also a binder, which suggests that binding may have taken place on the premises. Unbound quires would also be difficult to represent convincingly in a woodcut; the books in this picture may represent samples of bindings that the customer might then order.

A similar scene, though without the compositor, is shown in the printer's mark of Jodocus Badius Ascensius (Fig. 9), also known as Josse Bade. Among the many books in which the mark appears is John Major's *Historia Maioris Britanniae*, printed in Paris in 1521.[41] The text is in Latin and was presumably produced for a predominantly English readership of educated gentlemen. Here we see a press with a straight bar and small platen. The pressman pulls the handle of the press, and the printed pages are neatly laid out on a bench beside it. A man holding two ink-balls claps them together before the next inking. Scissors, a soft long-handled brush, a compass and another measuring tool hang from the press itself. At right, a customer peruses books (which again appear to be bound) for sale on a shelf.

Two final, late examples are from that most famous description of people at work, the *Eygentliche Beschreibung Aller Stände auff Erdenbuch*, or *Book of Trades*, by Hans Sachs, with woodcuts by Jost Amman, published in 1568 by Sigmund Feyerabend in Frankfurt at the press of Georg Raben.[42] The woodcut of the block-cutter (Fig. 10) shows a man at work at a draughting table, sitting in good light from a window and cutting a wood-block with a sharp tool. Among the implements on his desk are a sponge, a rule and possibly a stylus. An inkpot hangs by his table. The somewhat elliptical text supplied by Sachs gives further insight into the work at hand, explaining that the image is traced and then carefully cut. Using designs prepared by a draughtsman, the block-cutter engraves the image on wood. 'When the picture is printed, it is as clear as the original drawing,' claim the descriptive verses beneath.

Most scholars agree that the earliest woodcuts were executed on soft wood, probably pear. The design to be reproduced would be drawn or traced directly on the block, as here described, and the block-cutter would then cut away the surface of the block, leaving the lines which were to be printed in 'as high relief as possible consistently with their being sufficiently strong to stand the impression'.[43] When cutting the block, the cutter would try to follow the grain of

Fig. 9. Printer's mark of Jodocus Badius Ascensius. John Major, *Historia Maioris Britanniae* (Paris: Badius Ascensius, 1521), title-page. Collection of Martha W. Driver.

the wood. Breaks in English woodcuts tend to run up and down rather than across the block, and McKerrow comments that 'it seems to have been a general if not universal rule that the grain of the blocks should run vertically, and this rule was followed even in borders made up, as many were, of four separate pieces, in which we might have expected that, for the sake of obtaining greater strength in the top and bottom piece, the grain would there have been made to run horizontally'.[44]

The famous scene of the printers' shop from the *Book of Trades* (Fig. 11) again shows completed pages on a bench before the press. One printer examines a newly printed page as another inks the forme with two balls. Compositors standing before large cases are shown arranging type from compartments in the background. Similar scenes of printers with their presses are illustrated in books

Fig. 10. Block-cutter. Hans Sachs with
Jost Amman, *Eygentliche Beschreibung
Aller Stände auff Erdenbuch* (Frankfurt:
Georg Raben for Sigmund Feyerabend,
1568), sig. F1ʳ. BL C.57.b.25.

printed in England from the mid- to late sixteenth century.[45] Though we cannot
reconstruct the exact materials or even the precise processes of printing from
these images, we can get a general idea about the structure of the two-pull
wooden screw press, the job of the compositor, the inking of the forme and
the combined print shop and bookshop which were commonplace in the late
fifteenth and early sixteenth centuries. Pictures provide the only direct evidence
we have of the early printer's shop; the rest is conjecture or drawn from much
later historical records.

In addition to depicting social rituals and everyday activities, woodcut and
manuscript illustrations can also take us into the minds of late medieval people,
and reveal something of how they thought about and perceived their world.
Honoré de Balzac, that great observer of the human comedy, wrote in *The
Pursuit of the Absolute* (1834), 'The Events of human life, be they public
or private, are so intimately bound up with architecture, that the majority of
observers can reconstruct nations or individuals in the full reality of their
behavior, from the remnants of their public monuments or the examination of
their domestic remains.'[46] Like Balzac himself, the statement is extreme, even
grandiose, but there is truth in it. Can the same be said of woodcuts? Can we
'reconstruct nations or individuals in the full reality of their behavior' from some
of the illustrations found in their books? One historical theme that can be
recovered by careful reconstruction and observation of patterns of picture usage
is that of attitudes to black people in the era of the opening of trade routes to
Africa followed by the discovery of the New World.

While depictions of black figures in painting and sculpture have been traced in

Fig. 11. Printshop. Hans Sachs with Jost Amman, *Eygentliche Beschreibung Aller Stände auff Erdenbuch* (Frankfurt: Georg Raben for Sigmund Feyerabend, 1568), sig. F3ʳ. BL C.57.b.25.

monumental studies such as *The Image of the Black in Western Art*, very little attention has been paid to images of black people in prints.[47] The central focus here is a figure called 'the Horner' (Fig. 12) that I noticed some years ago in my study of the *Kalender of Shepherds*, a popular compendium that was printed and reprinted in France and in England during the late fifteenth and early sixteenth centuries. As we have seen elsewhere in this volume, pictures originally presented in the first editions of the *Kalender* published in France were especially influential on English book illustration, and were copied and recopied in a variety of contexts.[48] Trying to read this particular image to understand its original meaning is perhaps as difficult as trying to understand the more obscure jokes in Shakespeare or allusions in Joyce. Still, it is a valuable exercise to examine images like these, which were produced when perceptions of non-European people were pliable and plastic, before ideas about race became attached to slavery, and by implication, to an ideology of racial inferiority. Recently, the American historian Barbara Fields has eloquently argued that race is a social and historical construct. Fields reads race as ideology rather than biological fact: 'The view that Africans constituted a race ... must have arisen at a specific and ascertainable historical moment; and it cannot have sprung into being automatically at the moment when Europeans and Africans came into contact with each other.'[49] Early images of people of African descent were made during a period that Peter Mark calls 'a formative time for European racial attitudes toward blacks; it was also the last period before these attitudes would be affected by the transportation of hundreds of thousands of blacks into American slavery'.[50]

Like the other pictures we have examined in this chapter, the history of the

Fig. 12. Horner,
*Le compost et kalendrier
des bergiers* (Paris: Guy
Marchant, 1500), sig. n5ᵛ.
BL IB.39741.

Horner can be at least partly reconstructed by locating this particular image in the context of other related woodcuts, in this case by studying other images of black people that circulated in the late fifteenth and early sixteenth centuries. While there have been some recent historical and literary studies of race and ethnicity in the Middle Ages, very few recent sources consider images.[51] Older studies have focused on the development of the representations of black people in Italy, Germany, Portugal, Spain and the Low Countries; very little has been said about such representation in England and France, where the Horner appears.[52] This chapter will conclude with a closer look at the printer who first employed the image of the Horner.

Judging from its reprint history, the *Kalender of Shepherds* was extremely popular. It went through eight printings in Paris and Geneva between 1493 and

1500. The first English edition (actually a poor translation of the French text into Scots) appeared in 1503. According to the *STC*, following this edition, the *Kalender of Shepherds* remained in print in England in a variety of versions through 1631, going through some 19 editions.[53] The *Shepherd's Kalender* was a miscellany of shepherd's lore, tables for finding the dates of movable feasts, descriptions of the torments of Purgatory and explications of the Ten Commandments, Lord's Prayer and Creed. It was heavily illustrated, with pictures in the English editions deriving from woodcut models in the French editions, printed by Guy Marchant and published by Antoine Vérard. Copies were owned in France and England by aristocratic and middle-class readers.

Guy Marchant, the first printer of the *Kalender of Shepherds*, was also the first printer of the famous woodcut Dance of Death series, and as we have seen, books about death were popular in the late fifteenth century. In these books, the figure of Death is conventionally portrayed as a decaying corpse or skeleton, horrifying and all-powerful, a force no living thing can withstand. In the second edition of the *Kalendrier des bergiers*, published in Paris by Marchant in 1500, however, Death is shown as a young, barefoot black man in a tunic playing a horn and holding Death's dart in an illustration prefacing a poem titled *Dictie des trespassez en forme de balade et du iugement* ('Song of the dead in the form of a ballad, and of the judgement', see the Appendix to this chapter, p. 183). According to the *Oxford English Dictionary*, a horner may be 'One who blows or winds a horn', or 'One who cuckolds, a cuckold-maker', or, of course, a worker in horn, a material that is malleable and can be shaped much like wood.[54] Among the many things that might be made of horn in this period were drinking vessels and inkhorns. Leaves of horn, pounded thin, were used to line lanterns, and in England from the mid-fifteenth century, horn-books (made of paper fixed to a tablet and covered with a sheet of translucent horn to protect the surface) were used in schools.

In the French poem accompanying the illustration, there are many puns on the word *horn*, along with references to the unicorn's horn which was traditionally supposed to purify poisoned water, the trumpets blown by angels and the Last Trump at Judgement Day, ending with a prayer to St Michael to 'guard us from the horn'. The expression 'beware the horn' was apparently known as early as the thirteenth century in France and in England. Michael Camille, for example, has discussed an image in an early bestiary of a shepherd calling his sheep, with a text beside his head that says: 'ha ha ware le corn'.[55]

In the difficult and comparatively sophisticated French poem, there is persistent word play on *cors*, 'body', and *corne*, 'horn'. The poem is built on taking apart, then reconfiguring, these words in the French text, playfully reshaping the body of each stanza even as the poem presents its redemptive message. The English version of the poem, adapted by Robert Copland, which is accompanied by an English woodcut of the Horner (Fig. 13), may possibly have been inspired by the French one, though it is certainly not a direct translation. Titled 'How euery man and woman ought to cease of theyr synnes at [th]e

Fig. 13. Horner, *The Kalender of Shepardes*, trans. Robert Copland (London: T. Este for J. Wally, 1570?), sig. M5ᵛ. *STC* 22415. BL C.27.k.6.

sownynge of a dredable horne' (see Appendix, p. 184), the English verse does contain a similar message, though its presentation is quite different. As in the French poem, the Horner advises sinners to repent, though more emphatically. His horn warns of the Last Judgement: 'Take hede of my horne / totynge all alowde'. The English poem is less linguistically sophisticated than the French, relying mainly on alliteration ('Fle faynt falshod') and emphatic repetition for its effect. It even reproduces, like the text in the thirteenth-century bestiary, the 'ho ho' sound of the horn itself ('Ho / ho you blynde folke', 'Ho ho betyme'). In his text Copland 'substitutes anaphora and alliteration for the elaborate French punning'.[56] Copland's creation, in its language and rhetorical technique, is a very different poem from the French original.

The black Horner does not appear in the manuscript source for the *Kalendrier*, nor is he represented in the first imprint of the *Compost et kalendrier des bergiers* produced in 1493 by Guy Marchant.[57] But after his debut in the Marchant copy of 1500, he has a life in France of about seventy years and appears in many editions, including a copy of the 1529 edition printed by Nicolas le Rouge and in the 1569 edition printed for the widow of Jean Bonfons. In England, he appears in print through an edition printed *c.* 1585, where he actually appears twice, illustrating both the 'horner's song' and a poem of 'prouerbes'.[58]

In all these books, the Horner clearly represents Death, all-powerful in this mortal world. What did this image suggest about blacks and blackness to the original reader or audience? Did colour play a significant role in this depiction? Or is this a more contemporary reading? In the absence of other direct models (and the Horner may indeed originate in Marchant's second edition of the *Kalender*), let us turn now to some related images that might explain the iconography further.

The third Magus, who is identified either as Balthasar or Caspar, King of the Moors, was commonly portrayed as black in most of Europe by the fifteenth century, as Paul Kaplan and John Block Friedman, among others, have pointed out. The image of the Moorish Magus was first popularised by Johannes von Hildesheim in the *Historia Trium Regum*, or *The Three Kings of Cologne*, composed between 1364 and 1375, a work that describes the journey of the Magi to see the Christ child, and their meetings with St Thomas the Apostle and 'Preter Johan', the fabled Priest-King of Ethiopia. *The Three Kings of Cologne* further includes a life of 'seynt Elyn', or St Helena, mother of the Emperor Constantine. The Middle English version of this text, which dates from about 1400, describes 'Iaspar', the Ethiopian king, as 'in persone moost [largest] of hem, an Ethiope and blak'. This is thought to be 'the first explicit statement in Western literature that one of the Kings was black'. Prester John is also described at some length. He is the literate and fabulously wealthy 'lord of all þe Indes, writyng into this day in his lettris and epistles many diuers vertues & dignitees'.[59] The *Three Kings* circulated in manuscript and print editions not only in Germany but in France and England through the 1520s, and is thought to have popularised the image of the black king, along with another work, the *Travels* of Sir John Mandeville, written in the 1360s. Kaplan remarks: 'As no unimpeachable example of a painted or sculpted figure of a black Magus/King survives from earlier than the 1360s, the *Historia Trium Regum* and the *Travels* appear to have been essential to the development of this character in the visual arts during the late fourteenth century and first half of the fifteenth.'[60]

The first known depiction of the King of the Moors as African appears in Germany, and most of the earliest extant visual examples are German, probably connected with the Magi cult at Cologne. Though texts of the *Three Kings* and the *Travels* circulated in France and England, black people appear only rarely in visual representation. In England, Kaplan finds the earliest example of the black king in a church window at Great Malvern dating to the very end of the fifteenth century, while in France the figure of the black king does not appear until the

Fig. 14. Adoration of the Magi. *Horae in laudem beatiss[ime] semper virginis Mariae* (Paris: Geoffroy Tory, 1525), sig. F3ʳ. BL C.27.k.15.

Fig. 15. Adoration of the Magi. *Hore in laudem beatissime virginis Marie* (Paris: Geoffroy Tory, 22 October 1527), sig. k2ʳ. BL C.27.h.17.

1480s and is usually based on Flemish models.[61] The black Magus does appear, however, in several lesser-known French prints of the period, in woodcuts of the Adoration of the Magi (Figs 14, 15) illustrating Books of Hours printed in Paris from 1525 to *c.* 1531 by Geoffroy Tory.[62] In the first example, the two other Magi are clothed and wear sandals, while the young black king is partially nude and draped. Shown with his back toward the viewer, this Magus is barefoot, with bracelets on each of his calves. He also wears ankle bracelets and an earring. In the other example, the black Magus is shown in profile. He is again crowned, this time gesturing toward the Christ child and holding an urn or ointment pot. And, again, he is shown draped while the other (elderly) Magi are clothed. In both prints, he is portrayed as an exotic Ethiopian, a view of black people held since antiquity but particularly appropriate in a period when diplomatic and religious contacts between Ethiopia and Europe were increasing. Envoys from Ethiopia had reached Venice in 1402, and Ethiopian pilgrims visited Rome in 1408.[63] First in Germany, then in the Low Countries and Italy, the Three Kings became representative of the peoples of the world, including the black African.

Depictions of blacks are also used to represent humanity as a whole in art of the earlier fifteenth century, as part of the fascination with the exotic new world of Africa. Jean, Duke of Berry, was interested in both Africa and India. In about 1430 he sent three emissaries to Ethiopia, where one of them met an Italian named Pietro Rombulo, who had been sent there by the Emperor on business in 1407 and had married an Ethiopian woman.[64] It is not surprising, then, to find black figures painted by the brothers Limbourg in several miniatures in the *Très Riches Heures*. In the 1969 facsimile, the black Africans observing the elevation of Christ are described as 'probably symbolic of all mankind'. In the scene of the Exaltation of the Cross, three black monks adoring the Cross are representative of the descendants of Noah who came to live in Africa, one of the three known continents in the Middle Ages.[65]

In a prophetic preaching scene from the *Très Riches Heures*, titled 'David Foresees the Preaching of the Apostles', the listeners are Africans and Caucasians, none of whom 'seems overly interested in the teaching'. They are again identified in the picture caption as representing the people of the world.[66] A similar teaching scene occurs in an illumination from the breviary of Louis de Guyenne, made in Paris about 1413, which depicts the traditional scene of St Matthew preaching to the Ethiopians. The saint is shown holding a book and pointing to two dragons in the sky, with a speech gesture, before a group of black men, the first wearing a turban and crossing his arms. The others are shown with scimitars and looking upward. According to Élisabeth Lalou and Claudia Rabel, this is a typical example of the taste for exoticism that characterised Parisian illumination at the beginning of the fifteenth century.[67]

An earlier depiction of a black man, perhaps more closely allied with our Horner in his role as the black harbinger of death in the Marchant imprint, is that of the tormentor or executioner. He appears, for example, in scenes of the beheading of John the Baptist in an English psalter from Canterbury, dated *c.* 1200, and on the north portal of the Cathedral of Notre Dame in Rouen, dated *c.* 1260.[68] As Ruth Mellinkoff says: 'Since it was often difficult to find men willing to perform the grisly acts of torturer or executioner, convicts, slaves, Jews, and blacks were sometimes drafted for these tasks.'[69] Because commercial and diplomatic relations with Africa did not become frequent until the fourteenth century, it is rather difficult to imagine black executioners actually plying their trade in thirteenth-century Rouen or Canterbury, and these figures probably derive from literary or exegetical texts rather than historical reality.

Mellinkoff, however, does note the often ambivalent presentation of the executioner figure, commenting that 'the clothing represented on many of these executioners does not suggest a criminal or servile status'.[70] Another example, a miniature of 'The Martyrdom of Saint Mark' from the *Très Riches Heures*, is a case in point. According to the story in the *Golden Legend*, Mark was sent by Peter to Alexandria to spread the word of God. While Mark was celebrating the

Easter mass, heathens slipped a noose around his neck and dragged him out of the church and through the streets to prison. In the miniature, a black man is holding a rope that has been slung around the saint's neck, dragging Mark away from the altar. The man is handsomely arrayed in a conical hat, gold epaulettes and a gold-embroidered silk tunic. Costume in this case is a marker suggesting the world of hagiographical legend rather than realistic depiction.[71]

During the thirteenth century, depictions of black figures began to be used as heraldic devices. The first known coat of arms of the Three Kings of Cologne is found in the Gelre Book of Arms, the work of the Guelders herald Claes Heinen, made *c.* 1369-1395. The crest of Caspar is shown with the profile head of a bearded white man, while above the crowned helm of the crest of Balthasar is the profile head of a black African.[72] This fascination with exotic depictions of blacks is perhaps most evident in an ornate heraldic illustration in the Hours of Claude Molé, made in Paris *c.* 1500 and now in the Pierpont Morgan Library (Fig. 16). The final miniature in this manuscript is a full-page representation of 'two Moors supporting Molé's coat of arms, which is surmounted by a helmet and a wreath and mantling of his colors, and crested by a nude female with a scroll bearing his motto, "Cuider decoit" (Beware of deceit)'.[73]

With the invention of printing, heraldic depictions of black figures soon made the transition from illumination to woodcut. The Freising armorial, for instance, continues to appear in printed editions of the Freising Missal. The Freising arms are seen in a woodcut produced in 1487 depicting the patron saints of the bishopric, Mary, Korbinian and Sigismund, with a shield with the profile head of a black king placed prominently in the foreground. The woodcut illustrates the edition of the Freising Missal printed by Johann Sensenschmidt in Bamburg. A related woodcut (Fig. 17) appears in Erhardt Ratdolt's edition of the Freising Missal printed in Augsburg in 1492. Again, Mary is shown crowned holding the Christ Child, flanked by the patrons of the city, and the shield with the head of a black king appears in the foreground.[74]

These heraldic devices, I would suggest, with their noble and imperial associations, would also become models for later printers' marks in which similar emblems occur. For example, a printer's mark showing two full figures of black women in profile (Fig. 18), wearing fanciful head dresses and holding up a shield and helmet, crowned with the profile head of a black man, frequently appears in books printed by the Le Noir family of printer–publisher–booksellers active in Paris about 1486-1520. The printer's mark, in this case, occurs in the copy of *Le grant kalendrier et compost des bergiers*, the *Shepherd's Kalender* edition published by Philippe Le Noir in 1523, which also contains a very rough copy of the Marchant Horner. A similar printer's mark was sometimes also employed by Jehan Trepperel, who was related to the Le Noir publishing family by marriage, and then by Trepperel's nameless widow, who continued the business after her husband's death, producing 121 books in the late fifteenth and early sixteenth centuries. Another printer's mark with a shield crested by a black man's profile head and beside it the name 'M. LeNoir', for Philippe's brother

Fig. 16. Arms of Claude Molé. Hours (Paris, *c.* 1500), fol. 66[r].
Morgan MS M. 356. New York, Pierpont Morgan Library.

Fig. 17. Shield with Crowned Head of Black Man. Freisinger Missale
(Augsburg: Erhardt Ratdolt, 1492), fol. 1ᵛ. BL IB 6727.

Fig. 18. Printer's Mark. *Le grant kalendrier et compost des bergiers* (Paris: Philippe Le Noir, 1523), sig. R4ᵛ (last leaf). BL C.34.g.16.

Michel Le Noir, also a printer (Fig. 19), was used as well by Philippe, along with other printers in this productive family. These figures serve as visual puns on the printers' family name, and they are also exotic and memorable, like representations found on other distinctive printer's marks in France – the twin lions, for example, in the mark of Jehan Petit, or the elephant used in the printer's mark employed by François Regnault and later by his widow, Madeleine Boursette.[75] By borrowing the signs of nobility, printers publicised their wares, using pseudo-heraldic devices to promote their products, their publishing houses and themselves.

Perhaps one explanation for the mysterious origin of the Marchant Horner lies in its printer. Guy Marchant produced a number of important books, including the Dance of Death, though he was essentially an academic publisher of Latin tract volumes.[76] But perhaps more important for this study is the fact that in 1493 Marchant produced three variant impressions of the letter in which Columbus announced his discovery of the New World; he was the only French printer to publish the letter. The fact that Marchant published the letter three times seems a strong indication that he was himself interested in discoveries of new continents and new people.[77] There is another piece of pictorial evidence that seems to support this. Marchant employed several printers' marks, one of which represents him as Prester John, the literate priest-king of Ethiopia (Fig. 20). The mark appears, for example, on the first page of *Le compost et*

Fig. 19. Printer's Mark. Pierre Gringore, *Le Casteau damours*, 2d ed.
(Paris: Michel Le Noir, February 1500), sig. f6ᵛ (last folio). BL IA. 40470.

Kalendrier des bergeres, a rare copy of the Kalender of Shepherdesses printed by Marchant in 1499 and now in the British Library.[78] The device was used by Guy Marchant from 1499 until 1504 or 1505, when it passed to Jean Marchant.[79] The life of the image did not end there, however. We find it again used some forty years later to represent the Emperor (Fig. 21) in an English book, copied and reproduced in Robert Wyer's translation of Christine de Pizan, *Here foloweth the .C. Hystoryes of Troye.*[80] The picture of the Horner and the poem that accompanies it did not occur in the manuscript exemplar for the printed *Kalender of Shepherds*, nor did they appear in the first issue of the *Kalender*

Fig. 20. Prester John as Printer's Mark. *Le co[m]post et Kalendrier des bergeres* (Paris: G. Marchant for himself and J. Petit, 1499), sig. a1ʳ. BL IB. 39718.

Fig. 21. The Emperor. Christine de Pizan, *Here foloweth the .C. Hystoryes of Troye*, trans. Robert Wyer (London: Robert Wyer, *c.* 1540-1550), sig. U6ᵛ. *STC* 7272. BL C.21.a.34.

printed by Marchant in 1493. But, for the *Kalender* edition of 1500, Marchant has prepared a woodcut (and perhaps a text) that would be reprinted in France for some seventy years. A closely copied image of the Horner would also appear in England for about eighty years.

What did images like these suggest about black people and blackness to their original audiences? According to Ruth Mellinkoff, 'People with racial or ethnic features different from the majority elicited antipathy ..., but attitudes toward them were sometimes ambivalent or contradictory. A white-skinned society could tolerate a black magus and a black St Maurice because they represented an abstract piety, but more often white society viewed blacks as physically and morally ugly, and therefore inferior and despicable.'[81] Our examples, however, show the figure of the black man, often fancifully represented in exotic costume, as the wise and royal Magus, as a witness to Christ and the Cross, as a symbol of the African and more generally as a symbol of mankind. As Peter Mark observes, 'By the second third of the fifteenth century, dark Africans had appeared in the art of Italy, Germany and even France. Neither the writings nor the artistic representations of Negroid people of the period indicate any anti-black prejudice.'[82] This was a time when unfree people, including slaves, were

180

Fig. 22. Black Man in the Retinue of Margaret of York. Miscellany in French (Ghent, written by David Aubert, March 1475), fol. cxv^r. Bodleian Library MS Douce 365. By permission of the Bodleian Library, Oxford.

Fig. 23. Moorish Dancer. German, sculpted by Erasmus Grasser, *c.* 1480. Polychromed wood, from the ballroom of the Munich city hall (Münchner Stadtmuseum Ic/222).

mostly Europeans, when the image of the black African as a slave had not yet arisen, and when European traders and explorers had to be cautious and humble in their dealings with African chiefs.[83] Based upon the pattern of pictures examined here, social attitudes toward black people before the association of race with slavery in the New World seem to have been mainly positive. Certainly in the three main print examples under consideration, Marchant's Horner, the Magus in the Tory Hours and the pseudo-heraldic figures in the Le Noir family printers' marks, black people are shown as exotic emblems of power and prestige. During the periods of exploration and trade with west Africa, black people were portrayed with increasing frequency in art, and 'As Africans became more common in cities from southern Italy to the Low Countries, artists' approaches to the black man as subject matter underwent an evolution', becoming less focused on the exotic and tending toward realism.[84] We see, for example, a black man in the retinue of Margaret of York, duchess of Burgundy, from the manuscript collection of moral and religious treatises written at Ghent in 1475 by David Aubert (Fig. 22), and a lively Moorish dancer (Fig. 23), wearing kit that looks just like that of a contemporary morris dancer, from the ballroom of the Munich city hall, sculpted about 1480 by Erasmus Grasser.[85]

If we are agreed that art can serve to document the ideas and observations of artists and that representations of black people, like other types of representation, can provide historical information as well as ideas about and insight into attitudes toward Africans in western Europe in this period, we might then ask: What led printers such as Guy Marchant and members of the Le Noir family to produce and associate themselves with images of black men and women? Why does Marchant identify himself in an early printer's mark with the mythical king Prester John, who himself was often portrayed as black? Woodcuts like these reflect powerful late medieval fantasies which 'provide a key to distinctive drives at the heart of cultures: their force and intelligibility rely upon pervasive, well-established connections that don't require, and frequently resist, conscious explanation'.[86] By representing themselves as black and using similar depictions to market their books, these printers were perhaps embracing the idea of an earthly paradise, a kingdom of wealth beyond compare ruled by Prester John. And why are images of an exotically dressed young black man blowing a horn so pervasive and so long-lived, crossing the Channel to be copied and reprinted in English books? Perhaps we might attribute this to excitement over the opening of west Africa to trade and the discovery of the New World, and exclaim with Shakespeare's Miranda: 'How beauteous mankind is! / O brave new world / That has such people in't!'[87]

Considering the various examples presented here, we might say at the very least that pictures can help us reconstruct social custom as well as attitudes toward history, and that images may be used, with some care, to fill out the written historical record. Furthermore, there are many interesting contrasts between reality and depiction that are worth further consideration. Seemingly conventional marriage scenes, through their widespread circulation in print, helped to promote the religious aspect of the ritual that becomes increasingly prominent toward the beginning of the sixteenth century. Drawings that purport to record real events are taken, at least in part, from model books, though an accomplished artist can draw us into a visual world of knights and battles where the picture seems to reproduce the event. Simpler woodcut scenes introduce us to one man's historical journey to the Holy Land as told by his priest, and to an account of the siege of Troy which is seen as an actual occurrence, a turning-point in the history of the world. Both narratives, however, are illustrated with repeatable woodcuts. The late medieval idea of history, it seems, was more fluid than our own: it spilled over into other genres, among them literature and the visual arts. We have also seen how representations of tools are associated with, and become attributes of, specific occupations – tools that actually existed, and in some cases exist still, and that were put to very real uses in composing, studying and production of the written word. Evidence is available in plenty to show how woodcuts and other images picture a world of lives and practices that we should otherwise know only imperfectly and abstractly from report. In the examples of the representations of black people in particular, we glimpse a world in which the outsider is not defined by Western culture (as is conventionally thought) in terms of its own projection of fears, tensions and anxieties but is rather embraced as a reflection of the self, as a brother.

APPENDIX: THE HORNER'S SONG

I. From *Cy est le compost et kalendrier des bergiers nouuellement et autrement compose* ... (Paris: Guy Marchant, 1500)

Dictie des trespassez en forme de balade. et du iugement.

> Venimeuses tu qui portes la corne
> Tous escornans de ton escorne cor
> Au contraire d'une grande licorne
> Rendant le lieu plus intoxique encor
> Encor cornes cornement d'un grant cor
> Dont les cornars sen vont a la cornee
> Tous escornes nayas en leurs cors cor
> Auecques toute cornardie escornee
>
> Celle sera bien de corne cornee
> Dont luy fauldra sa grant cornete
> Quau monde n'est pas encor nee
> Et escoutant le hault son du cor nete
> Netz en espritz aussi netz du corps nete
> Dont vostre ame se sera encornee
> Du grant cornu qui sans cesse cornete
> Auecques toute cornardie escornee
>
> Escornee sera du cornement
> D'une tant terrible cornacion
> Fort cornante et se le cor ne ment
> Eschape nest encor nacion
> La nacion nest qui de ces cornetz
> Ainsi cornans en puist estre exemplee
> Car la seres infectz ou des corps netz?
> Auecques toute cornardie escornee.
>
> Encor ne naist nul exempt du cornu
> Ne de celle grande cornarderie
> Et quant chascun sera la du corps nu
> Garde naures quune cornardie rie
> Cornarderie naura quelque cornarde
> Ne escorne cornard a la iournee
> Donques prions a dieu que nos corps narde
> Auecques toute cornardie escornee.
>
> O sait michel garde nous du cornant
> De corps cornu car se le corne rompt
> Cornupetant nous venra escornant
> Quant les anges de leur cor corneront
> Le corps ne rompt iames aux bien cornez
> Aux oreilles cornans nuit et vespree
> Pour nous rendre de nos corps escornez
> Auecques toute cornardie escornee.

II. From the *Kalender of Shepardes*, translated by Robert Copland (transcribed from London, Julian Notary, 1518?: occurs in *STC* 22408, 22409, 22410, 22410, 22411, 22412, 22415, 22416; that is, in editions from 1506 to *c.* 1585)

How euery man and woman ought to cease of theyr synnes at ye sownynge of a dredable horne

> Ho / ho / you blynde folke / derked in ye clowde
> Of ignoraunt fumes / thycke & mystycall
> Take hede of my horne / totynge all alowde
> With boystous sownes / & blastes boryall
> Gyuynge you warnynge / of the Jogement fynall
> The whiche dayly is redy / to gyue sentence
> On peruers people / replete with neclygence.
>
> Ho / ho betyme / or that it be to late
> Cease whyle ye haue spake / and portunate
> Leue your folyes / or deth make you chekmate
> Cease your ignoraunt / incredulyte
> Clense your thoughtes / of immundycyte
> Cease of your / pecunyall pensement
> The whiche defyleth / your entendement. ...
>
> Fle faynt falshod / fykell fowle and fell
> Fle fatall flateres / full of fayrenes
> Fle fayre faynynge / fables of fauelle
> Fle folkes felawshyp / frequentyng falsenes
> Fle frantyke facers / fulfylled of frowardnes
> Fle foles falaces / fle fonde fancysyes
> Fle from fresshe bablers / faynynge flateryes.
> Thus endeth the horner.

Chapter 6

ICONOCLASM AND REFORM
THE SURVIVAL OF LATE MEDIEVAL
IMAGES AND THE PRINTED BOOK

Pictures contained in [the Revelation of John and in Moses and Joshua] we would paint on walls for the sake of remembrance and better understanding, since they do no more harm on walls than in books. It is to be sure better to paint pictures on walls of how God created the world, how Noah built the ark, and whatever other good stories they may be, than to paint shameless worldly things. Yes, would to God that I could persuade the rich and the mighty that they would permit the whole Bible to be painted on houses, on the inside and outside, so that all can see it.[1]

THESE WORDS of Martin Luther in his treatise 'Against the Heavenly Prophets' of 1524/5 stand in strong contrast to the well-known iconoclasm of the Reformation – the beheading or pulling down of statues of popes, saints and the Virgin Mary, the smashing of stained glass, the whitewashing of wall paintings, the desecration of places of pilgrimage and the like. Yet in fact, as the quotation shows, Luther was by no means opposed to all religious use of visual images. On the contrary, he followed the tradition of Gregory the Great's famous remark that 'what scriptures show to those who read, a picture shows to the illiterate people'. As David Freedberg has pointed out, 'Pictures were justified because they were the books of the illiterate … and writers like Luther (and to some extent Zwingli and Calvin too) emphasized the value of pictures which showed histories and were not cult images of Christ and the Virgin' that might promote misunderstanding among the unread. But, Freedberg continues, 'justifying images in terms of their value to the ignorant, the simple, and the illiterate clearly evaded many of the ontological issues that had been raised. … None of the writers, from Gregory to Luther, approved of the adoration of miracle-working images or cult images generally; but these were exactly the kinds of images that lay at the center of the religiosity of simple folk.'[2] From Gregory to Luther, as Freedberg points out, illiterate folk (that is, the uneducated lower classes) were generally thought to be excessively susceptible to the power of images and unable to discern between good and bad pictures or between symbol and reality. They were seen as being in need of guidance by those who could govern them better than themselves. This was why Protestants destroyed images that, in their view, instructed the people in false and misleading beliefs. It was a reason for them to censor, deface and gloss late medieval manuscripts, printed books and indulgence texts that contained material that they found objectionable, alongside other material that was still, from their point of view, instructive and spiritually elevating. Simultaneously, the reformers saw the value of using images to express their own beliefs, both as propaganda and as an aid to devotion – above all in printed books, which they exploited so thoroughly as a means of spreading Reformation doctrine. Particularly interesting to observe are the number of medieval books, religious and secular, in manuscript and print, that have been censored by later Protestant commentators and yet still survive to this day. Images in books, which we have seen developing out of single-leaf prints, acting as aids to readers, helping to market books and functioning as to illustrate and promote cultural values and social activities, also had a substantial impact upon and were themselves influenced by the social and political changes of the Reformation.

In 1522, Lucas Cranach the Elder and the goldsmith Christian Döring financed the printing of 5000 copies of Luther's New Testament, the first Protestant translation. The book appeared on 21 September and sold out within a few weeks; a second edition was printed three months later. The only illustrations in Luther's 'September Testament', woodcuts supplied by Cranach, appear in the Apocalypse. These were based on woodcuts made earlier by Albrecht Dürer and on medieval manuscript models.[3]

In his first preface to the Apocalypse, written in 1522, Luther could barely conceal his distaste for the book, commenting that it was difficult to understand and 'revealed nothing', and that St Jerome's praise for it 'at numerous places is far too generous'. But by 1530, when Luther wrote his second preface, he had become keenly aware of the book's propagandistic possibilities, a realisation that directly stemmed from Cranach's controversial illustrations for the September Testament, which were among the earliest instances of Protestant propaganda.[4]

In Cranach's illustrations, Babylon is depicted as Rome. The Whore of Babylon, the dragon, and the beast wear the papal tiara,[5] and in the woodcut of the beast vomiting frogs (Fig. 1), the beast is shown seated on the cushioned papal throne, again wearing the papal tiara. Dürer, whose earlier Apocalypse series was one model used by Cranach, omits this scene of the angels pouring out the seven bowls of wrath, described in Revelation 16. St Jerome does not mention it in his commentary, nor does Luther in his first preface. But in his second preface of 1530, Luther provides what seems to be a close description of the significance of the action in Cranach's picture: 'The throne of the beast – the pope's power – becomes dark and wretched and despised … three frogs, three foul spirits, issue from the mouth of the beast and stir up kings and princes against the gospel.'

Cranach's illustrations raised such an outcry that in the next edition of Luther's New Testament, published in December of 1522, the papal tiaras were scraped off the blocks, probably at the command of the Elector Frederick or Duke George of Saxony. This left what Colin Eisler aptly describes as a 'somewhat mystifying but inoffensive nimbus'.[6] In other, later editions, the papal crowns were sometimes painted over. However, the specific identification of the pope with Antichrist, indeed with all the evil characters in the Apocalypse, had

Fig. 1. Seven Bowls of Wrath Poured Out by Angels. Lucas Cranach, in Martin Luther, trans., *Das Neue Testament Deutsch* ['September Testament'] (Wittenberg: Melchior Lotter, 1522), opposite p. lxxxviii. BL 1562/285.

Fig. 2. The Two Witnesses.
Hans Holbein, in Martin
Luther, trans., *Das Neue
Testament Deutsch*
(Strassburg: Johann
Knobloch, 1524), sig. Ji2ʳ.
BL 3035.c.13.

taken hold. While Jerome had interpreted the general conflict in the Apocalypse as a confrontation between the Roman Empire and the Church, Luther saw no essential difference between them: the pope and the Roman Empire were one and the same, enemies to be defeated by Protestant reformers. A woodcut by Hans Holbein, reproduced in Luther's New Testament of 1524, shows the two witnesses and the beast, who again wears the papal crown (Fig. 2), as John measures the Temple in the background. Holbein's illustration is based on Cranach's original in the September Testament.

The illustrations by the monogrammist M.S. in the Luther Bibles of 1534 and 1538 show a slightly different version of the same scene (Fig. 3).[7] The Temple is an exact replica of the Castle Church at Wittenberg, with Luther's pulpit. The two witnesses speak, as they do in Revelation 11, with tongues of fire. Here they are dressed as evangelical preachers, and Luther likewise describes them, in his

Fig. 3. The Two Witnesses. Monogrammist M.S., in Martin Luther, trans.,
Das ist die Gantze Heilige Schrifft Deudsch, vol. 2 (Wittenberg:
Hans Lufft, 1534), sig. Kk3ʳ. BL I.b.10.

preface, as 'pious teachers and Christians'. The beast, or Antichrist, is once more portrayed wearing an elaborate papal mitre. In Roman Catholic Bibles of the same period, we see similar illustrations that are close in style to the illustration in Protestant Bibles, though without the virulent political commentary. In a woodcut from a Vulgate New Testament printed in Paris *c.* 1541 (Fig. 4), the image is clearly based on Holbein's version, but the papal tiara is missing entirely.[8]

In 1545, Luther formally instructed artists to use the Roman allusions in Revelation as a basis for antipapal caricature. This had, however, already begun as early as 1521. The *Passional Christi und Antichristi*, published in 1521, contains 26 woodcuts by Lucas Cranach contrasting the life of Christ with papal life and government – the Antichrist of the new Protestant polemic.[9] Woodcuts show Christ washing the feet of a disciple (opposite a scene of a man kissing the pope's foot), and Christ driving the money-changers from the temple as the pope counts his fortune, for example; other pairs of pictures illustrate the mocking of Christ with the Crown of Thorns facing a scene of the crowning of the Roman emperor, and finally, Christ ascending as King of Heaven as the Antichrist pope is flung into hell.[10] The seventh pair of images (Fig. 5) shows Christ on the left page

Fig. 4. The Two Witnesses. *Novvm testamentum* (Paris: Fran. Gryphius, 1541) sig. Q2^r. BL 3022.a.34.

preaching to the multitude. On the right, the pope, seated under a canopy, is enjoying a lavish meal (note the servant carrying three dishes at once) with a bishop, canon and monk. The text below describes bishops as too busy with their political affairs to preach God's word and as gluttonous 'animals' devoted only to living well.

Criticism, often explicit, of the gluttony, carnality and worldliness of the Catholic clergy reappeared in later Protestant polemical tracts. In a broadside (a later form of single-leaf print) based on the story of Dives and Lazarus, the pope is shown at the banquet table, embracing a nun, as a monk vomits in the foreground (Fig. 6). At the right, we see Lazarus, actually a portrait of Luther, pointing to an open book in his lap, emphasising the primacy of the word, while in the background, the naked pope, still wearing his tiara, is shown descending into the flames of hell. The text condemns the worldly concerns of the pope and his corrupt cronies, contrasting these with the virtues of Luther and his followers.[11]

Cranach's woodcuts, based on earlier models, alerted Luther to the possibilities afforded by the Book of Revelation for anti-Catholic propaganda and made him more keenly aware of the force of the image. Luther, a 'conservative' Reformer, understood the value of pictures to promote Protestant ideas, just as he advocated the suppression of other kinds of pictures. This ambivalence towards images is also seen in English examples of the period.

For example, a mixed response to the purpose and power of images is found in an English book *The ymage of loue*, which was first printed by de Worde for John Gough in 1525, and in its subsequent history.[12] 'Compyled by John Ryckes / bacheler in diuinite / an obseruant fryre', *The ymage of loue* was translated by Gough, an early sympathiser with the Reformation.[13] It was symptomatic of the

Fig. 5. Christ Preaching, the Pope Feasting. Lucas Cranach, *Passional Christi und Antichristi* (Wittenberg: Johann Grunenberg, 1521), sigs B3ᵛ-4ʳ. BL C.53.c.6.

1520s, when the lines between late medieval Catholic scruples and Protestant rejection of Catholicism had not yet been clearly drawn, that the book was printed for the learned nuns of the piously orthodox Bridgettine house of Syon. It was one of several books printed by de Worde for Gough, who seems to have sponsored books rather than printing them himself. Because of its criticism of images, the work was suspected of being heretical.[14] In 1524 de Worde was 'one of those warned by Bishop Tunstall against importing Lutheran books into England. ... A year later he was again summoned before the bishop with John Gough to answer a charge of having published a work called *The Image of Love*. De Worde confessed that he was one of those present in the previous year and that since that date he had printed *The Image of Love*, which was alleged to contain heresy, and had sent sixty copies to the nuns of Syon and had sold as many more. The two men were warned not to sell any more and to get back those they had already sold.'[15] *The ymage of loue* was presumably deemed heretical because of its iconoclastic subject.

The author, the 'observant friar' John Ryckes, says he wishes 'to gyue some

Fig. 6. The Pope as a Rich Man at Table. Engraving in anonymous German broadsheet, *c.* 1562. By permission of Arts, Prints, and Photographs, Kennedy Fund, New York Public Library.

goodly pyctures & ymages of our sauyour Jesu / of our blessed lady / or of some other holy sayntes', though there are no actual pictures in the second issue of this volume save that on the title-page. The images in this text are verbal, not visual. The author then criticises the false images drawn by 'dame Nature' whose 'colours faded / and dayly dyd dekaye'. Such images are 'also commune to fooles / to wyse men / to chrysten men / to hethen men / to beestes / to fowles & serpentes & lytell profyte commeth of them', especially because, the writer continues, making his most inflammatory statement, 'These ymages be often tymes paynted undiscretly & disceyuably / and dothe moche harme in the chyrche of god.'

The text is critical but also ambivalent about the use of images. They can be seductive and misleading, as is the image of carnal love, portrayed here as a beautiful woman with a high forehead, 'yelowe' hair, with 'skyn white as lilly' and a serpent's tail, who calls 'yonge persones in to her shoppe by flaterynge wordes saying. Comme to me goodly yonge gentylmen / I haue goodly pyctures and images for you / ye shal haue one of me for your love / it shall cost you nought.' Here images are associated with superficial, physical love, not with the true love of God. But later the writer echoes Gregory, arguing that images are the books of the laity and commenting further that inexpensive images are as good as costly ones for inspiring devotion: 'these ymages ben the bokes of laye people symple & unlerned / that be unperfyte in goostly lyfe / & yf they excite peoples myndes to deuocyon / as well that may be by suche as be of lytell pryce / as by them that be of great price & curiously wrought.' *The ymage of loue*, in other words, is not as iconoclastic as it would at first seem, arguing, as Luther himself also did, that images could have appropriate uses within the limits of Church doctrine.[16] However, the writer does conclude that the best images are those 'not … seen of the bodyly eyes' but glimpsed through a glass darkly and imprinted on the eternal soul.

In his *Dialogue to the Ymage of Love*, Thomas More referred to the author as 'the good holy man' who 'layeth sore against these carved and painted Ymages. … And he sheweth full well that ymages be but laymens bookes, and therefore that religious men … whould let all such dede ymages passe and labour onely for the lyvely quicke ymage of love.' These words, however, are placed in the mouth of the Messenger who represents the opponent, or devil's advocate, in More's text. Nonetheless (and because any publicity is apparently good publicity), it is thought that More's extended reference to the book prompted Gough to republish it later, 'in the safer days of Thomas Cromwell', with de Worde again as the printer.[17]

Gough would become known for his radical iconoclasm. He may have been involved in printing 'the first book that openly canvassed the cause of iconoclasm in English: a translation of Martin Bucer's *Das einigerlei Bild*' in 1535, and he certainly was one of a gang of men arrested for pulling down a popular holy image, the Rood of St Margaret Pattens in London, on 23 May 1538, and breaking it to bits.[18] And in 1541, Gough was imprisoned in the Fleet for printing seditious books.[19] He was also an overseer of de Worde's will in 1535 and received a legacy of books from de Worde, along with forgiveness of debts. Gough was perhaps the most outspoken and radical Protestant reformer with connections to de Worde's shop.

The woodcut of the Trinity on the title-page of *The ymage of love* (Chapter 3, Fig. 21) may have been made specifically for this volume.[20] Ironically, the title-page image of the Trinity was used to promote religious belief (and sell the book), even as the text condemned the unthinking worship of religious images. This curious and ambivalent historical document reveals the growing tensions between orthodox and reforming belief in the years just before the English Reformation. It is also interesting to note that while the first edition of 1525 contains several woodcut illustrations, the second edition of *The ymage of love*, published *c.* 1532, retains only the title-image and has no other pictures, a seeming consequence of the initial condemnation of the work for heresy.

Soon, however, images themselves would be seen as the outward and visible signs of Antichrist, objects to be destroyed by devout and fanatical Reformers in England and on the continent. That applied also to images in books, with an important difference – that very often the destruction or effacing of an image did not involve the destruction of the whole artefact.

Volumes originally intended for pious lay Catholics, or for nuns or priests, often fell into the hands of Protestants. A flyleaf of a Book of Hours printed in Paris for Antoine Vérard about 1503, now in the Pierpont Morgan Library, has an inscription in an early seventeenth-century hand: 'This Book was Brought from west Court itt is A Papist Book as I suppose and not To be made Use of.'[21] In some cases, Protestant revisers added to rather than destroyed the text. There are, for example, extensive and radical anti-Catholic commentaries (Fig. 7) on page after page of a Book of Hours in the Bodleian Library, an early de Worde imprint.[22] The same kind of virulent anti-Catholic marginalia, in a single seventeenth-century hand, are on many of the pages of the Pierpont Morgan Library copy of the *Mirror of Our Lady*, the English translation of the services of the Bridgettine nuns, printed by Richard Fawkes in 1530. On the title-page is written: 'A Glass wherein may bee seene þe Idollatry & Impiety superstition & Irreligion of þe Church of Roome & of þ(e) Followers of þe pope.' Beneath a woodcut of St Bridget on the verso of the title-page occurs this comment: 'you may take notice þat þe Idolatrus pappists þat pretend to own þe scripture and þat they might impose upon þe Ignorant ...' (Fig. 8). Beside the hymn to the Virgin Mary *Rubens rosa*, the glossator comments, 'This hymn is filled with their blasphemy and Idolatry.' And after the colophon occurs this anxious commentary: 'This booke though it bee sinne y[t] use of it was in ye monastery of Sion yet papists doie kepe for another day, and then we may see which an abominable seruice will bee obtruded uppon thee people.'[23] One wonders why this early seventeenth-century reader did not simply destroy his copy – and is immediately grateful he did not do so. Our commentator was apparently reading *Mirror of Our Lady* as standard Catholic dogma, studying the enemy to prepare against the day when Catholicism might reign again in England.

Catholic books might also be selectively defaced to remove material that was now thought objectionable, while preserving the rest. This was what many English owners of works of devotion did following the prohibition of the cult of St Thomas Becket. Protestant defacement of images and texts relating to Thomas Becket in England followed Thomas Cromwell's Injunctions of September 1538 against pilgrimage and the cults of saints and relics, and later, the 1539 desecration of the Becket shrine at Canterbury Cathedral. A clause attached to

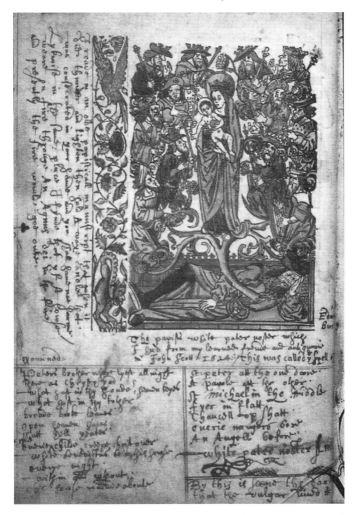

Fig. 7. 'The papist white Pater Noster'. *Horae ad usum Sarum* (London: de Worde, 1502), sig. A2ᵛ. *STC* 15898. Bodleian Library Arch. G.e.39. By permission of the Bodleian Library, Oxford.

Henry VIII's proclamation issued on 16 November 1538 against 'contentious and sinister opinions … by wrong teaching and naughty printed books' directly attacked Becket, whose shrine at Canterbury had been pillaged early in September and his bones scattered.[24] Denounced as a rebel against his king, Becket was no longer to be venerated as a saint, and his images and pictures were to be 'put down and avoided out of all churches, chapels and other places'. His name was to be erased from all liturgical books, and his office, antiphons and collects were to be said no more. The effect of this proclamation was immediate

Fig. 8. 'þe idolatrous papists'. *Mirror of Our Lady* (London: Richard Fawkes,
4 November 1530), title-page verso. *STC* 17542. PML 17691.
By permission of the Pierpont Morgan Library.

and pervasive. Book owners removed Becket's name from the calendars and his
prayers from the texts of their Books of Hours. We find, for example, Becket's
name removed from the calendar page of the Tilney Hours (Fig. 9), made in
England for the Tilney family in the last third of the fifteenth century, a
manuscript copied in Latin with English rubrics and now in the Pierpont
Morgan Library. In another example, from a fifteenth-century Hours now in the
Brotherton Library, University of Leeds (Fig. 10), the vellum page of prayers to
Becket has been virtually scraped clean. In MS Richardson 34, a Book of Hours

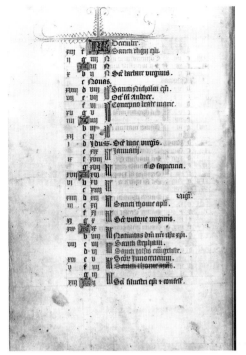

Fig. 9. Defaced calendar. The Tilney Hours (English, fifteenth century), fol. 9ᵛ. Morgan M. 1033. By permission of the Pierpont Morgan Library.

Fig. 10. Defaced page of prayers. English, fifteenth century. The Brotherton Library, Leeds, MS 15. By permission of the Brotherton Library, University of Leeds.

for Sarum use copied in the later fifteenth century and now housed in the Houghton Library, Harvard, the twelve spectacular illuminations remain untouched, but a Reformation censor has edited the book, removing the name of Becket and the word 'pope' fairly consistently in the calendar and crossing out prayers relating to Becket in the text.[25]

Effacement or partial erasure of Becket images is found as well in printed books of the late fifteenth century, perhaps even more consistently than in manuscript, though I have not done a complete survey. The hours for Becket are defaced, and the names of Becket and some popes deleted from the calendar pages of a Sarum Hours printed in Paris in 1495 that formerly belonged to the Carthusian house of Sheen.[26] Becket's face has been inked out in the scene of his murder from William Caxton's *Golden Legend* printed in 1483 (Fig. 11). A defaced woodcut of this scene occurs in the copy of Caxton's *Golden Legend* formerly in the Botsfield collection of Longleat House, and it is unusual to find it at all in surviving volumes. In the copies that I have examined in the New York Public Library and elsewhere, the Becket woodcut has been ripped out, an unequivocal and direct response to Henry's proclamation.[27]

Fig. 11. Becket Slain at the Altar. Jacobus de Voragine, *Legenda aurea* (Westminster: Caxton, 1483), fol. 105^r. *STC* 24873. Formerly in the collection of the Marquess of Bath, Longleat House, Warminster, Wiltshire.

The copy of Julian Notary's edition of the *Kalender of Shepherds* in the British Library, which was printed about 1518, includes a censored text that discusses the Ave Maria. The problematic portion of text in this case directs readers to pray to St Thomas Becket as an intercessor for the forgiveness of their sins.[28] In a Book of Hours for Sarum use printed in 1521 for Francis Byrkman, now in the Bodleian Library (Fig. 12), a prayer to Becket and the introduction to it have been cross-hatched, and his head in the accompanying illustration has been blotted with ink. On sig. D4^v, the border pieces around an illustration of the Annunciation are adorned with the Tudor rose and a shield with the arms of Henry VIII, celebrating Henry's coronation. A later sixteenth-century owner, probably the 'Johnis Bell' who wrote his name on the title-page of this volume ('Liber Johnis Bell ex dono Thame Bagsha'), wrote at the end of the text of Prime (sig. d1^v): 'This is a ranke Papis [*sic*] Booke.'[29] In another Sarum Hours printed in Paris for Francis Byrkman in 1519, now in Archbishop Marsh's Library, Dublin, prayers relating to Becket are again crossed out. The text is in a somewhat corrupt form of English which sometimes is found in French editions of English books, though the defacing hand is not correcting grammar or spelling. The censor of this volume has been particularly assiduous (Fig. 13), censoring images of the Virgin Mary and crossing out an indulgence granted by 'The rygth reuerent father in god laurence byshop', a description of a prayer as 'Ad deuowte

Fig. 12. Becket defaced. *Horae ad usum Sarum* (Paris, for Francis Byrkman, 1521),
sig. b7ᵛ. *STC* 15931. Bodleian Library Douce BB 135. By permission of the
Bodleian Library, Oxford.

prayer of the vii. sprytualle yoies of owre blessed lady showet vntho saynt thomas
of cantorberi', and another 'devote prayer' to the Virgin made by 'saint edmund
archebyscop of cantorberi' through which many miracles are said to have
occurred. The censored titles in the volume are in English, and the corrector,
if we may so call him, has left most of the Latin text alone. There is also a
seventeenth-century glossing hand which appears sporadically, writing such
comments as 'the popish collect' beside the printed text.[30]

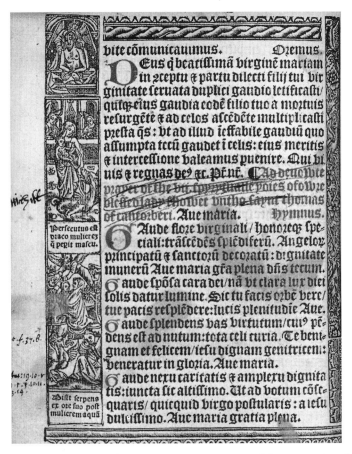

Fig. 13. Becket defaced. *Hore b[ea]tissime virginis Marie ad legitimum Sarisburiensis ecclesie ritum* (Paris: Nicholas Higman for François Regnault and Francis Byrckman, 1519), sig. D2r. Z1.2.8. *STC* 15924. By permission of the Governors and Guardians of Marsh's Library, Dublin.

The word 'pope' was stricken from Books of Hours, Bibles and the *Golden Legend* in accordance with a 1542 order to purge 'all manner of mention of the bishop of Rome's name, from all apocrypha, feigned legends, superstitious orations, collects, versicles and responses' that Thomas Cranmer, archbishop of Canterbury, obtained from the Convocation. Such censorship occurs, for example, in the British Library copy of the *Ordynarye of Crystyanyte*, printed by de Worde in 1502 (de Worde's later edition, which is similar though not identical, has been discussed previously as *ThOrdynary of Crysten Men*). In this vernacular religious handbook directed to lay readers, the word 'pope' has been inked out by a later reader, who is also concerned to censor the portion of text that explains confession and 'absolucyon [which] is reserued vnto the pope the whiche they ought to knowe and to note the whiche heren the confessyons'.[31]

Soon after Becket was outlawed and obedient subjects took to inking out or cutting out his images, along with pictures of papal mitres and the Virgin Mary, and removing the word 'pope' from their religious books, we also find reform affecting vernacular, non-religious texts. In a Cambridge University Library manuscript of the B-version of *Piers Plowman*, for example, a later italic hand has written 'nota howe fallshedd fyrst krept In by the pope and his flock' (20.58) and 'ipsa papa' as an interlinear gloss above 'anticryst' (20.53). The same hand has also drawn a marginal line next to the following six lines. In a copy of the C-text in the Huntington Library, the name 'Peres the plouhman' has been erased throughout, presumably because 'Peres' was read as 'Peter' or pope.[32] The word 'pope' is also typically crossed out in both manuscript and print copies of Chaucer's *Canterbury Tales*. In the copy of Caxton's *Golden Legend* in the Rare Book Room of the New York Public Library, all references to the pope have been obliterated by brown ink, and cross-hatchings appear throughout several saints' lives, in addition to that of Thomas Becket. Similarly, the word 'pope' with its related adjectives ('poperyche', 'poperiche') has been consistently crossed out in a copy of Ranulf Higden's *Polychronicon* in Durham University Library, printed by de Worde in 1495.[33]

One of the most interesting English examples of the censorship of the word 'pope' occurs in Glasgow University Library, MS Hunterian 5, S.1.5, a fifteenth-century manuscript of John Lydgate's *Fall of Princes*, in the portion of text describing Pope Joan. It has been suggested that the identification of the papacy with the Whore of Babylon in early Protestant polemic might have derived, in part, from the legend of Pope Joan, which retained some currency at the end of the Middle Ages. The story tells how Joan, who was either 'Ghiberta, daughter of a Mainz citizen' or possibly one 'Agnes of England', disguised herself as a man, learned Latin from her student-lover and travelled with him to England, where she took her doctorate, became a cardinal and then was elected pope on the death of Leo IV. Two years later, the pregnant pope 'unexpectedly gave birth near St John Lateran in the middle of a procession. Thereafter, no pope would pass in procession near this spot, and a special chair was created for papal elections, in which the pope had to display his male genitalia in order to prevent a woman ever again being elected.'[34]

The censor of the Hunterian manuscript has emended all of the feminine pronouns in the story to the masculine form and crossed out all other references to Joan's femaleness. For example, in the line 'No wight supposyng but that she was a man', the words 'she was a man' have been crossed out. In the lines 'Beyng a woman wherof Bochas toke hede, like a prelate shapyn was hir wede', the censor has crossed out the word 'woman' and emended 'hir' to 'his'. Two stanzas have been obliterated entirely. One would expect that this might be an orthodox censor objecting to the idea of the corruption of the papacy embodied by a female pope, but the censor has also crossed out all Roman references as well as

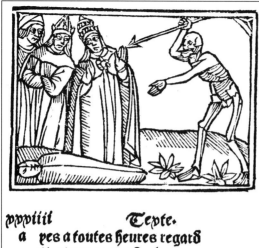

pppiiii   Texte.
a pes a toutes heures regars
A attropos et a son dart
Qui fiert et nespargne nul ame
Ce te fera penser de lame

Fig. 14. Death Strikes. Christine de Pizan, *Les cent histoires de troye* (Paris, Philippe Le Noir, 30 November 1522), sig. 3C^v. PML 41003. By permission of the Pierpont Morgan Library.

'the Pope' which 'called was Leon'. This is the most extensive censorship in the volume, seemingly by a prudish Protestant who misunderstood the propagandistic possibilities inherent in the story of Pope Joan.[35]

Another example of religious reform extending even to literary texts is found in the .C. *Hystoryes of Troye*, the English version of Christine de Pizan's *Letter of Othea to Hector*, which appeared between 1540 and 1550, translated into English and printed in London by Robert Wyer. Wyer, who was active from about 1523, had been brought before the bishop's vicar-general in 1527, and charged with both translating and printing a heretical book about the Apostles' Creed. However, he remained sufficiently prominent in the community to serve as churchwarden in the parish of St Martin-in-the-Fields, and printed some 145 known items over his career. For his edition of the .C. *Hystoryes*, Wyer used French texts of Christine's *Epistre* as models, particularly the *editio princeps* printed in Paris by Philippe Pigouchet *c.* 1500 and a second Paris edition, which appeared on 30 November 1522, printed by Philippe Le Noir.[36]

In Texte 34, Christine's discussion of Atropos, both French editions are illustrated by a woodcut (Fig. 14) showing Death as a skeleton striking with his dart a pope, a bishop and another man before a corpse lying on the ground sewn in its shroud. The woodcut is visual shorthand for a whole body of *ars moriendi* themes popular in the later Middle Ages. It calls up associations with the Dance of Death sequences popular with French printers from the 1470s, with their emphasis on the different estates and the portrayal of Death as a skeleton armed

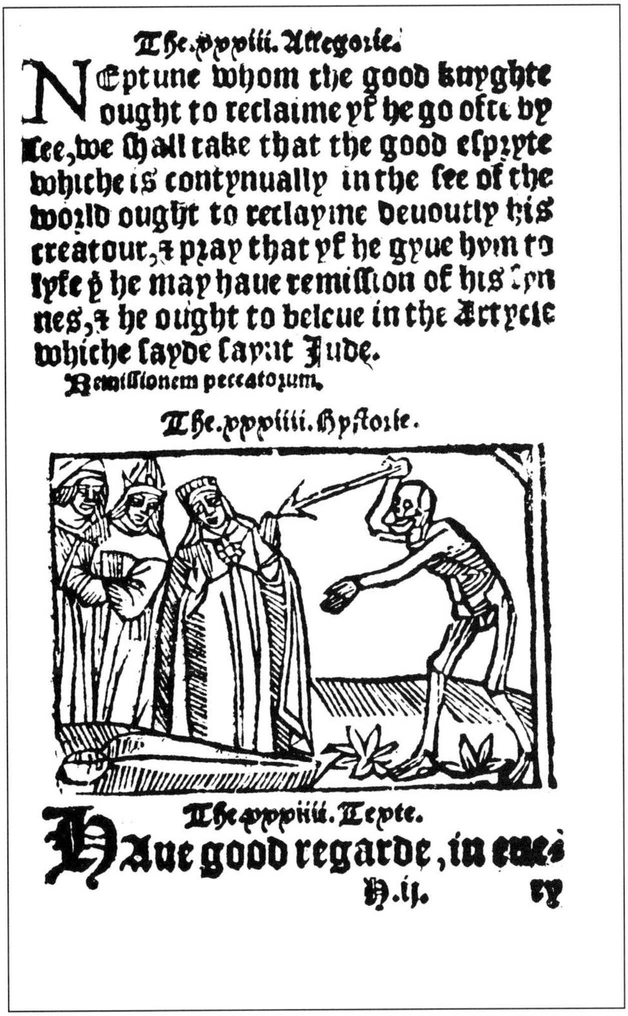

The.xxiiii. Allegorie.

Neptune whom the good knyghte ought to reclaime yf he go ofte by see, we shall take that the good espryte whiche is contynually in the see of the worlde ought to reclayme deuoutly his creatour, & pray that yf he gyue hym to lyfe y he may haue remission of his synnes, & he ought to beleue in the Artycle whiche sayde saynt Jude.

Remissionem peccatorum.

The.xxiiii. Hystorie.

The.xxiiii. Texte.

Haue good regarde, in eue ry

H.ij.

Fig. 15. Death Strikes. Christine de Pizan, *Here foloweth the .C. Hystoryes of Troye*, trans. Robert Wyer (London: Robert Wyer, *c.* 1540-1550), sig. H2r. *STC* 7272. BL C.21.a.34.

with an arrow or dart who leads everyone, rich and poor, noble and humble, men and women, to the grave. There is a suggestion in the woodcut, too, of the Legends of the Three Living and Three Dead – the three youths, kings or powerful men who must face their own mortality. The accompanying verse text in the French editions warns the reader, again conventionally, to remember that Death may strike at any hour and to consider his soul.

Wyer's illustration (Fig. 15) is a close but poor copy of the French model. Wyer's picture, however, omits the papal tiara on the first figure threatened by

Death. Given Wyer's own activity as publisher of at least one heretical work before the Reformation in England and his position as churchwarden in the Parish of St Martin-in-the-Fields afterwards, this omission seems particularly telling. The *STC* dates the *.C. Hystoryes* as *c.* 1540, though P. B. Tracy has suggested a date of 1550, based on the text type for the volume. During this decade, Protestantism was in full sway under Henry VIII and his son, Edward VI. Visual elements associated with Catholicism were undergoing a process of being redefined, if not entirely destroyed, by the Protestant Tudors. It would have been impolitic to publish a picture of the pope in this period (though a thoughtful propagandist might have made more of the original image of the pope shown as foremost among Death's victims). As we have seen, there are earlier examples of continental woodcuts showing the Beast of the Apocalypse, for example, wearing the papal tiara, in which the papal tiara was later literally scraped off the block, but Wyer has simply left it out of his copy of the picture, a sensible move in uncertain times. Wyer himself, like many printers, was clearly sympathetic to reform. He had earlier published 'several books for English reformers in the mid 1530s, notably William Marshall's translation of the *Defensor pacis* by Marsiglio of Padua – a work of great political significance and translated by one of Thomas Cromwell's circle'.[37]

Despite widespread censorship of Catholic images and texts, it is interesting to note the number of medieval books, religious and secular, in manuscript and print, which, though censored, defaced and annotated by later Protestant commentators, survive to this day, though some have been so badly damaged that they are scarcely decipherable. Given the Reformers' destructive impulses, it seems odd that so many Catholic books survive. Why not just destroy them? Why keep them and mark them up or deface only part and retain the rest? One answer might be that books continued to be valued as comparatively expensive commodities that were worth keeping. But another answer might be found in the complex relationships Protestantism had with Catholicism. The reformed religion was not made new out of whole cloth. Some of the complexities of this story may be seen when we look at indulgences in England and what becomes of them – namely, the defacing of their texts in existing manuscripts and printed books, their disappearance from newly printed Catholic as well as Protestant prayer-books and catechetical works, and yet the survival of many images associated with them.

The most popular indulgences in England were illustrated with the *arma Christi*, or Instruments of the Passion, and Christ as the Man of Sorrows (also known as the Image of Pity), with the indulgence referring to the Mass of St Gregory, or with the Wounds of Jesus, a related and popular devotion. Indulgences also included brief texts, such as a specific prayer to be said while contemplating a religious image or a list of prayers to be repeated for a set number of times (similar to a novena) in order to gain divine grace, an answer to a petition or a release from years spent in Purgatory. Indulgences were included in manuscript and printed Books of Hours, and circulated separately as single-

Fig. 16. Emblems of the Passion. Inserted into a Book of Hours (removed 1928)
(English, sixteenth century). Dodgson 18. *STC* 14077c.15. Bodleian Library
Arch.G.f.14. By permission of the Bodleian Library, Oxford.

leaf prints from the beginning of the fifteenth century. The Wounds of Jesus were
sometimes displayed emblematically with the Instruments of the Passion on a
heraldic shield (Fig. 16), for example, as they are on two single-leaf prints now
in the Bodleian Library. In the caption at the top, 'Ex domo Jhesu de Betheleem',
the ink is smudged at the beginning and the end, indicating that the caption
was either hand-stamped later on, or more likely produced in a second pull

205

through the press.[38] The caption itself 'refers to the Carthusian Priory of Sheen (Richmond), and the cuts are more likely to have been made for presentation or sale to visitors as souvenirs than as book-plates'.[39] Eamon Duffy has discussed the pervasiveness of Wounds iconography, with the emblem found 'carved on benchends, painted in glass, cast in brass or carved in slate to be placed on graves. It was also distributed in the form of cheap woodcuts, by the Charterhouses.'[40] Pilgrims acquired printed indulgences at holy shrines, or purchased them to support a charity or church foundation, often tacking them up on the walls of their houses. In some cases, we see that the texts have been crossed out by later censors, though the images remain intact.

Illustrations of the *arma Christi* and of the Man of Sorrows were both thought to reproduce actual historical artefacts and events. The *arma Christi*, for example, were believed to exist as actual relics. In a bull of 1243, Pope Innocent IV took the Sainte-Chapelle, along with its holy relics – the Crown of Thorns, a piece of the True Cross, the Lance, Sponge, Robe and vial of Holy Blood, among other items – under his protection.[41] The indulgence of the Mass of St Gregory dates from about 1400. While celebrating Mass in the church of Santa Croce in Gerusaleme in Rome, Pope Gregory the Great was supposed to have seen a vision of Christ seated on or standing in his tomb, displaying the wounds and surrounded by the instruments of Passion. This vision was said to have inspired the Pope to grant an indulgence to all who said five Paternosters and five Ave Marias before an image of the Man of Sorrows. The story probably derives from a Byzantine icon displayed in the church of Santa Croce which itself became an object of pilgrimage and was widely copied, appearing subsequently in late medieval prayer-books, manuscript miniatures and print.[42]

There are, for example, two surviving single-leaf prints of the Man of Sorrows surrounded by the Instruments of the Passion that are iconographically related. Both of them are preserved because they were bound into books, and both have Bridgettine associations. One woodcut (Fig. 17) has been inserted as fol. 1ᵛ into a copy of the *Directorium sacerdotum*, a version of the Sarum *Ordinale* containing rules for adapting the calendar to the services of each week. Clement Maydeston (fl. *c.* 1450), the author, was a member of the Bridgettine community at Syon, and the book itself was printed in 1486 in Westminster by Caxton.[43] The colophon of the *Directorium* says simply: 'Caxton me fieri fecit'. The other woodcut, which is very similar in iconography though different in style, is bound into Bodleian Library MS Rawlinson D. 403, a fifteenth-century paper manuscript with Bridgettine prayers (Fig. 18).[44] The print bound into the Maydeston volume is more elegantly rendered, perhaps continental in origin, and shows a half-figure of Jesus in a tomb. His eyelids are almost shut, and his wrists are crossed and bleeding heavily. Surrounding this central image is a border of 28 compartments containing the emblems of the Passion. In the Rawlinson woodcut, which is rougher in style, a frowning, sorrowful Jesus looks downward to the left, his eyes distinctly visible. Though Jesus is still flanked by the spear and sponge, as He is also in the first example, the tomb has disappeared, and the

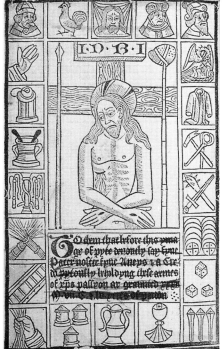

Fig. 17. Christ as the Man of Sorrows. Clement Maydeston, *Directorium sacerdotum* [Liturgy of Salisbury] (Westminster: William Caxton, *c.* 1487), inserted as fol. 1ᵛ. *STC* 14072. BL C.10.b.16.

Fig. 18. Christ as the Man of Sorrows. Anonymous, English, fifteenth century. Inserted as fol. 1ᵛ into MS Rawlinson D. 403. By permission of the Bodleian Library, Oxford.

28-compartment border has been reduced to 22 compartments. Missing from the border in this second example are the kiss of Judas and the Crown of Thorns, among the most readily recognisable Passion emblems.[45] The Rawlinson woodcut is perhaps a copy of a copy of the first, because the main figural elements are not reversed as they would have been if the image had been copied on to a woodblock and then printed.

These documents, too, have been censored by either crossing or rubbing out the indulgence panels beneath the images, even though the pictures themselves have been left intact.[46] In the *Directorium* text, there are further examples of censorship, most notably in the calendar where the name of Becket has been scratched out. We see similar defacement of the indulgence beneath the image in a Sarum Hours printed for Byrkman in 1521, now in the Bodleian Library (Fig. 19). The illustration of the Man of Sorrows (on sig. i6ʳ) and the heading that indicates that this is the prayer of Pope Gregory ('Or*atio* sancti Gregorii') remain

Fig. 19. Christ as the Man of Sorrows. *Horae ad usum Sarum* (Paris: for Francis
Byrkman, 1521), sig. i6ʳ. *STC* 15931. Bodleian Library Douce BB 135.
By permission of the Bodleian Library, Oxford.

untouched, though the text of the indulgence below has been emphatically
crossed out by a later reader.

Though indulgence texts and images circulated widely in pre-Reformation
prayer-books, they were subsequently removed when Catholicism returned to
England under the reign of Mary. Discussing Wayland's primer, printed during
the Counter-Reformation, Duffy comments on its 'sparer tone and less perfervid
atmosphere' and on 'the fact that every other primer produced in Mary's reign,
whether English or Latin, shares the same silence about indulgences or

miraculous legends. The wonder-world of charm, pardon, and promise in the older primers had gone for ever.'[47] In the case of indulgences, reform successfully excised the one area Luther found most objectionable, though in surviving English examples the pictures remain, attesting to the reverence still felt for the sacred events they represent. Other elements of Catholicism were also readily incorporated into Protestant practice, as we shall see in a final example.

Probably composed in the late fourteenth century, *The Fifteen Oes* are a series of fifteen prayers of meditation on Christ's suffering and his loneliness on the Cross, each beginning with the word 'O'. The text in William Caxton's first English printing of the prayers opens as follows: 'O Jhesu endles swetnes of louyng soules / O Jhesu gostly ioye passing & excedyng all gladnes and desires. O Jhesu helthe & tendre louer of al repentaunt sinners that likest to dwelle as thou saydest thy selfe with the children of men / For that was the cause why thou were incarnate / and made man in the ende of the worlde.'[48]

This invocation sets the emotional tone of the *Oes* prayers that follow. The emphasis throughout is on divine love and compassion, on the assurance of heavenly mercy rather than on divine judgement. The dominant image of the Crucifixion and the focus on Christ's physical pain were typical themes of late medieval devotional writing but were hardly central to Protestant reform. Yet what is remarkable about *The Fifteen Oes* is their survival throughout an age of doctrinal, political and social change. The prayers began to circulate in manuscript in the fifteenth century, both in England and on the continent, made the transition from manuscript to print, then continued to appear in both Catholic and Protestant prayer-books through the 1570s. The *Fifteen Oes* thus had an active life span of some 150 years.

Caxton does not tell us the source of the *Fifteen Oes*, nor does he ascribe them to Bridget. This casualness is not surprising, however, for the attribution of the *Oes* to St Bridget of Sweden was generally assumed in the fifteenth century. In fifteenth- and sixteenth-century manuscripts and in later printed books, the *Fifteen Oes* were always attributed (when they are attributed at all) to St Bridget. These fifteen prayers are not to be found, however, in any of the works written or dictated by Bridget herself, but became attached to her by association in manuscripts of the *Oes* copied or owned in England in the fifteenth century.[49]

In British Library Sloane MS 3548, a paper commonplace book copied in the fifteenth century, there is a poem which begins:

> A holy wooman that hight seynt Bryde
> Couetid to knowe the woundys wyde
> of Ihesu Cryste, howe fell thei woor,
> And often prayed hem therfor.
> Ihesu, that all goodnes be-gan,
> Apperid and bad this whoman than:
> Saye every daye vppon thi knees
> XV pater nosters and XV aues
> Vnto a 3ere fulli endid bee; ...'[50]

Fig. 20. St Bridget of Sweden. *Horae ad usum Sarum* (Paris: Francis Regnault, 1534), fol. lix^v. *STC* 15984. By permission of the Houghton Library, Harvard University.

In this poem Bridget has a vision of Jesus, modelled no doubt on the famous vision of St Gregory; Jesus tells her to say fifteen Paternosters and fifteen Aves daily for a year. He will then 'graunte wyth memory / XV soules out of purgatorye / And XV men that have dissesse / Of there old synne I am relesse.' The basic formula, praying for a year and releasing fifteen souls from Purgatory thereby, was picked up in later printings of the *Oes* in Sarum Hours. For

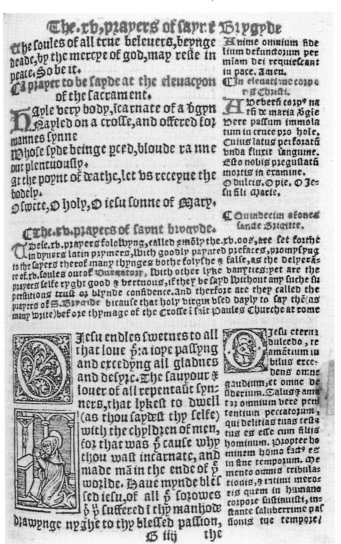

Fig. 21. Disclaimer. Prayer-book (London: Nicolas le Roux and Robert Redman, 1538), fol. Biv[r]. *STC* 16007. By permission of the Houghton Library, Harvard University.

example, the Books of Hours printed by Francis Regnault in 1527 and 1534 prefaced the *Fifteen Oes* (Fig. 20) with the caption: 'These be the .xv. oos the whyche the holy virgyn saint brygitte was wounte to say dayly before the holy rode in Saint Paules chyrche at Rome.' The rubric then becomes an indulgence, promising that 'who so say this a hole yere he shall delever .xv. soules out of purgatory of hys next kyndred: and converte other .xv. synners to gode lyf and other .xv. ryghtuouse men of his kynde shall persever in gode lyf'.[51]

By 1538, in the Protestant prayer-books printed by Nicolas le Roux and Robert Redman, the *Fifteen Oes* again appear (Fig. 21), but the indulgence text has been removed, and the prayers are prefaced by this disclaimer:

These .xv. Prayers folowyng / called commonly the .xv. Oos, are set forthe in dyuers latyn Prymers, with goodly paynted prefaces, promysynge to the sayers therof many thynges both folyshe and false, as the delyueraunce of .xv. soules out of Purgatory, with other lyke vanyties: yet are the prayers selfe ryght good and vertuous, yf they be sayde without any suche superstitious trust or blynde confydence. And therfore are they called the prayers of Saynt Brygide, by cause that holy vyrgyn vsed dayly to saye them (as many wryte) before the ymage of the Cross, in Saynt Paules churche at Rome.[52]

As we have seen in the earlier emendations of indulgences, the emphasis has shifted away from the prayers' miraculous efficacy to the historical religious event: St Bridget saying the prayers daily before the cross in St Paul's Church in Rome. Here the *Fifteen Oes* are given a context, though, like the vision of Pope Gregory or the Crown of Thorns at the Sainte-Chapelle, there is no external evidence that the story that has become attached to them is true.

A woodcut of St Bridget kneeling before a vision of Christ as the Man of Sorrows (Fig. 22) sets off the English translations of the *Oes* in Regnault's Sarum Hours of 1531 and 1534, which also contain Latin texts of the prayers. In fact, texts of the *Fifteen Oes* in both Latin and English began to appear regularly in the 1520s, again indicating the wide appreciation of the prayers in England. They were given in both Latin and English in Sarum Hours printed in Antwerp in 1525, and in Paris in 1525, 1531 and 1534; in the Rouen prayer-books of 1536 and 1538; in Bishop Hilsey's primer of 1539; and in the official Marian primer of 1555. The English texts in all of these, as well as those printed in later Protestant prayer-books, are based on the translation made around 1490 by William Caxton.[53] A work like the *Fifteen Oes* may have survived in Protestant prayer-books simply because the prayers were a familiar and beloved text in English read first by literate nuns and learned Catholic noblewomen, and later by Protestant laymen and women whose taste and sensibility may have differed very little from those of their Catholic predecessors.

Accounts of the destruction of images by Protestants in the throes of religious fervour are often horrifying. We read of statues and books burned in ceremonial fires, the smashing of images and glass, the pillaging of churches and monasteries.[54] Nonetheless, influenced by artists like Cranach and Dürer, Luther explored the potential of the image to promote Protestant ideas. In England, people were instructed by the state and from the pulpit to remove references to Becket, the popes and other Catholic elements from their books and households. But English owners of books deemed heretical were generally circumspect in their emendations, keeping the books and presumably continuing to use them while crossing out only the offending texts and, much less often, pictures. Even with images that are strongly associated with the old faith, in particular those

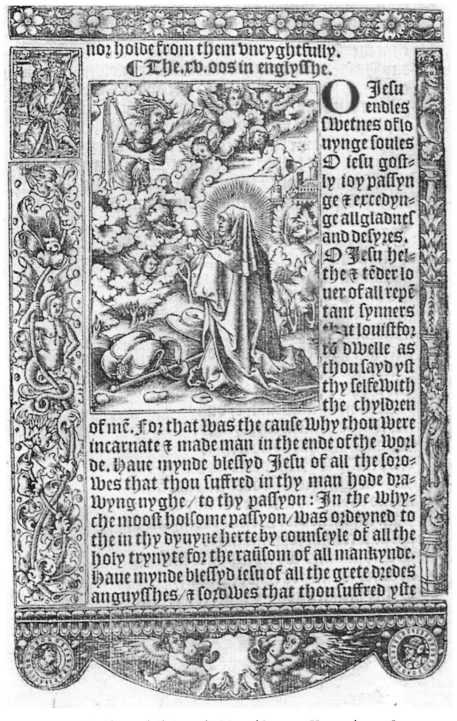

noz holde from them vnryghtfully.
℟ The .rb. oos in englysshe.

O Jesu endles swetnes of lo uynge soules O iesu gost ly ioy passyn ge & excedyn ge all gladnes and desyres. O Jesu hel the & tēder lo uer of all repē tant synners that louist for to dwelle as thou sayd yst thy selfe with the chyldren of mē. for that was the cause why thou were incarnate & made man in the ende of the worl de. Haue mynde blessyd Jesu of all the soro wes that thou suffred in thy man hode dra wyng nyghe / to thy passyon : In the why che moost holsome passyon / was ordeyned to the in thy dyuyne herte by counseyle of all the holy trynyte for the raūsom of all mankynde. Haue mynde blessyd iesu of all the grete dredes anguysshes / & sorowes that thou suffred yste

Fig. 22. St Bridget and Christ as the Man of Sorrows. *Horae ad usum Sarum* (Paris: Francis Regnault, 1534), fol. 185ᵛ. *STC* 15984. By permission of the Houghton Library, Harvard University.

illustrating indulgences and related texts, an emphasis on history, however apocryphal, rather than on the miraculous, may permit a picture (and sometimes the text too) to continue to circulate in Protestant contexts. Perhaps in the many examples included here we can also detect an impulse to preserve the medieval past while emending texts and images to fit contemporary religious and political trends in the early years of the Reformation.

NOTES

INTRODUCTION

1 Epigraph taken from *Selected Art Writings: James Schuyler*, ed. Simon Pettet (Santa Rosa, CA, 1998), p. 286. See L. M. J. Delaissé, 'The Importance of Books of Hours for the History of the Medieval Book', in *Gatherings in Honor of Dorothy E. Miner*, ed. Ursula E. McCracken, Lilian M. C. Randall, Richard H. Randall, Jr (Baltimore, 1974), pp. 203, 221; also Delaissé, *A Century of Dutch Manuscript Illumination* (Berkeley and Los Angeles, 1968). See further James H. Marrow, *Passion Iconography in Northern European Art of the Late Middle Ages and Early Renaissance: A Study of the Transformation of Sacred Metaphor into Descriptive Narrative* (Kortrijk, 1979); Mary Carpenter Erler, 'Devotional Literature', *The Cambridge History of the Book in Britain*, 7 vols, vol. 3: *1400-1557*, ed. Lotte Hellinga and J. B. Trapp (Cambridge, 1999-), pp. 508-509.

2 William M. Ivins, Jr, *Prints and Visual Communication* (Cambridge, MA, 1969), p. 19.

3 *STC* 17102-17111, 22407-22423.

4 According to the *STC*, following the edition printed by Antoine Vérard in Scots in 1503, the *Kalendar of Shepherds* remained in print in a variety of versions through 1631.

5 Ivins, *Prints and Visual Communication*, p. 24.

1. EARLY ILLUSTRATION IN PRINT

1 *STC* references are as follows: *Canterbury Tales* [*STC* 5082-5083], *The Parlement of Fowls* [*STC* 5091], *Polychronicon* [*STC* 13438], Bartholomeus Anglicus [*STC* 1536], *Golden Legend* [*STC* 24873-24875], *Fall of Princes* [*STC* 3175], *Pilgrimage of the Life of Man* [*STC* 6473], *The Siege of Thebes* [*STC* 17031], *The Churl and the Birde* [*STC* 17008-17009], *The Horse, the Sheep and the Goose* [*STC* 17018-17019], *The Temple of Glas* [*STC* 17032], *The Court of Sapyence* [*STC* 17015], *The lyf of our lady* [*STC* 17023-17024], *The medecyne of the stomache* [*STC* 12138]. For more on Lydgate copies in print, see Alexandra Gillespie, 'The Lydgate Canon in Print from 1476 to 1534', *Journal of the Early Book Society* 3 (2000), pp. 59-86. For information on early editions of Aesop in print, see Edward Wheatley, 'The Aesopic Corpus at War with Itself: A Literary Body and its Members', *Journal of the Early Book Society* 2 (1999), pp. 46-58; also Edward Wheatley, *Mastering Aesop: Medieval Education, Chaucer, and His Followers* (Gainesville, Fla., 2000). For background on the transition from manuscript to print, see Ernst Philip Goldschmidt, *Medieval Texts and Their First Appearance in Print* (1943, repr., New York, 1969), and Margaret B. Stillwell, *The Beginning of the World of Books, 1450 to 1470: A Chronological*

Survey of the Texts Chosen for Printing During the First Twenty Years of the Printing Art, with a Synopsis of the Gutenberg Documents (New York, 1972).

2   *STC* 5083. Shakespeare's sonnets, for example, circulated privately before their publication, as we learn from mention of them by Francis Meres who, in his *Palladis Tamia* (1598) refers to the passing of Shakespeare's 'sugared sonnets among his private friends'. Quoted in Richard Dutton, 'The Birth of the Author', *Texts and Cultural Change in Early Modern England*, ed. Cedric C. Brown and Arthur F. Marotti (New York, 1997), p. 165. This is true as well of the works of other court poets, including Sir Thomas Wyatt, Henry Howard, Earl of Surrey, and even John Donne (who had no compunction about rushing his sermons into print).

3   *STC* 5082, 5083. Caxton preface quoted in W. J. B. Crotch, *The Prologues and Epilogues of William Caxton* (1928; repr. New York, 1971), p. 91.

4   The *Canterbury Tales* portraits are discussed by Richard K. Emmerson, in 'Text and Image in the Ellesmere Portraits of the Tale-Tellers', pp. 143-170, and Betsy Bowden, 'Visual Portraits of the Canterbury Pilgrims, 1484 (?) to 1809', pp. 171-204, in *The Ellesmere Chaucer: Essays in Interpretation*, ed. Martin Stevens and Daniel Woodward (San Marino, Calif., 1995). See also David Carlson, 'Woodcut Illustrations of the *Canterbury Tales*, 1483-1602', *The Library*, 6th ser., 19 (1997), pp. 25-67.

5   *STC* 24762. Crotch, *Prologues and Epilogues*, p. 54. Woodcuts from *The Mirror of the World* have been reproduced by Hodnet (fig. 1), and in Janet Backhouse, Mirjam Foot and John Barr, comps., *William Caxton: An Exhibition to Commemorate the Quincentenary of the Introduction of Printing into England* (London, 1976), fig. 40, p. 48.

6   Richard S. Field, *Fifteenth-Century Woodcuts and Other Relief Prints in the Collection of The Metropolitan Museum of Art* (New York, 1977), unpaginated, item 61. For a useful study, see Mary C. Erler, 'Pasted-In Embellishments in English Manuscripts and Printed Books c. 1480-1533', *The Library*, 6th ser. 14, no. 3 (September, 1992), pp. 185-206. Early on, A. J. J. Delen, *Histoire de la gravure dans les anciens Pays-Bas et dans les provinces belges des origines jusqu'à la fin du XVIIIe siècle*, 2 parts (1924-1935), part 1, *Des origines à 1500* (Paris, 1924), noted: 'Nous trouvons encore des images religieuses collées à l'intérieur de ces coffrets de voyage où elles faisaient office de talisman et en même temps de retable portatif, devant lequel le voyageur s'agenouillait pour réciter ses prières journalières' (p. 31).

7   *American Heritage Dictionary of the English Language*, s.v. ephemerae, definition 2. Field, *Fifteenth-Century Woodcuts*, items 3-4, 13. Petrus Christus' *Portrait of a Female Donor*, now in the National Gallery of Art, Washington, D.C., Samuel H. Kress Collection, is reproduced in M. W. Ainsworth, *Petrus Christus: Renaissance Master of Bruges* (New York, 1994), p. 133. The prayer book of the anonymous noblewoman, with its one-column text and rubrication, is open and the pages are turning, but the woman stares out from the oak panel, her eyes lifted from the page and apparently transfixed by the now-missing holy scene that once appeared in a central panel. Other examples of the representation of prints in late medieval painting are described by Delen, *Histoire de la Gravure*, part 1, pp. 31-32, including an Annunciation by Robert Campion with a woodcut of St Christopher hung from the mantel of the chimney, and a triptych by Quentin Metsys depicting a scene from 'La Légende de Sainte Anne' in which 'en bas et à gauche du panneau central, un enfant jouant avec des manuscrits à miniatures et des estampes coloriées'.

8 Dodgson, *Ashm.*, item 38, p. 26. See also Schreiber, vol. 2, 1311-1313. Note that the spelling of 'Bridgettine' is variable: the version 'Brigittine' drawn from the Swedish spelling of Bridget's name, and 'Bridgettine' from the English spelling, are both correct. The English form is preferred in this volume as many of the examples presented are English in origin.

9 Schreiber, 1293a. The triptych woodcut of *Bridget Giving the Rule to Her Order* is described by Dodgson, *Ashm.*, item 37; and by Martha W. Driver in 'Bridgettine Woodcuts in Printed Books Produced for the English Market', in *Art into Life: Collected Papers from the Kresge Art Museum Medieval Symposia*, ed. Carol Garrett Fisher and Kathleen L. Scott (East Lansing, Mich., 1995), pp. 241-243, 263 n. 12. It has also been reproduced in Margaret Aston, *Lollards and Reformers: Images and Literacy in Late Medieval Religion* (London, 1984), pl. 4b.

10 Mary Erler, 'Devotional Literature', in *The Cambridge History of the Book in Britain, 1400-1557*, vol. 3, ed. Lotte Hellinga and J. B. Trapp (Cambridge, 1999), p. 513.

11 Barbara Obrist, 'The Swedish Visionary: Saint Bridget', in *Medieval Women Writers*, ed. Katharina M. Wilson (Athens, GA, 1984), p. 234.

12 Hodnett, item 2512. Of the later history of this image, which is reproduced by Tessa Watt in *Cheap Print and Popular Piety 1550-1640* (Cambridge, 1991), pl. 9, Watt comments, 'The "images of pity" disappeared around 1535, burnt up in the first fires of the Reformation' (p. 131).

13 See Dodgson, *Ashm.*, Bodl. 21, 22; Schreiber, 976, 608; Driver, 'Bridgettine Woodcuts', pp. 239-241.

14 A. I. Doyle, 'A Survey of the Origins and Circulation of Theological Writings in English in the 14th, 15th, and Early 16th Centuries with Special Consideration of the Part of the Clergy Therein' (Ph.D. dissertation, University of Cambridge, 1953), n. 61b. *STC* 14044.

15 See Allan Stevenson, 'The Quincentennial of Netherlandish Block Books', *British Museum Quarterly* 31 (1965), pp. 85-89; Allan Stevenson, 'The Problem of Blockbooks', in *Blockbücher des Mittelalters: Bilderfolgen als Lektüre*, ed. Cornelia Schneider (Mainz, 1991), pp. 229-261. Sandra Hindman, in 'The Illustrated Book: An Addendum to the State of Research in Northern European Art', *Art Bulletin* 68 (1986), pp. 536-542, comments, 'Apart from Stevenson, however, no one has submitted the block-books to an "archaeological" investigation, which might still yield evidence about their making. Nor has anyone studied the relationship between their texts and images to understand how and by whom they were actually meant to be read. Just because the block-book no longer holds the position of the harbinger of printing, which stands on the threshold of the modern world, we should not consign it to oblivion' (p. 541). Facsimile editions by Avril Henry, *The Mirour of Mans Saluacioune: A Middle English Translation of Speculum Humanae Salvationis* (Philadelphia, 1987) and *Biblia Pauperum: A Facsimile and Edition* (Aldershot, 1987), have begun to fill this scholarly gap.

16 The xylographic/typographic copy of the *Speculum humanae salvationis* (PML 20680) was shown in 'Netherlandish Manuscripts and Books 1470-1540', an exhibition at the Pierpont Morgan Library (January-April, 1987). The volume was then described in the accompanying exhibit case caption as 'peculiar, and indeed inexplicable'. Editions of the *Speculum* are discussed in Stevenson, 'The Problem of Blockbooks', pp. 251-257. See also Gerard van Thienen and John Goldfinch, *Incunabula Printed in the Low Countries: A Census* (Nieukoop, 1999), nos 2006-

2010. No. 2007 (p. 372) describes the second Latin edition. In addition to the copy in the Morgan, there are further copies in the John Rylands Library, the Bodleian Library, the British Library, and elsewhere; several of these are fragmentary. I examined Johannes Regiomontanus' *Calendarium* (Nuremberg, 1474; Venice, 1482) in the John Hay Library, Brown University, Providence, Rhode Island, as well as a copy of *Epytoma Joannis de monte Regio in Almagestum Ptolomaei*, printed in Venice by Johannes Hamman in 1496, in the Lownes Collection of Significant Books in the History of Science, John Hay Library, Brown University. The title-page of this epitome, begun by Georg von Peurbach and completed by his pupil Regiomontanus, includes woodcuts of Ptolemy and Regiomontanus, with a xylographic title. For basic background on Regiomontanus, see Colin Clair, *A History of European Printing* (New York, 1976).

17 Hind, vol. 1, pp. 216-254. For reproduction of the Fifteen Signs imagery in the margins of printed Books of Hours, see M. Driver, 'Picturing the Apocalypse in the Printed Book of Hours', *Harlaxton Medieval Studies*, ed. Nigel Morgan (forthcoming): see Bibliography, p. 282.

18 Nancy Lee Beaty, *The Craft of Dying: A Study on the Literary Tradition of the Ars moriendi in England* (New Haven, 1970), p. 2.

19 Paul Binski, *Medieval Death: Ritual and Representation* (Ithaca, N.Y., 1996), comments that 'The *Ars Moriendi* represents a lay appropriation both of a body of knowledge and of a body of procedure' (p. 41), describing it as 'a layperson's version of forms of preliminary ritual developed by the medieval Church. In some respects, as a text of pastoral reassurance, it resembled the *Ordo visitandi* of the priest' (p. 39). The late medieval text is preserved in over 300 Latin and vernacular versions. In its instructional capacity, the *Ars moriendi* further resembles the modern work of Elisabeth Kübler-Ross, a popular writer on the psychology of death. Her works include *On Death and Dying* (New York, 1969); *Death: The Final Stage of Growth* (Englewood Cliffs, N.J., 1975); *To Live Until We Say Good-bye* (Englewood Cliffs, N.J., 1978), and *AIDS: The Ultimate Challenge* (New York, 1987).

20 Sister Mary Catharine O'Connor, *The Art of Dying Well: The Development of the Ars moriendi* (New York, 1942), pp. 11-17. O'Connor supports her argument for the derivation of text by citing the simultaneity of xylographic and typographic reproduction: 'Investigation has now disclosed the fact that the use of woodblocks was coexistent with printing with movable type and that xylographic texts were often copies from typographic texts, just as manuscripts were copied from both.'

21 Ibid., p. 117.

22 Ibid., p. 119. Christopher Daniell, *Death and Burial in Medieval England, 1066-1550* (London, 1998), p. 40, mentions that representations of the Final Moment, in which angels are shown protecting the soul as demons fight to drag it away, are 'often incorporated in medieval tomb design', and the soul is commonly seen as 'a passive participant in the centre of a combat between angels and devils'.

23 O'Connor, *Art of Dying Well*, pp. 114-115.

24 Reproduced in Max Lehrs, *Geschichte und Kritischer Katalog des deutschen, niederländischen und französischen Kupferstichs im XV. Jahrhundert*, 9 vols (Vienna, 1908-1934; repr. 1969), vol. 2, item 179. See also Alan Shestack, *Master E. S.: Five Hundredth Anniversary Exhibition*, Philadelphia Museum of Art (Philadelphia, 1967), items 4-15.

25 John Macfarlane, in his catalogue *Antoine Vérard* (London, September 1900 for

1899), items 18, 19, describes Vérard's illustrations as 'imitated from the German block-books of the *Ars Moriendi*'. Macfarlane cites copies in the British Library, the Bibliothèque Nationale, and the Bibliothèque de l'Arsenal. There is another copy in the Bodleian Library, Douce 169, which has an odd colophon: 'Lequel a este imprime a paris le xii iour de feurier Mil.cccc.xxxx et xiii'. The French *Ars moriendi* images are discussed by Emile Mâle in *Religious Art in France: The Late Middle Ages, A Study of Medieval Iconography and Its Sources*, trans. Mathiel Mathews (Princeton, 1986), pp. 348-355.

26 *STC* 791.

27 *STC* 21430, 21430a. For their text, Pynson and de Worde used Caxton's translation (*STC* 21429). Pynson and de Worde reused some of the seven woodcut illustrations in Caxton's edition, but seem also to have looked at block-book and manuscript sources, expanding the traditional cycle in their version to 27 pictures. For other possible collaborations between Pynson and de Worde, see S. H. Johnston, 'A Study of the Career and Literary Productions of Richard Pynson' (Ph.D. diss., University of Western Ontario, 1977), items 90, 106.

28 In 'Notes on the Virtues and Vices', *Journal of the Warburg and Courtauld Institute* 26 (1963), pp. 264-303, Rosamund Tuve remarked that the picture cycle in *Somme le Roi* manuscripts was remarkably consistent: 'an unusually full set of directions to illuminators, to be found in several of the later copies, helped keep that tradition constant'. Manuscript illustrations in *Somme le Roi* manuscripts are also discussed by Tuve in *Allegorical Imagery: Some Mediaeval Books and Their Posterity* (Princeton, 1966), and by Ellen Kosmer in 'The "noyous humoure of lecherie"', *Art Bulletin* 57, no. 1 (March 1975), pp. 1-8.

29 For a discussion of de Worde's two editions (*STC* 5198, 5199), see M. Driver, 'Illustration in Early English Books: Methods and Problems', *Books at Brown* 33 (1986), pp. 25-32, n. 17. *Ars moriendi* images are also briefly discussed in Driver, 'Pictures in Print: Late Fifteenth- and Early Sixteenth-Century English Religious Books for Lay Readers', in *De Cella in Seculum: Religious and Secular Life and Devotion in Late Medieval England*, ed. M. G. Sargent (Cambridge, 1989), pp. 239-241.

30 For further discussion of title-page illustration and the binding of English books, see Chapter 3.

31 *STC* 792. Margaret M. Smith, in *The Title-Page: Its Early Development, 1460-1510* (London, 2000), describes the process: 'holes could be made so that something else could be inserted – another woodcut, or some text set in metal type, or both' (p. 76). The factotum is also defined by Philip Gaskell, *A New Introduction to Bibliography* (1972; repr. New Castle, Del., 1995), p. 155, as 'a square ornamental block with a hole through the middle into which a piece of type could be wedged, one block thus serving for any initial letter'. See also Driver, 'Illustration in Early English Books', pp. 32-41, figs 21, 22, 26, 27, 30, 32; Hodnett, pp. vii-viii. For further discussion of factotum printing, see below, Chapter 2.

32 *STC* 6033.5, 6034, 6035; 21336, 21337; 5609, 5609.5, 5610; 6932.

33 See Avril Henry, 'The Iconography of the Forty-Page Blockbook *Biblia Pauperum*: Form and Meaning', in Schneider, *Blockbücher des Mittelalters*, pp. 263-288.

34 See Mary J. Carruthers, *The Book of Memory: A Study of Memory in Medieval Culture* (Cambridge, 1990), pp. 221-229, 248-257, and Frances A. Yates, *The Art of Memory* (Chicago, 1966), pp. 82-104.

35 Carruthers, *Book of Memory*, pp. 78-79, 95, 229-230. See also A. R. Luria, *The Mind of a Mnemonist*, trans. Lynn Solotaroff (Cambridge, Mass., 1968).

36 'Typographic' here refers to printing with movable type. See *American Heritage Dictionary of the English Language*, s.v. typography, definition 1a.

37 Roger S. Wieck, intro., *Ars Memorandi: A Facsimile of the Text and Woodcuts* (Cambridge, Mass., 1981). In addition to studying the *Ars memorandi* in the Houghton Library at Harvard University and in the British Library (IB. 17, Germany, c. 1470), I have also examined the block-book *Ars memorandi* (PML 20582) in the Pierpont Morgan Library and a fascinating block-book edition of Publicius' *Ars memorativa* in the New York Public Library, which has memory diagrams with movable sections. For further interpretation of the *Ars memorandi*, see Franz Thoma, *The Relations between Petrus of Rosenheim to the Xylographa of the Ars Memorandi and to the Early Printings of the Rationarium Evangelistarium: A Bibliographical Study of the Literature of Mnemonics* (Leipzig, 1929).

38 See Anneliese Schmitt, 'Das Blockbuch – ein Volksbuch? Versuch einer Antwort', in *Blockbücher des Mittelalters*, pp. 215-220; Avril Henry, 'The Iconography of the Forty-Page Blockbook *Biblia Pauperum*', pp. 263-288.

39 Henry, *Biblia Pauperum*, p. 17.

40 Ibid., p. 17.

41 Rudolf Arnheim, *Visual Thinking* (Los Angeles, 1969), p. 234.

42 Ibid., p. 246.

43 Keith Moxey's important account of the cultural value of woodcuts may be found in the introduction to his *Peasants, Warriors and Wives: Popular Imagery in the Reformation* (Chicago, 1989), pp. 1-9.

44 Macfarlane, *Antoine Vérard*, item 163, cites only the vellum copy in the British Library (C.22.b.7) omitting mention of the paper fragment (C.36.f.5), which is misbound (signatures occur on verso instead of recto sides). In her introduction to the facsimile *Biblia Pauperum* (p. 39, n. 15), Henry briefly mentions Vérard's edition, along with a sixteenth-century block-book version produced by Vavassore in Italian. Publication of the *Biblia Pauperum* well into the sixteenth century seems to indicate its continued influence and popularity. For other recent editions and facsimiles see Henry, *The Mirour of Mans Saluacioune*, and Adrian Wilson and Joyce Lancaster Wilson, *A Medieval Mirror: Speculum Humanae Salvationis, 1324-1500* (Berkeley, 1985).

45 See Hodnett, p. 20. The metal-cuts used by de Worde may be rough copies of those illustrating a Book of Hours printed by Philippe Pigouchet in Paris, 1498, now in Lambeth Palace Library.

46 These lines are a crude variation on those penned by Chaucer in his 'ABC'. See Henry, 'Iconography of the *Biblia Pauperum*', p. 38, n. 160.

47 See Curt Bühler, 'The Apostles and the Creed', *Speculum* 28 (1953), pp. 335-339; James D. Gordon, 'The Articles of the Creed and the Apostles', *Speculum* 40 (1965), pp. 634-646; and Madeline Caviness, 'Fifteenth-Century Stained Glass from the Chapel of Hampton Court, Herefordshire: The Apostles' Creed and other subjects', *Walpole Society* 42 (1969-1970), pp. 35-60. Caviness cites seven sets of apostles in painted glass, three complete (p. 58). Ann Eljenholm Nichols, *Seeable Signs: The Iconography of the Seven Sacraments 1350-1544* (Woodbridge, 1994) mentions 'sets in manuscripts and particularly important for East Anglia, sets in glass and on rood screens in which each apostle held a scroll with "his" article inscribed thereon

(screens at Gooderstone, Mattishall, Ringland, Salle, and Weston Longville)' (p. 144, n. 43).

48 *STC* 3259, 3260.

49 For a consideration of Hours marginalia and their relationship to popular art, see Mâle, *Religious Art in France*, pp. 211-270. For a study of the presentation of sibyls and the Fifteen Signs in the marginalia of Books of Hours printed for French and English readers, see Driver, 'Picturing the Apocalypse in the Printed Book of Hours'.

50 Compare the reproduction of the same scene in Henry, *Biblia Pauperum*, p. 102. The *Book of Hours for Rome Use* was printed in Paris (n.d.) by Philippe Pigouchet and includes a calendar for 1489-1509, so was presumably printed prior to 1500. The copy referred to is Pierpont Morgan 19377 (ChL1476), sig. E7. Other versions of the same group of typological scenes occur in a *Book of Hours for Rome Use* printed in Paris by Simon Vostre in 1508. In Vostre's Hours, the marginal picture captions are supplied in French. A copy is in the Houghton Library (WKR 15. 2. 13) at Harvard University. The illustration shown here is from an *Hours for Sarum Use* printed by Philippe Pigouchet in 1494 in Paris.

2. WOODCUTS IN EARLY ENGLISH BOOKS

1 The illustrations in Caxton's *Golden Legend* of 1483 (*STC* 24873) are described in Hodnett, items 237-305.

2 De Worde commissioned a Book of Hours from a Parisian printer in 1497, but Books of Hours could be commissioned from as far away as Venice. A leaf from a *Horae ad usum Sarum*, printed in Venice and commissioned by two Flemish stationers in London, is reproduced in A. I. Doyle, Elizabeth Rainey and D. B. Wilson, *Manuscript to Print: Tradition and Innovation in the Renaissance Book* (Durham, 1975), fig. 24. In *English Books & Readers, 1475-1557: Being a Study in the History of the Book Trade from Caxton to the Incorporation of the Stationers' Company*, 2nd edn (Cambridge, 1969), H. S. Bennett remarks that 'Not less than 60% of all breviaries, books of hours (or primers), manuals, missals, etc., printed by 1557 came from overseas presses' (p. 66). Hind cites many Hours for the English market that were printed on the continent, vol. 2, p. 720 et passim. John Harthan, in the final chapter of *Books of Hours and Their Owners* (1977; repr. London, 1982), briefly comments on the export of printed Hours to England.

3 *STC* 2068. First Great Bible, rev. M. Coverdale, pr. Paris, F. Regnault, and London, R. Grafton and E. Whitchurch, 1539. See also my caption (p. 31) in Arthur Schlesinger, Jr, preface, *Censorship: 500 Years of Conflict* (New York, 1984): 'Since printing techniques in England were less advanced than those abroad, it was decided to print the book in Paris. French authorities protested and tried to stop the Bible from being printed. Sheets of the book, smuggled out of France in hats, were taken to England where the printing was completed.' In the collections of the New York Public Library is a 1538 broadside (*KVB 1538, *STC* 10086), titled 'Iniuntions for the clerge'. This proclamation of Thomas, Lord Cromwell (who is himself pictured on the title-page of the Great Bible, along with Henry VIII and Thomas Cranmer), threatens dire punishment of clergy who do not obey the king, and further stipulates that clergy must provide 'one boke of the hole byble of the largyest volume in Englysshe and the same set up in sum conuenient place wython the church … where as your parishoners may moste commodiously resorte to the same and read it'. The broadside also

includes the 'Item that you shall discourage no man priuely or apertly from readynge, or herynge of the sayde bible'.

4 E. Gordon Duff, *A Century of the English Book Trade* (London, 1948), p. 174. There are over nine hundred books cited in the 'Handlist of Publications by Wynkyn de Worde, 1492-1535', Appendix I, in H. S. Bennett's *English Books & Readers 1475 to 1557*, pp. 239-276. A few of these are certainly ghosts. To judge from titles in the *STC* and from general comparison of books I have seen with those examined by other scholars, the current estimated figure for de Worde's output is between nine hundred and one thousand separate editions. I am indebted to Ralph Hanna III for confirming this.

5 Links between illustration and literacy are discussed in M. Driver, 'Pictures in Print: Late Fifteenth- and Early Sixteenth-Century English Religious Books for Lay Readers', in *De Cella in Seculum: Religious and Secular Life and Devotion in Late Medieval England*, ed. Michael G. Sargent (Cambridge, 1989), pp. 229-244; see also Kathleen Kamerick, *Popular Piety and Art in the Late Middle Ages: Image Worship and Idolatry in England 1350-1550* (New York, 2002), pp. 155-196.

6 In his colophons de Worde tends to identify himself only as printer. In his will he describes himself as 'citizen and staciouner of london'. See M. Erler, 'Wynkyn de Worde's Will: Legatees and Bequests', *The Library*, 6th ser., 10 (1988), p. 118. Without straightforward documentary evidence, de Worde's precise role in the illustration of books produced in his shop is difficult to define. Here the assumption is made that de Worde was, to a large extent, responsible for the layout and page design of his books, as well as for acquiring and commissioning blocks to supplement those he inherited from Caxton.

7 Bennett, *English Books & Readers, 1475 to 1557*, p. 182. Henry R. Plomer, *Wynkyn de Worde and His Contemporaries from the Death of Caxton to 1535* (London, 1925), p. 61.

8 Malcolm Letts, 'The Source of Woodcuts in Wynkyn de Worde's Edition of *Mandeville's Travels*, 1499', *The Library*, 5th ser., 6 (1951), p. 156. J. W. Bennett, in her essay, 'The Woodcut Illustrations in the English Editions of *Mandeville's Travels*', *Papers of the Bibliographical Society of America* 47 (1953), pp. 59-69, points out Letts' errors in tracking de Worde's picture sources. However, his basic information on de Worde's shop remains unchallenged (if rather speculative).

9 'The Pilgrims at Table' in Caxton's *Canterbury Tales* (STC 5083) and its reuse in de Worde's *Assembly of Gods* (STC 17006) are discussed in Hind, vol. 2, pp. 710-711, fig. 446. James Moran, in *Wynkyn de Worde: Father of Fleet Street*, 2nd edn (London, 1976), claims the Canterbury pilgrims 'are recognisable' in the woodcut (p. 30); 'approximated' seems more accurate. While de Worde's appropriation of this image to represent the Feast of the Immortals has been much remarked on, what has not been discussed is its awkward presentation, sideways on the opening leaf, and the repetition of the cut, this time correctly positioned on the page, at the end of the volume. Placing the block sideways is certainly a mistake – perhaps a technical error – but its peculiar presentation is probably secondary to its value as a marketing device.

10 Prior to my visit to Brown University in the 1980s, where I curated a small exhibit of early printed materials in the John Hay Library, I had not been able to see these two prints together so had assumed that, though they were the same size, 'The Trinity Adored by the Assembly of Saints' cut in the *Nova legenda* was a copy of that in the

1493 *Golden Legend* (STC 24875). However, after I saw the prints side by side while placing the books in the exhibit case, it was evident that de Worde simply reused the same block for the *Nova legenda* frontispiece 23 years later. The *Nova legenda Angliae* (STC 4601) is listed under Capgrave in the *STC*, but is no longer attributed to him; the *STC* also does not cite the copy in the Annmary Brown Memorial collection at Brown University. The Assembly of Saints appeared as the prefatory woodcut in Caxton's first edition of this translation, printed 20 November 1483 (STC 24873-74; Hodnett, item 237) and reappeared in de Worde's editions of 1493, 1498 (STC 24875, 24876) and 1527 (24880), thereby linking them with the earlier Caxton best-seller. The two copies in the British Library (G.11925, C.48.h.2) open with the Assembly of Saints woodcut on both the recto and verso of the opening leaf. The woodcut is repeated at the end of the volume after the colophon with de Worde's printer's mark on the verso.

11 *STC* 20195, 13608.7, 24875.

12 Reproduced in Hodnett, fig. 21; items 375-378.

13 Hind, vol. 2, pp. 718-719; Hodnett, p. 6; and George D. Painter, *William Caxton, A Biography* (New York, 1977), p. 184. Painter reproduces the opening leaves of the *Fifteen Oes*, pl. 8. These are also reproduced in Janet Backhouse, Mirjam Foot and John Barr, comps., *William Caxton: An Exhibition to Commemorate the Quincentenary of the Introduction of Printing into England* (London, 1976), item 94, p. 87.

14 For further discussion, see Driver, 'The Illustrated de Worde: An Overview', *Studies in Iconography* 17 (1996), pp. 365-369, figs 9, 10, 11. M. J. Schretlen, *Dutch and Flemish Woodcuts of the Fifteen Century* (1925; repr. New York, 1969), p. 36. This Antwerp craftsman, says Schretlen, produced an enormous amount of work, and 'his woodcuts appeared for several decades in the Ludolphus editions in Antwerp and Zwolle, published by Petrus van Os from 1490 onwards'. Of the Master of the *Virgo inter Virgines*, Sandra Hindman has noted: 'There is still work to be done both from an attributional and iconographic viewpoint', in S. Hindman and James Douglas Farquhar, *Pen to Press: Illustrated Manuscripts and Printed Books in the First Century of Printing* (College Park, MD, 1977), p. 119.

15 PML 43. See also Gerard van Thienen and John Goldfinch, *Incunabula Printed in the Low Countries: A Census* (Nieukoop, 1999), no. 1309 (p. 239).

16 Van Thienen and Goldfinch, *Incunabula Printed in the Low Countries*, no. 1883 (p. 348). Lotte Hellinga, *Caxton in Focus: The Beginning of Printing in England* (London, 1982), p. 50. Veldener's ornately cut initials, which occur in his *Legenda aurea* (1480) as well as in his *Fasciculus temporum*, printed in Louvain '1476' (= 1475), served as prototypes for initials found at the beginning and end of de Worde's 1493 *Golden Legend*. For more on Veldener and his relationship with Caxton, see Wytze Hellinga and Lotte Hellinga, *The Fifteenth-Century Printing Types of the Low Countries* (Amsterdam, 1966); Hellinga, *Caxton in Focus*, pp. 49-51; Colin Clair, *A History of European Printing* (New York, 1976), p. 74; and Backhouse et al., *William Caxton*.

17 *STC* 9997, 13440b. Hodnett, assigns this (item 1312) to the 1497, 1498 and 1502 editions of the *Cronycle of Englonde*. The Morgan catalogue lists *The descrypcyon of Englonde*, which contains excerpts from the English translation of the *Polychronicon* paraphrased by William Caxton, under Ranulph Higden. This is bound with the Morgan copy of the *Cronycle of Englonde* (STC 9996).

18 *STC* 17103. For consideration of author and patron portraits, and their function in early printed books, see Mary C. Erler, 'Early Woodcuts of Skelton: The Uses of Convention', *Bulletin of Research in the Humanities* 87 (1986/87), pp. 17-28; Ruth Mortimer, *A Portrait of the Author in Sixteenth-Century France* (Chapel Hill, NC, 1980), pp. 1-50; Julie Smith, 'The Poet Laureate as University Professor: John Skelton's Woodcut Portrait', in *Renaissance Rereadings: Intertext and Context*, ed. M. C. Horowitz et al. (Urbana, Ill., 1988), pp. 159-183; and Julie A. Smith, 'Woodcut Presentation Scenes in Books Printed by Caxton, de Worde, Pynson', *Gutenberg Jahrbuch* 61 (1986), pp. 322-343.

19 The bishop woodcut is so close in style to the woodcut of a pope, which illustrates St Urban in de Worde's 1493 and 1498 editions of the *Golden Legend*, as well as Lyndewode in de Worde's 1499 edition of the *Constitutiones* (*STC* 17104), that Hodnett initially confused them. In item 373 he assigns the pope woodcut to the 1496 edition of Lyndewode, which he cites as *STC* 17103, though it is the bishop woodcut that actually occurs here. I have examined copies of the 1496 Lyndewode at the Annmary Brown Memorial collection, Brown University (AmBM 530), and in New York at the Pierpoint Morgan Library (Morgan 727, 733). The bishop appears on the title-pages of all three volumes. In Morgan 727 the woodcut has been coloured with gouache, water-colour and gold leaf. Hodnett corrects his error in *Additions and Corrections to English Woodcuts 1480-1535* (London, 1973), p. 63. There seem, however, to be more issues of the 1496 Lyndewode than the *STC* accounts for. Curt Bühler, 'Variants in English Incunabula', in *Bookmen's Holiday: Notes and Studies Written and Gathered in Tribute to Harry Miller Lyndenberg*, ed. Deoch Fulton (New York, 1943), p. 11, says that 'Morgan 727 is similar to the Harvard and Annmary Brown examples. These last two copies show that still further corrections were made while the work of printing was proceeding'. The title of the two Morgan copies is the same ('Constitutiones prouinciales'), though Morgan 727 has been heavily corrected in the first four quires. The first word of the title of AmBM 531 reads 'Constituciones'. It, too, shows corrections in quires 1-4. My thanks to Catherine Denning, curator of the Annmary Brown Memorial, for confirming this. The *STC* does not cite PML 727 or AmBM 531.

20 *STC* 15875, 17962. The unpainted woodcut is reproduced in Hodnett, fig. 18. For more on John Mirk, see Norman Blake, *Quattuor Sermones Printed by William Caxton*, Middle English Texts 2 (Heidelberg, 1975); and Susan Powell, 'Why Quattuor Sermones?' in *Texts and Their Contexts: Papers from the Early Book Society*, ed. Julia Boffey and V. J. Scattergood (Dublin, 1997), pp. 181-195.

21 *STC* 15876, 15900, 24877, 17958. See Hodnett, p. 6.

22 See Paul Needham, 'William Caxton and his Cologne Partners: An Enquiry based on Veldener's Cologne Type', in *Ars impressoria: Entstehung und Entwicklung des Buchdrucks: eine internationale Festgabe für Severin Corsten zum 65. Geburtstag*, ed. Hans Limburg, Hartwig Lohse and Wolfgang Schmitz (Munich, 1986), p. 14, n. 14. See also Paul Needham, *The Printer and the Pardoner* (Washington, D.C., 1986), p. 15. De Worde's edition is the first printed on English paper, made by John Tate the Younger. The *STC* does not cite the copies of Bartholomaeus which I examined in the Rare Book Room of the New York Public Library or in the John Hay Library, Brown University.

23 Hind, p. 605.

24 Van Thienen and Goldfinch, *Incunabula Printed in the Low Countries*, no. 349

(p. 61), *STC* 1536. Lotte Hellinga has contributed a recent description of the sources of the woodcuts in 'Wynkyn de Worde's Illustrations of Bartholomaeus Anglicus' *De Proprietatibus Rerum*', in *Three Lions and the Cross of Lorraine: Bartholomaeus Anglicus, John of Trevisa, John Tate, Wynkyn de Worde, and De Proprietatibus Rerum*, by Howell Heaney, Lotte Hellinga and Richard Hills (Newtown, Pa., 1992), pp. 34-40.

25 Hind, p. 620. Perhaps the most famous woodcut illustrations of surgery occur in the editions attributed to Johannes de Ketham of the *Fasciculus Medicinae* (Venice: Johannes and Gregorius de Gregoriis, 1491, 1493/4) (Goff K-13), which the Huss edition predates by at least ten years.

26 James Snyder, 'The Bellaert Master and *De Proprietatibus Rerum*', in *The Early Illustrated Book: Essays in Honor of Lessing J. Rosenwald*, ed. Sandra Hindman (Washington, D.C., 1982), pp. 41-62.

27 *STC* 5198, 5199.

28 *STC* 23876, 22411. For an account of the circulation of the Ten Commandments in Middle English, see Anthony Martin, 'The Middle English Versions of *The Ten Commandments*, with Special Reference to Rylands English MS 85', *Bulletin of the John Rylands University Library of Manchester* 64, no. 1 (Autumn, 1981), pp. 191-217.

29 Hodnett, p. 17. According to Hodnett, both the 1502 and 1506 Moses cuts appear in de Worde's 1528 edition of the *Kalender of shepeherdes*. This, however, seems to be an error, at least judging from the rather murky microfilm of the copy in the Huntington Library.

30 Moran, *Wynkyn de Worde*, p. 45. The existence of such presses might explain the typography of the Trees of Virtues and Vices that appear with very complex labels in de Worde's 1508 *Kalender* and in his *Boke named the Royall*. The 'tree of vyces' in de Worde's *Kalender*, for example, has eleven labels printed within scrolls on the tree itself (these are right side up and sideways left and right), then forty-two labels printed alongside, and nine labels printed sideways above.

31 *STC* 9996. Similar charts may be found in the *St Albans Chronicle* produced by the St Albans or Schoolmaster Printer as early as 1485 (*STC* 9995), a printer mentioned by de Worde in the colophon to his edition of the *Chronicles of England*: 'Here endyth this present cronycle of Englonde wyth the frute of tymes; compiled in a booke & also enprynted by one sometyme scole mayster of saynt Albons, on whoos soule God have mercy.'

32 Professor Robert Mathiesen (Brown University) first suggested to me Werner Rolewinck's *Fasciculus temporum* as a possible source for de Worde's *Chronicles* charts. Diane G. Scillia, 'The Master of The London Passional: Johann Veldener's "Utrecht Cutter"', in Hindman, *The Early Illustrated Book*, pp. 23-40, discusses the Veldener *Fasciculus*; this is on the whole a very useful article, though some of the similarities Scillia finds between woodcuts and paintings are not readily apparent.

33 *STC* 9997, 10000.5, 10001, 10002.

34 The woodcut from *The crafte to lyue well* is reproduced in Hodnett, fig. 46. The page seems to have been produced in one pull. The woodcut, with varying inset texts, appears in eight books produced by de Worde between 1506 and 1528 (ibid., item 477). In the *Boke named the Royall*, the prose explanation beneath the woodcut makes this comment on the Lord's prayer: 'It is moche shorte in wordes & moche longe in substaunce lyght to saye & subtyll for to understonde.' The *STC* does not list

the Longleat copy of the *Floure of the Commaundements* (STC 23876), though it is (incorrectly) cited in the 'Handlist of Publications by Wynkyn de Worde' in Bennett's *English Books and Readers, 1475 to 1557*, p. 250. Bennett dates the Longleat copy to 1505, labelling it STC 23875.1. According to the book's colophon, however, the Longleat edition is actually STC 23876. The colophon records the date of translation as 1509 and continues: 'Enprynted at London in Flete strete at the sygne of the sonne by Wynkyn de Worde. The seconde yere of ye reygne of oure moost naturell souerayne lorde kynge Henry The eyght of that name. Fynysshed the yere of oure lorde. M. CCCCC .x. the .xiiii. daye of Septembre.' (My thanks to Kate Harris, Librarian and Archivist to the Marquess of Bath, for confirming my suspicions about Bennett's dating and for sending me her transcription of the colophon.)

35 STC 791. Translated from 'franch' by 'Samoth Notgnywel' (Thomas Lewyngton), the text is very odd, perhaps most closely resembling Dutch (?), though an argument has been put forward that it is in Scots. The example in the Bodleian Library, Douce MM 402, lacks its opening and final leaves.

36 Van Thienen and Goldfinch, *Incunabula Printed in the Low Countries*, no. 1674 (p. 308). The Pierpont Morgan Library copy of the *Boeck des gulden throens* (PML 77100) is described by Paul Needham and Anna Lou Ashby in the *Twentieth Report to the Fellows of the Pierpont Morgan Library 1981-83* (1984), p. 47. There is a slightly later copy printed by Bellaert in Harlem in 1484 [BL IB. 48505]; Bellaert does not use factotums in his *Boec des gulden throens*. The figures of the Elder and Soul throughout are repeated with some variation in the Elder. The soul looks to have been copied from tC's earlier edition.

37 There is a painted copy of this volume in the Annmary Brown Memorial collection, Brown University, Providence, R.I. See also British Library IB. 47094.

38 Schretlen, *Dutch and Flemish Woodcuts of the Fifteenth Century*, p. 32. See also Hind, vol. 2, p. 562.

39 GW 5593, 5595, 5596.

40 Plate reproduced in Hind, vol. 1, fig. 153. Woodcuts from Grüninger's Terence are also reproduced in M. Driver, 'Illustration in Early English Books: Methods and Problems', *Books at Brown* 33 (1987), fig. 25; T. M. MacRobert, *Fine Illustrations in Western European Printed Books* (London, 1969), pl. 17; and Dale Roylance, *European Graphic Arts* (Princeton, 1986), p. 18. A copy of Grüninger's Terence is housed in the Pierpoint Morgan Library (Morgan 64); the Annmary Brown Memorial has one leaf (Goff T-94).

41. Hind, vol. 1, p. 342, fig. 152, reproduces a composite woodcut from the Terence (Goff T-91).

42 Hind remarks that Vérard's 'illustrations are based on the *Terence* printed by Grüninger at Strassburg, 1496' (Goff T. 106, BMC VIII, p. 94). There are copies of Vérard's Terence in the Spencer Collection at the New York Public Library and of *Le Jardin de Plaisance* in the Beinecke Library, Yale University. Woodcuts from Vérard's Terence are reproduced in Driver, 'Illustration in Early English Books', figs 26, 27. A two-volume facsimile of *Le Jardin de Plaisance*, with introduction and notes by E. Droz and A. Piaget, was published by the Société des anciens textes français (Paris, 1910-1925).

43 Hind, vol. 2, p. 669.

44 As Mary Beth Winn has further pointed out, 'Only the initial work in the anthology

corresponds to the title, the *Amoureux transy*', in *Anthoine Vérard, Parisian Publisher 1485-1512: Prologues, Poems, and Presentations* (Geneva, 1997) p. 81. For more on Bouchet's work, see Jennifer Britnell, *Jean Bouchet* (Edinburgh, 1986). (This painted copy is now in the Huntington Library.)

45 *STC* 22407, 22409, 22409.3, 22409.5, 22409.7. Bibliographical background is supplied by H. Oskar Sommer in his edition of *The Kalender of Shepherdes, The Edition of Paris 1503 in Photographic Facsimile: A Faithful Reprint of R. Pynson's Edition of London 1506*, vol. 1: *Prolegomena* (London, 1892). On the editions produced by Guy Marchant, see Sandra L. Hindman, 'The Career of Guy Marchant (1483-1504): High Culture and Low Culture in Paris', in *Printing the Written Word: The Social History of Books, circa 1450-1520*, ed. Hindman (Ithaca, N.Y., 1991), pp. 68-100. For a brief overview of English editions and their relationships to French sources, see Julia Boffey, 'Wynkyn de Worde, Richard Pynson, and the English Printing of Texts Translated from French', in *Vernacular Literature and Current Affairs in the Early Sixteenth Century: France, England, Scotland*, ed. Richard Britnell and Jennifer J. Britnell (Aldershot, 2000), pp. 177-181.

The date given for the first issue of de Worde's *The Kalender of shepeherdes* in Hind, Hodnett, Sommer, *Kalender of Shepherdes*, Bennett, 'Handlist of Publications by Wynkyn de Worde', and the old *STC* is 8 December 1508, though *STC* has revised that date to *c.* 1516, based apparently on McKerrow's dating of devices rather than on the book's colophon. See Ronald B. McKerrow, *Printers & Publishers' Devices in England & Scotland 1485-1640* (London, 1913). In this case, however, it seems better to go with the majority and place de Worde's competing edition of the *Kalender* within two years or so of Pynson's edition. The colophon of the first issue of de Worde's *Kalender*, extant only in one example, which I examined in Magdalen College, Oxford, reads as follows: 'Thus endeth the Kalender of Shepherdes newly translated out of frensshe in to Englysshe. Enprynten at London in ye Fletestrete at the sygne of the Sonne by Wynkyn de Worde in the yere of our lorde. M.CCCCC.viii. the .viii. day of December. The .xxiiii. yere of our moost redoubted & natural lorde kynge Henry the seueth.'

46 In *A Descriptive Catalogue of the Manuscripts in the Fitzwilliam Museum* (Cambridge, 1814), M. R. James provides a list of illuminations in Fitzwilliam MS 167, *Le Calendrier des Bergers* (pp. 368-372), many of which are close in iconography and detail to the later woodcut series illustrating the printed volumes. Fitzwilliam MS 167 includes figures of solar and lunar eclipses from 1486 to 1544 and seems to have been produced *c.* 1485-1486. The manuscript was acquired by the Fitzwilliam in 1814. Compare plates 27 and 26 in Driver, 'Ideas of Order: Wynkyn de Worde and the Title Page', in *Texts and Their Contexts: Papers from the Early Book Society*, ed. Julia Boffey and V. J. Scattergood (Dublin, 1997). Emile Mâle, in *Religious Art in France, The Late Middle Ages: A Study of Medieval Iconography and Its Sources*, trans. Marthiel Matthews, Bollingen Series XC:3 (Princeton, 1986), p. 430, mentions a Latin edition of this work dating from 1480 (Bibliothèque Nationale de France, ms. fr. 20107).

47 *STC* 21430, 21430a. The type and capitals point to de Worde rather than to Pynson as the actual printer, and many of the woodcuts in the *Boke named the Royall* are repeated in other de Worde editions, but not in those printed by Pynson.

48 *STC* 22409, 10606, 10606.5. The Everyman figure is reproduced in A. W. Pollard,

English Miracle Plays, Moralities and Interludes (Oxford, 1923), p. 77.

49 *STC* 10604, 10604.5. Unfortunately, the two surviving copies of these editions are fragmentary; the Bodleian has a few leaves of *STC* 10604 (sig. C4) and the British Library copy of *STC* 10604.5 lacks A6. See Pollard's discussion in *English Miracle Plays*, p. 202, as well as the reproduction and brief mention in Pollard's 'Woodcuts in English Plays Printed Before 1660', in *Old Picture Books with Other Essays on Bookish Subjects* (1902; repr. New York, 1970), pp. 182-184.

50 Letts, 'The Source of Woodcuts in Wynkyn de Worde's Edition of *Mandeville's Travels*', p. 156. The copy of the *Boke named the Royall* (*STC* 21430) in the Rare Book Room of the New York Public Library has de Worde's name in the colophon. The British Library has copies with the colophon of de Worde and also of Pynson (*STC* 21430a).

51 *STC* 15258. Portions of *The fyftene Joyes* are quoted in *Poems / Robert Copland*, ed. Mary Carpenter Erler (Toronto, 1993), pp. 113, 118-119. I examined de Worde's second edition of *The fyftene Joyes* in the Pierpont Morgan Library (PML 21589). The colophon reads: 'Thus endeth the .xv. Joyes of maryage. Enprynted in London in Flete strete at þe sygne of the sonne/by me Wynkyn de Worde. The yere of our lorde. M.CCCCC. and .ix.' Faith Gildenhuys, in her recent edition of a later English prose adaptation (sometimes attributed to Thomas Dekker) entitled *The Bachelor's Banquet*, comments that the earlier version printed by de Worde 'has little literary merit and its language has more in common with Chaucer than with Shakespeare or Dekker' (Binghamton, N.Y., 1993), p. 23.

52 *STC* 5095, 20108.

53 *STC* 14519, 21286.3. The *Gesta Romanorum* of *c.* 1510 has been reproduced in facsimile in *Wynkyn de Worde's Gesta Romanorum* (Exeter, 1974) from the unique copy in the possession of St John's College, Cambridge (A.2.18).

54 *STC* 10839, 17014.7.

55 *STC* 14039. Reproduced in Pollard, *English Miracle Plays*, p. lxviii.

56 *STC* 18475, 12948. Nevill's *The Castell of Pleasure* is one of four books perhaps printed by Robert Copland for de Worde. On fol. a1ᵛ, Copland identifies himself as 'Coplande the prynter' (see also Hodnett, p. 55; Erler, *Copland*, p. 58). The Everyman figure and copies of it occur as well in *The Pastime of Pleasure* (*STC* 12949) printed by de Worde in 1517. A facsimile from the unique volume in the Morgan Library is included in *The Works of Stephen Hawes*, intro. Frank J. Spang (Delmar, N.Y., 1975).

57 *STC* 14111. *STC* dates *Thenterlude of Youth* to *c.* 1530.

58 In the Vérard copy of *Le Jardin de plaisance Et fleur de Rethoricque* in the British Library [C.6.b.8 (impf.)], printed *c.* 1503, the text is illustrated with elaborate composites, including the figures of Everyman and Everywoman which are both repeated. In the later edition of Michel Le Noir, printed in Paris *c.* 1510 [BL C.57.i.4.], the Everywoman figure reappears. She appears again in the edition printed by the widow of Jean Trepperel with John Jehannot of *c.* 1515 [BL 87.b.18 (I)].

59 *STC* 3383.

60 Roberta D. Cornelius, ed., *The Castell of Pleasure* (London, 1930), p. 53.

61 De Worde employs the same double image in his 1509 edition of *The fyftene Joyes of maryage* (*STC* 15258). Sandra Hindman, in *Text and Image in Fifteenth-Century Illustrated Dutch Bibles* (Leiden, 1977), p. 79, describes a scene in a Brussels Bible representing 'two women boiling their children [for food] after the siege and famine related in the apocryphal Destruction of Jerusalem'.

62 *STC* 7571, 7572 (this, however, dated *c.* 1560? by *STC*).

63 *STC* 21286.3, 10001.

64 *STC* 14109. *STC* dates the British Library copy 1525?

65 Pynson's edition of the *Kalender of shepherdes* (*STC* 22408) 'borrowed most of the blocks used by Vérard in 1503' (Hind, vol. 2, p. 651). In *The crafte to lyue well*, de Worde uses clusters of woodcuts; these, however, do not function in quite the same way as composites. Hodnett reproduces a two-compartment woodcut used by de Worde in the *Boke of Comforte* (*STC* 3295), dated *c.* 1505 (fig. 12), but again, this is not a true composite. Another work that comes to de Worde via Pynson and is originally printed by Vérard is the *Castell of Laboure*. De Worde's edition (*STC* 12381) makes use of composites in depicting the Virtues and Vices, though whether this is an early (and failed) experiment or an attempt to maximise the number of blocks (and later apply them to other uses) is uncertain. I studied a copy of de Worde's *The crafte to lyue well* (*STC* 792) in the library of the Marquess of Bath, Longleat House.

66 Cornelius, *Castell of Pleasure*, p. 52. Another odd example of de Worde's experimentation with movable pictures occurs in his *Exornatorium curatorum* (1516, *STC* 10627.5): on the title-page, two woodcuts, one of a man kneeling in prayer, the other of Christ gesturing, appear left to right (Hodnett, fig. 30, item 443). On the verso of the title-page, these prints are reversed, with the Christ figure now on the left and the kneeling man on the right. Here, Christ seems to beckon to the reader as the kneeling man gestures toward the text.

67 See Bennett, *English Books & Readers, 1475 to 1557*, p. 185.

68 *STC* 7272, 7271. John Skot was also an early publisher of Christine in England, printing her *body of polycye* in 1521 (*STC* 7270).

69 Duff, *A Century of the English Book Trade*, p. 176; Erler, *Copland*, p. 158. For further background on Wyer, see also Henry R. Plomer, *Robert Wyer, Printer and Bookseller* (London, 1897).

70 Wyer, on occasion, does appropriate text. See Erler, *Copland*, p. 158, who discusses 'Robert Wyer's publication of his *Compost of Ptholomeus* around 1530 (*STC* 20480). ... This short book is taken entirely from the *Kalender of shepeherdes*, a work revised, edited and partly retranslated by [Robert] Copland in 1508' for Wynkyn de Worde. Wyer took the prologue of this work from Julian Notary's edition of the *Kalender*, printed *c.* 1518?, though Notary's edition was itself a compilation of the two earlier editions of the *Kalender* produced by Pynson and de Worde–Copland. As Erler comments: 'there are no pieces in Wyer that are not in Notary: that is, Wyer took nothing *directly* from Copland', an example of borrowing perhaps necessary to a popular printer who published approximately 145 known items. Erler, *Copland*, p. 158. For a redating of books printed by Wyer, many of which are undated or have been dated differently by the *STC*, see P. B. Tracy, 'Robert Wyer: A Brief Analysis of His Types and a Suggested Chronology for the Output of His Press', *The Library*, 6th ser., 2 (1980), pp. 294-303. Wyer's plagiarism is also discussed by H. B. Lathrop, 'Some Rogueries of Robert Wyer', ibid., 3rd ser., 5 (1914), pp. 349-364. Wyer's edition of *The .C. Hystoryes of Troye* is briefly discussed in George F. Warner, ed., *The Epistle of Othea to Hector or The Boke of Knyghthode, Translated from the French of Christine de Pisan With a Dedication to Sir John Fastolf, K.G.* (London, 1904), who comments: 'there is no doubt that it is taken from Pigouchet's French edition of 1490, or one of the reprints; in fact, it copies the same title in French, merely omitting the imprint "a Paris". Many of its rough woodcuts, one of

which accompanies each "texte", also come from the same source, being generally reversed, but others are independent and their subjects often have no connexion whatever with the text' (p. xli). There is, however, a logical correlation between image and text in Wyer's translation.

71 Wyer's Apologia has been transcribed in full in Driver, 'Christine de Pisan and Robert Wyer: The *.C. Hystoryes of Troye*, or *L'Epistre d'Othea* Englished', *Gutenberg-Jahrbuch* 72 (1997), pp. 126-127.

72 For example, publicity for the film *Terms of Endearment* focused on its two female leads, Debra Winger and Shirley MacLaine, rather than on the author of the novel from which the story came; Larry McMurtry was mentioned only in small type, when at all. (In more egregious instances, Choderlos de Laclos, author of *Les liaisons dangereuses*, made into the hit movie *Dangerous Liaisons*, was entirely omitted from the movie publicity and most movie reviews, and was not mentioned during the Academy Awards ceremony in which the film won several awards. *The Age of Innocence*, originally a novel by Edith Wharton, has become identified only as a film by Martin Scorsese, while in the publicity for *Othello*, the name William Shakespeare was not mentioned, and the film was described instead as by Oliver Stone.)

73 Curt F. Bühler, in his edition *The Epistle of Othea Translated from the French Text of Christine de Pisan by Stephen Scrope* (New York, 1970), cites at least four French printed editions which survive today, the others known from descriptions only: 'The *editio princeps* is Paris: Philippe Pigouchet [c1499], *GW* 6646. Three early sixteenth-century editions are listed by Jacques-Charles Brunet, *Manual du libraire et de l'amateur de livres*, vol. 1 (Paris, 1860), 1856, viz: Paris, [*sine nota*]; Lyon 1519; and Paris: Philippe Le Noir 1522 (PML 41003). These have the title *Cent histoires de Troye*. There is an undated edition, printed at Rouen by Raulin Gautier, at the Biblioteca Colombina, Seville; this is entitled 'Lepistre de othea'. Two more undated editions, with the same title, are credited to the Parisian press of 'Jehan Trepperel's widow' (p. xii n. 2). The editions by Trepperel's widow have been described by P. G. C. Campbell, 'L' Épître d'Othéa', *Étude sur les sources de Christine de Pisan* (Paris, 1924), p. 17.

74 The *Epistre* had been translated into English earlier by Stephen Scrope from a French illuminated manuscript made for Sir John Fastolf in 1450. Scrope's elegant translation is extant in several de luxe manuscripts made for the nobility. Pierpont Morgan Library MS M. 773, for example, seems originally to have been made for a noblewoman: 'the text in the Morgan MS was dedicated to some unknown noble lady. It was clearly not rededicated to Sir John Astley, for whom the manuscript seems to have been written prior to 1461' (from the unpublished Morgan catalogue). For Wyer's alteration of an image in the *.C. Hystoryes* with a religious theme, presumably so as to avoid trouble in the highly charged religious atmosphere of England in the 1540s, see below, pp. 202-204.

75 Philippe Le Noir was only a printer on occasion. He came from a family of publisher–printer–booksellers, of whom his brother Michel Le Noir, active in Paris about 1486-1520, was the more productive and famous. It is Michel's mark that appears on the title-page of *Les cent hystoires*. For more on Philippe Le Noir, see Cynthia J. Brown, 'Text, Image, and Authorial Self-Consciousness in Late Medieval Paris', in Hindman, *Printing the Written Word*, pp. 126, 129, 142.

76 *STC* 4815.

77 Hodnett, p. 59. For discussion of the Bridget portrait, see Chapter 4, pp. 146-149;

Driver, 'Pictures in Print', pp. 241-244; for more on Catherine, see Driver, 'Bridgettine Woodcuts in Printed Books Produced for the English Market', in *Art into Life: Collected Papers from the Kresge Art Museum Symposium*, ed. Carol Garrett Fisher and Kathleen L. Scott (East Lansing, Mich., 1995), pp. 248ff.

3. WYNKYN DE WORDE AND THE TITLE-PAGE

1 *STC* 6897, 15948, 3309. Other examples of de Worde's device are reproduced in Hind, 2:725, fig. 458; R. B. McKerrow, *Printers' and Publisher's Devices in England and Scotland 1485-1640* (London, 1913), and E. Gordon Duff et al., *Hand-Lists of Books Printed by London Printers, 1501-1556*, part 1 (London, 1913). The copy of the *Book of Hawking, Hunting, and Heraldry* in the Pierpont Morgan Library, in which the device is printed in red ink, was formerly in the possession of Richard Bennett. See A. W. Pollard, S. J. Aldrich, E. G. Duff and R. G. C. Proctor, *Catalogue of Manuscripts and Early Printed Books From the Libraries of William Morris, Richard Bennett, Bertram, Fourth Earl of Ashburnham, and Other Sources, Now Forming a Portion of the Library of J. Pierpont Morgan: Early Printed Books*, 4 vols (London, 1906-1907), vol. 3, item 732. According to this catalogue, the type is unusual, having been acquired by de Worde 'from Govaert van Ghemen, about 1491, when the latter removed to Copenhagen'.

2 *STC* 11615.5, 25479, 25480.3.

3 *STC* 10450.6, 16169. I examined a copy of the 1497 missal, printed in red and black, with woodcuts of the Crucifixion (sig. M6^v) and Resurrection (sig. O1), in the Huntington Library (PR 8305.3X). There is also a copy in the BL (IB. 40686). The colophon reads in part: '... hoc missale diuinorum offictorum vigilanti studio emendatum & reuisum: iussu & impensis prestantissimorum virorum vvinkin de vvorde & Michael mo rin: necnon Petri leueti: Impressus Parisius per Udalricum Gering. & Magistrum Berchtoldum Renbolt lociorum felicii numine explicitum est. Anno domini. M.cccc.xcvii. secunda Januarii.' Gering and Rembolt were printers to the University of Paris, while Levet was one of the many printers employed by Vérard. See Colin Clair, *A History of European Printing* (New York, 1976), p. 67. E. Gordon Duff, in *A Century of the English Book Trade* (London, 1948), describes Michael Morin as a London stationer, 'first mentioned in 1497 (1498) when Pierre Levet printed at Paris an edition of the *Destructorium Vitiorum* of Alexander Anglus "expensis Joh. Cobelens, Petri Levet, et Michaelis Morin"' (p. 107). Morin collaborated with de Worde on, or perhaps they helped fund, an edition of Terence printed in 1504 at Paris by Badius Ascensius and sold in London 'in edibus W. de Worde, Michael Morin et Johannis Brachii'. There is a copy of this in the British Library [C.48.i.5, Terence (Terentius Publius), *Comoedie*, 1504]. A grammatical text of Iodocus Badius Ascensius, attributed on its title-page to Sulpicius, *Quinta recognitio atque additio ad gramaticen Sulpitianam cum textu Ascensiano*, was printed for de Worde in Paris by Jean Barbier in 1511. There is a copy in the BL [625.g.24]. In 1506, Thielmann Kerver also printed a Sarum Breviary for Morin and de Worde. Other books commissioned by de Worde from Paris include a 1497 Book of Hours and a liturgical book ostensibly printed in York (*STC* 16160). See also *STC*, 3, p. 187.

4 Alfred W. Pollard, *Last Words on the History of the Title-Page with Notes on Some Colophons and Twenty-Seven Fac-Similes of Title-Pages* (1891; repr. New York, 1971), p. 15.

5 *STC* 24873, 20195, 15375.

6 *STC* 5065.

7 *STC* 14507, 1536. Margaret M. Smith, *The Title-Page: Its Early Development 1460-1510* (London, 2000), pp. 59-60, 77. For more on Bartholomaeus, see Chapter 2, esp. pp. 40-46.

8 See, for example, Hodnett, figs 372, 22, 54, 66. On woodcuts, see Driver, 'Pictures in Print: Late 15th- and Early 16th-Century English Religious Books for Lay Readers', in *De Cella in Seculum: Religious and Secular Life and Devotion in Late Medieval England*, ed. Michael G. Sargent (Cambridge, 1989), pp. 241ff; and 'Nuns as Patrons, Artists, Readers: Bridgettine Woodcuts in Printed Books Produced for the English Market', in *Art into Life: Collected Papers from the Kresge Art Museum Medieval Symposia*, ed. Carol Garrett Fisher and Kathleen L. Scott (East Lansing, Mich., 1995), pp. 244-257. This subject is also explored in Driver, 'The Illustrated de Worde: An Overview', *Studies in Iconography*, Medieval Institute Publications, 17 (Spring 1996), pp. 359-361.

9 *STC* 21259, 21260, 20875.5, 20876. *The Remedy Against the Troubles of Temptations* does, however, include a few Rolle quotations. Samuel Halkett and John Laing, *A Dictionary of Anonymous and Pseudonymous Publications in the English Language, 1475-1640*, 3rd rev. edn (New York, 1980), say of the *Contemplacyons of the drede and loue of God* that 'Rolle's name appears in none of the many early MSS, and the treatise contains a reference to one of his authentic works in terms most unlikely to have been used by him' (p. 137). The attribution of *The Remedy Against the Troubles of Temptations* to Rolle 'arises from the appearance of his name in a MS (Trinity Coll., Dublin, MS 154) containing this treatise, but more probably the name relates to another part of the MS. ... The work is possibly by William Sangham (fl. 1260), to whom a piece entitled *Of the remedies against temptations* is ascribed by John Stephens' (R53).

10 A. I. Doyle, 'A Survey of the Origins and Circulation of Theological Writings in English in the 14th, 15th, and Early 16th Centuries with Special Consideration of the Part of the Clergy Therein' (Ph.D. diss., University of Cambridge, 1953), p. 187.

11 *STC* 6895. The transcription of the opening of *The mirroure of golde* has been taken from the 1526 copy in the Fitzwilliam, which is not cited in the *STC*. I have also examined another 1522 copy in the Cambridge University Library [*STC* 6895] and the 1526 de Worde issue in the British Library [*STC* 6897]. For excerpts, see Alexandra Barratt, ed., *Women's Writing in Middle English* (New York, 1992), pp. 303-310.

12 *STC* 10902, 10903, 10891. For a description of the Fisher woodcut, see Hodnett, item 895. Reproductions of the image and of all the title-pages of Fisher's works printed by de Worde may be found in F. S. Ferguson's picture file, of which a copy is kept in the Houghton Library, Harvard University.

13 *STC* 10900, 10901.

14 Hodnett, p. 26.

15 *STC* 10894, 10894.5, 10895.

16 The Holbein drawing has been reproduced in *Holbein and the Court of Henry VIII* (London, 1978), item 15; in E. E. Reynolds, *Saint John Fisher*, 2nd edn (Wheathampstead, 1972); and in Brendan Bradshaw and Eamon Duffy, eds, *Humanism, Reform and the Reformation: The Career of Bishop John Fisher* (Cambridge, 1989). There is an early copy in the British Museum and another copy

in oil on paper in the National Portrait Gallery.

17 Hodnett, pp. 26ff.

18 *STC* 15258, 21286.3, 7571, 18808, 19119. Judging from the *STC*, Lydgate's translations and writings were printed and reprinted by Caxton, de Worde and other printers. *STC* attributes the translation to Lydgate. For more on Lydgate copies in print, see Alexandra Gillespie, 'The Lydgate Canon in Print from 1476 to 1534', *Journal of the Early Book Society* 3 (2000), pp. 59-86.

19 *STC* 6470. The only copy known is in the Pierpont Morgan Library (PML 21135).

20 Hodnett cites the title image, item 1122, and reproduces it as fig. 103. He does not, however, include a main listing for *Syr Degore* in his catalogue and misdates it as 'before 3 Dec., 1517'. The BL copy of the *Dystruccyon of Jherusalem* [C.25.k.5] has a composite illustration comprised of three figures labelled 'Uaspasyan', 'Archlylaus' and 'Pylate' on the title-page with the title in a banderole or scroll: 'The dystruccyon of Jherusalem by Vaspazian and Tytus'. The end-leaf of this volume, with the woodcut on the recto and the printer's mark on the verso, typifies the way early printed books were enclosed by printed wrappers prior to binding. See further discussion in this chapter.

21 Gerard van Thienen and John Goldfinch, *Incunabula Printed in the Low Countries: A Census* (Nieukoop, 1999), no. 1903 (p. 353). *STC* 792, 5198, 5199. I examined the illuminated edition printed by Couteau and Menard for Vérard in the Huntington Library. For more on the French editions and *ThOrdynary of Crysten Men*, see Chapter 1; Driver, 'Pictures in Print', pp. 232, 239; and Driver, 'The Image Redux: Pictures in Block-books and What Becomes of Them', in *Blockbücher des Mittelalters: Bilderfolgen als Lektüre* (Mainz, 1991), pp. 342-345. For the identification of Andrew Chertsey as translator, see Mary Carpenter Erler, *Poems / Robert Copland: Poems* (Toronto, 1993) pp. 73-74. A woodcut from the Leeu edition is reproduced in M. J. Schretlen, *Dutch and Flemish Woodcuts of the Fifteenth Century* (1925: repr. New York, 1969), pl. 40A. The Leeu edition is also mentioned in Ann Eljenholm Nichols, *Seeable Signs: The Iconography of the Seven Sacraments 1350-1544* (Woodbridge, 1994), p. 50. For more on de Worde's use of block-book sources, see Driver, 'Pictures in Print', plates 15-19, pp. 239-240.

22 Vérard republished illustrations directly copied from the block-book *Biblia pauperum* in *Les figures du vieil Testament et du nouuel*, which appeared c. 1504. Block-book images also influenced the iconography in Vérard's editions of *L'Art de bien mourir*, though their relationship to these images (as well as their links with *Biblia pauperum* models) requires further inquiry.

23 The *Ars moriendi* block-book series is known in at least 21 printings reproduced from thirteen distinct sets of blocks. See Sister Mary Catharine O'Connor, *The Art of Dying Well: The Development of the Ars moriendi* (New York, 1942), pp. 114-115. Translated from 'franch' by 'Samoth Notgynwell' (Thomas Lewyngton), the text [*STC* 791] is very odd.

24 *STC* 6034, 6035, 21336, 21337. In the 1507 edition of *The deyenge creature*, which I examined at Cambridge University Library, the title-cut is repeated on the verso of the last leaf of text, appearing with the printer's mark. In *The Rote or myrour*, the title-cut is the only illustration in the volume.

25 *STC* 21471.5, 21472. According to *STC*, there are two editions of *The ymage of loue*, the first a quarto with several more illustrations than appear in the second edition. These woodcuts are cited and reproduced in Hodnett (see item 442, fig. 63; item 436,

fig. 61; item 453, fig. 58, item 430). *STC* 21471.5 was printed 7 October 1525, and there is a copy in the Huntington Library. The copy I examined in the Bodleian Library (*STC* 21472), an octavo, was published *c.* 1532; the title image is the only picture in the volume.

26 Margaret Aston, *Lollards and Reformers: Images and Literacy in Late Medieval Religion* (London, 1984), p. 229, p. 230 n. 46. De Worde printed Gough's first books. According to Duff, Gough 'seems to have done little or no practical printing himself' (*A Century of the English Book Trade*, p. 58). Among other reforming printers associated with de Worde or with his house were John Byddell (or Salisbury), who worked for de Worde and for whom de Worde also printed books. Byddell was another of the executors of de Worde's will and was imprisoned in 1543 'in the Poultry Compter for printing unlawful books' (*Acts of the Privy Council*, N.S. vol. 1, pp. 107, 117), but was liberated after a fortnight's detention. Following de Worde's death, his London establishment passed to John Byddell. After Byddell's death in 1545, the house and its possessions passed into the hands of Edward Whitchurch, who stopped printing in the reign of Mary: 'Under Queen Mary Whitchurch was in trouble and was excluded from pardon in the proclamation at her coronation, and during her reign he ceased to print' (Duff, *A Century of the English Book Trade*, pp. 20, 169).

27 James Moran, *Wynkyn de Worde: Father of Fleet Street* (1960; repr. London, 1976), p. 41. See also A. W. Reed, *Early Tudor Drama: Medwall, The Rastells, Heywood, and the More Circle* (1926; repr. New York, 1969), pp. 166-174, who points out that the Vicar-General warned de Worde and Gough 'to appear before him in Consistory on the third day after St. Hilary to reply to articles concerning suspicion of heresy' (p. 167).

28 See Hodnett, item 430. Compare, however, ibid., fig. 186, which illustrates *A devout Intercescion*, with Fig. 21 here. Apparently, the title cut from *The ymage of loue* came into the hands of Richard Fawkes (or possibly was lent by Fawkes to de Worde), who used it to illustrate *A devout Intercescion*, dated 1525? by Hodnett and *c.* 1530 by the *STC* (14546.7). Hodnett comments, 'A similar *Salvator mundi* occurs in *A devout Intercescion*, assigned to the same year [as *The ymage of love*], together with a Crucifixion (no. 860) borrowed from de Worde' (p. 54). For further discussion of the passages in *The ymage of loue* dealing with pictures, as well as of Gough's and de Worde's troubles with the church authorities, see below, pp. 190-194.

29 There are four editions of *The thre kynges of Coleyn*, published *c.* 1496? (*STC* 5572), after July 1499 (*STC* 5573), in 1511 (*STC* 5574) and 1526 (*STC* 5575). I have examined copies in the Bodleian, Cambridge University Library, and the Pierpont Morgan Library. The 1496? copy in the Bodleian lacks A1. A recent edition of the *Three Kings of Cologne* has been edited by Frank Schaer (Heidelberg, 2000). *The thre kynges* is further discussed in Chapter 5, pp. 172-173.

30 *STC* 15922, 15934, 15948; *STC* 3266, 3267. The title image of the 1526 edition of *The thre kynges of Coleyne* (*STC* 5575) is reproduced by Hodnett, fig. 60, item 795.

31 *STC* 5574; *STC* 3263.5, 3264. The title-cut in de Worde's 1511 issue of *The thre kynges* is reproduced by Hodnett, fig. 23.

32 Elizabeth Salter, *Nicholas Love's 'Myrrour of the Blessed Lyf of Jesu Christ'*, ed. James Hogg (Salzburg, 1974), pp. 164ff. See also Michael G. Sargent, ed., *Nicholas Love's Mirror of the Blessed Life of Jesus Christ: A Critical Edition Based on Cambridge University Library Add. MS 6578 and 6686* (New York, 1992), p. 43.

33 *STC* 19213. Hodnett, p. 13. The unpainted woodcut is reproduced in Pollard, *Last Words on the History of the Title-Page*, pl. 6. Pollard, less impressed by the style and execution of the woodcut, comments, 'The deprecating attitude of Pauper is perhaps the best thing in the cut. ... Of the landscape it can only be said that it is highly conventionalized, and a small prize might safely be offered for a correct identification of the flowers growing on the hillside' (p. 19). The conventional representation of plants in early woodcuts is actually very typical in continental as well as English books. The Morgan copy lacks the title-page, A1, and parts of the tabula, but the New York Public Library copy has both title-page and end-leaf. The work was formerly ascribed to Henry Parker, but the *STC* in a note to Pynson's 1493 edition (*STC* 19212) says 'Prob. not by Parker'.

34 *STC* 792. The work was translated from French by Andrew Chertsey. Mary Erler has suggested to me in passing that the central image of the cart may be a play on Chertsey's name (cart = chart = Chertsey?). The OED notes that carts were formerly used for conveying convicts to the gallows and also for the chastisement and public exposure of offenders. The *STC* does not cite the copy at Longleat. See also mention of Chertsey by another contemporary, Robert Copland, in Erler, *Copland*, pp. 74-75.

35 *STC* 25007. Francis Henry Cripps-Day, *The Manor Farm* (London, 1931), p. xi. This edition includes a facsimile of de Worde's imprint; I examined the original copy in Cambridge University Library. See also Dorothea Oschinsky, ed., *Walter of Henley and Other Treatises on Estate Management and Accounting* (Oxford, 1971). For more on the author of the *Boke of Husbandry*, see N. Denholm-Young, 'Walter of Henley', in *Medievalia et Humanistica* 14 (April 1962), pp. 61-65. According to the opening text, the *Boke of Husbandry* was translated from French into English by Robert Grosseteste: 'HEre begynneth a treatyse of husbondry whiche mayster Groshede somtyme bysshop of Lyncoln made / & translated it out of Frensshe in to Englysshe /.' The *STC* comments: 'The attribution of the trans. to Grosseteste is dubious.'

36 *STC* 18566; *STC* 3259. The woodcut of the Deposition is reproduced in Hodnett, fig. 13, item 346.

37 *STC* 1966. For more on the manière criblée, see Hind, vol. 1, pp. 20-23; for an example of an early metal engraved relief plate, see William M. Ivins, Jr, *How Prints Look* (Boston, 1958), p. 25. *The chirche of the euyll men and women* is not cited in Hodnett. The metalcut of the Image of Pity is close in style to other such images occurring, for example, in editions of Hours produced by or for Thielman Kerver. Compare, for example, pl. 582, Figure of Pity, from *Horae Ad Usum Romanum*, printed by Kerver for Gillet Remacle in Paris, 14 May 1501, in Pollard et al., *Catalogue of Manuscripts and Early Printed Books from the Libraries of William Morris ...*, vol. 3. Other related illustrations are described by Ruth Mortimer in *Harvard College Library Department of Printing and Graphic Arts Catalogue of Books and Manuscripts Part I: French 16th Century Books*, vol. 2 (Cambridge, Mass., 1974), pp. 374-375.

38 Watson worked for de Worde, as he says in his preface to the 1518 edition of *Olyuer of Castylle* (Oliver of Castille): 'J. Henry Watson apprentice of London trustynge in the grace of god, hathe enterprysed for to translate this present hystorye out of frensshe into Englysshe, oure moders tonge, at the comaundement of my worshypfull

mayster Wynkyn de Worde.' Duff cites Bagford as the source for a reference to a *Donatus* 'Impressum Londiniis juxta Charing Crosse per me Hugonem Goes et Henery Watson', and continues, 'The only book now known printed by Goes is the *Directorium* of 1509 printed at York with W. de Worde's type who in the same year printed the York *Manual*' (*A Century of the English Book Trade*, pp. 166-167). Watson and printer's waste related to his shop are further discussed in Franklin B. Williams (ed.), *The Gardyners passetaunce* (London, 1985), pp. 42-50, 54-56.

39 See *STC* 1966, vol. 1, p. 82.

40 *STC* 14082. The single surviving example of *The way to the holy lande* is housed in the Pierpont Morgan Library. The border piece on the title-page resembles those in the *Fifteen Oes* (*STC* 20195), printed by Caxton (*c.* 1491), and in de Worde's Sarum Hours of 1494 (*STC* 15875).

41 *STC* 14546.3, 17537. Further careful study and comparison of the banderoles used in de Worde's books may reveal clearer patterns of use and reuse. The examples in the Ferguson file are not always to size, being cut mainly from sales catalogues, but breaks in the blocks, indicative of wearing, are often discernible. I am grateful to Katherine Pantzer for first introducing me to the Ferguson file, and for our subsequent conversations about using banderoles and woodcuts for dating undated printed books.

42 De Worde's editions of Aesop's *Fables* were printed in 1503 (*STC* 169), *c.* 1514 (*STC* 169.5), 1516 (*STC* 170) and 1535 (*STC* 171). For Pynson's edition (*STC* 176), see Hodnett, p. 93.

43 The colophon reads: 'Londonii, Apud Winandum de VVorde. Anno. M.D. xxxv'. There is a woodcut pasted in at the end of FABVLAE POGGII, of a fox and heron, with a speckled background. I examined the Caxton and de Worde editions in the Bodleian Library. The Caxton edition has 186 woodcuts, with many repeats. It is reproduced in facsimile in Edward Hodnett, *The History and Fables of Aesop Translated and Printed by William Caxton 1484: Reproduced in Facsimile from the Copy in the Royal Library, Windsor Castle* (London, 1976).

44 For Italian and humanist influence on de Worde and other English printers, see David R. Carlson, *English Humanist Books: Writers and Patrons, Manuscripts and Print, 1475-1525* (Toronto, 1993), pp. 135-141. Some models may be found in *Italian Renaissance Books, 1478-1587* (Provo, UT, 1988), pp. 95, 97.

45 W. J. Ong, *Ramus, Method, and the Decay of Dialogue* (Cambridge, Mass., 1958), p. 313. For the use of title-pages in manuscripts, see: Smith, *The Title-Page*, pp. 25-34; H. J. Hermann, *Die Handschriften und Inkunabeln der Italienischen Renaissance* (Leipzig, 1932), figs 12, 17, 22, 62-64; Giordana Mariana Canova, *La miniatura veneta del Rinascimento 1450-1500* (Venice, 1969); J. J. G. Alexander, *Italian Renaissance Illuminations* (London, 1977); and Tammaro de Marinis, *La biblioteca napoletana dei re d'Aragona*, vol. 4 (Milan, 1947). Albinia de la Mare spent a very instructive day with me at the Bodleian and made many suggestions about the development of the title-page in Italy. For the use of the title-page after the introduction of printing, see Pollard, *Last Words on the History of the Title-Page*; and Rudolph Hirsch, 'The Earliest Development of Title-Pages 1470-1479', in *The Printed Word: Its Impact and Diffusion* (London, 1978), pp. 1-13.

46 Walter J. Ong, *Orality and Literacy: The Technologizing of the Word* (New York, 1982), pp. 126-127.

47 Howard M. Nixon, 'William Caxton and Bookbinding', *Journal of the Printing*

Historical Society 11 (1976/77), p. 92; Paul Needham, *Twelve Centuries of Book-bindings 400-1600* (New York, 1979), p. 89.

48 Nixon, 'William Caxton and Bookbinding', pp. 94-96. See also A. I. Doyle, 'The Work of a Late Fifteenth-Century English Scribe, William Ebesham', *Bulletin of the John Rylands Library* 39, 2 (March 1957), pp. 298-325.

49 Needham, *Twelve Centuries of Bookbinding*, p. 90.

50 Nixon, 'William Caxton and Bookbinding', p. 95. The 1503 edition of Joannes de Janua's *Catholicon*, printed in Lyon by Nicholas Wolff, which contains de Worde waste of 1502, is currently housed in Corpus Christi College, Oxford. The binding of this book is reproduced in E. Gordon Duff, *William Caxton* (1905; repr. New York, 1970), frontispiece. See also Paul Needham, 'Johann Gutenberg and the Catholicon Press', *Papers of the Bibliographical Society of America* 76 (1983), pp. 341-371.

51 Howard M. Nixon and Mirjam M. Foot, *The History of Decorated Bookbinding in England* (Oxford, 1992), p. 11.

52 Mirjam M. Foot, *Studies in the History of Bookbinding* (Brookfield, Vt., 1994), p. 148.

53 Needham, *Twelve Centuries of Bookbindings*, p. 89. For more on the identity of the Caxton binder, see Howard M. Nixon, 'Caxton, His Contemporaries and Successors in the Book Trade from Westminster Documents', *The Library*, 5th ser., 31, no. 4 (December 1976), pp. 323-326.

54 W. H. James Weale, *Bookbindings and Rubbings of Bindings in the National Art Library South Kensington Museum*, 2 vols (London, 1894-1898), vol. 1, p. xxxii.

55 M. Erler, 'Wynkyn de Worde's Will: Legatees and Bequests', *The Library*, 6th ser., 10 (1988), pp. 121, 119.

56 Nixon, 'William Caxton and Bookbinding', p. 92.

57 Henry R. Plomer, 'An Inventory of Wynkyn de Worde's House "The Sun in Fleet Street" in 1553', *The Library* 6 (1915), p. 231.

58 Erler, 'Wynkyn de Worde's Will', p. 119; Duff, *A Century of the English Book Trade*, pp. 53-54.

59 E. Gordon Duff, *The Printers, Stationers, and Bookbinders of Westminster and London from 1476 to 1535* (1906; repr. New York, 1971, 1977), p. 113. Duff's 1899 lectures were first printed in a small edition under the title: *The Printers, Stationers and Bookbinders of London and Westminster in the Fifteenth Century* (Aberdeen, 1899).

60 See Chapter 2, note 4.

61 Weale, *Bookbindings and Rubbings* II, item 158; G. D. Hobson, *Bindings in Cambridge Libraries* (Cambridge, 1929), pl. XIX, no. 15, pp. 58-59. I wish to thank Muriel McCarthy, Librarian, Archbishop Marsh's Library, Dublin, for calling my attention to the 1511 Jehan Petit imprint.

62 Hobson's descriptions are generally confusing. He seems to posit three examples (*Bindings*, p. 59): one French binding panel with a four-compartment panel of St John the Evangelist, St Barbara, St Katherine and St Claude (his note says 'This saint has not previously been identified: he also figures at the end of Books of Hours'); the binding made by 'Pierre Gipot', a French binding panel with St John Evangelist, St Barbara, St Katherine and St Nicholas (which I strongly suspect is the same as the first binding he describes); and an English binding that is related. Other descriptions of the Gipot binding panel (now attributed to Guiot) sometimes describe the fourth saint as St Claude, and at other times, as St Nicholas. See notes following.

63 Ibid., p. 58.

64 Mortimer, *Harvard College Library Department of Printing and Graphic Arts Catalogue of Books and Manuscripts*, vol. 1, item 31. The folio edition of the *Golden Ass* of Apuleius Madaurensis was edited by F. Beroaldo and J. Kierher, and printed by J. Philippi for L. Hornken and G. Hittorp at Paris and Cologne, 1512. Mortimer describes the binding this way: 'blind-stamped with panel in four compartments of saints John the Evangelist, Barbara, Catherine, and Nicholas on front cover'. The front panel is signed with the initials PG: 'The reading of this name is discussed by Goldschmidt (no. 55), who adopted the form "Pierre Gipot", but the name has since been reread and accepted as "Pierre Guiot". ... The saints panel corresponds to the Goldschmidt example.'

65 E. Ph. Goldschmidt, *Gothic & Renaissance Bookbindings*, 2 vols (Amsterdam, 1967), vol. 1, p. 177. See also *The History of Bookbinding, 525-1950 A.D.; An Exhibition Held at the Baltimore Museum of Art, November 12, 1957, to January 12, 1958*, organised by the Walters Art Gallery and presented in cooperation with the Baltimore Museum of Art (Baltimore, 1957). Goldschmidt describes the binding panel on a quarto of Ricardus de Sancto Victore, *De Trinitate*, printed 1510 in Paris by H. Stephanus. He says the printer's name is 'Pierre Gipot' and that he was active about 1510, describing the panel this way: 'On front cover a panel (164 × 102 mm.) in four compartments: S. John the Evangelist, S. Barbara, S. Catherine and S. Nicholas, standing each under a canopy against a starry background; in the two lower compartments the binder's initials, p.g.' This French binding panel is 'Not in Weale' (p. 178). Goldschmidt further cites other French occurrences of the binding, including one described in the *Catalogue of Early Printed Books in the Pierpont Morgan Library*: 'a specimen of these panels is described from a Horae, Paris, Kerver for G. Remackle, 1500-1 (No 581)'. There are actually three examples of this binder's work in the Pierpont Morgan Library. The example cited in Mortimer is also described in the Walters Art Gallery catalogue, *The History of Bookbinding 525-1950 AD*, reproduced as pl. xxxvii, description, p. 80. The 'lower cover' is not reproduced here, though it appears in Goldschmidt, *Gothic & Renaissance Bookbindings*, pl. xxiii, and there is this further comment: 'the sharp condition of the present example confirms the correct reading as Guiot – doubtless a member of a French family of booksellers. The names on French panels seem always to be those of publishers or booksellers, rather than of individual binders, in contrast to Flemish practice – although this does not exclude the possibility of a bindery being connected with the establishment.'

66 The Image of Pity illustration from *Horae Ad Usum Romanum* (PML 581, ChL 1515), printed in Paris, by Thielman Kerver for G. Remacle, 5 January 1500-1501, is reproduced in the *Catalogue of Manuscripts and Early Printed Books From the Libraries of William Morris ...*, vol. 2, no. 581, where the binding panel is also described: 'Original brown calf, stamped on the upper side with a panel in four compartments, in each of which stands a saint (SS. John the Evangelist, Katherine, Barbara, Claudius), the lower compartments bearing the initials of the binder, p and g; on the lower side with a centre panel made up of five floral rolls, surrounded by a border of vines and birds, and motto on the scrolls: "En // Dieu tout // bon // aduis // esperence //" and the name of the binder, Pierre Gipot (the third letter of surname doubtful)' (p. 22). Note the confusion of Nicholas with Claude or Claudius in describing the fourth panel, and the earlier attribution to 'Gipot'. The colophon of

this Book of Hours reads: 'Ces presentes heures a lusaige de Romme furent acheuees le.v.iour de ianuier.Lan.M.CCCCC. par Thielman keruer pour Gillet remacle libraire demouran*t* sur pont saint michiel a lenseigne de la licorne.' The French border panels occur only on the front and back, along with other borders, of the binding of an Hours for Rome use, printed by Philippe Pigouchet for Simon Vostre (PML ChL 1478A) in 1496.

67 Hobson, *Bindings*, p. 58.

68 Weale, *Bookbindings and Rubbings*, vol. 2, item 158. Cyril Davenport, in *Cameo Book-Stamps Figured and Described* (London, 1911), item LXXXVI, pp. 116-117, includes this description: 'The border has at the top a bird between oak sprays; at each side are a wyvern and alternate sprays of artichoke and oak; at the bottom are the initials of the designer SG formed by two monsters tied together between two birds; and in each corner is a large artichoke.' The pineapple was a rarity up to the reign of Charles II, though these seem to appear, for example, on the monument of Edmund Harman, barber and servant to Henry VIII, erected in 1570, along with pictures of Indians, the earliest representation in England of the original inhabitants of America (St John the Baptist Church, Burford, Oxfordshire).

Comparison of my photographs of Marsh's bindings with reproductions of the French and English panels in Mortimer and Hobson shows that the borders of the French and English versions are similar but certainly not the same. In English examples, the border always occurs along with the four-compartment panel, and it substitutes acorns and what look to be pineapples, or artichokes, for grapes. There are no banderoles in the English version.

69 J. Basil Oldham, *Shrewsbury School Library Bindings* (1943; rev. edn, New York, 1990), p. 87: 'in all examples known to me there is a rectangular mark at the top of the panel and across part of the signature at the bottom (see under F.VI.4), but of which in the Weale collection of rubbings in the Victoria and Albert Museum there are rubbings of two examples, in one of which, unfortunately with no reference attached to it, the panel appears in its undamaged state. How to account for these strange marks I can make no suggestion whatever.'

70 Oldham, *Shrewsbury School Library*, p. 86; Hobson, *Bindings*, p. 58.

71 The flyleaves from the de Worde edition of *The thre kynges of Coleyne* seem closest to the 1511 edition (*STC* 5574). Hobson says he has found the panel in bookbindings in the Society of Antiquaries (London, 1515); British Museum (C.24.9.38) (London, 1518); a 1530 Paris Missal now in Oxford (Bodley Gough Missal 117); a 1530 copy printed in London (BM C.11.b.8); an undated empty binding (Bagford scrapbook, Harley 5943); and a sixteenth-century manuscript in the Public Record Office (catalogue 1926, case F, no. 62). He attributes four of these editions to Wynkyn de Worde (1514 Marsh, 1515 Society of Antiquaries, 1518 British Museum C.24.9.38 and 1530 British Museum C.11.b.8), though only three of these have been printed by de Worde (*Bindings*, p. 58). The two examples I have found in the BL are *Synonyma* (*STC* 11617) and *Myroure of our Lady* (C.11.b.8, *STC* 17542), the latter printed by Fawkes.

72 Georg Wolff worked 'first at Gering's house at the Soleil d'Or', then 'au Chasteaupers, prope collegium bonae curiae', and finally in 1493 at the sign of Ste Barbe in the rue St Jacques. He went into partnership with Thielmann Kerver by 1498. His career is briefly described and his printer's mark is reproduced from an edition of Masilius Ficinus in *Catalogue of Manuscripts and Early Printed Books From the Libraries of*

William Morris ..., vol. 2, item 517. Hind (vol. 2, p. 782) says Georg Wolff was a printer about 1489-1500, who worked with Kerver after 1497.

73 *STC* 16125. Comparison of the printer's waste with the four editions of *The thre kynges of Coleyne,* published *c.* 1496? (*STC* 5572), after July 1499 (*STC* 5573), in 1511 (*STC* 5574) and in 1526 (*STC* 5575), indicates that it is closest to the 1511 issue. For a discussion of a ghost edition of *The thre kynges of Coleyne,* see Driver, 'Nuns as Patrons, Artists, Readers', pp. 266-267, n. 46.

74 Foot, *Studies in the History,* p. 106.

75 Nixon, 'William Caxton and Bookbinding', p. 106.

4. SAINTLY WOMEN

1 André Vauchez, *Sainthood in the Later Middle Ages,* trans. Jean Birrell (Cambridge, 1997), p. 411. Vauchez further makes the point that late medieval mystics (of the fourteenth and fifteenth centuries) were concerned less with the common folk than with addressing themselves and telling their visions to 'kings, popes, at a pinch bishops and superiors of orders'.

2 See the discussion of single-leaf prints in Chapter 1, pp. 8-12. The reader may also compare woodcuts from *The Orcharde of Syon* and Bridget portraits in my essay, 'Pictures in Print: Late Fifteenth- and Early Sixteenth-Century English Religious Books for Lay Readers', in *De Cella in Seculum: Religious and Secular Life and Devotion in Late Medieval England,* ed. M. Sargent (Cambridge, 1989), figs 20-24.

3 Tessa Watt, *Cheap Print and Popular Piety, 1550-1640* (Cambridge, 1991), p. 131. Rudolf Hirsch, in *Printing, Selling and Reading 1450-1550* (1964; repr. Wiesbaden, 1974), p. 4, comments further that 'these woodcuts ... were produced in sizable quantities'. W. L. Schreiber, the best-qualified writer on the subject, estimated they were printed in editions of 200-300 copies, figures corresponding to those of early printed books. 'They were sold during pilgrimages, in front of churches, in market places, at fairs, and probably from house to house' (Schreiber, p. 4.). He continues: 'The very concept of pictures with an explanatory text (instead of a text to which illustrations are subordinated) presumes the existence of buyers with a limited ability to read' (ibid.).

4 According to Hind, vol. 1, p. 91. Ysenhut's work is further cited in Richard S. Field, *Fifteenth Century Woodcuts and Metalcuts from the National Gallery of Art* (Washington, D.C., 1965), no. 78. Field points out that the immediate source for this image (Schreiber ix.506aa, Rosenwald Collection 1959.16.15) is an engraving by Master E. S., now in the British Library, which is reproduced in Alan Shestack, *Master E. S. Five Hundredth Anniversary Exhibition, Philadelphia Museum of Art* (Philadelphia, 1967), item 18. See also Max Lehrs, *Geschichte und kritischer Katalog des deutschen, niederländischen und französischen Kupferstichs im XV. Jahrhundert,* 9 vols (Vienna, 1908-1934), no. 33. The woodcut appears in a unique printed altarpiece created in Basel by Lienhart Ysenhut about 1490. 'In this portable altarpiece, printed on parchment, the woodcut copy of the E. S. engraving is pasted between two pages of text, forming a triptych.' The woodcut is further discussed in H. Diane Russell with Bernadine Barnes, *Eva/Ave: Woman in Renaissance and Baroque Prints,* National Gallery of Art, Washington (New York, 1990), p. 96, item 54.

5 See Russell with Barnes, *Eva/Ave: Woman in Renaissance and Baroque Prints,* item

47 (pp. 96-97), who compares an extant example of an impression pasted into a surviving box in a sales catalogue by Arsène Bonafous-Murat, *Estampes 1490-1989* (Paris, 1989), no. 1. The image is of the Virgin as the woman of the Book of Revelation, surrounded by the rays of the sun and standing on a crescent moon. See further A. J. J. Delen, *Histoire de la gravure dans les anciens Pays-Bas et dans les provinces belges des origines jusqu'à la fin du XVIIIe siècle*, part 1: *Des origines à 1500* (Paris, 1924), who reproduces the same picture as fig. 1 (p. 151): 'Coffret de voyage avec gravure sur bois á l'intérieur du couvercle (Cabinet des Estampes, Paris).'

6 David Landau and Peter Parshall, *The Renaissance Print 1470-1550* (New Haven, 1994), p. 2. Such craftsmen were also most likely responsible for designing metal and wooden moulds with religious scenes that were used to make marzipan or gingerbread, often produced in monastic houses for sacral purposes. There are, for example, two sixteenth-century metal moulds, one of the Virgin and Child, the other of the Annunciation, which were produced in Germany, currently on display in the Musée national du Moyen-Age, Thermes de Cluny, in Paris (Rothschild legacy).

7 See M. Driver, 'Nuns as Patrons, Artists, Readers: Bridgettine Woodcuts in Printed Books Produced for the English Market', in *Art into Life: Collected Papers from the Kresge Art Museum Medieval Symposia*, ed. Carol Garrett Fisher and Kathleen L. Scott (East Lansing, Mich., 1995), pp. 237-238, 262 n. 5. Edmund Colledge, 'A Syon Centenary', *Life of the Spirit* 15 (1960), pp. 1-35. The most recent edition is *The Myroure of Oure Ladye*, ed. John Henry Blunt (London, 1873). Vincent Gillespie has recently edited Thomas Betson's catalogue for Syon, *Syon Abbey*, published in one volume with *The Libraries of the Carthusians*, ed. A. I. Doyle (London, 2001).

8 For more on vernacular reading at Syon, see Arthur Jefferies Collins, in his Introduction to *The Bridgettine Breviary of Syon Abbey*, Henry Bradshaw Society 96 (Worcester, Stanbrook Abbey Press, 1969), p. xxxi, who cites the case of Mary Champney, professed at Mishagen after the second suppression when the Bridgettine nuns had fled to Belgium. Champney was 'there placed to learne her Songe and her Grammer, for vnderstandinge of her lattin service, for her preparacion to be fitt for Religion'. Barbara J. Harris, in her study of 1200 aristocratic couples and their children, which includes a survey of wills and thousands of letters written by aristocratic Englishwomen between 1450 and 1550, has 'not found evidence of a single laywoman of this class who learned Latin before the reign of Henry VIII'. See Harris, *English Aristocratic Women 1450-1550: Marriage and Family, Property and Careers* (Oxford, 2002), p. 37. For further remarks on reading at Syon, see Collins, Introduction to *The Bridgettine Breviary of Syon Abbey*, pp. xxxi-xxxvii; Christopher de Hamel, 'The Library: The Medieval Manuscripts of Syon Abbey, and Their Dispersal', in *Syon Abbey: The Library of the Bridgettine Nuns and Their Peregrinations after the Reformation* (Otley, 1991), pp. 48-158; Ann M. Hutchison, 'What the Nuns Read: Literary Evidence from the English Bridgettine House, Syon Abbey', *Mediaeval Studies* 57 (1995), pp. 205-222; and Ann M. Hutchison, 'Devotional Reading in the Monastery and in the Late Medieval Household', in Sargent, *De Cella in Seculum*, pp. 215-227. De Hamel, 'The Library', notes that the sacristan of Syon Abbey had the responsibility 'for the upkeep of "thynges longyne to the chirche" and her equipment for this, as assigned by the abbess, included "penners, pennes, ynke, ynkehornes, tables and suche other"' – implements essential to the writing of documents and books (p. 70). De Hamel is here citing George James Aungier, *The History and Antiquities of Syon Monastery, the Parish of Isleworth, and*

the *Chapelry of Hounslow* (London, 1840), p. 367.

9 Dodgson, *Ashm.*, item 39, p. 27, describes the woodcut as a 'Late impression, coloured in fifteenth-century style'. On the verso are manuscript prayers in Latin. Dodgson says further: 'I believe the woodcut here described in two states to be an early work of Burgkmair, about 1499-1501, and I attribute the Oxford woodcut, in which the Man of Sorrows is freely repeated in reverse, with a considerable change in the position of the arms, also to Burgkmair.' For brief background on Burgkmair and some examples of his work, see Christiane Andersson and Charles Talbot, eds, *From a Mighty Fortress: Prints, Drawings, and Books in the Age of Luther 1483-1546* (Detroit, 1983), cat. nos 112, 114-116.

10 Schreiber 1154. This woodcut has been reproduced in Landau and Parshall, *The Renaissance Print 1470-1550*, item 2, p. 3, who remind us that 'Holy images of the kind manufactured by these workshops were undoubtedly meant for both the religious community and its lay public' (p. 2).

11 Hodnett, *Additions & Corrections to English Woodcuts 1480-1535* (London, 1973), items 2513, 2512. See Dodgson, *Ashm.*, p. 34. Hodnett is more cautious, dating the Man of Sorrows cut as 'ca. 1500?' and ascribing it to 'printer unknown' (*Additions and Corrections*, p. 46). Of the *Pietà* (Schreiber 976), Hodnett further comments, 'It is difficult to see what compulsion led to such duplication of blocks that were available and in good condition' (*Additions and Corrections*, p. 28). Hodnett cites close copies of the *Pietà* that were used to illustrate Wynkyn de Worde's edition of the *Imytacion of cryst* (STC 23956), printed around 1518. De Hamel, 'The Library', echoing Hodnett, says the manuscript has been 'written by an unpractised scribe Johannes, "cuius habitacio est in syon", (and) opens with three bound-in woodcuts, at least two of them English' (p. 100).

12 There are 27 surviving single-leaf Images of Pity made in England (STC 14077c.6-.23b), probably representing 'thousands of paper images of Christ, Our Lady and various saints, which were for sale at cathedrals and shrines' (Watt, *Cheap Print and Popular Piety*, p. 131). The texts beneath the Man of Sorrows and *Pietà* woodcuts were most likely scratched out by a later sixteenth-century owner, though this may have occurred at the same time the indulgences were incorporated as ready-made illustrations into the manuscript. For further discussion of the censorship of single-leaf prints, see Chapter 6.

13 STC 14077c.18. STC attributes the print to Pynson (*c.* 1510) and says, 'Presumably issued for the Brigittine Convent of Syon, near Isleworth'. This image is also discussed in Dodgson, *Ashm.*, pp. 34ff, item 15. Hind, vol. 2, p. 738, says that 'The type used in the *Last Judgment* has not been definitely assigned to any printer, but has letters which are found in both Wynkyn de Worde and Pynson. The cut has something of the character of the blocks in Wynkyn's Bartholomaeus, *De Proprietatibus Rerum*, 1495.'

14 Collins, *The Bridgettine Breviary of Syon Abbey*, p. xvi nn. 5, 27, 29. A similar image of Christ seated on a rainbow and displaying his wounds appeared, imprinted in beaten gold on a black cloth of majesty and 'at every corner a shield of France and England quarterly', above the funeral image of Richard III as part of the ceremony of his reburial at Fotheringay in 1476, at which his mother, Cicely, Duchess of York 'was the foremost participant'. C. A. J. Armstrong, 'The Piety of Cicely, Duchess of York: A Study in Late Medieval Culture', in *For Hilaire Belloc, Essays in Honor of His 71st Birthday*, ed. Douglas Woodruff (New York, 1942), p. 72.

15 De Hamel, 'The Library', p. 100, also cites another Syon manuscript with added woodcuts, St Paul's Cathedral MS. 5, which 'has four historiated initials formed by pasting woodcuts into an added surround (fols 57^r, 69^r, 69^v and 84^r)'. Oxford, St John's College MS 164 is cited in David N. Bell, *What Nuns Read: Books and Libraries in Medieval English Nunneries* (Kalamazoo, Mich., 1995), p. 40. Satoko Tokunaga, in 'The Use of Books Owned by Medieval Women: A Contribution to a Study of Medieval Nuns' Reading in Late Medieval England' (M.A. thesis, University of Birmingham, 2000), pp. 71-72, comments that 'a metal cut image of the Holy family and the Magi is fittingly pasted on the margin'. For further reference to books in convents, see N. R. Ker, *Medieval Libraries of Great Britain: A List of Surviving Books*, 2nd edn (London, 1964), and Andrew G. Watson, *Medieval Libraries of Great Britain: A List of Surviving Books: Supplement to the Second Edition* (London, 1987). Mary Erler includes two brief appendices in *Women, Reading, and Piety in Late Medieval England* (Cambridge, 2002), 'Surviving Religious Women's Books Not Listed in Ker-Watson or Bell,' pp. 139-146, and 'Multiple Book Ownership by Religious Women', pp. 147-149.

16 'Dotted prints' are discussed by Hind, vol. 1, pp. 20-21, 175-197.

17 Millard Meiss, *Painting in Florence and Siena after the Black Death: The Arts, Religion, and Society in the Mid-Fourteenth Century* (Princeton, 1978), p. 111, quoting from *I Miracoli di Caterina di Iacopo da Siena*, ed. Francesco Valli (Siena, 1936). See also Field, *Fifteenth Century Woodcuts and Metalcuts from the National Gallery of Art*, cat. 346. This image is reproduced in Russell with Barnes, *Eva/Ave: Woman in Renaissance and Baroque Prints*, item 58 (Schreiber 2519m, Rosenwald Collection 1943.3.704). Field further cites this artist in connection with another metal-cut now in the Metropolitan Museum of Art, New York, in *Fifteenth-Century Woodcuts and Other Relief Prints in the Collection of the Metropolitan Museum* (New York, 1977), item 42.

18 Catherine M. Mooney, ed., *Gendered Voices: Medieval Saints and Their Interpreters* (Philadelphia, 1999), p. 13.

19 *STC* 24873-24874. Though there were illustrated copies of the *Golden Legend* produced on the continent, no direct model for Caxton's illustrations has been found among them. His pictures may, instead, have been drawn from English ivories which sometimes give a similar, rather crude, impression of immobility.

20 Acts 1:14, 2:17-18 (RSV). Gerard van Thienen and John Goldfinch, *Incunabula Printed in the Low Countries: A Census* (Nieukoop, 1999), no. 1312 (pp. 240-241).

21 Van Thienen and Goldfinch, *Incunabula Printed in the Low Countries*, no. 1503 (p. 275). Isa Ragusa and Rosalie B. Green, eds, *Meditations on the Life of Christ: An Illustrated Manuscript of the Fourteenth Century, Paris, Bibliothèque Nationale, MS. Ital. 115*, trans. Isa Ragusa (Princeton, 1961), p. xxiii. See also the Introduction to *Iohannis de Cavlibvs, Meditaciones Vite Christi*, ed. M. Stallings-Taney (Turnholt, 1997), pp. ix-xviii.

22 BNF MS fr. 992. See Millard Meiss and Elizabeth H. Beatson, eds, *La Vie de Nostre Benoit Sauveur Ihesuscrist & La Saincte vie de nostre Dame* (New York, 1977), pp. x, xiii n. 4. Meiss cites C. Perrat, 'Barthélemy Buyer et les débuts de l'imprimerie á Lyon', *Humanisme et Renaissance*, II (1935), pp. 103ff, though 'The *Vie de Nostre Sauveur* is not [specifically] mentioned by Perrat'. See also *Early Printed Books: Major Acquisitions of The Pierpont Morgan Library 1924-1974* (New York, 1974), item 10, which dates the Morgan copy, one of three surviving copies, of *La Vie de*

Notre Benoit Sauveur Ihesuscrist to c. 1479.

23 BNF MS fr. 1686. In the copy of *La Passion Jhesuscrist*, the manuscript text has been written on the rectos of leaves, with the engravings on the versos. Mary Beth Winn, in *Anthoine Vérard: Parisian Publisher, 1485-1512, Prologues, Poems and Presentations* (Geneva, 1997), item 18, pp. 406-409, describes the manuscript as follows: 'Facing the [manuscript] text are the twelve engraved pictures of Israhel van Meckenem's Large Passion, imprinted on the versos of fols. 1 to 12 and overpainted in a subdued palette.' Several other books are known in which spaces intended for miniatures were filled with engravings by van Meckenem. See Henry Meier, 'Some Israhel Van Meckenem Problems', *Print Collector's Quarterly*, vol. 27, no. 1 (February, 1940), p. 67.

24 Another famous example of a printed book illustrated with engravings is Laurent de Premierfait's translation of Boccaccio's *De casibus illustrium virorum et mulierum*, a luxuriously laid-out book published in 1476 by Colard Mansion with spaces provided for ten illustrations – probably originally intended to be miniatures – one for the introduction and nine others at the start of each of the nine books. Nine copper engravings with Boccaccio subjects then came into Mansion's hands, and he included them in some editions. Several illustrated copies are extant: one in the Museum of Fine Arts in Boston (formerly in the collection of the Marquess of Lothian at Newbattle Abbey), another in the Bibliothèque d'Amiens, and another copy in private hands in Schweinfurt, Germany. Loose engravings have also survived. See M. Driver, 'Printing the *Confessio Amantis*', in *Re-visioning Gower*, ed. R. F. Yeager (Asheville, NC, 1998), pp. 274-279, 275 n. 14.

25 The *STC* and Cambridge University Library catalogue date Caxton's first edition to c. 1484, though it is dated 1486 by Hodnett, p. 75, and by Elizabeth Salter, *Nicholas Love's 'Myrrour of the Blessed Lyf of Jesu Christ'* (Salzburg, 1974), p. 18. STC 3259, 3260.

26 See Hodnett, p. 5, and N. F. Blake, *Caxton: England's First Publisher* (New York, 1976), p. 150.

27 National Library of Scotland, Advocates 18.1.7, Pierpont Morgan Library M. 648. See Jonathan Alexander, 'William Abell 'lymnour' and 15th Century English Illumination', in *Kunsthistorische Forschungen: Otto Pächt zu seinem 70. Geburtstag*, ed. Artur Rosenauer and Gerold Weber (Vienna, 1972), pp. 166-170. A typically cryptic remark of A. I. Doyle apparently supports a manuscript exemplar for Caxton's illustrations: 'Only a few (manuscripts) have explicit ascription to Love, and only one was to have pictures, though those in the printed editions may be derived from another.' A. I. Doyle, 'A Survey of the Origins and Circulation of Theological Writings in English in the 14th, 15th, and Early 16th Centuries with Special Consideration of the Part of the Clergy Therein' (Ph.D. diss., University of Cambridge, 1953), p. 143 n. 16.

28 Doyle, 'A Survey of the Origins and Circulation of Theological Writings in English', p. 142. The household ordinance of Cicely, Duchess of York, mother of Edward IV and Richard III, specifies that Love's text was to be often read aloud during meals. Cicely herself owned a copy of the *Mirror of the Blessed Life* bound together with Walter Hilton's *Epistle on Mixed Life*, 'which she bequeathed to her grand-daughter, Anne de la Pole, Prioress of Syon, as 'a book of Bonaventure and Hilton in the same in English'. Cited in Armstrong, 'The Piety of Cicely, Duchess of York', p. 78.

29 Michael G. Sargent, ed., *Nicholas Love's Mirror of the Blessed Life of Jesus Christ:*

A Critical Edition Based on Cambridge University Library Additional MS 6578 and 6686 (New York, 1992), p. lxiii. See also Sargent's discussion of the manuscript groups of this text, pp. lxxii-lxxxv.

30 *STC* 3262, 3263, 3263.5, 3264, 3266, 3267. See also Lotte Hellinga, 'Nicholas Love in Print', in *Nicholas Love at Waseda: Proceedings of the International Conference 20-22 July 1995*, ed. Shoichi Oguro, Richard Beadle and Michael G. Sargent (Cambridge, 1997), pp. 144-162.

31 Blake, *Caxton: England's First Publisher*, p. 150. Blake argues that the woodcuts Caxton uses to illustrate Love's *Speculum* are 'a set', in 'Caxton's Reprints', originally published in *The Humanities Association Review*, 26 (1975), pp. 169-179, and reprinted in *William Caxton and English Literary Culture* (London, 1991), pp. 115-116. Here Blake opines that 'in the period 1481-4 Caxton had artists available at Westminster, later in his career he appears to have imported woodcuts from the Continent. This fact has never received the consideration it deserves. ... It was clearly much easier to buy sets of religious blocks from Continental suppliers than sets of other subjects.' Blake further suggests that Caxton chose books to print based on the availability of blocks to illustrate them: 'If he had acquired a set of cuts dealing with the life of Christ, his choice of a suitable text in English in which to use them would be limited; hence he chose *Speculum Vitae Christi*. Although he used individual cuts from this series in other of his translations, the existence of the series probably led him to issue a reprint when the first edition sold out.'

32 Hodnett, item 333, p. 150. For a detailed description of Corpus Christi processions, see Miri Rubin, *Corpus Christi: The Eucharist in Late Medieval Culture* (Cambridge, 1991), pp. 243-271.

33 Hodnett, item 323, p. 146.

34 Sargent, *Nicholas Love's Mirror of the Blessed Life of Jesus Christ*, pp. 92, 95-96. The rubric for this woodcut appears somewhat earlier in the text, and Caxton does not include a caption here to set off the picture.

35 Hodnett, p. 5, and Blake, *Caxton: England's First Publisher*, p. 150, describe the blocks as Flemish. The catalogue compiled by Janet Backhouse, Mirjam Foot and John Barr, *William Caxton: An Exhibition to Commemorate the Quincentenary of the Introduction of Printing into England, British Library Reference Division, 24 September 1976-31 January 1977* (London, 1976), says that Caxton probably ordered the blocks 'from Flanders in 1485; the twenty-five cuts of the *Life of Christ* are French in style' (p. 85). George D. Painter, in *William Caxton* (New York, 1977), p. 155, says Caxton ordered the blocks 'from Flanders in 1485 at the same time as his new types, ... the *Speculum* cuts are northern French in their simple elegance'. According to the *STC*, the edition was published in 1484, and there are actually 29 pictures with two repeats.

36 Backhouse, Foot and Barr, *William Caxton: An Exhibition*, pp. 28-29.

37 Diane G. Scillia has argued convincingly that the 'Utrecht Cutter', an important woodcut designer associated with Veldener's shop, was also the Master of the London Passional. 'The Master of the London Passional: Johann Veldener's "Utrecht Cutter"', in *The Early Illustrated Book: Essays in Honor of Lessing J. Rosenwald*, ed. Sandra Hindman (Washington, D.C., 1982). This artist has been described by Delaissé as 'perhaps the most prolific miniaturist active at Utrecht around 1460'. L. M. J. Delaissé, *A Century of Dutch Manuscript Illumination* (Berkeley, 1968), p. 72. In a talk at the International Congress on Medieval Studies, Western Michigan

University, in 1992, I analysed the hats that appear in Caxton's woodcut illustrations in the *Speculum*, which provide one clue to the source of these images. For example, the curled rim and high crown of the hat worn by Jairus in the woodcut of Jesus raising his daughter from the dead closely resembles the hat worn by Lamech in a paper Bible manuscript produced in Utrecht in 1439 (Staatsbibliothek, Munich, COD German 1102, fol. 11ᵛ) reproduced by Delaissé in *A Century of Dutch Manuscript Illumination*, plates 45 and 46, as well as by Sandra Hindman in *Text and Image in Fifteenth-Century Illustrated Dutch Bibles* (Leiden, 1977), plate 17. Hats similar to that worn by Jairus also occur in the block-book *Biblia pauperum*. For more on hats, see Avril Henry, 'The Prophet's Hats', in her *Biblia Pauperum: A Facsimile and Edition* (Aldershot, 1987), pp. 177-178. For background on depiction of eastern, Islamic and Jewish hats, see Joyce Kubiski, 'Orientalizing Costume in Early Fifteenth-Century French Manuscript Painting (*Cité des Dames* Master, Limbourg Brothers, Boucicaut Master, and Bedford Master)', *Gesta* (International Center of Medieval Art), 40, no. 2 (2001), pp. 161-180.

38 A. I. Doyle, 'A Survey of the Origins and Circulation of Theological Writings in English', p. 158.

39 Elizabeth Salter, 'The Manuscripts of Nicholas Love's *Myrrour of the Blessed Lyf of Jesu Christ* and Related Texts', in *Middle English Prose: Essays on Bibliographical Problems*, ed. A. S. G. Edwards and Derek Pearsall (New York, 1981), p. 120.

40 Doyle, 'A Survey of the Origins and Circulation of Theological Writings in English', finds copies of the 1505 de Worde edition 'among the books pledged among certain students of Canterbury College, Oxford' (p. 157). Henry Dane, a layman 'presumably of contemplative inclination' owned the Caxton fragment now in Cambridge University Library. An early Pynson edition belonged to 'Robard Spencer', a layman leading a religious life, who describes himself as 'lederseller of London Aremit of the chapell of Sant Katheryn at charyng crosse'. These and other editions are discussed by Doyle, pp. 156-158.

41 IB. 55119, *STC* 3260, ownership mark cited in Doyle who says the name is 'Susan Pureseye', p. 157, though Ann Hutchison has more recently cited the name as 'Susan Purefoy' in 'What the Nuns Read', p. 215. She says the copy 'bears the inscription "Susan purefeye owethe thys booke"' and that 'Susan Purefoy was professed after 1518 and remained with the community until her death in exile in 1570'. Erler, *Women, Reading, and Piety*, identifies the owner she calls 'Susan Purefeye' as the niece of the three Fettyplace sisters, two of whom became nuns at Syon (p. 124). See also Carol M. Meale, '"Oft siþis with grete deuotion I þought what I miȝt do pleysyng to god": The Early Ownership and Readership of *Love's Mirror*, with Special Reference to its Female Audience', in *Nicholas Love at Waseda: Proceedings of the International Conference 20-22 July 1995*, ed. Shoichi Oguro, Richard Beadle and Michael G. Sargent (Cambridge, 1997), pp. 19-46.

42 Bell, *What Nuns Read*, p. 33, comments that ten of seventeen printed books in the vernacular which have been traced to the possession of English nuns or nunneries are known to have been owned by the nuns at Syon. Erler, *Women, Reading, and Piety*, has uncovered four, and perhaps five, further examples (pp. 141-143). See also Driver, 'Pictures in Print', pp. 229-244; 'Bridgettine Woodcuts', pp. 237-267.

43 The edition of *L'Art de bien vivre et de bien mourir* printed by Le Rouge in 1492 is described by John Macfarlane, *Antoine Vérard* (London, September 1900 for 1899), item 18, pp. 8-10. Macfarlane cites this copy as BL C.53.g.8. Winn explains, in

Anthoine Vérard: Parisian Publisher 1485-1512, p. 86 n. 22, that 'Vérard employed Pierre Le Rouge to print Part I, but Gillet Couteau and Jean Ménard for Parts II-IV of this four-part volume'.

44 Hodnett, fig. 47, no. 538. Compare the even closer copy of the Vérard original in Hodnett, fig. 117, no. 1358, which appeared first in the collaboratively produced copy of the *Golden Legend* printed by de Worde and Pynson in 1507. The block was then used later by Pynson (but not by de Worde) in his 1512 and 1520 editions of the *Missale ad usum Sarum* (*STC* 16190, 16202).

45 This is sometimes shown in medieval painting and sculpture. In a related scene of the inception of the Virgin, the pregnant Anne is shown reading as the foetus within appears to look on. One such miniature occurs in the Da Costa Hours (Morgan M. 399, fol. 351ᵛ), illuminated by Simon Bening of Bruges *c.* 1515; related miniatures appear in the Grimani Breviary and in another book of hours in the Pierpont Morgan Library (Morgan M. 451, fol. 69ᵛ), written and illuminated in Bruges by Simon Bening in 1531. See also Driver, 'Mirrors of a Collective Past: Re-Considering Images of Medieval Women', in *Women and the Book: Assessing the Pictorial Evidence*, ed. Lesley Smith and Jane Taylor (London, 1997), pp. 86, 92 n. 25, fig. 36.

46 There are copies of the edition printed on 15 December 1492 by Gillet Couteau and Jean Ménard for Antoine Vérard in the Huntington and British Libraries. The Huntington copy has been printed on vellum and hand-coloured. The British Library copy (IB. 40027) is complete and has been printed on paper. The concluding colophon says: 'Cy finist le liure de bien viure Imprime at paris le xv iour de decembre mil.cccc.nonante & deux/pour anthoine verard libraire ...'.

47 Isaiah 7:14-15. Mary began to be shown with a book at the Annunciation from the late fourteenth century.

48 See Paul Saenger, 'Silent Reading: its Impact on Late Medieval Script and Society', *Viator*, 13 (1982), pp. 367-414. See also Saenger, 'Books of Hours and the Reading Habits of the Later Middle Ages', in *The Culture of Print: Power and the Uses of Print in Early Modern Europe*, ed. Roger Chartier, trans. L. G. Cochrane (Cambridge, 1989), pp. 141-173, in which he makes a seeming connection between reading and looking at a picture as a form of 'comprehension literacy': 'to decode a written text silently, word by word, and to understand it fully in the very act of gazing upon it'. See, further, Saenger, *Space Between Words: The Origins of Silent Reading* (Stanford, Calif., 1997). Speech scrolls do appear in later medieval manuscripts, for example, in the illuminations in Pierpont Morgan Library, MS M. 815, a Sarum Book of Hours written and illuminated in Paris *c.* 1471-1485, and probably owned by Henry VII of England.

49 For further discussion of *lectio divina*, see Beryl Smalley, *The Study of the Bible in the Middle Ages* (Notre Dame, Ind., 1964), pp. 27-196, passim, and Brian Stock, *After Augustine: The Meditative Reader and the Text* (Philadelphia, 2001).

50 The *Golden Legend* further describes Jerome as leading a penitential life in the desert for four years, after which he went to the town of Bethlehem, where 'He reread his own books, which he had kept safely stowed away, and other books as well'. See Jacobus de Voragine, *The Golden Legend*, trans. W. G. Ryan, vol. 2 (Princeton, 1993), pp. 213, 215. Smalley, *The Study of the Bible*, p. 29. Smalley comments further that St Jerome 'was more than a channel for Greek learning. He followed Origen's example in studying Hebrew and consulting Jews. ... As a Hebrew scholar and humanist he brought the Bible closer to the Latin-speaking world' (p. 21).

51 *STC* 14507. Hodnett, item 800, fig. 22, p. 245. Mary Erler has identified women's ownership inscriptions in the John Rylands copy of *Vitas Patrum* (*STC* 14507), translated by Caxton and published by de Worde in 1495. The first is of Joan Regent, widow of a Bristol mayor, beside the story of Paula, mother of Eustochium: 'mi owne gud ladi pole pray for your ione regent & dam agnes mi doter of sion i prai you for god sake'. Joan Regent's daughter Agnes and her friend, Katherine Pole (a grand-daughter of Cecil Neville, Duchess of York) also wrote their names in this copy. Erler, 'Devotional Literature', in *The Cambridge History of the Book in Britain*, 7 vols (Cambridge, 1999-2002), vol. 3: *1400-1557*, ed. Lotte Hellinga and J. B. Trapp, pp. 522-523. See also Erler, *Women, Reading, and Piety*, pp. 125-128.

52 De Worde's colophon states: 'Thus endyth the moost vertuouse hystorye of the devoute and right renommed lyves of holy faders lyvynge in deserte, worthy of remembraunce to all well dysposed persones, whiche hath be translated out of Frensshe in to Englysshe by Wyllyam Caxton of Westmynstre late deed, and fynysshed it at the laste daye of his lyff.' The text is 'wrongly ascribed to St. Jerome'; Caxton based his translation on a collection of saints' lives 'Printed by Nicolaus Philippi and Jean Dupré, 15 January "1486", i.e. 1487 by the modern calendar, at Lyons'. See Painter, *Caxton*, p. 187 n. 1. See also M. Driver, 'The Illustrated de Worde: An Overview', *Studies in Iconography*, Medieval Institute Publications 17 (1996), p. 354.

53 Alberto Manguel, *A History of Reading* (New York, 1997), p. 59. According to de Fournival, 'Memory has two gates of access, sight and hearing, and a road particular to each of these portals. These roads are called *peinture* and *parole*.' See M. J. Carruthers, *The Book of Memory* (Cambridge, 1990), pp. 223-224. See also M. T. Clanchy, *From Memory to Written Record, England 1066-1307*, 2nd edn (London, 1993), pp. 283-284. For more discussion of prayerful looking, see Kathleen Kamerick, *Popular Piety and Art in the Late Middle Ages: Image Worship and Idolatry in England, 1350-1500* (New York, 2002), pp. 145-154.

54 Smalley, in *The Study of the Bible*, p. 2, quoting Roger P. Hinks, *Carolingian Art* (London, 1935), pp. 82-83. For a powerful image of a viewer peering through a lattice, see Song of Songs 2: 8-13 (RSV).

55 Michael Baxandall, *Painting and Experience in Fifteenth-Century Italy: A Primer in the Social History of Pictorial Style*, 2nd edn (Oxford, 1972), pp. 45, 47.

56 *STC* 4815; Hodnett, items 862, 863-869. The prologue is addressed to the 'relygyous moder and deuoute sustren ... at the house of Syon' and ends with 'Lenuoye of Dane James the translater' who welcomes his female audience to the orchard in which are planted 'Helthefull fruytes and herbes ... full delectable to þe soule'. He then directs his readers to 'serche this ghostly meet with besy and ofte redynge / taste you then with medyacyon and inwarde thynkyng after medyacyon / sauour them well and chewe them well in your soules with deuoute prayer'. The title-image is reproduced in Hodnett, fig. 66. The copy in the British Library (C.11.b.6) has the title-page printed in two colours, red and black. The portrait of Catherine with her nuns appears on the verso of the title-page and again on the end-leaf of the volume. At the end of each book, the explicits have been typeset into shapes, for example, into a diamond at the end of book four (sig. o5), into a triangle at the end of book five (sig. x4) and into a diamond with triangle at the end of book six (sig. z2), another example of the compositor's expertise.

57 *STC* spells the saint's name 'Catharine of Siena'; the title-page says 'Katheryne of

Sene'. Suzanne Noffke, trans., *Catherine of Siena, The Dialogue* (New York, 1980), p. 66. The depiction of the visionary praying before an open book as her vision is shown occurring around her continues particularly in women's devotional representation well into the seventeenth century. There is, for example, a remarkable mural in the refectory at the Abbaye Royale de Fontevraud, painted by Thomas Pot in the seventeenth century, which shows several prominent nuns of the order, their likenesses distinct and recognisable, praying before their open books as visions of scenes from the lives of the Virgin and Christ progress cinematically around them.

58 Ibid., pp. 80-81.

59 Ibid., pp. 67, 73, passim. De Worde includes Virtue and Vice trees in his 1508 *Kalender of shepeherdes* (STC 22409) and in his *Boke named the Royall* (STC 21430). The woodcuts are printed with some dexterity. The 'tree of vyces' in de Worde's *Kalender*, for example, has eleven labels printed within scrolls on the tree itself (these are right side up and sideways left and right), the type set within the wood-block for the illustration, along with 42 labels printed beside the image, and nine labels printed sideways above.

60 Walter Hilton, *The Scale of Perfection*, trans. J. P. H. Clark and R. Dorward (New York, 1991), pp. 295, 296.

61 Noffke, *Catherine of Siena*, pp. 155-156.

62 Ibid., p. 249.

63 Ibid., p. 235.

64 The illuminated end-leaf is from the copy formerly in Longleat House, Warminster, Wiltshire. The painting appears to be contemporary, as demonstrated by a painted-over page mending at the start of Book Four. Illuminated borders have been added to the woodcut illustrations and also to the opening page of text. The book was one of those formerly in the Beriah Botfield collection auctioned at Christie's on 13 June 2002. See *Printed Books & Manuscripts from Longleat* (London: Christie's, 2002), item 17, pp. 70-71, which comments, 'Although the Botfield copy contains no contemporary inscription of ownership, it was clearly intended for presentation, perhaps to Sutton as publisher or, more likely, to [Syon] abbey itself. The arms in the painted border at the beginning of the work are those of the Passion; the Bridgettine order is dedicated to the Passion.' For more about the role of illustrations in early binding practice, see Driver, 'Wynkyn de Worde and the Title Page', in *Texts and Their Contexts: Papers from the Early Book Society*, ed. John Scattergood and Julia Boffey (Dublin, 1997), pp. 104-114, as well as Chapter 3, pp. 106-114.

65 There are earlier examples of manuscripts moving outward from religious to lay communities. Kelly Parsons discusses one example in 'The Red Ink Annotator of The Book of Margery Kempe and His Lay Audience', in *The Medieval Professional Reader at Work: Evidence from Manuscripts of Chaucer, Langland, Kempe, and Gower,* ed. Kathryn Kerby-Fulton and Maidie Hilmo (Victoria, 2001). Annotations in British Library MS Additional 61823, copied by a scribe named Salthows between 1440 and 1450, a manuscript that was owned and extensively annotated by Carthusians at Mount Grace Priory in Yorkshire, suggest that the so-called 'Red Ink Annotator' was shaping Margery's narrative for an audience of laywomen. Parsons comments that 'many of the red ink annotations seem to have been tailored for female consumption' and 'The pastoral care of women can be inferred from these anno-tations; a married woman's identification with the married (and child-bearing) Margery would enhance the effectiveness of the *Book* as a tool of pastoral care' (pp.

146-147). The manuscript includes several devotional images drawn by the Red Ink Annotator indicating 'that our Mount Grace annotator understood and approved of the devotional use of images. We find drawings of hearts, hands, a pillar and, of particular interest, a graphic depiction of "flames of divine love"' (p. 151). Nicholas Watson, also in this volume, has commented on the *Book*'s *ex libris* which suggests that it 'was loaned for use outside the walls of the monastery' (p. 153).

66 Ellen Catherine Dunn, '*The Myroure of Oure Ladye*: Syon Abbey's Role in the Continuity of English Prose', in *Diakonia: Studies in Honor of Robert T. Meyer*, ed. Thomas Halton and J. P. Williman (Washington, D.C., 1986), p. 116. See also Ann Hutchison, 'Devotional Reading in the Monastery', who cites the Bridgettine Rule as allowing 'an unlimited supply of books for study' (p. 217).

67 Marguerite Tjader Harris, *Birgitta of Sweden: Life and Selected Revelations*, trans. Albert Ryle Kezel (New York, 1990), p. 72.

68 Birgit Klockars, *Birgittas svenska värld* (Stockholm, 1976), p. 32.

69 Harris, *Birgitta of Sweden*, p. 68.

70 For the Zeninger print, see Schreiber, p. 1290. Field describes the woodcut in *Fifteenth-Century Woodcuts and Metalcuts from the National Gallery of Art*, fig. 210. I have examined a damaged copy of Zeninger's edition in the British Library, which lacks the opening woodcut, and a complete edition in the Pierpont Morgan Library. The fifteenth-century painting is reproduced in Engelbert Kirschbaum, ed., *Lexikon der christlichen Ikonographie*, vol. 5 (Freiburg, 1973), p. 402. The woodcut of Bridget reproduced here originally appeared on the title-page of William Bonde's *Pylgrimage of perfection* printed in London by de Worde on 23 February 1531 (*STC* 3278). For more on Bridgettine iconography, see Driver, 'Bridgettine Woodcuts', pp. 248-249.

71 Bridget Morris, *St Birgitta of Sweden* (Woodbridge, 1999), p. 105.

72 Field, *Fifteenth-Century Woodcuts and Metalcuts from the National Gallery of Art*, fig. 210.

73 For more on the *Fifteen Oes* (*STC* 20195) and its subsequent censorship, see Chapter 6. See also Eamon Duffy, *The Stripping of the Altars: Traditional Religion in England c. 1400-c. 1580* (New Haven, 1992), pp. 249-256; and Driver, 'Bridgettine Woodcuts', pp. 252-261, 265-267 nn. 33-51.

74 Harris, *Birgitta of Sweden*, p. 161.

75 Hodnett was perplexed by the purpose of the Bridget woodcut, describing it as it occurs in Pynson's edition of Bonde's *Pylgrimage of perfection* (*STC* 3277), as 'de Worde's useful St Bridget, a borrowing that is even harder to explain than most' (p. 46). I discovered its function some years ago and discuss this further in 'Pictures in Print', pp. 243-244. Bonde, a fellow of Pembroke College, Cambridge, and a Syon monk, began to compose this work in Latin but was persuaded to write it in English so that his readers could understand the text. See Jan T. Rhodes, 'Syon Abbey's Religious Publications in the Sixteenth Century', *Journal of Ecclesiastical History*, 44 (1993), p. 21.

76 *STC* 17532. Part II of *The Mirror of Our Lady*, on the 'Deuoute redyng of holy Bokes', describes for the Syon nuns how to read devoutly by choosing appropriate reading material, opening the mind to receive it ('in redynge god spekyth to man. and therfore he oughte reuerently to be herde'), rereading for proper understanding, for gaining knowledge, and for developing discretion. Like the *Orcharde of Syon*, the text attests to the importance given spiritual and devotional reading at Syon. For

further discussion, see Hutchison, 'Devotional Reading in the Monastery', pp. 221-225.

77 *STC* 17542, 14553. John Fewterer, along with William Bonde, was a fellow of Pembroke College, Cambridge, and a university preacher.

78 See earlier arguments presented in 'Pictures in Print', pp. 243-244, and in 'Bridgettine Woodcuts', pp. 249-252.

79 Noffke, *Catherine of Siena*, p. 211.

80 Reproductions of the frontispiece of BL Harley MS 4431 occur on the dust-jacket of Smith and Taylor, *Women and the Book*; on the cover of Eileen Power, *Medieval Women*, ed. M. M. Postan (Cambridge, 1975); and in Maureen Quilligan, *The Allegory of Female Authority: Christine de Pizan's Cité des Dames* (Ithaca, N.Y., 1991), fig. 36. Books owned by Elizabeth Woodville are also cited briefly by Margaret Kekewich, in 'Edward IV, William Caxton, and Literary Patronage in Yorkist England', *Modern Language Review* 66, 3 (July 1971), p. 486. Harris, *English Aristocratic Women*, further mentions a copy of French Grail romances bequeathed by Sir Richard Roos to his niece, Eleanor, who 'subsequently gave the book to her first cousin, Elizabeth Woodville' (p. 37).

81 Christine is shown reading from an open book and instructing her son in miniatures illustrating *The Moral Teachings* in BL Harley MS 4431, fol. 261ᵛ, and instructing four men in Harley MS 4431, fol. 259ᵛ. Woodcut illustrations in *The boke of the Cyte of Ladyes* (STC 7271), trans. B. Anslay and printed in 1521 by Pepwell, are discussed in M. Driver, 'Christine de Pisan and Robert Wyer: the *.C. Hystoryes of Troye*, or *L'Epistre d'Othea* Englished', *Gutenberg-Jahrbuch* 72 (1997), pp. 125, 136-137.

82 Christine describes her reading of Mathéolus (and her negative reaction) at the beginning of the *Book of the City of Ladies*. To sample the antifeminist flavour of Jehan Le Fèvre's translation of *The Lamentations of Mathéolus*, probably the version read by Christine, see Alcuin Blamires, ed., *Woman Defamed and Woman Defended: An Anthology of Medieval Texts* (Oxford, 1992), pp. 175-197.

83 The woodcut of Christine has been reproduced in Hodnett, fig. 231 (J. Skot, no. 2281). See also earlier discussion of this woodcut in Chapter 2. The random placement of books in the Christine woodcut was apparently typical practice. John Updike in 'Groaning Shelves', *The New Yorker* (4 October 1999), p. 107, comments that medieval 'books were propped on tilted surfaces like modern music stands or lecterns. Woodcut representations of fifteenth-century scholars at work show random book dispersal over all available surfaces.'

5. RECONSTRUCTING SOCIAL HISTORIES

1 Keith Moxey, 'Motivating History', *Art Bulletin* 77 (1995): 396. For further discussion of this idea, see Driver, 'Mirrors of a Collective Past: Reconsidering Images of Medieval Women', in *Women and the Book: Assessing the Visual Evidence*, ed. Jane H. M. Taylor and Lesley Smith (London, 1997), pp. 75-93.

2 Christopher N. L. Brooke, *The Medieval Idea of Marriage* (Oxford, 1989), pp. 248-257, devotes a chapter to discussion of the church porch as the most probable location of most marriages. He argues that one of the main functions of the late medieval porch 'was to provide an appropriate setting for weddings', pointing out further that church porches 'must have been especially associated, in the minds of many of the clergy, of many patrons of such buildings, and of countless married folk,

with the ceremonies of marriage at church door' (pp. 253-254).

3 No matter where the marriage ceremony took place, witnesses were key to confirmation that the marriage ceremony had actually occurred. After analysis of evidence from church courts at Ely, Canterbury and York produced in the fourteenth and early fifteenth centuries, Michael Sheehan and Richard Helmholz found, not unpredictably, that in the majority of marriages in which lawsuits were subsequently brought, the marriages had been contracted outside the church, though before witnesses. Richard H. Helmholz, *Marriage Litigation in Medieval England* (Cambridge, 1978), pp. 28-30, 159, 166ff; Michael M. Sheehan, 'The Formation and Stability of Marriage in Fourteenth-Century England: Evidence of an Ely Register', *Mediaeval Studies* 33 (1971), pp. 228-263. For clandestine marriages, see Ann Eljenholm Nichols, *Seeable Signs: The Iconography of the Seven Sacraments 1350-1544* (Woodbridge, 1994) pp. 283-286. Brooke, *The Medieval Idea of Marriage*, p. 250.

4 Françoise Piponnier and Perrine Mane, *Dress in the Middle Ages*, trans. Caroline Beamish (New Haven, 1997), p. 110.

5 R. H. Helmholz, *Marriage Litigation in Medieval England*, pp. 28-29. Piponnier and Mane, *Dress in the Middle Ages*, p. 111, say that the floral coronet worn by the bride and sometimes by members of the wedding party symbolises the wedding's 'festive atmosphere rather than the solemnisation of marriage'. See, for example, Song of Solomon 1:1, 5-7; 2:1-7. The wearing of the marriage garland is much older than the Middle Ages. It is referred to by Sappho, for example. See *Sappho*, trans. Mary Barnard (Berkeley, 1958), lyrics 10, 83.

6 Nichols, *Seeable Signs*, p. 169.

7 British Library IB. 40027. In the edition dated 1493, also in the British Library (C.22.b.3 [imperf.]), the marriage scene occurs on sig. h8ᵛ. The copy of the woodcut in *The crafte to lyue well* (STC 792), printed by de Worde in 1505, occurs on sig. h5ʳ.

8 Nichols, *Seeable Signs*, p. 279. Book of Tobit, 7:15. For further mention of the wedding of Sarah and Tobit as a model of marriage, see Brooke, *The Medieval Idea of Marriage*, pp. 30, 43, 188n., 194n. Salley Vickers includes a novelised account of the story of Tobias in *Miss Garnet's Angel* (New York, 2002). Married couples are often indicated solely through an icon of clasped hands in genealogical representations. See, for example, figs 9 and 10, from John Speed's *The Genealogies Recorded in Sacred Scripture* (1610), in Driver, 'Mapping Chaucer: John Speed and the Later Portraits', *Chaucer Review* 36, no. 3 (2002).

9 See reproductions of similar wedding scenes in Georges Duby, ed., *A History of Private Life II. Revelations of the Medieval World* (Cambridge, Mass., 1988), pp. 126, 129, 130; Erika Uitz, *The Legend of Good Women: Medieval Women in Towns and Cities*, trans. Sheila Marnie (Mount Kisco, N.Y., 1990), pp. 104-105; Piponnier and Mane, *Dress in the Middle Ages*, p. 110, fig. 43; Nichols, *Seeable Signs*, pls 31, 74-80.

10 The woodcut illustrating the title-page of *The fyftene Joyes of maryage* (1509, STC 15258) has a particularly long history. It was repeated in de Worde's editions of the *Knyght of the swanne* (1512, STC 7571), the *Gesta Romanorum* (before 1518, STC 21286.3, 21286.5) and in the 1518 edition of *Olyuer of Castylle* (STC 18808), as well as in the surviving copy of *The payne and sorowe of euyll maryage* (c. 1530, STC 19119) in the Huntington Library. See Hodnett, pp. 308-309, item 1264.

11 British Library, MS Cotton Julius E.IV, Article 6. The drawing of the marriage of

Henry V with Katherine of Valois is Pageant 43 in the manuscript.

12 The butterfly veils worn in the Pageant depicting Joan of Navarre observing a tournament are rather anachronistic, since they did not come into fashion until the 1450s. They remained popular well into the 1480s, when the Pageants were made. For more on the Beauchamp Pageants, see: E. M. Thompson, 'The Pageants of Richard Beauchamp, Earl of Warwick, Commonly Called the Warwick MS.', *Burlington Magazine* 1 (March 1903):, pp. 151-164; *The Pageants of Richard Beauchamp Earl of Warwick, Reproduced in Facsimile from the Cottonian MS Julius E.IV, in the British Museum*, introd. William, Earl of Carysfort, K.P. (Oxford, 1908), which largely quotes Thompson; *Pageant of the Birth Life and Death of Richard Beauchamp Earl of Warwick K.G. 1389-1439*, ed. Viscount Dillon and W. H. St John Hope (London, 1914); K. L. Scott, 'The Beauchamp Pageants', in *The Caxton Master and His Patrons* (Cambridge, 1976), pp. 55-66, who attributes the illustration, no doubt rightly, to the Caxton Master. The Beauchamp Pageants are generally thought to have been made for Anne Neville, Countess of Warwick, and daughter of Richard, who survived to the beginning of the year 1493 (see Thompson, 'The Pageants', p. 160).

13 Morgan M. 775 has been discussed by C. F. Bühler, 'Sir John Paston's Grete Boke, a Fifteenth-Century Best-Seller', *MLN* 56 (1941), pp. 345-351; and extensively by G. A. Lester, 'Sir John Paston's "Grete-Boke": A Bespoke Book or Mass-Produced?' *English Studies* 66 (1985), pp. 93-104, and in *Sir John Paston's Grete Boke* (Woodbridge, 1984), pp. 31-34, pp. 93-95. In the latter volume, Lester explores the complex connections between Paston's Grete Boke and the Morgan manuscript (pp. 31, 32, 33-45, 47-48), describing it as 'a composite manuscript', with the arms of Astley on fols 25, 131 and 274. Lester believes the Astley MS very probably served as one important copy text for the Paston volume: 'Pierpont Morgan Library MS 775 is probably the very book from which the first parts of Lansdowne were copied' (p. 7). Morgan M. 775 was later owned by Edward VI when Prince of Wales, as shown by the present English stamped-calf binding with the motto 'Ich Dien'. Apparently the book originally consisted of the Vegetius and ended with the *Othea*, with other texts added to these after the fashion of a commonplace book (ibid., p. 32). The date of the original text is thought to be *c.* 1450-1460. Internal evidence indicates Astley acquired the volume 'before 1461', owning it until his death in 1486 (ibid., p. 33). For related manuscripts, see David Anderson, ed., *Sixty Bokes Olde and Newe* (Knoxville, Tenn., 1986), items 55, 57.

14 Michael Baxandall has further pointed out that verbal 'description has only the most general independent meaning and depends for such precision as it has on the presence of the picture', *Patterns of Intention: On the Historical Explanation of Pictures* (New Haven, 1985), p. 11. On disjunction between text and image, see M. Foucault, *This Is Not a Pipe*, trans. J. Harkness (Berkeley, 1982), pp. 28-55. For a basic introduction to heraldry, with definitions of the coat of arms, the device, and the crest, see Piponnier and Mane, *Dress in the Middle Ages*, pp. 131-135.

15 Hodnett includes a few examples, including item 883, fig. 115, from the *Coronacyon of Henry the eyght* (STC 12953) by Stephen Hawes, printed by de Worde in 1509. This print has a criblée background, which shows the simultaneous crowning of Henry and Katherine by four bishops. The Tudor rose and a large pomegranate hang over their heads. Later in the Tudor period, woodcut portraiture began in earnest. John N. King, in *Tudor Royal Iconography: Literature and Art in an Age of Religious*

Crisis (Princeton, 1989) includes examples of woodcut portraits of Henry VIII, figs 8 and 14; Edward VI, figs 21, 24 and 27; and Elizabeth I, figs 30 and 50.

16 *STC* 12549. Hodnett, item 1622, British Library G. 6719. Guilford himself died in Jerusalem about midway through this pilgrimage account. *The hystorye / Sege and dystruccyon of Troye* (*STC* 5579) was printed by Pynson in 1513. David Benson has pointed out that in the Middle Ages Guido's Trojan history was 'considered factually true'. References to the siege of Troy as an actual event occur in the *Brut* chronicles, *Sir Gawain and the Green Knight*, and in John Hardyng's *Chronicle*, among other works. The story of Troy was used to supply factual context for the founding of Britain and to trace the lineage of her kings. As Benson notes, Lydgate's *Troy Book* and Caxton's *Recuyell of the Historyes of Troye*, two fictions, became the standard English sources through which medieval traditions about Troy continued into the Renaissance. See C. David Benson, *The History of Troy in Middle English Literature: Giudo delle Colonne's Historia Destructionis Troiae in Medieval England* (Woodbridge, 1980), pp. 5, 96.

17 I have argued that women's work can be partially reconstructed from manuscript miniatures, in 'Mirrors of a Collective Past', pp. 75-93. Woodcuts of women at work, for example, illustrate *De re metallica* (1556), by Georgius Agricola, the standard work on mining and metallurgy until the end of the eighteenth century. These show women employed in oreworks, panning for gold and sorting precious metal from stone in silver mines (ibid., p. 82).

18 See, for example, the title-cut of Walter of Henley's *Boke of Husbandry* (*STC* 25007), printed by Wynkyn de Worde *c.* 1508 (Chapter 3, Fig. 25). Two men stand in a stylised forest (which seems to foreshadow the cinematic forest, with its brittle artificiality, in Eric Rohmer's *Perceval le Gallois* [Gaumont-Films du Losange, 1981]), swinging axes, which are shown in such detail that the maker's mark is visible on each blade. Illustrations of building scenes, with hammers, awls and trowels, occur in various books. See T. M. MacRobert, *Fine Illustrations in Western European Printed Books* (London, 1969), fig. 16; Hodnett, item 882, fig. 90.

19 *STC* 175. For information on early editions of Aesop in print, see Edward Wheatley, 'The Aesopic Corpus at War with Itself: A Literary Body and Its Members', *Journal of the Early Book Society* 2 (1999): 46-58; also Edward Wheatley, *Mastering Aesop: Medieval Education, Chaucer, and His Followers* (Gainesville, Fla., 2000).

20 Examples of English inkhorns of the early sixteenth century may be seen at the Royal Ontario Museum, Toronto (926.29.4, 926.29.5). There is a leather case for an ink container, probably Italian in origin and dating from the Middle Ages, in the Metropolitan Museum of Art. Christopher de Hamel, *Medieval Craftsmen: Scribes and Illuminators* (Toronto, 1992), reproduces a picture of a late medieval leather inkwell (p. 32, pl. 25). See also *The Age of Chivalry: Art in Plantagenet England 1200-1400*, ed. Jonathan Alexander and Paul Binski (London, 1987), p. 383, item 423, which includes a photograph of a fourteenth-century leather penner now in the Museum of London (4670).

21 For background on Chaucer portraits, see Derek Pearsall, *The Life of Geoffrey Chaucer: A Critical Biography* (Oxford, 1992), Appendix 1, 'The Chaucer Portraits', pp. 285-305. Chaucer's penner appears in numerous Chaucer portraits, including those in Ellesmere (The Henry E. Huntington Library, MS EL 26.C.9, fol. 153^v); British Library MS Harley 4866 (fol. 88^r); BL MS Royal 17.D.vi (fol. 93^v); the Rosenbach forgery, MS 1083/10 (fol. 72^v); BL MS Additional 5141; many panel

paintings; and in the portrait frontispiece by John Speed prefacing *The Workes of our Antient and lerned English Poet* (1598), among others. For more on Chaucer portraits in print, see Driver, 'Mapping Chaucer: John Speed and the Later Portraits', pp. 228-249; on the penner itself, see p. 247 n. 11.

22 Hodnett reproduces or describes schoolmaster woodcuts (which originate in Germany) in books printed by de Worde (figs 75-80, items 918-923) and Pynson (figs 139-141, items 1507a, 1508). De Worde's examples occur in a large number of Latin grammars and other works, including the following for just one schoolmaster woodcut (item 918): Donatus, *Accedence*, 1495 (STC 23153.4); William Horman, *Introductorium lingue latine*, 1495 (STC 13809); Donatus, *Donatus minor cum Remigio*, c. 1496? (STC 7016); Donatus, *Accedence*, 1499 (STC 23153.5); Lydgate, *The chorle & the byrde*, 1497, 1500? (STC 17011, 17012); Aesop, *Fabule Esopi cum commento*, 1503 (STC 169); and Alexander grammaticus, *Textus Alexandri cum sententiis & constructionibus*, 1503 (STC 319). This partial list would seem to indicate that both Lydgate and Aesop were promoted as schoolbooks. Item 920, fig. 77 in Hodnett, which is also reproduced here as Fig. 7, illustrates numerous Latin editions of John Stanbridge's *Vocabula*, the Synonyms of John of Garland, and the Latin grammar of Robert Whittinton. The woodcuts employed by Pynson also illustrate schoolbooks. Both de Worde and Pynson also occasionally use the schoolmaster woodcut to illustrate their editions of the *Expositio hymnorum secundum vsum Sarum*.

23 Michael T. Clanchy, *From Memory to Written Record, England 1066-1307*, 2nd edn (London, 1993), p. 224. Alfred W. Pollard, 'Es tu Scholaris', in *Old Picture Books with Other Essays on Bookish Subjects* (1902; repr. New York, 1970), pp. 99-105, esp. pp. 103-104. The book of Latin dialogues further includes discussion of 'the four chief books in use in grammar schools, the "Tabula" or horn-book on which was written the Lord's Prayer, the moral sayings of Cato, the accidence of Donatus, and the syntax and prosody of Alexander Gallus' (p. 101).

24 Norman Davis, ed., *Paston Letters and Papers of the Fifteenth Century*, 2 vols (Oxford, 1971-1976), vol. 2, p. 32. Barbara A. Hanawalt, *Growing Up in Medieval London: The Experience of Childhood in History* (New York, 1993), pp. 84-85, quoting from H. E. Salter, ed., *Records of Mediaeval Oxford: Coroners' Inquests, the Walls of Oxford* (Oxford, 1912), p. 10.

25 R. A. B. Mynors, ed., *Catalogue of the Manuscripts of Balliol College, Oxford* (Oxford, 1963), item 354, pp. 352-354. The memorandum book of Richard Hill, citizen and grocer of London (born shortly before 1490), was probably compiled in the first third of the sixteenth century. Titled 'A Boke of dyueris tales and balettes and dyueris Reconynges etc', the MS also includes the *Gesta Romanorum*, *The Seven Sages of Rome*, excerpts from John Gower's *Confessio Amantis*, an Anglo-French vocabulary, and one of the most famous of carols, the Corpus Christi Carol. The schoolboy poem is partially quoted by Hanawalt, *Growing Up in Medieval London*, p. 82, and Nicholas Orme, *Medieval Children* (New Haven, 2001), p. 154.

26 Patricia Basing, *Trades and Crafts in Medieval Manuscripts* (New York, 1990), p. 108. Jo Ann Hoeppner Moran, *The Growth of English Schooling 1340-1548: Learning, Literacy and Laicization in Pre-Reformation York Diocese* (Princeton, 1985), p. 216. For more on the later petty schools in England, see the classic works by T. W. Baldwin, *William Shakspere's Petty School* (Urbana, Ill., 1943) and *William Shakspere's Small Latine and Lesse Greeke*, 2 vols (Urbana, Ill., 1944).

27 Orme, *Medieval Children*, p. 101.

28 Alberto Manguel, *A History of Reading* (New York, 1997), says that in the medieval classroom 'The teacher usually sat at an elevated lectern, or sometimes at a table, on an ordinary bench (chairs did not become common in Christian Europe until the fifteenth century)', p. 75.

29 David Cressy, *Literacy and the Social Order: Reading and Writing in Tudor and Stuart England* (Cambridge, 1980), p. 35. Cressy here outlines the basic educational skills acquired by English children in school, though he focuses mainly on examples from the later sixteenth and seventeenth centuries.

30 Moran, *The Growth of English Schooling*, pp. 71-74, 77. Compare the comment made by Shulamith Shahar, in *Childhood in the Middle Ages*, trans. Chaya Galai (London, 1990), p. 190: 'the teaching profession, particularly in the lower school, was not considered a prestigious one, and for the more talented masters constituted an interim stage in their careers'.

31 Churchill Babington, ed., *The Repressor of Over Much Blaming of the Clergy, by Reginald Pecock* (London, 1860).

32 Moran suggests 'that a school at Harwood (W. Riding) that was attended circa 1505 by Richard Robynson, yeoman, when he was about ten years old, was offering a reading education' (ibid., p. 68). Hanawalt, *Growing Up in Medieval London*, p. 82, remarks that 'The number of schools to teach Latin, which were controlled by the bishop of London, doubled by the fifteenth century, growing from three to six'. For more on types of schools in the Middle Ages, see also Orme, *Medieval Children*, pp. 144-157, 240-242.

33 We do have some account records of William Caxton and Wynkyn de Worde's will, which are certainly helpful in reconstructing the work of their shops. But there is no detailed description of day-to-day work or of printing equipment until Moxon. His work is reprinted by Herbert Davis and Harry Carter, eds, *Mechanick Exercises on the Whole Art of Printing by Joseph Moxon (1683-4)* (London, 1958).

34 Ronald B. McKerrow, *An Introduction to Bibliography for Literary Students* (Oxford, 1928; rev. edn, New Castle, Del., 1994), p. 8, n. 1. McKerrow cites two early articles on woodcut illustrations of printers by Falconer Madon, 'Early Representations of the Printing Press', *Bibliographica* 1 (1895): 223-248, 499, and 3 (1897): 475. Madan subsequently published a larger list of depictions of the press (1499-1600) in *The Bodleian Quarterly Record* 4 (1923-1925): 165-167.

35 McKerrow, *An Introduction to Bibliography*, p. 20 n. 1.

36 For more on the inking process, see Michael Twyman, *The British Library Guide to Printing: History and Techniques* (London, 1998), p. 39; Colin H. Bloy, *A History of Printing Ink Balls and Rollers 1440-1850* (London, 1967; repr. 1972), p. 53. For another, perhaps somewhat fanciful, recounting of the process of inking with ink-balls, see 'The Printing Press and Printer's Ink,' in Albert Kapr, *Johann Gutenberg: The Man and his Invention*, trans. Douglas Martin (Aldershot, 1996), pp. 135-137, esp. pp. 135-136.

37 Kapr, *Johann Gutenberg*, p. 135; Seán Jennett, *The Making of Books* (London, 1951), p. 119.

38 For a basic description of the printing press, see Twyman, *The British Library Guide to Printing*, fig. 5, pp. 8-17, pp. 21-42. See also Kapr, *Johann Gutenberg*, pp. 132-135.

39 Janet Ing, *Johann Gutenberg and His Bible* (New York, 1988), p. 78.

40 Seán Jennett, *The Making of Books*, p. 118. Kapr, *Johann Gutenberg*, p. 133, says of the textile press: 'Cloth would have been fed along the bed of the press, a coloured pattern block placed face downward on a predetermined spot, and then the platen forced down upon the woodblock with a single heave on a lever, impressing the pigment deeply into the fabric. Bookbinders and papermakers were also using their own presses by then. It simply came down to choosing, from a range of available models, the version most suitable to further development to print pages of type.'

41 The copy in my collection has marginal annotations throughout in English and Latin. The binding is contemporary with publication and has the stamps of the English printer John Reynes, along with the arms of Henry VIII. For further description of the press illustrated in the mark of Jodocus Badius Ascensius, see Kapr, *Johann Gutenberg*, p. 133.

42 A Latin version also published by Feyerabend in Frankfurt am Main the same year, with text by Hartmann Schoper, was entitled *Panoplia Omnium Artium*. There is a copy in the collection of the Metropolitan Museum of Art (Rogers Fund).

43 McKerrow, *An Introduction to Bibliography*, p. 119.

44 Ibid., p. 119.

45 McKerrow reproduces woodcuts of later sixteenth-century English presses from the *Ordinary for all faithful Christians* (London, printed by Anthony Scoloker, *c.*1548), and from Stephen Bateman's *Doom warning all men to the Judgement* (London, printed by R. Newbery, 1581), in *An Introduction to Bibliography*, fig. 12, p. 43. He further provides detailed descriptions of composition, printing and imposition, as well as information about the early printing press, ibid., pp. 6-52. First published in 1927, McKerrow's book remains one of the best resources for understanding these processes.

46 Quoted by Arthur C. Danto in his introduction to Honoré de Balzac, *The Unknown Masterpiece* and *Gambara*, trans. Richard Howard (New York, 2001), p. vii.

47 Jean Devisse, *The Image of the Black in Western Art II, From the Early Christian Era to the 'Age of Discovery'*, trans. William Granger Ryan, vol. 1 (Cambridge, Mass., 1979); Jean Devisse and Michel Mollat, *The Image of the Black in Western Art II, From the Early Christian Era to the 'Age of Discovery'*, trans. William Granger Ryan, vol. 2 (Cambridge, Mass., 1979).

48 See discussion in Chapter 2, also Chapter 2, Figs 35, 36, 37, 39.

49 Barbara J. Fields, 'Ideology and Race in American History', *Region, Race, and Reconstruction: Essays in Honor of C. Vann Woodward*, ed. J. Morgan Kousser and James M. McPherson (Oxford, 1982), pp. 151-152. Fields points out earlier in her essay that 'To assume, by intention or default, that race is a phenomenon outside history is to take up a position within the terrain of racist ideology and to become its unknowing – and therefore uncontesting – victim' (p. 144).

50 Peter Mark, *Africans in European Eyes: The Portrayal of Black Africans in Fourteenth and Fifteenth Century Europe* (Syracuse, 1974), pp. iii-iv.

51 See, for example, *Journal of Medieval and Early Modern Studies*, 31, no. 1 (Winter 2001), ed. Thomas Hahn, particularly the essays by Thomas Hahn, 'The Difference the Middle Ages Makes: Color and Race before the Modern World', pp. 1-38; Robert Bartlett, 'Medieval and Modern Concepts of Race and Ethnicity', pp. 39-56; and William Chester Jordan, 'Why "Race"?', pp. 165-173. See also the *William and Mary Quarterly*, 3rd ser., 54 (January 1997), which includes several pertinent essays, including Benjamin Braude, 'The Sons of Noah and the Construction of Ethnic and

Geographical Identities in the Medieval and Early Modern Periods', pp. 103-142.

52 These include Henri Baudet, *Paradise on Earth: Some Thoughts on European Images of Non-European Man*, trans. Elizabeth Wentholt (New Haven, 1965); Jacqueline de Weever, *Sheba's Daughters: Whitening and Demonizing the Saracen Women in Medieval French Epic* (New York, 1998); John Block Friedman mentions the Ethiopian king Caspar in 'Monstrous Men as Noble Savages' in J. B. Friedman, *The Monstrous Races in Medieval Art and Thought* (Cambridge, Mass., 1981), pp. 163-177; Paul Friedman explores Judaeo-Christian origin myths of black people in *Images of the Medieval Peasant* (Stanford, Calif., 1999), pp. 86-104. See also Kim F. Hall, *Things of Darkness: Economies of Race and Gender in Early Modern England* (Ithaca, N.Y., 1995), which discusses the portrayal of black people in the later Tudor and early modern period; Paul H. D. Kaplan, *The Rise of the Black Magus in Western Art* (Ann Arbor, 1985); Jan Nederveen Pieterse, *White on Black: Images of Africa and Blacks in Western Popular Culture* (New Haven, 1992; repr. 1996). Frank M. Snowden, Jr, in *Before Color Prejudice: The Ancient View of Blacks* (Cambridge, Mass., 1991), examines attitudes toward black people in the classical world.

53 Bibliographical background on *The Kalender of Shepherds* is supplied by H. Oskar Sommer, *The Kalender of Shepherdes, The Edition of Paris 1503 in Photographic Facsimile: A Faithful Reprint of R. Pynson's Edition of London 1506*, 3 vols (London, 1892), vol. 1: *Prolegomena*. See also Driver, 'When is a Miscellany not Miscellaneous? Making Sense of the *Kalender of Shepherds*', *Yearbook of English Studies* 33, ed. Phillipa Hardman, Modern Humanities Research Association (2003), pp. 199-214. According to *STC*, vol. 2, p. 329, following the edition printed by Vérard in Scots in 1503, the *Kalendar of Shepherds* remained in print in a variety of versions through 1631, going through some nineteen editions, as follows. For more on the Scots copy, see also Sommer, *Kalender of Shepherdes*, vol. 1, *Prolegomena*, p. 67. *STC* cites these: *The kalendayr of the shyppars*, trans. from 'Le Compost et Kalendrier des Bergiers' into Scots (Paris: for A. Vérard, 1503) (*STC* 22407); Claudius Ptolemy, *Here begynneth the Compost of Ptholomeus*, trans. oute of Frenche (R. Wyer, [1530?] (*STC* 20480), consists of extracts from *STC* 22407; for further editions by Wyer, see *STC* 20480a [1540?], 20481 [1550?], 20481.3 [1552?], 20481.7 (pr. T. Colwell [1562?]), 20482 (M. Parsons for H. Gosson, sold by E. Wright [1638?]). Another edition, rev. into English: *Here begynneth the Kalender of shepherdes* (R. Pynson, 1506) (*STC* 22408). Another edition, rev. by R. Copland: *The kalender of shepeherdes* (W. de Worde, 8 December 1508 [1516]) (*STC* 22409); the cuts and device (McK. 19) are in a state *c.* 1516. Another edition of *STC* 22409 printed by de Worde, 1511 (*STC* 22409.5). Other editions of 22408 (R. Pynson, 1517?) (*STC* 22409.3, 22409.7). Another edition: *Here begynneth the kalender of shepardes* (J. Notary, 1518?) (*STC* 22410). Another edition: *The kalender of shepeherdes* (W. de Worde, 24 January 1528) (*STC* 22411). Another edition (W. Powell, 1556) (*STC* 22412). Another edition: (W. Powell for J. Walley, 1559) (*STC* 22413); (T. Este for J. Wally [1570?]) (*STC* 22415); (J. Charlewood for John Wally [*c.* 1580]) (*STC* 22416); (J. Charlewood and G. Robinson for John Wally [*c.* 1585]) (*STC* 22416.5); *STC* 22417 = 22418; (V. S[immes], assigned by T. Adams [1595?]; ass'd to R. Walley, 7 March 1591; to T. Adams, 12 October 1591) (*STC* 22418); (V. Simmes for T. Adams? 1600?) (*STC* 22419); (G. Elde for T. Adams, 1604) (*STC* 22420); (for T. Adams, 1611) (*STC* 22421); (for T. Adams, 1618) (*STC* 22422); (Eliot's Court Press for J. Wright, 1631; ass'd to A. Hebb, 6 May 1625) (*STC* 22423).

54　There seem to be several inside jokes in the poem that may refer to a guild of workers in a craft or confraternity of fools, horns representing cuckoldry as well as being worn typically in fool's motley. 'Les Co[r]nards', the horned ones, or cuckolds, was the name of a confraternity of young people in sixteenth-century Rouen. In England, the horners' guild was quite important early on. The earliest documents of the London Horners' Company were written in 1391, in which the horners describe themselves as 'the pour men of the littell crafte of the Horneris'. See Arthur MacGregor, 'Antler, Bone and Horn', in *English Medieval Industries: Craftsmen, Techniques, Products*, ed. John Blair and Nigel Ramsay (London, 1991), who cites finds in York, London, Bristol, Exeter, Oxford and elsewhere that have been interpreted as medieval horners' workshops (pp. 371-373). See further Frederick Jack Fisher, *A Short History of the Worshipful Company of Horners* (1936), pp. 19-22.

55　Michael Camille, 'Seeing and Reading: Some Visual Implications of Medieval Literacy and Illiteracy', *Art History* 8, no. 1 (March 1985), pp. 26-49, fig. 10, reproduces an image of a shepherd calling to his sheep (some of which are black) with a text similar to that in Marchant's *Kalendrier*. The shepherd wears a hooded cape and has a horn slung around his neck; with one hand he reaches out with his crook, and with the other, he holds a lamb. A text beside his head says, 'ha ha ware le corn'. The illustration occurs in an early thirteenth-century Latin bestiary (Cambridge University Library, MS Kk.4.25, fol. 58ᵛ), illuminated by an English artist. Camille comments: 'It is ... an unusual surprise to come across a colloquial utterance, the very sound of the marketplace, in the pages of an early thirteenth-century Latin Bestiary', though he goes on to qualify this seeming 'sound of the marketplace' as 'the Anglo-Norman French of a ruling Norman elite' (p. 39).

56　Mary Carpenter Erler, ed., *Poems / Robert Copland* (Toronto, 1993), p. 56. The text of Copland's poem, 'How euery man and woman ought to cease of theyr synnes at the sownynge of the dredable horne' is reproduced ibid., pp. 52-53.

57　One manuscript source for the *Kalendar* prints which I identified sometime ago is Fitzwilliam Museum, MS 167. Written in French, with later notations in Italian, this illuminated manuscript is dated *c.*1486. Its text and iconography provide an immediate source for Marchant and Vérard, and indirectly for the English printers who copy them. See the description of this manuscript in M. R. James, *A Descriptive Catalogue of the Manuscripts in the Fitzwilliam Museum* (Cambridge, 1914), pp. 368-372. The Fitzwilliam manuscript is further discussed in Chapter 2, see especially n. 46.

58　I examined all these editions in the British Library. Many leaves are missing from John Wally's late sixteenth-century edition, titled *HEERE BEGINNETH the Kalender of Sheepehards: Newly Augmented and Corrected* (C.131.h.7). The introduction occurs on sig. A 2ʳ⁻ᵛ. The end verses are appended to another poem beginning 'O ye Clearkes famous and eloquent'. *LE grant kalendrier & compost des Bergiers* (British Library 34.b.4), printed by Le Rouge in 1529, includes some copies of the Marchant woodcuts. On sig. J1ᵛ he includes a newly designed woodcut of the Horner: a black figure with a partial turban, dressed in a tunic with a knotted rope belt, blowing a horn and holding a spear. He stands on an architectural pedestal flanked by two arches in the lower portion of the image and topped by the fleur-de-lis. This presentation seems to suggest that the image was drawn from a statue (in church?) standing in a niche or on a pedestal. The copy produced by 'la vefue Jean Bonfons' in Paris in 1569 (British Library C.97.b.13) is a small quarto with very rough copies of

Marchant's woodcuts, including the Horner on sig. xi.

59 Frank Schaer, ed., *The Three Kings of Cologne Edited from London Lambeth Palace MS 491* (Heidelberg, 2000), pp. 26-27, 69, 162; for Prester John, see ibid., pp. 93ff. Schaer states (ibid., pp. 26-27) that this was a popular version, 'extant in twenty-one copies (mostly in Midland dialects) in manuscripts of varied contents, as well as at least four prints by Wynkyn de Worde' (*STC* 5572, 5573, 5574, 5575). The Queen of Sheba, who is also sometimes shown as black in works of art and is thought to be one model for the black Magus, is also mentioned in the *Three Kings* text. The gifts brought by the Magi are said to have been obtained from her: 'And vndirstondith that thes .iij. Kynges out of her kyngdomes broght with hem ricchest and noblest iewels, ornementis, and yeftis to offre to our Lord ... & also all the ornamentis which the qwene Saba had in the temple Salamon of vessell ...' (ibid., pp. 70-71). Prester John is described on pp. 93-94ff.

60 Kaplan, *Black Magus*, p. 19.

61 Ibid., p. 114.

62 Examples of this print in copies of Tory's *Horae* in the British Library appear in a 1525 edition printed by 'Simon Colinaevs Parisiis' for 'G. Tory', C.27.k.15, and in a 1527 edition printed 'Par maistre Simon du bois imprimeur pour maistre Geofroy Tori de Bourges', C.27.h.17. Other examples of the black Magus in prints are provided in *Harvard College Library Department of Printing and Graphic Arts Catalogue of Books and Manuscripts*, Part 1: *French 16th Century Books*, compiled by Ruth Mortimer, under the supervision of Philip Hofer and William A. Jackson, 2 vols (Cambridge, Mass., 1964-1974). In no. 304 (vol. 2, p. 396), Mortimer reproduces a scene of the black Magus at the Adoration wearing a crown and loin cloth (sigs. k1ᵛ-k2ʳ) from *Horae B.M.V. Hore in laudem beatissime virginis Marie: secundum consuetudinem ecclesie parisiensis*, printed in Paris by S. Du Bois for G. Tory on 22 October 1527. This is the same as British Library C.27.h.17. She comments further: 'The black king in the Adoration of the Magi and the black horse in the Triumph of Death offer another link with the Italian woodcut, specifically with the Florentine cut of the 1490's, where the black ground or the black figure with white detail provides dramatic contrast to the clear line and areas of white. ... These Horae blocks are so striking as to inspire a search for other examples – whether independent of or influenced by Tory – throughout the sixteenth century' (pp. 395-396). She remarks further that 'The Ethiopians in the 1549 Gérard d'Euphrate are perhaps the most commanding figures of this type (no. 246)'.

   A print from *Le premier liure de l'histoire & ancienne croniqve de Gerard d'Evphrate* (Paris, E. Groulleau, 1549) is reproduced ibid., no. 246, p. 298: 'Of particular interest is the use of black figures with white details, in the third block, for the Ethiopians at the throne of the king of the underworld.' The Tory woodcut of the black Magus occurs as well ibid., item 123, p. 153, reused in the *Sapphicae hore* printed in Lyons for G. and J. Huguetan in 1538.

63 Pieterse, *White on Black*, p. 28. Braude, 'The Sons of Noah', p. 126. Paul Friedman, in *Images of the Medieval Peasant*, cites earlier examples of Ethiopian exoticism including 'the Isis cult and in Origen's commentaries. ... In 1324 the spectacular pilgrimage to Mecca of Mansa Musa, king of Mali, dazzled not only the Islamic but the European Christian world with a magnificent display of gold and slaves' (p. 93).

64 Mark, *Africans in European Eyes*, p. 34. Intermarriage between black women and European travellers is also reported in later accounts. See Baudet, *Paradise on Earth*,

p. 20, who describes the fate of Pedro de Covilha, sent by John II of Portugal in search of Prester John: 'After many wanderings, de Covilha eventually reached Ethiopia, where he was received with honor. The Ethiopians had developed their own image of the outside world, however, and he was refused permission to leave. According to the reports of later Portuguese travelers he finally resigned himself to his fate, married an Ethiopian wife, and settled down with his family.'

65   Jean Longon, with preface by Millard Meiss, *The Très Riches Heures of Jean, Duke of Berry* (New York, 1969), figs 23 (fol. 27^v, David imagines Christ elevated) and 133 (fol. 193^r, Exaltation of the Cross). The caption for the latter image says: 'Three Negro monks wearing cloaks of the same color as their faces have come to adore [the Cross]', exemplifying the descriptive style of the late 1960s. A lively discussion of the division of the world into three continents linked to the three sons of Noah is presented by Braude, 'The Sons of Noah', pp. 109-126.

66   Ibid., fig. 24 (fol. 28^r).

67   Èlisabeth Lalou and Claudia Rabel, *'Dedens mon livre de pensee ...': De Grégoire de Tours á Charles d'Orléans, Une histoire du livre médiéval en région Centre* (Paris, 1997). The early fifteenth-century breviary was probably made for Louis de Guyenne in Paris (Châteauroux, BM, MS 2, fol. 337^v).

68   De Weever, in *Sheba's Daughters*, points out that figures of power sometimes appear as black in medieval romances and epics, while guardians and inhabitants of the underworld are also occasionally shown as black. Sebilla, encountered by Eneas at the entrance to Avernus, in the twelfth-century romance *Eneas,* is thus described: 'She sat before the entrance, / Quite hoary and dishevelled; / Her face was quite clouded / Her skin black and wrinkled' (pp. 79-80). The images discussed here are reproduced in Devisse, *The Image of the Black in Western Art II*, vol. 2; figs 25, 31. The illumination of the Beheading of John the Baptist illustrates the Canterbury Psalter (fol. 2^v), made about 1200, now in the Bibliothèque nationale de France, MS. lat. 8846. The sculpture of the Beheading of John the Baptist appears on the right side of the lower register of a carved tympanum dating from about 1260 on the north portal of the west façade of the Cathedral of Notre-Dame, Rouen.

69   Ruth Mellinkoff, *Outcasts: Signs of Otherness in Northern European Art of the Late Middle Ages*, 2 vols (Los Angeles, 1993), vol. 1, p. 185 n. 41.

70   Mellinkoff, *Outcasts: Signs of Otherness*, p. 186.

71   Longon with Meiss, *The Très Riches Heures*, fig. 18, fol. 19^v.

72   Gelre Armorial, Brussels, Bibliothèque Royale Albert Ier MS 15652-15656. Kaplan, *Black Magus*, pp. 91, 93. Devisse and Mollat, in *The Image of the Black in Western Art II*, vol. 2, p. 13, further cite 'twenty-nine examples identified by P. Adam-Even, in which seigneurial arms include Moors', as well as other medieval examples from Bavaria, Swabia, Austria, Brabant, Flanders, Holland, Jülich and Gelderland, Berg and Hesse, Holstein, Poland, England, France, Scotland and Aragon. See also P. Adam-Even, 'L'armorial universel du héraut Gelre (1370-1395): Claes Heinen, roi d'armes des Ruyers', *Archives héraldiques suisses* (1971), pp. 28, 31, 37, 38. The arms of the Three Kings from the Gelre Armorial, fol. 28^v, are reproduced in Devisse and Mollat, *The Image of the Black in Western Art II*, vol. 2, p. 9, fig. 1, p. 13, fig. 7. Other heraldic Moors from the Armorial of the Gelre Herald (fols 90^v, 74^r, 106^r, 97^r, 74^r, 82^v, 48^v, 107^r), are reproduced ibid., p. 13, fig. 7. A related Flemish manuscript is the Bellenville Armorial (BNF, MS. fr. 5230), made about the same date as the Gelre Armorial, which has similar black figures.

73 Devisse and Mollat, *The Image of the Black in Western Art II*, vol. 2, p. 10.
Reproductions of the armorial bearings appear ibid., p. 9, fig. 1, p. 10, fig. 2. *Liber
praediorum* (1316), fols 1, 94, Munich, Archiv des Erzbistums von München und
Freising.

73 Roger Wieck, *Painted Prayers: The Book of Hours in Medieval and Renaissance Art*
(New York, 1997), p. 9, item 9. The Hours of Claude Molé, lord of Villy-le-Maréchal,
were illuminated by the Master of Petrarch's Triumphs. Pierpont Morgan Library MS
M. 356, fol. 66^r.

74 A copy of the Freising Missal, published by Johann Sensenschmidt in 1487, may be
examined in the Diözesanmuseum, Freising.

75 For more on the Le Noir family of printers, see Cynthia J. Brown, *Poets, Patrons, and
Printers: Crisis of Authority in Late Medieval France* (ithaca, N.Y., 1995), pp. 31-32,
48-49, 83, 89-90, 187-191, 193, 255-259, 265, also p. 84, fig. 2.9. For early printers'
marks employed by women printers, see Driver, 'Women Printers and the Page, 1477-
1541', *Gutenberg-Jahrbuch* (1998), pp. 139-153.

76 Sandra Hindman, 'The Career of Guy Marchant (1483-1504): High Culture and Low
Culture in Paris,' in *Printing the Written Word: The Social History of Books, circa
1450-1520*, ed. Sandra L. Hindman (Ithaca, N.Y., 1991), pp. 68-100. This article
contains a helpful preliminary checklist of imprints citing 149 books printed by
Marchant from 1492 to 1507. Hindman argues that Marchant was essentially an
academic, scholarly publisher of Latin tract volumes with a close relationship to the
College of Navarre, founded by Jeanne de Navarre, wife of Philip the Fair, in 1304
(p. 81). Hindman further cites 'the copy of the Shepherd's Calendar, printed by
Marchant for Vérard, on which the emblem and arms of King Charles VIII appear'
(p. 87). This was printed in 1493 (BNF, Réserve Vélins 518, Blois 130). Mary Beth
Winn describes this volume more fully in *Anthoine Vérard Parisian Publisher 1485-
1512 Prologues, Poems, and Presentations* (Geneva, 1997), p. 114.

77 Wilberforce Eames, 'Columbus' Letter on the Discovery of America (1493-1497)',
Bulletin of the New York Public Library 28, no. 8 (August 1924), pp. 595-599.

78 Hindman, 'The Career of Guy Marchant', p. 92, points out that 'the 1499 edition of
the Shepherdesses' Calendar in the British Library records the names of members of
a family from Essex with a note in English proclaiming that the present owner stole
the book at Morlaix in Brittany'. There are many marginal markings in Latin and
English at the beginning of this text, also marginalia in English in a sixteenth-century
hand. Some inscriptions I was able to decipher include: sig. a1^v, 'A state of landes
soulde by the executors … J. R. de N., mercer'; sig. a3^v, 'Be it knowne unto all men
by that …'; sig. i3^r, 'No man can sarue two maisters eyther he must hearme? to the
one and dispyse the other or …'. This volume is worth another look.

79 For reproductions of both of Marchant's printer's marks, see Philippe Renouard,
Les marques typographiques parisiennes des xve et xvie siècles (Paris, 1926), p. 707.
Another printer's mark employed by Marchant shows shoemakers at work in a
shop, perhaps a reference to the occupation of the printer's family. See Hindman, 'The
Career of Guy Marchant', p. 77; Mortimer, *Harvard College Library Department of
Printing*, vol. 2, p. 622.

80 *STC* 7272.

81 Mellinkoff, *Outcasts: Signs of Otherness*, p. li.

82 Mark, *Africans in European Eyes*, p. 53. See also Hahn, 'The Difference the Middle
Ages Makes', p. 28, n. 7, p. 32, nn. 37-39. Black figures are also increasingly

illustrated in travel literature. See, for example, the travel journal of Arnold von Harff, Account of Travels in 1496-1499 (Oxford, Bodleian Library, MS Bodley 972 [28066]), a 1554 copy of the original of *c.* 1500, with pen and ink drawings of black Arabs and Africans (fols 74ᵛ, 80ʳ, 81ʳ, 88ʳ, 92ʳ, 96ʳ, 97ʳ, 104ᵛ).

83   Fields, 'Ideology and Race', p. 147. Barbara Fields remarks pointedly that 'No trader who had to confront and learn to placate the power of an African chief could in practice believe that Africans were docile, childlike or primitive. The practical circumstances in which the Europeans confronted Africans in Africa make nonsense of any attempt to encompass Europeans' reactions to Africans within the literary stereotypes that scholars have traced through the ages as discrete racial attitudes.' See also Friedman, *Images of the Medieval Peasant*, p. 93. Braude, 'Sons of Noah', p. 133. There are, however, many fifteenth-century and later representations of the young black servant. For an unusual and little-known example, see the Tapestry of the Black Squire in the Salles des gardes, a fragment from a Nine Worthies series, reproduced in Jean Favier, *The Tapestries of the Chateau of Langeais*, trans. Lisa Davidson (Paris: Beaux Arts Magazine, n.d.), fig. 28. This late fifteenth-century tapestry was woven in wool for a chateau of the Chabannes family in Auvergne. The handsome young man wears a headband or partial turban similar to that seen in the Marchant woodcut, an earring and a jewelled neckband, and has a scimitar at his waist. He is leading a large grey horse wearing face armour with a jewelled breastplate.

84   Mark, *Africans in European Eyes*, p. 74.

85   Lotte Hellinga-Querido, 'Reading an Engraving: William Caxton's Dedication to Margaret of York, Duchess of Burgundy', in *Across the Narrow Seas: Studies in the History and Bibliography of Britain and the Low Countries*, ed. Susan Roach (London, 1991), pp. 4-5, provides a brief description of the miniature in *Les Traités moraux et religieux*, copied by David Aubert and dated March 1475. The miniature 'showing Margaret in prayer accompanied by two kneeling ladies and a male figure standing in the background' has been ascribed to the Master of Mary of Burgundy. The curly dark hair and dark-skinned face of this male figure in the background are not noted in this description. For discussion of the dress of morris dancers, see John Forrest, *The History of Morris Dancing 1458-1750* (Toronto, 1999), pp. 52-55, 62-65, 136-137, 153-167, passim.

86   Hahn, 'The Difference the Middle Ages Makes', p. 25.

87   *The Tempest*, V.1.182-3.

6. ICONOCLASM AND REFORM

1   Martin Luther, 'Against the Heavenly Prophets', in Jaroslav Pelikan and Helmut T. Lehmann, gen. eds, *Luther's Works*, 55 vols (St Louis and Philadelphia, 1955-1976), vol. 44, p. 99. Luther concludes his argument concerning the positive didactic use of images in a characteristically compelling way: 'For whether I will or not, when I hear of Christ, an image of a man hanging on a cross takes form in my heart, just as the reflection of my face naturally appears in the water when I look into it. If it is not a sin but good to have the image of Christ in my heart, why should it be a sin to have it in my eyes?' (pp. 99-100). See also Driver, '"Sweet as Honey": Albrecht Dürer as Protestant Propagandist', *American Book Collector* 7 (1986), pp. 3-10. For discussion of later wall painting in England, see Tessa Watt, 'Stories for Walls', in *Cheap Print and Popular Piety, 1550-1640* (Cambridge, 1991), pp. 178-216.

2 David Freedberg, *The Power of Images: Studies in the History and Theory of Response* (Chicago, 1989), pp. 398-399. For further background, see Carl G. Christensen, *Art and the Reformation in Germany* (Athens, OH, 1979); Craig Harbison, 'Reformation Iconography, Problems and Attitudes', *Print Review* 5 (1976): 78-87; R. W. Scribner, *Popular Culture and Popular Movements in Reformation Germany* (London, 1987). For visual responses to religious and social problems by early Protestant artists, see also the first chapters of Ralph E. Shikes, *The Indignant Eye: The Artist as Social Critic in Prints and Drawings from the Fifteenth Century to Picasso* (Boston, 1969), which remains a classic; *From a Mighty Fortress: Prints, Drawings, and Books in the Age of Luther, 1483-1546*, ed. Christiane Andersson and Charles Talbot (Detroit, 1983); and Jeffrey Chipps Smith, *Nuremberg: A Renaissance City, 1500-1618* (Austin, Tex., 1983). Richard G. Cole, in 'The Use of Reformation Woodcuts by Sixteenth-Century Printers as a Mediator Between the Elite and Popular Cultures', *Journal of Popular Culture* 21, no. 3 (Winter 1987), pp. 111-130, has commented: 'Much remains to be done on the Reformation woodcut as a historical source' (p. 128).

3 See Driver, 'Sweet as Honey', p. 7.

4 Luther's 1522 and 1530 prefaces to Revelation are in Pelikan and Lehmann, *Luther's Works*, vol. 35, pp. 399ff.

5 For further description of Cranach's woodcuts for the Apocalypse, see R. W. Scribner, *For the Sake of Simple Folk: Popular Propaganda for the German Reformation* (Cambridge, 1981), pp. 169-187.

6 Colin Eisler, *The Master of the Unicorn: The Life and Work of Jean Duvet* (New York, 1977), p. 60. A Protestant English New Testament, the Coverdale version, printed in Antwerp by Matthew Crom in 1538 (*STC* 2837), illustrates Revelation with images similar to those used in the Knobloch Bible of 1524. In the illustrations of the English New Testament, which are copies of Holbein's copies of Cranach, the dragon and the Whore of Babylon clearly once wore papal crowns. These were inadequately removed from the blocks, and traces still remain, giving the nimbus effect described by Eisler.

7 Illustrations by Monogrammist M.S. occur in Luther's two-volume translation of the Bible, *Biblia: das ist die gantze Heilige Schrifft: Deudsch Auffs New zugericht. D. Mart. Luth. Begnadet mit Kürfürstlicher zu Sachsen Freiheit*, printed in Wittenberg by Hans Lufft in 1534 and 1541. I examined these volumes in the Rare Book Room of the New York Public Library (*KB + 1534). For more on the 1541 edition, see Andersson and Talbot, *From a Mighty Fortress*, item 211, pp. 375-377.

8 A similar illustration sans tiara occurs in a New Testament published in Dresden by Wolffgang Stöckel in 1527, a copy of which is in the New York Public Library (*KB + 1527). The illustrations in both the Paris and Dresden editions have been directly drawn from those produced by Cranach.

9 See Scribner, *For the Sake of Simple Folk*, pp. 150-155, who comments, 'This little book is an extremely complex work. ... The religion of Christ is contrasted to that of human laws and externals. The testimony of the Word of God in Scripture is opposed to that of the pope in canon law and to the mendacious Donation of Constantine. A third theme found in both visual and printed text is the highly emotive issue of anticlericalism' (155). *Passional Christi und Antichristi* is discussed briefly by Christiane Andersson in 'Polemical Prints during the Reformation', in *Censorship: 500 Years of Conflict* (New York, 1984), pp. 46-47; and by Richard K. Emmerson,

Antichrist in the Middle Ages: A Study of Medieval Apocalypticism, Art, and Literature (Seattle, 1981), pp. 226-227. Research on the *Passional*'s later publication in France is being conducted by Jonathan Reid and William Kemp, whose paper 'Multi-Genre Narratives in the *c.* 1535 French Adaptation of the 1521 *Passional Christi und Antichristi*' was presented at 'Telling Stories: The Book and the Art of Narrative', the seventh biennial conference of the Early Book Society, held at University College, Cork, 2001.

10 In England, the equation of the pope with the Antichrist was explicitly made by John Wycliffe and his followers. Printed English tracts about the Antichrist, though in some cases orthodox, further prepared the ground for later attacks on the pope during the Reformation. There are a number of these. For example, following his usual pattern of republishing works that had originally appeared in French, de Worde published *A lytell tretyse called the Lucydarye* in an English translation by Andrew Chertsey, printed in 1507 (*STC* 13685.5) and again about 1523 (*STC* 13686), which provides a detailed life of Antichrist. A woodcut series illustrating the life of Antichrist also appears in de Worde's *The arte or crafte to lyue well*, also translated by Chertsey and printed in 1505 (*STC* 792, BL C.6.A.19), in which 'The treatyse of þe comynge of Antecryst' occurs on sigs. Hh6-Kk3. Another work printed by de Worde, which is essentially orthodox, titled *Here begynneth the byrthe and lyfe of the moost false and deceytfull Antechryst*, appeared *c.* 1525 (*STC* 670) again with woodcut illustrations, many repeated from *The arte or crafte to lyue well*. The unique copy is in Cambridge University Library (Syn. 7.52.17). See Richard K. Emmerson, 'Wynkyn de Worde's *Byrthe and Lyfe of Antechryst* and Popular Eschatology on the Eve of the English Reformation', *Mediaevalia* 14 (1991), pp. 281-311; also Joseph Martin Ricke, 'The Antichrist "Vita" at the End of the Middle Ages: An Edition of "The Byrthe and Lyfe of the Moost False and Deceytfull Antechryst"' (Ph.D. diss., Rice University, 1982). Ricke has traced several of the woodcuts to an earlier French work, *L'Avenement et du Mauvais Antechrist*, printed in Lyons in 1495 (pp. 85-86, 105-107, 206-213). The copy I examined in the British Library (IB 42340) contains full-page woodcuts on the verso of each leaf. The text is Latin with French verses. Four of de Worde's woodcuts are also related iconographically to the fifteenth-century German block-book *vitae Antichristi*.

11 See also Andersson, 'Polemical Prints', fig. 8, pp. 44-46.

12 *STC* 21471.5, 21472. According to the *STC*, there are two editions of *The ymage of loue*, the first a quarto with several more illustrations than appear in the second edition. These woodcuts are cited and reproduced by Hodnett: see item 442, fig. 63; item 436, fig. 61; item 453, fig. 58, item 430. *STC* 21471.5 was printed on 7 October 1525, and there is a copy in the Huntington. The copy I examined in Bodley (*STC* 21472), an octavo, was published *c.* 1532; the title-page image is the only picture in the volume.

13 Margaret Aston, *Lollards and Reformers: Images and Literacy in Late Medieval Religion* (London, 1984), p. 229.

14 Ibid., p. 230 n. 46. See also above, Chapter 3, note 27.

15 James Moran, *Wynkyn de Worde: Father of Fleet Street* (1960; repr. London, 1976), p. 41.

16 According to Susan Foister, 'Paintings and Other Works of Art in Sixteenth-Century English Inventories', *Burlington Magazine*, 123, no. 938 (May 1981), pp. 273-282, pictures of the Virgin Mary, the Passion and the saints continued to be revered in

private houses through the early years of the reign of Elizabeth I: 'The inventories do not bear out the assumption often made that religious pictures vanished during the latter part of the reign of Henry VIII and in the iconoclastic reign of his son Edward VI. ... The Virgin Mary, the Passion and various saints were common subjects' (p. 276).

17 STC 18084. Library of Congress BX1780 .M6 1529. *A dyaloge of syr T. More ... wherin be treatyd dyuers maters, as of the veneration & worship of ymagys & relyques, prayng to sayntys* (London: John Rastell, 1529). See also A. W. Reed, *Early Tudor Drama: Medwall, The Rastells, Heywood, and the More Circle* (1926; repr. New York, 1969), p. 168; W. E. Campbell and A. W. Reed, eds, *A Dialogue Concerning Heresies and Matters of Religion made in 1528 by Sir Thomas More* (London, 1927).

18 Aston, *Faith and Fire: Popular and Unpopular Religion, 1350-1600* (London, 1993), pp. 276-278: 'As one of the more famous images in London, [the Rood] had for some while been the butt of denigration and suspect invective' (p. 277).

19 Aston, *Lollards and Reformers*, p. 251 n. 28.

20 See chapter 3, note 28.

21 PML 590. The writing continues, rather confusedly, 'As is one or 2 more which I can not find'.

22 This is a Sarum Hours printed on vellum by de Worde in 1502 (Bodleian Library, Gough Missal 173 = Arch.G.e.39, *STC* 15898) that uses the Crucifixion woodcut series described by Hodnett and discussed above, Chapter 2, p. 36, notes 12, 13; the woodcut of the Jesse Tree is one of this series.

23 STC 17542. For a description of the original audience for this book and of reading practice more generally at Syon, see Ann Hutchison, 'Devotional Reading in the Monastery and in the Late Medieval Household', in *De Cella in Seculum: Religious and Secular Life and Devotion in Late Medieval England*, ed. Michael G. Sargent (Cambridge, 1989), pp. 215-227. The seventeenth-century reader's added comment about keeping the book 'for another day' seems extraordinarily prescient. Eamon Duffy points out, in *The Stripping of the Altars: Traditional Religion in England c. 1400-c. 1580* (New Haven, 1992), pp. 526-564, that the Marian articles and injunctions advocated similar censorship of Protestant images: 'Texts or pictures painted on the walls and which "chiefly and principally do tend to the maintenance of carnall liberty" by attacking fasting, clerical celibacy, the value of good works, or the veneration of the Blessed Sacrament, were to be blotted out' (p. 545).

24 Paul L. Hughes and James F. Larkin, *Tudor Royal Proclamations* (New Haven, 1964), 30 Henry VIII, no. 186. See also Margaret Aston, *England's Iconoclasts*, vol. 1: *Laws Against Images* (Oxford, 1988), pp. 391, 379-382, 393; Duffy, *The Stripping of the Altars*, pp. 405-413.

25 PML M. 1033, Brotherton Library MS 15. MS Richardson 34 is briefly described by Roger S. Wieck, *Late Medieval and Renaissance Illuminated Manuscripts 1350-1525 in the Houghton Library* (Cambridge, Mass., 1983), item 45; and in Harvard College Library, *Illuminated and Calligraphic Manuscripts* (Cambridge, Mass., 1955) 21, no. 63, though neither catalogue describes the censored passages in the text. The risqué miniature of the Flagellation featuring one tormentor who takes down his hose and shows his bare buttocks has been left untouched by the censor. Censorship of Becket-related materials and of the word 'pope' is found in many fifteenth-century English manuscripts, whether religious or secular, in the collections of Harvard, the British

Library and elsewhere.

26 For a description of Bodleian Library Douce 24, see Alan Coates and Kristian Jensen, 'The Bodleian Library's Acquisition of Incunabula with English and Scottish Medieval Monastic Provenances', in *Books and Collectors 1200-1700: Essays Presented to Andrew Watson*, ed. James P. Carley and Colin G. C. Tite (London, 1997), p. 252, item 18.

27 The copy of Caxton's 1483 *Golden Legend* (STC 24873) in the Rare Book Room of the New York Public Library lacks several of its opening leaves; others are fragmentary. The woodcut illustrating the murder of Becket is missing entirely. However, the copy formerly at Longleat House, which I have also examined, is intact, though the Becket woodcut is partially inked over; many of its other cuts have been hand-coloured. Like one of the copies of the *Orcharde of Syon* discussed in Chapter 4, the Longleat copy of the *Golden Legend* was one of those formerly in the Beriah Botfield collection auctioned at Christie's on 13 June 2002. See *Printed Books and Manuscripts from Longleat* (London, Christie's, 2002), item 41, p. 109, for a reproduction of the censored woodcut. A woodcut of Becket appears twice clean and intact in the British Library copy of Caxton's *Golden Legend* (C.11.d.8), illustrating 'The lyf of saynt Thomas of Caunterburye' at sig. N8^r (fol. cv) and also 'Here foloweth the translacion of Seynt Thomas of caunterbury' (sig. B4^r, fol. ccxii), though the text has been partially inked over on fol. ccxiii (sig. B5^r). The word 'pope' has also been sporadically crossed out (see sig. E4^v, for example). The censor's pen has also been busy elsewhere in this copy. See also John N. King, in *English Reformation Literature: The Tudor Origins of the Protestant Tradition* (Princeton, N.J., 1982), who describes extensive deletions in the Denchworth and British Library copies of the *Golden Legend* (pp. 147-149): in British Library C.11.d.8, 'B5^r was stricken out by hand in order to delete references to St. Thomas Becket' (p. 147 n. 24). Texts pertaining to Becket in books on other subjects are also regularly censored; one finds prayers to him crossed out in the British Library copy of *Missale Secundum vsum Insignis Ecclesie Sarum*, the prayer-book printed for de Worde in Paris in 1497 (for example, fol. xv^v).

28 This is a copy of the fourth edition of the *Kalendar of Shepherds* in the British Library (C.71.f.2., STC 22410), which combines the earlier texts of Pynson and de Worde. The censored text occurs on sig. f6, and I assume that here 'saynt Thomas' refers to Becket: 'And if thou demaunde howe thou mayste than praye to other saynts. I say to the thou must pray as our moder holy churche prayeth in saynge to saynt peter. Holy saynt Peter praye for vs / saynt Thomas praye for vs / and saynt katheryne for vs. That they maye praye to god to gyue vs grace / and that he forgyue vs our synnes. ...' The idea that the saints can intercede with God for the salvation of sinners and the Marian material in the passage may have contributed to its defacement. H. Oskar Sommer also describes a copy in the Bodleian Library in a note in *The Academy*, no. 972 (20 December 1890) (unpaginated), 'Notary's edition is of extreme rarity.' A variant version of this text also appears in Pynson's edition; see H. Oskar Sommer in *The Kalender of Shepherdes, The Edition of Paris 1503 in Photographic Facsimile: A Faithful Reprint of R. Pynson's Edition of London 1506*, pt 1: 'Prolegomena' (London, 1892), pp. 115-117.

29 The texts and images in the 1521 Byrkman Hours in the Bodleian Library (Douce BB 135, Hoskins 59, STC 15931) have been thoroughly censored in other ways as well. The word 'pope' has been assiduously removed throughout. On signature S1^r, the Tudor rose reappears in the borders along with the shields of the English kings from

William the Conqueror and William Rufus to Henry VII.

30 This example is found in Marsh's Library, Dublin (Z1.2.8 Hours, STC 15924), titled in part: *Hore beatissime virginis Marie ad legitimum Sarisburiensis ecclesie ritum: cum quindecim orationibus beate Brigitte*. This volume was printed in Paris by 'Nicolaus hicqman impensis Francisci Byrkman', in 1519. The device of François Regnault appears on the last page. The title-page has a woodcut of the Jesse Tree with censored images of the Virgin and another Old Testament figure. The word 'pape' has been erased throughout the calendar, along with names of popes and all indulgences. In the introduction to the *Fifteen Oes* text, a censor has simply crossed out 'Rome' and 'whoso says'. The censor tends to avoid the Latin texts in the volume, censoring only the English headings, one indication that he may not have read Latin. The Jesse Tree illustration has been repeated at the end of the Suffrages and there has definitely been another attempt at erasure of the picture of the Virgin, after which the censor's hand ceases its labours.

31 Duffy, *The Stripping of the Altars*, p. 432, p. 432 n. 22. In *Here foloweth a notable treatyse ... named the Ordynarye of crystyanyte or of crysten men*, translated by Chertsey from *L'ordinaire des chrestiens*, and printed by de Worde in 1502 (STC 5198, British Library G 1739 [11.739]), much of the 'fourth parte' of the volume, which explains confession, has been censored by a later reader. The word 'pope' has been scratched out and the text inked over (see especially sigs. t1^v-t3^r).

32 Cambridge University Library MS Cg.iv.31, Huntington Library MS HM 143. See *The Manuscripts of 'Piers Plowman': The B-version*, ed. C. David Benson and Lynne S. Blanchfield, with Marie-Claire Uhart (London, 1998), p. 25. In a discussion of marginal notation of *Piers* manuscripts by later readers, Benson and Blanchfield point out that 'surprisingly few Protestant sentiments are found in the later annotations of the B-manuscripts' (pp. 24-25), though Carl James Grindley has found that this is not necessarily the case in his study of the annotation of the C-texts. Grindley has found that polemical responses to the text in British Library MS Add. 35157, for example, 'make up a large proportion of that manuscript's marginalia' (p. 89). See his 'Reading Piers Plowman C-Text Annotations: Notes toward the Classification of Printed and Written Marginalia in Texts from the British Isles 1300-1641', in *The Medieval Professional Reader at Work: Evidence from Manuscripts of Chaucer, Langland, Kempe, and Gower*, ed. Kathryn Kerby-Fulton and Maidie Hilmo (Victoria, 2001), pp. 73-141. See also Derek Pearsall, *Piers Plowman by William Langland: An Edition of the C-text* (Berkeley, 1978), p. 24.

33 Bamburgh Sel. 13 (STC 13439). The copy of Higden's *Polychronicon*, printed by de Worde in Westminster on 13 April 1495, has mid-sixteenth century brown calf covers with blind roll impressions, possibly of a Norfolk binder but over reused wooden boards that perhaps originate in the Caxton–de Worde workshop. The volume contains sixteenth-century notations made by members of the Heydon family of Baconsthorp, Norfolk. Cited in A. I. Doyle, Elizabeth Rainey, Sheila Hingley, '*To se, and eek for to be seye': A Display of Manuscripts and Printed Books at Durham University Library, 11 July 2003 for a Conference of the Early Book Society* (pamphlet), item 39.

34 Scribner, *For the Sake of Simple Folk*, p. 171. Like Morgan MS M. 126, a de luxe manuscript of John Gower's *Confessio Amantis*, MS Hunterian 5, S.I.5, has been copied in the hand of Ricardus Franciscus. See my comments on this scribe in 'Printing the *Confessio Amantis*: Caxton's Edition in Context', in *Re-visioning*

Gower, ed. R. F. Yeager (Asheville, NC, 1998), pp. 280-281 n. 21; and Lisa Jefferson, 'Two Fifteenth-Century Manuscripts of the Statutes of the Order of the Garter', in *English Manuscript Studies 1100-1700*, ed. Peter Beal and Jeremy Griffiths, vol. 5 (London, 1995), pp. 18-35.

35 The censored passages in the Hunterian manuscript occur on fols 197-211. In addition to obliterating the Roman Catholic references, our prudish censor also deleted the lines 'Quick with childe the houre cam on hir than Was delyuered. at seynt John Lateran'. For another example of censorship more focused on the profane than the religious, see David Landau and Peter Parshall, *The Renaissance Print 1470-1550* (New Haven, 1994), p. 225. The printer, artist and illuminator Hans Guldenmund was accused before the Nuremberg council in 1535 of owning 'a most shameful and sinful little book, containing many obscene pictures of unconventional lovemaking'. He confessed that he had received nine copies of this book from the Augsburg woodblock cutter Hans Schwarzenberger 'on the understanding that they be taken on consignment to Frankfurt and sold there. ... This information comes down to us in a letter written from the Nuremberg council to its counterpart in Augsburg warning of the publication, "since lustful images alone can provoke great scandal and incite the young to sinful vices".'

36 For discussion and redating of books printed by Wyer, many of which are undated or have been dated differently by the *STC*, see P. B. Tracy, 'Robert Wyer: A Brief Analysis of His Types and a Suggested Chronology for the Output of His Press', *The Library*, 6th ser., no. 2 (1980), pp. 294-303. Some of the composite illustrations found in the .C. Hystoryes are discussed in Chapter 2 (Figs 48, 49).

37 *STC* 17817. For Wyer's Protestant publications, see Jean Preston, 'The Pricke of Conscience (Paris I-III) and Its First Appearance in Print', *The Library*, 6th ser., no. 4 (December 1985), p. 314.

38 Bodleian Library Arch. G. f.14, 15. Both prints were probably preserved by being bound into the Sarum Hours printed in Paris in 1495 (*STC* 15880), now Douce 24. The prints were removed in 1928, but neither is original to Douce 24. The woodcut reproduced here is briefly described by Coates and Jensen, 'The Bodleian Library's Acquisition of Incunabula', pp. 252-253, item 18.

39 Hind, 2: 738. Hind remarks further that these single-leaf prints were 'detached from a Sarum Hours printed by Pigouchet, Paris 1495'.

40 Duffy, *The Stripping of the Altars*, discusses the Wounds, pp. 238-246, and reproduces Arch. G. f.14 as plate 99. Duffy adds that the Sheen woodcut was 'a devotional card circulated by the Carthusians'. Whether the woodcuts were originally intended to be circulated by the Carthusians at Sheen among lay people as well is not entirely clear, as these are sole surviving examples, preserved, no doubt, by being bound into a book. For further discussion of single-leaf prints and their circulation, see Chapters 1 and 4, also *STC* 14077c.6-.23B.

41 The famous relics acquired by St Louis for which he built the Sainte-Chapelle were featured in an exhibition 'Le trésor de la Sainte-Chapelle' at the Louvre, 1 June-27 August 2001 (catalogued in *Le trésor de la Sainte-Chapelle* [Paris, 2001]. It was particularly interesting to see pictures of the relics, which further include the head of John the Baptist, and the breast milk of the Virgin Mary, reproduced in manuscripts and then in early printed books of the fifteenth century, along with the documents with numerous wax seals verifying the provenance of the relics. Flora Lewis, 'The Wound in Christ's Side and the Instruments of the Passion: Gendered Experience and

the Response', in *Women and the Book: Assessing the Visual Evidence*, ed. Jane H. M. Taylor and Lesley Smith (London, 1996), pp. 204-229, mentions 'indulgences for the *arma christi* granted by Innocent' (p. 208). For discussion of the popularity of images of the Sacred Heart, Five Wounds, Holy Face and Holy Name (or sacred monogram), see John Block Friedman, *Northern English Books, Owners, and Makers in the Late Middle Ages* (Syracuse, N.Y., 1995). Readers wishing to gain God's mercy through affective devotion were advised to focus on religious images and to 'imagine themselves bystanders at or even participants in the events they contemplate' (ibid., p. 149). See also Kathleen Kamerick, *Popular Piety and Art in the Late Middle Ages: Image Worship and Idolatry in England 1350-1550* (New York, 2002), pp. 169-180.

42 Duffy, *The Stripping of the Altars*, p. 238.

43 British Library C.10.b.16, *STC* 14077c.6. The Image of Pity print is *STC* 14072 and Hodnett, item 381. The *Directorium* is described by E. Gordon Duff, *William Caxton* (1905; repr. New York, 1970), p. 66, pl. XIV, and by Henry Bradshaw, *Collected Papers of Henry Bradshaw* (Cambridge, 1889), pp. 255ff.

44 For more on the single-leaf prints bound into MS Rawlinson D. 403 and their Bridgettine associations, see Chapter 4. The Rawlinson Image of Pity print is *STC* 14077c.13 (Dodgson 6), and Hodnett, item 2513 (Supplement), fig. 17. See also Dodgson *Ashm.*, p. 34; Dodgson 'Bodl.', item 9.

45 A similar border comprised of emblems of the Passion surrounds the single-leaf *Pietà* (*STC* 14077c.22, *c*. 1500, Dodgson 13) bound in as fol. 1ᵛ to Bodleian MS Rawlinson D. 403 (Hodnett, item 2512). Its indulgence text has also been crossed out. For a brief description, see pp. 9-12, and Chapter 1, Fig. 6. This single-leaf print seems to have served as a model for other woodcuts (Hodnett, figs 27, 28). De Worde later employed it in his editions of Thomas à Kempis (*STC* 23956, 23960), and here, too, the images perhaps served as markers of Bridgettine production or influence.

46 In the Rawlinson example, the indulgence text is crossed out, though it is still somewhat legible, including the usual formula of five Paternosters, five Aves and the Creed; the last line has been obliterated. A label has been pasted over the indulgence panel of the woodcut inserted into the *Directorium*, the text of which seems to have been scraped away previously. The modern label cites D. Middleton's 'Dissertation on the Origin of Printing' which (incorrectly) states, 'This is the only Book printed in Latin by Caxton, and which is not mention'd in any Catalogue of his Works. ...' Bradshaw, in *Collected Papers*, pp. 256-257, describes another single-leaf Image of Pity bound into the Lambeth Palace copy of a Sarum Hours printed by de Worde *c*. 1494 (*STC* 15875). As in the *Directorium*, the text of this Hours copy shows signs of censorship: 'The word *pape* is erased in the kalendar, but St Thomas of Canterbury remains; a fact which shows that the book was withdrawn from sight between 1534 and 1538. The devotional pictures fastened into it must have been inserted much earlier than the XVIth century.' In the print, Jesus stands in a tomb, his hands crossed, and in this case, tied. Emblems of the Passion appear around this central figure, 'loose, as in the Dutch prints, not in compartments, as in Caxton's treatment of the subject'. In this case again, the single-leaf print seems to have Bridgettine associations. The other surviving illustrations include a copper-engraving of St Katherine of Sweden, the daughter of St Bridget. Bradshaw comments that the book 'bears marks of having contained eighteen of these inserted pictures. ... When I first saw the book at Lambeth, only three were still in existence.' This is not cited in *STC*.

47 Duffy, *The Stripping of the Altars*, pp. 539-540.

48 *STC* 20195.

49 Duffy, in *The Stripping of the Altars*, p. 249, says of the *Oes*, 'They are English in origin, probably composed either in the devotional world of the Yorkshire hermitages associated with figures like Richard Rolle and his disciples, or in the circle of the English Brigittines' – which seems a particularly likely source. Duffy also comments on connections between the *Oes* and the cult of the Wounds. Nicholas Rogers, in 'About the 15 O's, The Brigittines and Syon Abbey', *St. Ansgar's Bulletin* 80 (1984), focuses on six of the *Oes* manuscripts copied or owned in England in the fifteenth century. Only one includes the rubric '15 orationes sancte Brigitte' before the prayers; the other manuscripts, however, have illustrations of Bridget at the start of the *Oes*, include references to Bridget elsewhere in the text, or are known to have been owned by people associated with the Bridgettine house of Syon Abbey. As Rogers remarks, there is 'a good degree of circumstantial evidence to support Brigittine origin of the Fifteen O's' (pp. 29-30).

50 Reprinted in W. P. Cumming, ed., *Revelations of St. Birgitta*, Early English Text Society, old ser. 178 (1929), p. xxxviii (fol. 118ᵛ). The poem 'is written on a blank leaf in a word-list of Latin synonyms, and may have been copied from a manuscript containing the *Fifteen Oes*, to which it served as the introduction'. Cumming briefly mentions the passing down of manuscript copies of Bridget's *Revelations* from mother to daughter and from women to other women. The most famous example is that of Cecily, Duchess of York, who left a copy to her daughter Anne de la Pole in 1495: 'Also I geve to my daughter Anne, priores of Sion, a boke of Bonaventure and Hilton in the same Englishe, and a boke of the Revelations of Saint Burgitte.'

51 *STC* 15949, 15950 (1527), 15951, 15984 (1534).

52 *STC* 16004, 16007, 16008. I have examined the copies at the Bodleian Library, Oxford, and the Houghton Library, Harvard University.

53 *STC* 15970, 15973; 15984; 20195. See Helen C. White, *The Tudor Books of Private Devotion* (Madison, 1951), p. 219. For more on Caxton's printing of the *Oes*, see Henry Bradshaw, 'Notice of a Fragment of the *Fifteen Oes* and Other Prayers Printed at Westminster by William Caxton about 1490-91, Preserved in the Library of the Baptist College, Bristol', in his *Collected Papers*, pp. 341-349; Lotte Hellinga, *Caxton in Focus: The Beginning of Printing in England* (London, 1982), p. 44, figs 13, 14; George D. Painter, 'Caxton Through the Looking-Glass: An Enquiry into the Offsets on a Fragment of Caxton's *Fifteen Oes*, with a Census of Caxton Binding', *Gutenberg-Jahrbuch* (1963), pp. 73-88.

54 One seventeenth-century diary account describes the activities of a gang of men who at Stoke-by-Nayland 'brake down an 100 superstitious pictures; and took up 7 superstitious Inscriptions on the Grave-Stones, *ora pro nobis*, &c', and who, three days later at Barham, 'brake down the 12 Apostles in the Chancel, and 6 superstitious more there; and 8 in the Church, one a Lamb with a Cross X on the back, and digged down the [altar] Steps ...' from *The Journal of William Dowsing of Stratford*, ed. C. H. Evelyn White (Ipswich, 1885), p. 16. For more on later destruction of images, especially that of the Cheapside Cross in January 1642, which was described in contemporary pamphlets 'as a sentient being, as if it had a voice and social identity of its own. ... as a heathen idol, a popish monument, a foolish Catholic' and which 'was gendered as female and tied to the "womanish" faith of Roman Catholicism' (p. 235), see David Cressy, 'The Downfall of Cheapside Cross: Vandalism, Ridicule,

and Iconoclasm', in *Agnes Bowker's Cat: Travesties and Transgressions in Tudor and Stuart England* (Oxford, 2000), pp. 234-250, and Duffy, *The Stripping of the Altars*, pp. 569-570, 575-580.

BIBLIOGRAPHY

SELECTED PRIMARY SOURCES

Following are selected primary printed sources discussed in the text of this book. These are grouped by the names of authors, or in the case of anonymous works, by keywords taken from the titles. Titles of English works are cited as they appear in the *STC*, with *STC* numbers, place of publication and date. Shelfmarks of books held in The British Library are also given.

Aesop. *Fables of Esope*, trans. William Caxton. Westminster: William Caxton, 26 March 1484. *STC* 175. BL C.11.c.17.

Aesop. *Fabule Esopi cum commento*. London: Wynkyn de Worde, 1535. *STC* 171.

Ars memorandi. Pforzheim: Thomas Anshelm, 1502. BL 689.C.7.

Ars moriendi block-book, 1st edition. Rhine district: *c.* 1465. BL IB.18.

Ars moriendi. London: Wynkyn de Worde, 1506. *STC* 788.

L'Art de bien vivre et de bien mourir. Paris: for Antoine Vérard, October 1492. BL IB.40027.

L'Art de bien viure et de bien mourir. Paris: Gillet Couteau and Jean Menard for Antoine Vérard, 15 December 1492.

L'Art de bien viure et de bien mourir. Paris: A. Bocard for Antoine Vérard, 12 February 1493. BL C.22.b.3.

The book intytulyd the art of good lywyng and good deyng. Paris: for Antoine Vérard, 1503. *STC* 791. BL C.70.g.14.

Bartholomaeus Anglicus. *De proprietatibus rerum*. Haarlem: Bellaert, 1485. BL IB.48508.

Bartholomaeus Anglicus. *De proprietatibus rerum*. Lyons: Mathias Huss, 12 October 1485. BL IB.41702.

Bartholomaeus Anglicus. *De proprietatibus rerum*. Toulouse: Heinrich Mayer, 1494. BL IB.42456.

Bartholomaeus Anglicus, *De proprietatibus rerum*. Westminster: Wynkyn de Worde, 1495. *STC* 1536. BL IB.55242.

Beaufort, Margaret, trans. *The mirroure of golde for the Synfull soule*. London: Wynkyn de Worde, 29 March 1522. *STC* 6895. BL G.12042.

Biblia Latina [Gutenberg Bible]. Mainz: Johann Gutenberg, *c.* 1454-1455. BL C.9.d.3, 4.

Biblia pauperum. Netherlands: *c.* 1470. BL G.12090.

Les figures du Vieil Testament et du Nouuel. Paris: for Antoine Vérard, *c.* 1504. BL C.22.b.7.

Bible. *Das Neue Testament Deutsch* ['September Testament'], trans. Martin Luther. Wittenberg: Melchior Lotter, 1522. BL 1502/591.

Bible. *Das Neue Testament Deutsch*, trans. Martin Luther. Strassburg: Johann Knobloch, 1524. BL 3035.c.13.

Bible. *Das ist die Gantze Heilige Schrifft Deudsch*, trans. Martin Luther, vol. 2. Wittenberg: Hans Lufft, 1534. BL I.b.10.

Bible. *Novvm testamentum*. Paris: Fran. Gryphius, 1541. BL 3022.a.34.

Boccaccio, Giovanni. *De Casibus Virorum Illustrium*. Lyons: Mathias Huss and Iehan Schabeler, 1483. BL 86.h.18.

Bonde, William. *Pylgrimage of perfection*. London: Wynkyn de Worde, 23 February 1531. *STC* 3278. BL 22.3.K.1.

Boorde, Andrew. *The Fyrste Boke of the Introduction of Knowledge*. London: William Copland, *c.* 1562. *STC* 3383.

Bouchet, Jean. *L'amoureux Transy sans Espoir*. Paris: for Antoine Vérard, *c.* 1502/1503. BL C.34.g.6 (1).

Catherine of Siena. *The Orcharde of Syon*, trans. Dane James. London: Wynkyn de Worde, 1519. *STC* 4815. BL C.11.b.6.

Chaucer, Geoffrey. *Canterbury Tales*. Westminster: William Caxton, 1483. *STC* 5083. BL G.11586, IB. 55095.

The Chronicles of England. London: Wynkyn de Worde, 1520. *STC* 1000.

Cronycle of Englonde. Westminster: Wynkyn de Worde, 1497. *STC* 9996. BL C.11.b.1. (1).

The descrypcyon of Englonde. Westminster: Wynkyn de Worde, 1498. *STC* 13440b.

The complaynt of a louers lyfe. London: de Worde, *c.* 1531. *STC* 17014.7.

Contemplacyons of the drede and loue of God. London: Wynkyn de Worde, 1506. *STC* 21259. BL G.12058, C.21.c.22.

The crafte to lyue well and to dye well. London: Wynkyn de Worde, 1505. *STC* 792. BL C.132.h.40, C.53.e.4.

Cranach, Lucas. *Passional Christi und Antichristi*. Wittenberg: Johann Grunenberg, 1521. BL C.53.c.6.

La grante danse macabre. Lyons: Mathias Huss, 18 February 1499. BL IB.41735.

Syr Degore. London: Wynkyn de Worde, *c.* 1528. *STC* 6470.

Destruction of Jerusalem. London: Wynkyn de Worde, 1528. *STC* 14519.

The deyenge creature. London: Wynkyn de Worde, 1514. *STC* 6035.5. BL c.21.c.29.

Erasmus, Desiderius. *Familiarium colloquiorum*. London: Wynkyn de Worde, 1519. *STC* 10450.6.

Erasmus, Desiderius. *Familiarium colloquiorum*. Westminster: Wynkyn de Worde, 1520. *STC* 10450.7.

Expositio hymnorum totius anni secundum usum Sarum; *Expositio Sequentiarum*. London: Wynkyn de Worde, 12 June 1514; 8 July 1514. *STC* 16125.

Fisher, John. *the fruytfull saynges of Dauyd ... in the seuen penytencyall psalmes*. London: Wynkyn de Worde, 1508, 1509. *STC* 10902, 10903. BL G.12026.

Fisher, John. *A mornynge remembraunce*. London: Wynkyn de Worde, 1509. *STC* 10891. BL G. 1202.

Fisher, John. *Sermon agayn M. Luther*. London: Wynkyn de Worde, 1522. *STC* 10894.5. BL c.25.e.20.

Floure of the Commaundements of God, trans. Andrew Chertsey. London: de Worde, 1510. *STC* 23876. BL Huth 30.

Gough, John, trans. *The ymage of loue*. London: Wynkyn de Worde for John Gough, 1525. *STC* 21471.5.

Gough, John, trans. *The ymage of loue*. London: Wynkyn de Worde for John Gough, 1532. *STC* 21472.

Gringore, Pierre. *Le chasteau d'amours*. Paris: Michel Le Noir, 4 February 1500. BL IA. 40470.

Pylgrymage of Sir R. Guylforde Knyght. London: Richard Pynson, 1511. *STC* 12549. BL G.6719.

Hildesheim, Joannes of. *The thre kynges of Coleyne*. London: Wynkyn de Worde, 1526. *STC* 5575.

Henley, Walter of. *Boke of Husbandry*. London: Wynkyn de Worde, *c.* 1508. *STC* 25007.

Horace. *Opera*. Strassburg: Johann Grüninger, 1498. BL IB. 1471.

Heures de nostre dame. Paris: for Antoine Vérard, *c.* 1499.

Horae ad usum Sarum. Paris: Philippe Pigouchet, 1494. BL IA.40311.

Hore beate Marie v[ir]g[in]is secundum usum Sarum. Paris: Thielmann Kerver for Jean Richard, 1497. *STC* 15885.

Horae ad usum Sarum. London: Wynkyn de Worde, 1502. *STC* 15898.

Hore presentes ad usum Sarum. Paris: for Simon Vostre, 1507. *STC* 15905.

Hore beate marie virginis ad usum insignis ac p[rae]clare ecclesie Sarum. London: Wynkyn de Worde, 1514. *STC* 15919.

Hore b[ea]tissime virginis Marie ad legitimum Sarisburiensis ecclesie ritum. Paris: Nicholas Higman for Francis Regnault and Francis Byrckman, 1519. *STC* 15924.

Horae ad usum Sarum. Paris: for Francis Byrkman, 1521. *STC* 15931.

Horae in laudem beatiss[ime] semper virginis Mariae. Paris: Geoffroy Tory, 1525. BL C.27.k.15.

Hore in laudem beatissime virginis Marie. Paris: Geoffroy Tory, 22 October 1527. BL C.27.h.17.

Horae ad usum Sarum. Paris: Francis Regnault, 1534. *STC* 15984. BL C.354.h.11.

Jerome (attrib.). *Vitas Patrum*. Westminster: Wynkyn de Worde, before 21 August 1495. *STC* 14507. BL C.11.b.3.

Kalender. *Le compost et Kalendrier des bergeres*. Paris: Guy Marchant for himself and J. Petit, 1499. BL IB. 39718.

Kalender. *Le compost et kalendrier des bergiers*. Paris: Guy Marchant, 1500. BL IB.39741.

Kalender. *Le grant kalendrier et compost des bergiers*. Paris: Philippe Le Noir, 1523. BL C.34.g.16.

Kalender. *The Kalendayr of the shyppars*. Paris: for Antoine Vérard, 1503. *STC* 22407. BL C.132.i.2.

Kalender. *Here begynneth the Kalender of shepherdes*. London: Richard Pynson, 1506. *STC* 22408.

Kalender. *The Kalender of shepeherdes*. London: Wynkyn de Worde, *c.* 1508 [1516]. *STC* 22409.

Kalender. *Here begynneth the kalender of shepardes*. London: Julian Notary, 1518? *STC* 22410.

Kalender. *The kalender of shepeherdes*. London: Wynkyn de Worde, 24 January 1528. *STC* 22411.

Kalender of Shepardes. London: T. Este for John Wally, 1570? *STC* 22415.

The knyght of the swanne. London: William Copland, *c.* 1560. *STC* 7572.

La Sale, Antoine de. *The fyftene Joyes of maryage*. London: Wynkyn de Worde, 1509. *STC* 15258.

Laurent, Dominican. *Boke named the Royall*, trans. William Caxton. London: Wynkyn de Worde and Richard Pynson, 1507. *STC* 21430, 21430a. BL C.11.a.23, C.21.c.1.

Love, Nicholas. *Speculum vitae Christi*. Westminster: William Caxton, 1484. *STC* 3259.

Love, Nicholas. *Speculum vitae Christi*. Westminster: William Caxton, 1490. *STC* 3260. BL IB.55119.

Love, Nicholas. *Speculum vitae Christi*. London: Wynkyn de Worde, 1494. *STC* 3261.

Love, Nicholas. *Speculum vitae Christi*. London: Richard Pynson, 1494. *STC* 3262.

Love, Nicholas. *Speculum vitae Christi*. London: Richard Pynson, 1506. *STC* 3263.

Love, Nicholas. *Speculum vitae Christi*. London: Wynkyn de Worde, 1507. *STC* 3263.5.

Ludolphus de Saxonia. *Vita Christi. Tboeck vanden leven Jhesu Christi*. Antwerp: Gerard Leeu, 3 Nov. 1487. BL IB.49767.

Lyndewode, William. *Constitutiones provinciales ecclesie Anglicanae*. Westminster: Wynkyn de Worde, 1496. *STC* 17103. BL IA.55185.

Major, John. *Historia Maioris Britanniae*. Paris: Badius Ascensius, 1521.

Maydeston, Clement. *Directorium sacerdotum* [Liturgy of Salisbury]. Westminster: William Caxton, 1486. *STC* 14072. BL C.10.b.16.

Mirk, John. *Liber festivalis*. Westminster: Wynkyn de Worde, 1496. *STC* 17962. BL C.11.a.20.

Mirror of Our Lady. London: Richard Fawkes, 4 November 1530. *STC* 17542.

Freisinger Missale [Freisingen Missal]. Augsburg: Erhardt Ratdolt, 1492. BL IB. 6727.

Missale Secundum vsum Insignis Ecclesie Sarum. Paris: for Wynkyn de Worde, 1497/1498. *STC* 16169. BL IB.40686.

More, Thomas. *A dyaloge of syr T. More ... wherin be treatyd dyuers maters, as of the veneration & worship of ymagys & relyques, prayng to sayntys*. London: John Rastell, 1529. *STC* 18084.

Nevill, William. *The Castell of Pleasure*. London: Wynkyn de Worde, n.d. *STC* 18475.

Ordynarye of Crystyanyte or of Crysten Men, trans. A. Chertsey. London: Wynkyn de Worde, 1502. *STC* 5198. BL G.11739.

ThOrdynary of Chrysten Men, trans. Andrew Chertsey. London: Wynkyn de Worde, 1506. *STC* 5199. BL C.25.f.7.

Parker, Henry [attrib.]. *Diues & Pauper*. Westminster: Wynkyn de Worde, 3 December 1496. *STC* 19213. BL C.11.b.4.

Passau, Otto von. *Dat boeck des gulden throens*. Utrecht: tC, 1480. BL IB. 47094.

Pizan, Christine de. *Here begynneth the boke of the Cyte of Ladyes*, trans. B. Anslay. London: Henry Pepwell, 26 October 1521. *STC* 7271. BL C.13.a.18.

Pizan, Christine de. *Les cent histoires de troye*. Paris: Philippe Le Noir, 30 Nov. 1522.

Pizan, Christine de. *Here foloweth the .C. Hystoryes of Troye*, trans. Robert Wyer. London: Robert Wyer, c. 1540-1550. *STC* 7272. BL C.21.a.34.

The noble hystory of ... kynge Ponthus. London: Wynkyn de Worde, 1511. *STC* 20108.

The Remedy Against the Troubles of Temptations. London: Wynkyn de Worde, 1508. *STC* 20875.5. BL G.12058, C.21.c.22.

Rolewinck, Werner. *Fasciculus Temporum*. Utrecht: Jan Veldener, 1480. BL IB. 47086.

The Rote or myrour of consolacyon & conforte. London: Wynkyn de Worde, 1511. *STC* 21336. BL C.37.e.6.(2.).

Sachs, Hans. *Eygentliche Beschreibung Aller Stände auff Erdenbuch*. Frankfurt: Georg Raben for Sigmund Feyerabend, 1568. BL C.57.b.25.

Sermones in parabolum filii glutonis profusi atque. Paris: Jehan Petit, 1511.

Stanbridge, John. *Vocabula magistri stanbrigi*. London: Wynkyn de Worde, 1510. *STC*

23178. BL G.7559.

Terence. *Comoediae*. Strassburg: Johann Grüninger, 1496. BL C.3.c.16.

Therence en françois. Paris: for Antoine Vérard, *c.* 1500. BL IB. 41244.

Tynemouth, John of. *Nova legenda Angliae*. London: Wynkyn de Worde, 1516. *STC* 4601. BL G.11925, C. 48.h.2.

Voragine, Jacobus de. *Legenda aurea*, trans. William Caxton. Westminster: William Caxton, 20 November 1483. *STC* 24873-24874. BL C.11.d.8, IB.55161.

Voragine, Jacobus de. *Legenda aurea sanctorum*. Zwolle: Peter van Os, 1490.

Voragine, Jacobus de. *Legenda Aurea*. Westminster: Wynkyn de Worde, 1493. *STC* 24875.

Watson, Henry, trans. *The chirche of the euyll men and women*. London: Wynkyn de Worde, 1511. *STC* 1966.

The way to the holy lande. London: Wynkyn de Worde, 1515. *STC* 14082.

SECONDARY SOURCES

Ainsworth, M. W., *Petrus Christus: Renaissance Master of Bruges* (New York: The Metropolitan Museum of Art, 1994).

Alexander, J. J. G., 'William Abell "lymnour" and 15th Century English Illumination', in *Kunsthistorische Forschungen: Otto Pächt zu seinem 70. Geburtstag*, ed. Artur Rosenauer and Gerold Weber (Vienna: Residenz Verlag, 1972), pp. 166-170.

Italian Renaissance Illuminations (London: Chatto & Windus, 1977).

Alexander, J. J. G., and Paul Binski, eds, *The Age of Chivalry: Art in Plantagenet England 1200-1400* (London: Weidenfeld and Nicolson with the Royal Academy of Arts, 1987).

Anderson, David, ed., *Sixty Bokes Olde and Newe* (Knoxville: University of Tennessee Press, 1986).

Andersson, Christiane, 'Polemical Prints during the Reformation', in *Censorship: 500 Years of Conflict* (New York: New York Public Library, 1984), pp. 35-51.

Andersson, Christiane, and Charles Talbot, eds, *From a Mighty Fortress: Prints, Drawings, and Books in the Age of Luther 1483-1546* (Detroit: Detroit Institute of Arts, 1983).

Armstrong, C. A. J., 'The Piety of Cicely, Duchess of York: A Study in Late Medieval Culture', in *For Hilaire Belloc, Essays in Honor of His 71st Birthday*, ed. Douglas Woodruff (New York: Sheed & Ward, 1942).

Arnheim, Rudolf, *Visual Thinking* (Los Angeles: University of California Press, 1969).

Aston, Margaret, *Lollards and Reformers: Images and Literacy in Late Medieval Religion* (London: Hambledon Press, 1984).

England's Iconoclasts, vol. 1: *Laws Against Images* (Oxford: Clarendon Press, 1988).

Faith and Fire: Popular and Unpopular Religion, 1350-1600 (London: Hambledon Press, 1993).

Augustine, Saint, *Confessions*, trans. R. S. Pine-Coffin (Harmondsworth: Penguin, 1961; repr. 1970).

Aungier, George James, *The History and Antiquities of Syon Monastery, the Parish of Isleworth, and the Chapelry of Hounslow* (London: J. B. Nichols & Son, 1840).

Backhouse, Janet, Mirjam Foot and John Barr, comps., *William Caxton: An Exhibition to Commemorate the Quincentenary of the Introduction of Printing into England*, British Library Reference Division (London: British Museum Publications, 1976).

Baldwin, T. W., *William Shakspere's Petty School* (Urbana: University of Illinois Press, 1943).

    William Shakspere's Small Latine and Lesse Greeke, 2 vols (Urbana: University of Illinois Press, 1944).

Barratt, Alexandra, ed., *Women's Writing in Middle English* (New York: Longman, 1992).

Bartlett, Robert, 'Medieval and Modern Concepts of Race and Ethnicity', *Journal of Medieval and Early Modern Studies*, 31, no. 1 (Winter 2001), ed. Thomas Hahn, pp. 39-56.

Basing, Patricia, *Trades and Crafts in Medieval Manuscripts* (New York: New Amsterdam Books by arrangement with The British Library, 1990).

Baudet, Henri, *Paradise on Earth: Some Thoughts on European Images of Non-European Man*, trans. Elizabeth Wentholt (New Haven, Conn.: Yale University Press, 1965).

Baxandall, Michael, *Painting and Experience in Fifteenth-Century Italy: A Primer in the Social History of Pictorial Style*, 2nd edn (Oxford: Oxford University Press, 1972; repr. 1988).

    Patterns of Intention: On the Historical Explanation of Pictures (New Haven, Conn.: Yale University Press, 1985).

Beaty, Nancy Lee, *The Craft of Dying: A Study on the Literary Tradition of the Ars moriendi in England*, Yale Studies in English, 175 (New Haven, Conn.: Yale University Press, 1970).

Bell, David N., *What Nuns Read: Books and Libraries in Medieval English Nunneries*, Cistercian Studies Series 158 (Kalamazoo, Mich.: Cistercian Institute, 1995).

Bennett, H. S., *English Books & Readers 1475 to 1557: Being a Study in the History of the Book Trade from Caxton to the Incorporation of the Stationers' Company*, 2nd edn (London: Cambridge University Press, 1969).

Bennett, J. W., 'The Woodcut Illustrations in the English Editions of *Mandeville's Travels*', *Papers of the Bibliographical Society of America* 47 (1953), pp. 59-69.

Benson, C. David, *The History of Troy in Middle English Literature: Giudo delle Colonne's Historia Destructionis Troiae in Medieval England* (Woodbridge: Boydell & Brewer, 1980).

Benson, C. David, and Lynne S. Blanchfield, with Marie-Claire Uhart, eds, *The Manuscripts of 'Piers Plowman': The B-version* (London: D. S. Brewer, 1998).

Binski, Paul, *Medieval Death: Ritual and Representation* (Ithaca, N.Y.: Cornell University Press, 1996).

Blake, N. F., 'Caxton's Reprints', originally published in *The Humanities Association Review*, 26 (1975), pp. 169-179, and reprinted in *William Caxton and English Literary Culture* (London: The Hambledon Press, 1991), pp. 100-117.

    Caxton: England's First Publisher (New York: Harper & Row, 1976).

    ed., *Quattuor Sermones Printed by William Caxton*, Middle English Texts 2 (Heidelberg: Carl Winter, 1975).

Blamires, Alcuin, ed., *Woman Defamed and Woman Defended: An Anthology of Medieval Texts* (Oxford: Clarendon Press, 1992).

Bloy, Colin H., *A History of Printing Ink Balls and Rollers 1440-1850* (London: The Wynkyn de Worde Society, 1967; repr. 1972).

Blunt, John Henry, ed., *The Myroure of oure Ladye*, Early English Text Society, extra ser., 19 (London: Trübner, 1873).

Boffey, Julia, 'Wynkyn de Worde, Richard Pynson, and the English Printing of Texts

Translated from French', in *Vernacular Literature and Current Affairs in the Early Sixteenth Century: France, England, Scotland*, ed. Richard Britnell and Jennifer J. Britnell (Aldershot: Ashgate, 2000), pp. 171-183.

Bonafous-Murat, Arsène, *Estampes 1490-1989* (Paris: Arsène Bonafous-Murat, 1989).

Bowden, Betsy, 'Visual Portraits of the Canterbury Pilgrims, 1484 (?) to 1809', in *The Ellesmere Chaucer: Essays in Interpretation*, ed. Martin Stevens and Daniel Woodward (San Marino, Calif.: Huntington Library, 1995), pp. 171-204.

Bradshaw, Brendan, and Eamon Duffy, eds, *Humanism, Reform and the Reformation: The Career of Bishop John Fisher* (Cambridge: Cambridge University Press, 1989).

Bradshaw, Henry, *Collected Papers of Henry Bradshaw* (Cambridge: Cambridge University Press, 1889).

Braude, Benjamin, 'The Sons of Noah and the Construction of Ethnic and Geographical Identities in the Medieval and Early Modern Periods', *William and Mary Quarterly*, 3rd ser., 54 (January 1997), pp. 103-142.

Britnell, Jennifer, *Jean Bouchet* (Edinburgh: Edinburgh University Press, 1986).

Brooke, Christopher N. L., *The Medieval Idea of Marriage* (Oxford: Oxford University Press, 1989; repr. 1990).

Brown, Cynthia J., 'Text, Image, and Authorial Self-Consciousness in Late Medieval Paris', in *Printing the Written Word : The Social History of Books, circa 1450-1520*, ed. Sandra L. Hindman (Ithaca, N.Y.: Cornell University Press, 1991), pp. 103-142.

Poets, Patrons, and Printers: Crisis of Authority in Late Medieval France (Ithaca, N.Y.: Cornell University Press, 1995).

Brunet, Jacques-Charles, *Manuel du libraire et de l'amateur de livres*, vol. 1 (Paris: Firmin-Didot, 1860).

Bühler, C. F., 'Sir John Paston's Grete Boke, a Fifteenth-Century Best-Seller', *MLN* 56 (1941), pp. 345-351.

'Variants in English Incunabula', in *Bookmen's Holiday: Notes and Studies Written and Gathered in Tribute to Harry Miller Lyndenberg*, ed. Deoch Fulton (New York: New York Public Library, 1943).

'The Apostles and the Creed', *Speculum* 28 (1953), pp. 335-339.

ed., *The Epistle of Othea Translated from the French Text of Christine de Pisan by Stephen Scrope* (New York: Oxford University Press, 1970).

Camille, Michael, 'Seeing and Reading: Some Visual Implications of Medieval Literacy and Illiteracy', *Art History* 8, no. 1 (March 1985), pp. 26-49.

Campbell, P. G. C., 'L'Epitre d'Othea', *Etude sur les sources de Christine de Pisan* (Paris: E. Champion, 1942).

Carlson, David R., *English Humanist Books: Writers and Patrons, Manuscripts and Print, 1475-1525* (Toronto: University of Toronto Press, 1993).

'Woodcut Illustrations of the *Canterbury Tales*, 1483-1602', *The Library*, 6th ser., 19 (1997), pp. 25-67.

Carruthers, Mary J., *The Book of Memory: A Study of Memory in Medieval Culture* (New York: Cambridge University Press, 1990).

Catalogue of Manuscripts and Early Printed Books from the Libraries of William Morris, Richard Bennett, Bertram, Fourth Earl of Ashburnham, and Other Sources, Now Forming a Portion of the Library of J. Pierpont Morgan, 4 vols (London: Chiswick Press, 1906-1907).

Catherine of Siena, Saint, *Catherine of Siena, The Dialogue*, trans. Suzanne Noffke (New York: Paulist Press, 1980).

Caviness, Madeline, 'Fifteenth-Century Stained Glass from the Chapel of Hampton Court, Herefordshire: The Apostles' Creed and other subjects', *Walpole Society* 42 (1969-1970), pp. 35-60.

Censorship: 500 Years of Conflict (New York: The New York Public Library, 1984).

Christensen, Carl G., *Art and the Reformation in Germany*, Studies in the Reformation 2 (Athens, OH: Ohio University Press, 1979).

Clair, Colin, *A History of European Printing* (New York: Academic Press, 1976).

Clanchy, Michael T., *From Memory to Written Record, England 1066-1307*, 2nd edn (London: Blackwell, 1993).

Coates, Alan, and Kristian Jensen, 'The Bodleian Library's Acquisition of Incunabula with English and Scottish Medieval Monastic Provenances', in *Books and Collectors 1200-1700: Essays Presented to Andrew Watson*, ed. James P. Carley and Colin G. C. Tite (London: The British Library, 1997), pp. 237-259.

Cole, Richard G., 'The Use of Reformation Woodcuts by Sixteenth-Century Printers as a Mediator Between the Elite and Popular Cultures', *Journal of Popular Culture* 21, no. 3 (Winter 1987), pp. 111-130.

Colledge, Edmund, 'A Syon Centenary', *Life of the Spirit* 15 (1960), pp. 1-35.

Collins, Arthur Jefferies, ed., *The Bridgettine Breviary of Syon Abbey*, Henry Bradshaw Society 96 (Worcester: The Stanbrook Abbey Press, 1969).

Copland, Robert, *Poems / Robert Copland*, ed. Mary Carpenter Erler (Toronto: University of Toronto Press, 1993).

Cornelius, Roberta D., ed., *The Castell of Pleasure*, Early English Text Society 179 (London: Oxford University Press, 1930).

Cressy, David, *Literacy and the Social Order: Reading and Writing in Tudor and Stuart England* (Cambridge: Cambridge University Press, 1980).

'The Downfall of Cheapside Cross: Vandalism, Ridicule, and Iconoclasm', in *Agnes Bowker's Cat: Travesties and Transgressions in Tudor and Stuart England* (Oxford: Oxford University Press, 2000), pp. 234-250.

Cripps-Day, Francis Henry, ed., *The Manor Farm* (London: Quaritch, 1931).

Crotch, W. J. B., *The Prologues and Epilogues of William Caxton* (1928; repr. New York: Burt Franklin, 1971), p. 91.

Cumming, W. P., ed., *Revelations of St. Birgitta*, Early English Text Society, original ser. 178 (1929; repr. Oxford: Early English Text Society / Kraus Reprint, 1971).

Daniell, Christopher, *Death and Burial in Medieval England, 1066-1550* (London: Routledge, 1998).

Danto, Arthur C., introduction to Honoré de Balzac, *The Unknown Masterpiece and Gambara*, trans. Richard Howard (New York: New York Review of Books, 2001), vii-xxvii.

Davenport, Cyril, *Cameo Book-Stamps Figured and Described* (London: E. Arnold, 1911).

Davis, Norman, ed., *Paston Letters and Papers of the Fifteenth Century*, 2 vols (Oxford: Clarendon Press, 1971-1976).

De Hamel, Christopher, *Medieval Craftsmen: Scribes and Illuminators* (Toronto: University of Toronto Press, 1992).

'The Library: The Medieval Manuscripts of Syon Abbey, and Their Dispersal', in *Syon Abbey: The Library of the Bridgettine Nuns and Their Peregrinations after the Reformation* (Otley: Roxburghe Club, 1993), pp. 48-158.

Delaissé, L. M. J., *A Century of Dutch Manuscript Illumination* (Berkeley: University of

California Press, 1968).

'The Importance of Books of Hours for the History of the Medieval Book', in *Gatherings in Honor of Dorothy E. Miner,* ed. Ursula E. McCracken, Lilian M. C. Randall, and Richard H. Randall, Jr (Baltimore: Walters Art Gallery, 1974), pp. 203-226.

Delen, A. J. J., *Histoire de la gravure dans les anciens Pays-Bas et dans les provinces belges des origines jusqu'à la fin du XVIIIe siècle,* part 1: *Des origines à 1500* (Paris: G. Van Oest, 1924).

Denholm-Young, N., 'Walter of Henley', in *Medievalia et Humanistica* 14 (April 1962), pp. 61-65.

Devisse, Jean, *The Image of the Black in Western Art II, From the Early Christian Era to the 'Age of Discovery',* trans. William Granger Ryan, vol. 1 (Cambridge, Mass.: Harvard University Press, 1979).

Devisse, Jean, and Michel Mollat, *The Image of the Black in Western Art II, From the Early Christian Era to the 'Age of Discovery',* trans. William Granger Ryan, vol. 2 (Cambridge, Mass.: Harvard University Press, 1979).

De Weever, Jacqueline, *Sheba's Daughters: Whitening and Demonizing the Saracen Women in Medieval French Epic* (New York: Garland, 1998).

Dillon, Viscount, and W. H. St. John Hope, eds, *Pageant of the Birth Life and Death of Richard Beauchamp Earl of Warwick K.G. 1389-1439* (London: Longmans, Green, 1914).

Doyle, A. I., 'A Survey of the Origins and Circulation of Theological Writings in English in the 14th, 15th, and Early 16th Centuries with Special Consideration of the Part of the Clergy Therein' (Ph.D. diss., University of Cambridge, 1953).

'The Work of a Late Fifteenth-Century English Scribe, William Ebesham', *Bulletin of the John Rylands Library* 39, 2 (March, 1957), pp. 298-325.

Doyle, A. I., Elizabeth Rainey and D. B. Wilson, *Manuscript to Print: Tradition and Innovation in the Renaissance Book* (Durham: University of Durham, Library, 1975).

Doyle, A. I., Elizabeth Rainey and Sheila Hingley, '*To se, and eek for to be seye': A Display of Manuscripts and Printed Books at Durham University Library, 11 July 2003 for a conference of the Early Book Society* (Durham: Palace Green Library, 2003).

Driver, Martha, 'Illustration in Early English Books: Methods and Problems', *Books at Brown* 33 (1986), pp. 1-57.

'"Sweet as Honey": Albrecht Dürer as Protestant Propagandist', *American Book Collector* 7 (1986), pp. 3-10.

'Pictures in Print: Late Fifteenth- and Early Sixteenth-Century English Religious Books for Lay Readers', in *De Cella in Seculum: Religious and Secular Life and Devotion in Late Medieval England,* ed. Michael G. Sargent (Cambridge: D. S. Brewer, 1989), pp. 229-244.

'The Image *Redux*: Pictures in Block-books and What Becomes of Them', in *Blockbücher des Mittelalters: Bilderfolgen als Lektüre,* ed. Cornelia Schneider (Mainz: Gutenberg-Museum, 1991), pp. 341-352.

'Nuns as Patrons, Artists, Readers: Bridgettine Woodcuts in Printed Books Produced for the English Market', in *Art into Life: Collected Papers from the Kresge Art Museum Medieval Symposia,* ed. Carol Garrett Fisher and Kathleen L. Scott (East Lansing: Michigan State University Press, 1995), pp. 244-257.

'The Illustrated de Worde: An Overview', *Studies in Iconography,* Medieval Institute

Publications, 17 (Spring 1996), pp. 349-403.

'Christine de Pisan and Robert Wyer: The *.C. Hystoryes of Troye*, or *L'Epistre d'Othea* Englished', *Gutenberg-Jahrbuch* 72 (1997), pp. 125-139.

'Ideas of Order: Wynkyn de Worde and the Title Page', in *Texts and Their Contexts: Papers from the Early Book Society*, ed. Julia Boffey and V. J. Scattergood (Dublin: Four Courts Press, 1997), pp. 87-149.

'Mirrors of a Collective Past: Re-Considering Images of Medieval Women', in *Women and the Book: Assessing the Visual Evidence*, ed. Lesley Smith and Jane Taylor, The British Library Studies in Medieval Culture (London: British Museum Publications, 1997), pp. 75-93.

'Printing the *Confessio Amantis*', in *Re-visioning Gower*, ed. R. F. Yeager (Asheville, N.C.: Pegasus Press, 1998), pp. 269-303.

'Women Printers and the Page, 1477-1541', *Gutenberg-Jahrbuch* 73 (1998), pp. 139-153.

'Medievalizing the Classical Past in Pierpont Morgan MS M. 876', in *Middle English Poetry: Texts and Traditions, Essays in Honour of Derek Pearsall*, ed. A. J. Minnis (York: York Medieval Press with Boydell and Brewer, 2001), pp. 211-239.

'Mapping Chaucer: John Speed and the Later Portraits', *Chaucer Review* 36, no. 3 (2002), pp. 228-249.

'When Is a Miscellany not Miscellaneous? Making Sense of the *Kalendar of Shepherds*', *Yearbook of English Studies* 33, ed. Phillipa Hardman, Modern Humanities Research Association (2003), pp. 199-214.

'Picturing the Apocalypse in the Printed Book of Hours', in *Prophecy, Apocalypse and the Day of Doom, Proceedings of the 2000 Harlaxton Symposium*, Harlaxton Medieval Studies XII, ed. Nigel Morgan (Stamford, Lincs.: Paul Watkins, 2004).

Droz, E., and A. Piaget, introd., *Le Jardin de Plaisance*, 2 vols, Société des anciens textes français (Paris: Firmin-Didot, 1910-1925).

Duby, Georges, ed., *A History of Private Life II: Revelations of the Medieval World* (Cambridge, Mass.: The Belknap Press of Harvard University Press, 1988).

Duff, E. Gordon, *The Printers, Stationers and Bookbinders of London and Westminster in the Fifteenth Century* (Aberdeen: privately printed, 1899).

William Caxton (1905; repr. New York: Burt Franklin, 1970).

The Printers, Stationers, and Bookbinders of Westminster and London from 1476 to 1535 (1906; repr. New York: Arno Press, 1971, 1977).

Hand-Lists of Books Printed by London Printers, 1501-1556, part 1 (London: Blades, East & Blades, for the Bibliographical Society, 1913).

A Century of the English Book Trade (London: Oxford University Press for the Bibliographical Society, 1948).

Duffy, Eamon, *The Stripping of the Altars: Traditional Religion in England c. 1400-c. 1580* (New Haven, Conn.: Yale University Press, 1992).

Dunn, Ellen Catherine, '*The Myroure of Oure Ladye*: Syon Abbey's Role in the Continuity of English Prose', in *Diakonia: Studies in Honor of Robert T. Meyer*, ed. Thomas Halton and J. P. Williman (Washington, D.C.: Catholic University of America Press, 1986), pp. 111-133.

Dutton, Richard, 'The Birth of the Author', in *Texts and Cultural Change in Early Modern England*, ed. Cedric C. Brown and Arthur F. Marotti (New York: St Martin's Press, 1997), pp. 153-178.

Eames, Wilberforce, 'Columbus' Letter on the Discovery of America (1493-1497)',

Bibliography

Bulletin of the New York Public Library 28, no. 8 (August 1924), pp. 595-599.

Early Printed Books: Major Acquisitions of The Pierpont Morgan Library 1924-1974 (New York: The Pierpont Morgan Library, 1974).

Eisler, Colin, *The Master of the Unicorn: The Life and Work of Jean Duvet* (New York: Abaris Books, 1977).

Emmerson, Richard K., *Antichrist in the Middle Ages: A Study of Medieval Apocalypticism, Art, and Literature* (Seattle: University of Washington Press, 1981).

'Wynkyn de Worde's *Byrthe and Lyfe of Antechryst* and Popular Eschatology on the Eve of the English Reformation', *Mediaevalia* 14 (1991), pp. 281-311.

'Text and Image in the Ellesmere Portraits of the Tale-Tellers', in *The Ellesmere Chaucer: Essays in Interpretation*, ed. Martin Stevens and Daniel Woodward (San Marino, Calif.: Huntington Library, 1995), pp. 143-170.

Erler, Mary C., 'Early Woodcuts of Skelton: The Uses of Convention', *Bulletin of Research in the Humanities* 87 (1986/87), pp. 17-28.

'Wynkyn de Worde's Will: Legatees and Bequests', *The Library*, 6th ser., 10 (1988), pp. 107-121.

'Pasted-In Embellishments in English Manuscripts and Printed Books *c.* 1480-1533', *The Library*, 6th ser., 14, no. 3 (September 1992), pp. 185-206.

'Devotional Literature', in *The Cambridge History of the Book in Britain*, 7 vols (Cambridge: Cambridge University Press, 1999-2002), vol. 3: *1400-1557*, ed. Lotte Hellinga and J. B. Trapp, pp. 495-525.

Women, Reading, and Piety in Late Medieval England (Cambridge: Cambridge University Press, 2002).

Favier, Jean, *The Tapestries of the Chateau of Langeais*, trans. Lisa Davidson (Paris: Beaux Arts Magazine, n.d.).

Field, Richard S., *Fifteenth Century Woodcuts and Metalcuts from the National Gallery of Art* (Washington, D.C.: The National Gallery of Art, 1965).

Fifteenth-Century Woodcuts and Other Relief Prints in the Collection of the Metropolitan Museum (New York: The Metropolitan Museum of Art, 1977).

Fields, Barbara J., 'Ideology and Race in American History', *Region, Race, and Reconstruction: Essays in Honor of C. Vann Woodward*, ed. J. Morgan Kousser and James M. McPherson (Oxford: Oxford University Press, 1982), pp. 143-177.

Fisher, Frederick Jack, *A Short History of the Worshipful Company of Horners* (Croyden: privately printed, 1936).

Foister, Susan, 'Paintings and Other Works of Art in Sixteenth-Century English Inventories', *Burlington Magazine* 123, no. 938 (May 1981), pp. 273-282.

Foot, Mirjam M., *Studies in the History of Bookbinding* (Brookfield, Vt.: Scolar Press, 1993).

Forrest, John, *The History of Morris Dancing 1458-1750* (Toronto: University of Toronto Press, 1999).

Foucault, M., *This Is Not a Pipe*, trans. J. Harkness (Berkeley, Calif.: University of California Press, 1982).

Freedberg, David, *The Power of Images: Studies in the History and Theory of Response* (Chicago: University of Chicago Press, 1989).

Friedman, John Block, *The Monstrous Races in Medieval Art and Thought* (Cambridge, Mass.: Harvard University Press, 1981).

Northern English Books, Owners, and Makers in the Late Middle Ages (Syracuse, N.Y.: Syracuse University Press, 1995).

Friedman, Paul, *Images of the Medieval Peasant* (Stanford, Calif.: Stanford University Press, 1999).

Gaskell, Philip, *A New Introduction to Bibliography* (1972; repr. New Castle, Del.: Oak Knoll, 1995).

Wynkyn de Worde's Gesta Romanorum, Exeter Medieval English Texts (Exeter: University of Exeter, 1974).

Gildenhuys, Faith, ed., *The Bachelor's Banquet*, Publications of the Barnabe Riche Society 2 (Binghamton, N.Y.: Medieval & Renaissance Texts & Studies, 1993).

Gillespie, Alexandra, 'The Lydgate Canon in Print from 1476 to 1534', *Journal of the Early Book Society* 3 (2000), pp. 59-86.

Gillespie, Vincent, ed., *Syon Abbey*, published in one volume with *The Libraries of the Carthusians*, ed. A. I. Doyle, Corpus of British Medieval Library Catalogues 9 (London: British Library in association with the British Academy, 2001).

Goldschmidt, Ernst Philip, *Medieval Texts and Their First Appearance in Print* (1943; repr. New York: Biblio and Tannen, 1969).

Gothic & Renaissance Bookbindings, 2 vols (Amsterdam: N. Israel, 1967).

Grindley, Carl James, 'Reading Piers Plowman C-Text Annotations: Notes toward the Classification of Printed and Written Marginalia in Texts from the British Isles 1300-1641', in *The Medieval Professional Reader at Work: Evidence from Manuscripts of Chaucer, Langland, Kempe, and Gower*, ed. Kathryn Kerby-Fulton and Maidie Hilmo, English Literary Studies Monograph Series no. 85 (Victoria: University of Victoria, 2001), pp. 73-141.

Hahn, Thomas, 'The Difference the Middle Ages Makes: Color and Race before the Modern World', *Journal of Medieval and Early Modern Studies*, 31, no. 1 (Winter 2001), ed. Thomas Hahn, pp. 1-38.

Haile, H. G., *Luther: An Experiment in Biography* (Princeton, N.J.: Princeton University Press, 1983).

Halkett, Samuel, and John Laing, *A Dictionary of Anonymous and Pseudonymous Publications in the English Language, 1475-1640*, 3rd rev. edn (New York: Longman, 1980).

Hall, Kim F., *Things of Darkness: Economies of Race and Gender in Early Modern England* (Ithaca, N.Y.: Cornell University Press, 1995).

Hanawalt, Barbara A., *Growing Up in Medieval London: The Experience of Childhood in History* (New York: Oxford University Press, 1993).

Harbison, Craig, 'Reformation Iconography, Problems and Attitudes', *Print Review* 5 (1976), pp. 78-87.

Harris, Barbara, *English Aristocratic Women 1450-1550: Marriage and Family, Property and Careers* (Oxford: Oxford University Press, 2002).

Harris, Marguerite Tjader, *Birgitta of Sweden: Life and Selected Revelations*, trans. Albert Ryle Kezel (New York: Paulist Press, 1990).

Harthan, John, *Books of Hours and Their Owners* (1977; repr. London: Thames and Hudson, 1982).

Harvard College Library, *Illuminated and Calligraphic Manuscripts* (Cambridge, Mass.: Harvard College Library, 1955).

Hawes, Stephen, *The Works of Stephen Hawes*, ed. F. J. Sprang (Delmar, N.Y.: Scholars' Facsimiles & Reprints, 1975).

Hawkins, Rush C. (collected by), and Alfred W. Pollard (catalogued by), *Catalogue of Books mostly from the Presses of the First Printers showing the Progress of Printing*

with Movable Metal Types through the Second Half of the Fifteenth Century
(Oxford: privately printed at the University Press, 1910; deposited in the Annmary
Brown memorial, Providence, R.I.).

Hellinga, Lotte, *Caxton in Focus: The Beginning of Printing in England* (London: British
Library, 1982).

'Reading an Engraving: William Caxton's Dedication to Margaret of York, Duchess of
Burgundy', in *Across the Narrow Seas: Studies in the History and Bibliography
of Britain and the Low Countries*, ed. Susan Roach (London: The British Library,
1991), pp. 1-15.

'Wynkyn de Worde's Illustrations of Bartholomaeus Anglicus' *De Proprietatibus
Rerum*', in *Three Lions and the Cross of Lorraine: Bartholomaeus Anglicus, John of
Trevisa, John Tate, Wynkyn de Worde, and De Proprietatibus Rerum*, ed. Howell
Heaney, Lotte Hellinga and Richard Hills (Newtown, Pa.: Bird & Bull Press, 1992),
pp. 34-40.

'Nicholas Love in Print', in *Nicholas Love at Waseda: Proceedings of the International
Conference 20-22 July 1995*, ed. Shoichi Oguro, Richard Beadle and Michael G.
Sargent (Cambridge: Brewer, 1997), pp. 144-162.

Hellinga, Wytze, and Lotte Hellinga, *The Fifteenth-Century Printing Types of the Low
Countries* (Amsterdam: Menno Hertzberger, 1966).

Helmholz, Richard H., *Marriage Litigation in Medieval England* (Cambridge: Cambridge
University Press, 1978).

Henry, Avril, ed., *Biblia Pauperum: A Facsimile and Edition* (Aldershot: Scolar Press,
1987).

ed., *The Mirour of Mans Saluacioune: A Middle English Translation of Speculum
Humanae Salvationis* (Philadelphia: University of Pennsylvania Press, 1987).

'The Iconography of the Forty-Page Blockbook *Biblia Pauperum*: Form and Meaning',
in *Blockbücher des Mittelalters: Bilderfolgen als Lektüre*, ed. Cornelia Schneider
(Mainz: Gutenberg-Museum, 1991), pp. 263-288.

Hermann, H. J., *Die Handschriften und Inkunabeln der Italienischen Renaissance*
(Leipzig: n.p., 1932).

Hilton, Walter, *The Scale of Perfection*, trans. J. P. H. Clark and R. Dorward (New York:
Paulist Press, 1991).

Hindman, Sandra, *Text and Image in Fifteenth-Century Illustrated Dutch Bibles* (Leiden:
Brill, 1977).

'The Illustrated Book: An Addendum to the State of Research in Northern European
Art', *Art Bulletin* 68 (1986), pp. 536-542.

'The Career of Guy Marchant (1483-1504): High Culture and Low Culture in Paris',
in *Printing the Written Word: The Social History of Books, circa 1450-1520*, ed.
Sandra L. Hindman (Ithaca, N.Y.: Cornell University Press, 1991), pp. 68-100.

Hindman, Sandra, and James Douglas Farquhar, *Pen to Press: Illustrated Manuscripts
and Printed Books in the First Century of Printing* (College Park: Art Department,
University of Maryland, 1977).

Hinks, R., *Carolingian Art* (London: Sidgwick & Jackson, 1935).

Hirsch, Rudolf, *Printing, Selling and Reading 1450-1550* (1964; repr. Wiesbaden: Otto
Harrassowitz, 1974).

'The Earliest Development of Title-Pages 1470-1479', in *The Printed Word: Its Impact
and Diffusion* (London: Variorum Reprints, 1978).

The History of Bookbinding 525-1950 AD: An Exhibition Held at the Baltimore Museum of Art (Baltimore: Trustees of the Walters Art Gallery, 1957).

Hobson, G. D., *Bindings in Cambridge Libraries* (Cambridge: Cambridge University Press, 1929).

Hodnett, Edward, *English Woodcuts 1480-1535* (1935; repr. Oxford: Oxford University Press, 1973).

   (bound with) *Additions and Corrections to English Woodcuts 1480-1535* (London: The Bibliographical Society, 1973).

   The History and Fables of Aesop Translated and Printed by William Caxton 1484: Reproduced in Facsimile from the Copy in the Royal Library, Windsor Castle (London: Scolar Press, 1976).

Holbein and the Court of Henry VIII (London: The Queen's Gallery, Buckingham Palace, 1978).

Hughes, Paul L., and James F. Larkin, *Tudor Royal Proclamations* (New Haven, Conn.: Yale University Press, 1964).

Hutchison, Ann M., 'Devotional Reading in the Monastery and in the Late Medieval Household', in *De Cella in Seculum*, ed. Michael G. Sargent (Cambridge: D. S. Brewer, 1989), pp. 215-227.

   'What the Nuns Read: Literary Evidence from the English Bridgettine House, Syon Abbey', *Mediaeval Studies* 57 (1995), pp. 205-222.

Ing, Janet, *Johann Gutenberg and His Bible* (New York: The Typophiles, 1988).

Ivins, William M., Jr, *How Prints Look* (Boston: Beacon Press, 1943).

   Prints and Visual Communication (Cambridge, Mass.: MIT Press, 1969; repr. 1982).

Jacobus de Voragine, *The Golden Legend*, trans. W. G. Ryan, vol. 2 (Princeton, N.J.: Princeton University Press, 1993).

James, M. R., *A Descriptive Catalogue of the Manuscripts in the Fitzwilliam Museum* (Cambridge: Cambridge University Press, 1914).

Jefferson, Lisa, 'Two Fifteenth-Century Manuscripts of the Statutes of the Order of the Garter', in *English Manuscript Studies 1100-1700*, ed. Peter Beal and Jeremy Griffiths, vol. 5 (London: British Library, 1995), pp. 18-35.

Jennett, Seán, *The Making of Books* (London: Faber & Faber, 1951; repr. 1967).

Johnston, S. H., 'A Study of the Career and Literary Productions of Richard Pynson' (Ph.D. diss., University of Western Ontario, 1977).

Jordan, William Chester, 'Why "Race"?', *Journal of Medieval and Early Modern Studies*, 31, no. 1 (Winter 2001), ed. Thomas Hahn, pp. 165-173.

Kamerick, Kathleen, *Popular Piety and Art in the Late Middle Ages: Image Worship and Idolatry in England, 1350-1500* (New York: Palgrave, 2002).

Kaplan, Paul H. D., *The Rise of the Black Magus in Western Art* (Ann Arbor, Mich.: UMI Research Press, 1985).

Kapr, Albert, *Johann Gutenberg: The Man and his Invention*, trans. Douglas Martin (Aldershot: Scolar Press, 1996).

Kekewich, Margaret, 'Edward IV, William Caxton, and Literary Patronage in Yorkist England', *Modern Language Review* 66, no. 3 (July 1971), pp. 481-487.

Kerr, N. R., ed., *Medieval Libraries of Great Britain: A List of Surviving Books*, 2nd edn, Royal Historical Society Guides and Handbooks, 3 (London: Royal Historical Society, 1964).

King, John N., *English Reformation Literature: The Tudor Origins of the Protestant Tradition* (Princeton, N.J.: Princeton University Press, 1982).

   Tudor Royal Iconography: Literature and Art in an Age of Religious Crisis (Princeton,

N.J.: Princeton University Press, 1989).

Kirschbaum, Engelbert, ed., *Lexikon der christlichen Ikonographie*, vol. 5 (Freiburg: Herder, 1973).

Klockars, Birgit, *Birgittas svenska värld* (Stockholm: Natur och Kultur, 1976).

Kosmer, Ellen, 'The "noyous humoure of lecherie",' *Art Bulletin* 57 no. 1 (March, 1975), pp. 1-8.

Kubiski, Joyce, 'Orientalizing Costume in Early Fifteenth-Century French Manuscript Painting (*Cité des Dames* Master, Limbourg Brothers, Boucicaut Master, and Bedford Master)', *Gesta* (International Center of Romanesque Art) 40, no. 2 (2001), pp. 161-180.

Kuryluk, Ewa, *Veronica and Her Cloth: History, Symbolism, and Structure of a 'True Image'* (Oxford: Basil Blackwell, 1991).

Lalou, Élisabeth, and Claudia Rabel, *'Dedens mon livre de pensee ...': De Grégoire de Tours á Charles d'Orléans, Une histoire du livre médiéval en région Centre* (Paris: Somogy éditions d'art with CNRS-IRHT, 1997).

Landau, David, and Peter Parshall, *The Renaissance Print 1470-1550* (New Haven, Conn.: Yale University Press, 1994).

Lathrop, H. B., 'Some Rogueries of Robert Wyer', *The Library*, 3rd ser., 5 (1914), pp. 349-364.

Lehrs, Max, *Geschichte und Kritischer Katalog des deutschen, niederländischen und franzosischen Kupferstichs im XV. Jahrhundert*, 9 vols (Vienna: Gesellschaft für vervielfältigende Kunst, 1908-1934; repr. 1969).

Lester, G. A., *Sir John Paston's Grete Boke* (Woodbridge: Boydell & Brewer, 1984).

'Sir John Paston's "Grete-Boke": A Bespoke Book or Mass-Produced?' *English Studies* 66 (1985), pp. 93-104.

Letts, Malcolm, 'The Source of Woodcuts in Wynkyn de Worde's Edition of *Mandeville's Travels*, 1499', *Transactions of the Bibliographical Society*, 5th ser., 6 (1951), pp. 154-161.

Lewis, Flora, 'The Wound in Christ's Side and the Instruments of the Passion: Gendered Experience and the Response', in *Women and the Book: Assessing the Visual Evidence*, ed. Jane H. M. Taylor and Lesley Smith (London: The British Library, 1996), pp. 204-229.

Lewis, Suzanne, 'Picturing Other Visions', in *Reading Images: Narrative Discourse and Reception in the Thirteenth-Century Illuminated Apocalypse* (Cambridge: Cambridge University Press, 1995).

Longon, Jean, with preface by Millard Meiss, *The Très Riches Heures of Jean, Duke of Berry* (New York: George Braziller, 1969).

Luria, A. R., *The Mind of a Mnemonist*, trans. Lynn Solotaroff (Cambridge, Mass.: Harvard University Press, 1968).

Luther, Martin. *Luther's Works*, ed. Jaroslav Pelikan and Helmut T. Lehmann, 55 vols (St Louis: Concordia Publishing House, and Philadelphia: Muhlenberg Press, 1955-1976).

Lyons, Albert S., and R. Joseph Petrucelli, *Medicine: An Illustrated History* (New York: Harry N. Abrams, 1987).

Macfarlane, John, *Antoine Vérard* (London: Printed for the Bibliographical Society at the Chiswick Press, September 1900 for 1899).

MacGregor, Arthur, 'Antler, Bone and Horn', in *English Medieval Industries: Craftsmen, Techniques, Products*, ed. John Blair and Nigel Ramsay (London: Hambledon Press,

1991), pp. 355-378.

McKerrow, Ronald B., *Printers' and Publisher's Devices in England and Scotland 1485-1640* (London: Bibliographical Society at the Chiswick Press, 1913).

An Introduction to Bibliography for Literary Students (Oxford: The Clarendon Press, 1928; rev edn, New Castle, Del.: Oak Knoll Press, 1994).

McLuhan, Marshall, *The Gutenberg Galaxy: The Making of Typographic Man* (Toronto: University of Toronto Press, 1962; repr. 1986).

MacRobert, T. M., *Fine Illustrations in Western European Printed Books* (London: Her Majesty's Stationery Office, 1969).

Madon, Falconer, 'Early Representations of the Printing Press', *Bibliographica* 1 (1895) and 3 (1897).

Mâle, Emile, *Religious Art in France: The Late Middle Ages, A Study of Medieval Iconography and Its Sources*, trans. Marthiel Mathews, Bollingen Series XC.3 (Princeton, N.J.: Princeton University Press, 1986).

Manguel, Alberto, *A History of Reading* (New York: Penguin Books, 1997).

Mariana Canova, G., *La miniatura veneta del Rinascimento 1450-1500* (Venice: Alfieri, 1969).

Marinis, Tammaro de, *La biblioteca napoletana dei re d'Aragona*, vol. 4 (Milan: Hoepli, 1947).

Mark, Peter, *Africans in European Eyes: The Portrayal of Black Africans in Fourteenth and Fifteenth Century Europe*, Foreign and Comparative Studies/Eastern Africa XVI (Syracuse: Maxwell School of Citizenship and Foreign Affairs, Syracuse University, 1974).

Marrow, James H., *Passion Iconography in Northern European Art of the Late Middle Ages and Early Renaissance: A Study of the Transformation of Sacred Metaphor into Descriptive Narrative* (Kortrijk: Van Ghemmert, 1979).

Martin, Anthony, 'The Middle English Versions of *The Ten Commandments*, with Special Reference to Rylands English MS 85', *Bulletin of the John Rylands University Library of Manchester* 64, no. 1 (Autumn, 1981), pp. 191-217.

Meale, Carol M., '"Oft siþis with grete deuotion I þought what I miȝt do pleysyng to god": The Early Ownership and Readership of *Love's Mirror*, with Special Reference to its Female Audience', in *Nicholas Love at Waseda: Proceedings of the International Conference 20-22 July 1995*, ed. Shoichi Oguro, Richard Beadle and Michael G. Sargent (Cambridge: Brewer, 1997), pp. 19-46.

Meier, Henry, 'Some Israhel Van Meckenem Problems', *Print Collector's Quarterly* 27, no. 1 (February, 1940), pp. 27-67.

Meiss, Millard, *Painting in Florence and Siena after the Black Death: The Arts, Religion, and Society in the Mid-Fourteenth Century* (Princeton, N.J.: Princeton University Press, 1978).

Meiss, Millard, and Elizabeth H. Beatson, eds, *La Vie de Nostre Benoit Sauveur Ihesuscrist & La Saincte vie de Nostre Dame* (New York: New York University Press for the College Art Association of America, 1977).

Mellinkoff, Ruth, *Outcasts: Signs of Otherness in Northern European Art of the Late Middle Ages*, 2 vols (Los Angeles: University of California Press, 1993).

Mooney, Catherine M., ed., *Gendered Voices: Medieval Saints and Their Interpreters* (Philadelphia: University of Pennsylvania Press, 1999).

Moran, James, *Wynkyn de Worde: Father of Fleet Street*, 3rd edn (London: The British Library and New Castle: Oak Knoll Press, 2003).

Bibliography

Moran, Jo Ann Hoeppner, *The Growth of English Schooling 1340-1548: Learning, Literacy and Laicization in Pre-Reformation York Diocese* (Princeton, N.J.: Princeton University Press, 1985).

Morris, Bridget, *St Birgitta of Sweden*, Studies in Medieval Mysticism, vol. 1 (Woodbridge: Boydell, 1999).

Mortimer, Ruth, *A Portrait of the Author in Sixteenth-Century France*, Hanes Foundation Lecture Series (Chapel Hill: University of North Carolina Press, 1980).

comp., *Harvard College Library Department of Printing and Graphic Arts Catalogue of Books and Manuscripts*, 2 vols (Cambridge, Mass.: The Belknap Press of Harvard University Press, 1964-1974).

Moxey, Keith, *Peasants, Warriors and Wives: Popular Imagery in the Reformation* (Chicago: University of Chicago Press, 1989).

'Motivating History', *Art Bulletin* 77 (1995), pp. 392-401.

Moxon, Joseph, *Mechanick Exercises on the Whole Art of Printing by Joseph Moxon (1683-4)*, ed. Herbert Davis and Harry Carter (London: Oxford University Press, 1958; repr. 1962).

Mynors, R. A. B., ed., *Catalogue of the Manuscripts of Balliol College, Oxford* (Oxford: Clarendon Press, 1963).

Needham, Paul, *Twelve Centuries of Bookbindings 400-1600* (New York: Pierpont Morgan Library with Oxford University Press, 1979).

'Johann Gutenberg and the Catholicon Press', *Papers of the Bibliographical Society of America* 76 (1983), pp. 341-71.

The Printer and the Pardoner (Washington, D.C.: Library of Congress, 1986).

'William Caxton and his Cologne Partners: An Enquiry based on Veldener's Cologne Type', in *Ars Impressoria: Entstehung und Entwicklung des Buchdrucks: Eine internationale Festgabe für Severin Corsten zum 65. Geburtstag*, ed. Hans Limburg, Hartwig Lohse and Wolfgang Schmitz (Munich: K. G. Saur, 1986), pp. 103–131.

Needham, Paul, and Anna Lou Ashby, *Twentieth Report to the Fellows of the Pierpont Morgan Library 1981-83* (New York: Pierpont Morgan Library, 1984).

Nichols, Ann Eljenholm, *Seeable Signs: The Iconography of the Seven Sacraments 1350-1544* (Woodbridge: Boydell Press, 1994).

Nixon, Howard M., 'Caxton, His Contemporaries and Successors in the Book Trade from Westminster Documents', *The Library*, 5th ser., 31, no. 4 (December 1976), pp. 323-326.

'William Caxton and Bookbinding', *Journal of the Printing Historical Society* 11 (1976/77), pp. 92-113.

Nixon, Howard M., and Mirjam M. Foot, *The History of Decorated Bookbinding in England* (Oxford: Clarendon Press, 1992).

Obrist, Barbara, 'The Swedish Visionary: Saint Bridget', in *Medieval Women Writers*, ed. Katharina M. Wilson (Athens, GA: University of Georgia Press, 1984).

O'Connor, Sister Mary Catharine, *The Art of Dying Well: The Development of the Ars moriendi* (New York: Columbia University Press, 1942).

Oldham, J. Basil, *Shrewsbury School Library Bindings* (1943; rev edn, New York: Garland, 1990).

Ong, Walter J., *Ramus, Method, and the Decay of Dialogue* (Cambridge, Mass.: Harvard University Press, 1958).

Orality and Literacy: The Technologizing of the Word (New York: Methuen, 1982).

Orme, Nicholas, *Medieval Children* (New Haven, Conn.: Yale University Press, 2001).

Oschinsky, Dorothy, ed., *Walter of Henley and Other Treatises on Estate Management and Accounting* (Oxford: Clarendon Press, 1971).

Painter, George D., 'Caxton Through the Looking-Glass: An Enquiry into the Offsets on a Fragment of Caxton's *Fifteen Oes*, with a Census of Caxton Binding', *Gutenberg-Jahrbuch* (1963), pp. 73-88.

William Caxton, A Biography (New York: Putnam, 1977).

Parkes, M. B., 'The Literacy of the Laity', in *Literature and Western Civilization: The Medieval World*, ed. David Daiches and Anthony Thorlby (London: Aldus, 1973), pp. 555-578.

Scribes, Scripts and Readers: Studies in the Communication, Presentation and Dissemination of Medieval Texts (London: Hambledon Press, 1991).

Parsons, Kelly, 'The Red Ink Annotator of The Book of Margery Kempe and His Lay Audience', in *The Medieval Professional Reader at Work: Evidence from Manuscripts of Chaucer, Langland, Kempe, and Gower,* ed. Kathryn Kerby-Fulton and Maidie Hilmo, English Literary Studies Monograph Series no. 85 (Victoria: University of Victoria, 2001).

Pearsall, Derek, *Piers Plowman by William Langland: An Edition of the C-text* (Berkeley: University of California Press, 1978).

The Life of Geoffrey Chaucer: A Critical Biography (Oxford: Blackwell, 1992; repr. 1994).

Pecock, Reginald, *The Repressor of Over Much Blaming of the Clergy, by Reginald Pecock*, ed. Churchill Babington, Great Britain Public Record Office, Chronicles and Memorials of Great Britain and Ireland During the Middle Ages, no. 19 (London: Longman, Green, Longman, and Roberts, 1860).

Perrat, C., 'Barthélemy Buyer et les débuts de l'imprimerie á Lyon', *Humanisme et Renaissance* 2 (1935), pp. 103-126.

Pieterse, Jan Nederveen, *White on Black: Images of Africa and Blacks in Western Popular Culture* (New Haven, Conn.: Yale University Press, 1992; repr. 1996).

Piponnier, Françoise, and Perrine Mane, *Dress in the Middle Ages*, trans. Caroline Beamish (New Haven, Conn.: Yale University Press, 1997).

Plomer, Henry R., *Robert Wyer, Printer and Bookseller* (London: For the Bibliographical Society, by Blades, East & Blades, 1897).

'An Inventory of Wynkyn de Worde's House "The Sun in Fleet Street" in 1553', *The Library*, 3rd ser., 6 (1915), pp. 228-234.

Wynkyn de Worde and His Contemporaries from the Death of Caxton to 1535 (London: Grafton, 1925).

Pollard, Alfred W., *Last Words on the History of the Title-Page with Notes on Some Colophons and Twenty-Seven Fac-Similes of Title-Pages* (1891; repr. New York: Burt Franklin, 1971).

'Es tu Scholaris', in *Old Picture Books with Other Essays on Bookish Subjects* (1902; repr. New York: Burt Franklin, 1970), pp. 99-105.

'Woodcuts in English Plays Printed Before 1660', in *Old Picture Books with Other Essays on Bookish Subjects* (1902; repr. New York: Burt Franklin, 1970), pp. 182-199.

English Miracle Plays, Moralities and Interludes (Oxford: Clarendon Press, 1923).

Pollard, A. W., S. J. Aldrich, E. G. Duff and R. G. C. Proctor, *Catalogue of Manuscripts and Early Printed Books From the Libraries of William Morris, Richard Bennett, Bertram, Fourth Earl of Ashburnham, and Other Sources, Now Forming a Portion of the Library of J. Pierpont Morgan: Early Printed Books*, 4 vols (London: Chiswick Press, 1906-1907).

Powell, Susan, 'Why Quattuor Sermones?' in *Texts and Their Contexts: Papers from the Early Book Society*, ed. Julia Boffey and V. J. Scattergood (Dublin: Four Courts Press, 1997), pp. 181-195.

Power, Eileen, *Medieval Women*, ed. M. M. Postan (Cambridge: Cambridge University Press, 1975).

Preston, Jean, 'The Pricke of Conscience (Paris I-III) and Its First Appearance in Print', *The Library*, 6th ser., 7, no. 4 (December, 1985), pp. 303-314.

Printed Books & Manuscripts from Longleat (London: Christie's, 2002).

Quilligan, Maureen, *The Allegory of Female Authority: Christine de Pizan's Cité des Dames* (Ithaca, N.Y.: Cornell University Press, 1991).

Ragusa, Isa, and Rosalie B. Green, eds, *Meditations on the Life of Christ: An Illustrated Manuscript of the Fourteenth Century, Paris, Bibliothèque Nationale, MS. Ital. 115*, trans. Isa Ragusa (Princeton, N.J.: Princeton University Press, 1961).

Reed, A. W., *Early Tudor Drama: Medwall, The Rastells, Heywood, and the More Circle* (1926; repr. New York: Octagon Books, 1969).

Reid, Jonathan, and William Kemp, 'Multi-Genre Narratives in the *c.* 1535 French Adaptation of the 1521 *Passional Christi und Antichristi*', paper presented at 'Telling Stories: The Book and the Art of Narrative', the seventh biennial conference of the Early Book Society, University College, Cork, 2001.

Renouard, Philippe, *Les marques typographiques parisiennes des xve et xvie siècles* (Paris: Librairie Ancienne Honoré Champion, 1926).

Reynolds, E. E., *Saint John Fisher*, 2nd edn (Wheathampstead: Anthony Clarke Books, 1972).

Rhodes, Jan T., 'Syon Abbey's Religious Publications in the Sixteenth Century', *Journal of Ecclesiastical History* 44, 1 (1993), pp. 11-25.

Ricke, Joseph Martin, 'The Antichrist "Vita" at the End of the Middle Ages: An Edition of "The Byrthe and Lyfe of the Moost False and Deceytfull Antechryst"' (Ph.D. diss., Rice University, 1982).

Rogers, Nicholas, 'About the 15 "O"s, The Brigittines and Syon Abbey', *St. Ansgar's Bulletin* 80 (1984), pp. 29-30.

Rohmer, Eric, *Perceval le Gallois* (Gaumont-Films du Losange, 1978).

Roylance, Dale, *European Graphic Arts* (Princeton, N.J.: Princeton University Press, 1986).

Rubin, Miri, *Corpus Christi: The Eucharist in Late Medieval Culture* (Cambridge: Cambridge University Press, 1991; repr. 1992).

Russell, H. Diane, with Bernadine Barnes, *Eva/Ave: Woman in Renaissance and Baroque Prints*, National Gallery of Art, Washington (New York: The Feminist Press at the City University of New York, 1990).

Saenger, Paul, 'Silent Reading: its Impact on Late Medieval Script and Society', *Viator* 13 (1982), pp. 367-414.

'Books of Hours and the Reading Habits of the Later Middle Ages', in *The Culture of Print: Power and the Uses of Print in Early Modern Europe*, ed. Roger Chartier, trans. L. G. Cochrane (Cambridge: Polity Press, 1989), pp. 141-173.

Space Between Words: The Origins of Silent Reading (Stanford, Calif.: Stanford University Press, 1997).

Salter, Elizabeth, *Nicholas Love's 'Myrrour of the Blessed Lyf of Jesu Christ'*, *Analecta*

Cartusiana, ed. James Hogg (Salzburg: Institut für Englische Sprache und Literatur, Universität Salzburg, 1974).

'The Manuscripts of Nicholas Love's *Myrrour of the Blessed Lyf of Jesu Christ* and Related Texts', in *Middle English Prose: Essays on Bibliographical Problems*, ed. A. S. G. Edwards and Derek Pearsall (New York: Garland, 1981), pp. 115-127.

Salter, H. E., ed., *Records of Medieval Oxford: Coroners' Inquests, the Walls of Oxford* (Oxford: Oxford Chronicle Company, 1912).

Sappho, trans. Mary Barnard (Berkeley: University of California Press, 1958).

Sargent, Michael G., ed., *Nicholas Love's Mirror of the Blessed Life of Jesus Christ: A Critical Edition Based on Cambridge University Library Additional MS 6578 and 6686* (New York: Garland, 1992).

Schaer, Frank, ed., *The Three Kings of Cologne Edited from London Lambeth Palace MS 491*, Middle English Texts 31 (Heidelberg: Winter, 2000).

Schmitt, Anneliese, 'Das Blockbuch – ein Volksbuch? Versuch einer Antwort', in *Blockbücher des Mittelalters: Bilderfolgen als Lektüre*, ed. Cornelia Schneider (Mainz: Gutenberg-Museum, 1991), pp. 215-220.

Schretlen, M. J., *Dutch and Flemish Woodcuts of the Fifteenth Century* (1925; repr. New York: Hacker Art Books, 1969).

Schuyler, James, *Selected Art Writings: James Schuyler*, ed. Simon Pettet (Santa Rosa, Calif.: Black Sparrow Press, 1998).

Scillia, Diane G., 'The Master of The London Passional: Johann Veldener's "Utrecht Cutter"', in *The Early Illustrated Book: Essays in Honor of Lessing J. Rosenwald*, ed. Sandra Hindman (Washington, D.C.: Library of Congress, 1982), pp. 23-40.

Scott, K. L., 'The Beauchamp Pageants', in *The Caxton Master and His Patrons*, Cambridge Bibliographical Society Monograph 8 (Cambridge: Cambridge Bibliographical Society, 1976), pp. 55-66.

Scribner, R. W., *For the Sake of Simple Folk: Popular Propaganda for the German Reformation* (Cambridge: Cambridge University Press, 1981).

Popular Culture and Popular Movements in Reformation Germany (London: Hambledon Press, 1987).

Shahar, Shulamith, *Childhood in the Middle Ages*, trans. Chaya Galai (London: Routledge, 1990).

Shestack, Alan, *Master E. S.: Five Hundredth Anniversary Exhibition, Philadelphia Museum of Art* (Philadelphia: Philadelphia Museum of Art, 1967).

Sheehan, Michael M., 'The Formation and Stability of Marriage in Fourteenth-Century England: Evidence of an Ely Register', *Mediaeval Studies* 33 (1971), pp. 228-263.

Shikes, Ralph E., *The Indignant Eye: The Artist as Social Critic in Prints and Drawings from the Fifteenth Century to Picasso* (Boston: Beacon Press, 1969).

Smalley, Beryl, *The Study of the Bible in the Middle Ages* (Notre Dame: University of Notre Dame Press, 1964).

Smith, Jeffrey Chipps, *Nuremberg: A Renaissance City, 1500-1618* (Austin: University of Texas Press, 1983).

Smith, Julie A., 'Woodcut Presentation Scenes in Books Printed by Caxton, de Worde, Pynson', *Gutenberg-Jahrbuch* 61 (1986), pp. 322-343.

'The Poet Laureate as University Professor: John Skelton's Woodcut Portrait', in *Renaissance Rereadings: Intertext and Context*, ed. M. C. Horowitz et al. (Urbana: University of Illinois Press, 1988), pp. 159-183.

Smith, Lesley, and Jane Taylor, ed., *Women and the Book: Assessing the Visual Evidence*,

Bibliography

The British Library Studies in Medieval Culture (London: British Museum, 1997).

Smith, Margaret M., *The Title-Page: Its Early Development, 1460-1510* (London: The British Library, 2000).

Smythe, Sara Lanier, 'Woodcuts in English Books, 1536-1560' (Ph.D. diss., The University of North Carolina at Chapel Hill, 1973).

Snowden, Frank M., Jr, *Before Color Prejudice: The Ancient View of Blacks* (Cambridge, Mass.: Harvard University Press, 1991).

Snyder, James, 'The Bellaert Master and *De Proprietatibus Rerum*', in *The Early Illustrated Book: Essays in Honor of Lessing J. Rosenwald*, ed. Sandra Hindman (Washington, D.C.: Library of Congress, 1982).

Sowell, Madison U., *Italian Renaissance Books, 1478-1587* (Provo, Utah: Friends of the Brigham Young University Library, 1988).

Sommer, H. Oskar, letter to *The Academy*, no. 972 (20 December 1890) (unpaginated).

ed., *The Kalender of Shepherdes, The Edition of Paris 1503 in Photographic Facsimile: A Faithful Reprint of R. Pynson's Edition of London 1506*, 3 vols (London: Kegan Paul, Trench, Trübner & Co., 1892).

Stallings-Taney, M., ed., *Iohannis de Cavlibvs, Meditaciones Vite Christi* (Turnholt: Brepols, 1997),

Stevenson, Allan, 'The Quincentennial of Netherlandish Block Books', *British Museum Quarterly* 31 (1965), pp. 85-89.

'The Problem of Blockbooks', in *Blockbücher des Mittelalters: Bilderfolgen als Lektüre*, ed. Cornelia Schneider (Mainz: Gutenberg-Museum, 1991), pp. 229-261.

Stillwell, Margaret B., *The Beginning of the World of Books, 1450 to 1470: A Chronological Survey of the Texts Chosen for Printing During the First Twenty Years of the Printing Art, with a Synopsis of the Gutenberg Documents* (New York: Bibliographical Society of America, 1972).

Stock, Brian, *After Augustine: The Meditative Reader and the Text* (Philadelphia: University of Pennsylvania Press, 2001).

Thienen, Gerard van, and John Goldfinch, *Incunabula Printed in the Low Countries: A Census* (Nieukoop: De Graaf Publishers, 1999).

Thoma, Franz, *The Relations between Petrus of Rosenheim and the Xylographa of the Ars Memorandi and to the Early Printings of the Rationarium Evangelistarium: A Bibliographical Study of the Literature of Mnemonics* (Leipzig, 1929).

Thompson, E. M., 'The Pageants of Richard Beauchamp, Earl of Warwick, Commonly Called the Warwick MS.', *Burlington Magazine* 1 (March 1903), pp. 151-164.

Tokunaga, Satoko, 'The Use of Books Owned by Medieval Women: A Contribution to a Study of Medieval Nuns' Reading in Late Medieval England' (M.A. thesis, University of Birmingham, 2000).

Tracy, P. B., 'Robert Wyer: A Brief Analysis of His Types and a Suggested Chronology for the Output of His Press', *The Library*, 6th ser., 2 (1980), pp. 294-303.

Le trésor de la Sainte-Chapelle (Paris: Réunion des musées nationaux, 2001).

Tuve, Rosemond, 'Notes on the Virtues and Vices', *Journal of the Warburg and Courtauld Institute* 26 (1963), pp. 264-303.

Allegorical Imagery: Some Mediaeval Books and Their Posterity (Princeton, N.J.: Princeton University Press, 1966).

Twyman, Michael, *The British Library Guide to Printing: History and Techniques* (London: The British Library, 1998).

Uitz, Erika, *The Legend of Good Women: Medieval Women in Towns and Cities*, trans.

Sheila Marnie (Mount Kisco, N.Y.: Moyer Bell, 1990).

Updike, John, 'Groaning Shelves', *The New Yorker* 75, 29 (October 4, 1999), pp. 106-110.

Valli, Francesco, ed., *I miracoli di Caterina di Iacopo f Siena* (Siena: R. Università, 1936).

Vauchez, André, *Sainthood in the Later Middle Ages*, trans. Jean Birrell (Cambridge: Cambridge University Press, 1997).

Vickers, Salley, *Miss Garnet's Angel* (New York: Plume, 2002).

Warner, George F., ed., *The Epistle of Othea to Hector or The Boke of Knyghthode, Translated from the French of Christine de Pisan With a Dedication to Sir John Fastolf, KG* (London: J. B. Nichols and Sons, 1904).

Watson, Andrew G., *Medieval Libraries of Great Britain: A List of Surviving Books: Supplement to the Second Edition*, Royal Historical Society Guides and Handbooks, 15 (London: Royal Historical Society; University of London, 1987).

Watt, Tessa, *Cheap Print and Popular Piety, 1550-1640* (Cambridge: Cambridge University Press, 1991).

Weale, W. H. James, *Bookbindings and Rubbings of Bindings in the National Art Library South Kensington Museum*, 2 vols (London: Printed for Her Majesty's Stationery Office by Eyre and Spottiswoode, Printers to the Queen's Most Excellent Majesty, 1894-1898).

Wheatley, Edward, 'The Aesopic Corpus at War with Itself: A Literary Body and its Members', *Journal of the Early Book Society* 2 (1999), pp. 46-58.

Mastering Aesop: Medieval Education, Chaucer, and His Followers (Gainesville: University Press of Florida, 2000).

White, C. H. Evelyn, ed., *The Journal of William Dowsing of Stratford* (Ipswich: Pawsey & Hayes, 1885).

White, Helen C., *The Tudor Books of Private Devotion* (Madison: University of Wisconsin Press, 1951).

Wieck, Roger S., introduction, *Ars Memorandi: A Facsimile of the Text and Woodcuts* (Cambridge, Mass.: Harvard University Department of Printing and Graphic Arts, 1981).

Late Medieval and Renaissance Illuminated Manuscripts 1350-1525 in the Houghton Library (Cambridge, Mass.: Department of Printing and Graphic Arts, Harvard College Library, 1983).

Painted Prayers: The Book of Hours in Medieval and Renaissance Art (New York: George Braziller, 1997).

William, Earl of Carysfort, K.P., introd., *The Pageants of Richard Beauchamp Earl of Warwick, Reproduced in Facsimile from the Cottonian MS Julius E.IV in the British Museum* (Oxford: Roxburghe Club, 1908).

Williams, Franklin B., ed., *The Gardyners passetaunce* (London: Roxburghe Club, 1985).

Wilson, Adrian, and Joyce Lancaster Wilson, *A Medieval Mirror: Speculum Humanae Salvationis, 1324-1500* (Berkeley: University of California Press, 1985).

Winn, Mary Beth, ed., *Anthoine Vérard, Parisian Publisher 1485-1512: Prologues, Poems, and Presentations* (Geneva: Librairie Droz, 1997).

Yates, Frances A., *The Art of Memory* (Chicago: University of Chicago Press, 1966).

GENERAL INDEX

INDEX OF BOOKS, AUTHORS
AND MANUSCRIPTS